Programming Windows™ Games with Borland® C++

Programming Windows™ Games with Borland® C++

Nabajyoti Barkakati

A Division of Prentice Hall Computer Publishing
11711 North College, Carmel, Indiana, 46032 USA

To Leha, Ivy, Emily, and Ashley

Copyright © 1993 by Sams Publishing

FIRST EDITION

All rights reserved. No part of this book shall be reproduced, stored in a retrieval system, or transmitted by any means, electronic, mechanical, photocopying, recording, or otherwise, without written permission from the publisher. No patent liability is assumed with respect to the use of the information contained herein. Although every precaution has been taken in the preparation of this book, the publisher and author assume no responsibility for errors or omissions. Neither is any liability assumed for damages resulting from the use of the information contained herein. For information, address Sams Publishing, 11711 N. College Ave., Carmel, IN 46032.

International Standard Book Number: 0-672-30292-6

Library of Congress Catalog Card Number: 92-82084

96 95 94 93   4 3 2 1

Interpretation of the printing code: the rightmost double-digit number is the year of the book's printing; the rightmost single-digit, the number of the book's printing. For example, a printing code of 93-1 shows that the first printing of the book occurred in 1993.

Composed in Palatino and MCPdigital by Prentice Hall Computer Publishing

Printed in the United States of America

Trademarks

All terms mentioned in this book that are known to be trademarks or service marks have been appropriately capitalized. Sams Publishing cannot attest to the accuracy of this information. Use of a term in this book should not be regarded as affecting the validity of any trademark or service mark. Borland C++ is a registered trademark of Borland International, Inc. Windows is a trademark of Microsoft Corporation.

Publisher
Richard K. Swadley

Acquisitions Manager
Jordan Gold

Acquisitions Editor
Stacy Hiquet

Development Editor
Dean Miller

Senior Editor
Tad Ringo

Production Editor
Nancy Albright

Editorial Coordinators
Rebecca S. Freeman
Bill Whitmer

Editorial Assistants
Rosemarie Graham
Sharon Cox

Technical Reviewer
Tim Moore

Marketing Manager
Greg Wiegand

Cover Designers
Tim Amrhein
Kathy Hanley

Director of Production and Manufacturing
Jeff Valler

Production Manager
Corinne Walls

Imprint Manager
Matthew Morrill

Book Designer
Michele Laseau

Production Analyst
Mary Beth Wakefield

Proofreading/Indexing Coordinator
Joelynn Gifford

Graphics Image Specialists
Dennis Sheehan
Sue VandeWalle

Production
Christine Cook
Mitzi F. Gianakos
Howard Jones
John Kane
Sean Medlock
Roger Morgan
Juli Pavey
Angela M. Pozdol
Linda Quigley
Michelle M. Self
Suzanne Tully
Barbara Webster
Phil Worthington

Indexer
John Sleeva

Overview

Preface	xiii
Introduction	xvii

Part I
Basics of Game Programming with Borland C+

1	Game Programming for Windows	3
2	Windows Programming with Borland C++	21
3	Graphics Programming with the Windows API	57
4	Understanding Image File Formats	95
5	Animating Images	149
6	Generating Sound	189

Part II
Sample Games

7	SPUZZLE—A Spelling Puzzle	205
8	3-D Graphics	275
9	BLOCKADE—A Game of Modern Naval Simulation	317

Index	495

Contents

Introduction		xvii

Part I
Basics of Game Programming with Borland C++

1   Game Programming for Windows   3

    An Overview of Computer Games 5
        Common Themes in Computer Games 8
        Common Elements of Computer Games 15
    Issues in Game Programming for Windows 18
        Color 18
        Multimedia Games for Windows 19
    Summary 20
    Further Reading 20

2   Windows Programming with Borland C++   21

    Microsoft Windows Programming
      with Borland C++ Classes 23
        Model-View-Controller (MVC) Architecture 24
        A Windows Application
            Using OWL and CLASSLIB 26
    Borland C++ Class Libraries 40
        Breakdown of the CLASSLIB Classes 41
        Template-Based Container Classes 46
        OWL Classes 50
    Summary 54
    Further Reading 54

3   Graphics Programming with the Windows API   57

    Windows Graphics Device Interface 58
        Device Context 59
        GDI Coordinate Systems 65

Drawing with GDI Functions	68
Drawing Points	69
Drawing Lines	69
Drawing Closed Figures	70
Manipulating Rectangles	72
Regions	74
Drawing Mode	76
Text Output	77
Handling Color	80
System Palette	81
Logical Palette	81
Bitmaps	86
Device-Dependent Bitmaps	86
Device-Independent Bitmap (DIB) Format	92
Summary	93
Further Reading	94

4 Understanding Image File Formats — 95

Image File Formats	96
Common Characteristics of Image Files	97
Some Common Formats	99
C++ Classes for Handling Image Files	100
ImageData Class	101
Image Class	105
BMPImage Class	113
TGAImage Class	119
PCXImage Class	125
ImageView—A Windows Image Viewer	136
Running ImageView	136
ImageViewApp Class	136
ImageViewFrame and *ImageViewWindow* Classes	139
Building ImageView	145
Summary	146
Further Reading	146

5 Animating Images — 149

Animation Techniques	150
Sprite Animation	150

    C++ Classes for Sprite Animation 152
        Sprite Class 152
        SpriteAnimation Class 162
    A Sample Animation Program 178
        AnimationWindow Class 178
        The ANIMATE Application 186
        Building ANIMATE.EXE 187
    Summary 188
    Further Reading 188

6   Generating Sound   189

    Sound under Windows 190
        Programming for Sound 190
    A Sample Program 197
    Summary 201
    Further Reading 201

Part II
Sample Games

7   SPUZZLE—A Spelling Puzzle   205

    Playing SPUZZLE 206
        Starting SPUZZLE 207
        Building a Puzzle 208
        Keeping Score 209
        Controlling Sound Output 209
        Adding a New Word 210
    Designing SPUZZLE 211
        Window Hierarchy 212
        Assigning the Responsibilities 213
        Maintaining Information about the Puzzles 213
    Implementing SPUZZLE 214
        SpuzzleApp Class 214
        PuzzleFrame Class 216
        PuzzleWindow Class 232
        LetterWindow Class 245
        ToolWindow Class 252
        StatusWindow Class 259
        Data Structures for Puzzle Information 265

	High Scores Dialog Box	267
	Resources for SPUZZLE	271
	Help File	272
	Other Files	273
	Summary	273

8 3-D Graphics — 275

Modeling 3-D Objects	276
3-D Cartesian Coordinates	276
Boundary Representation of 3-D Objects	277
Constructing Objects with Polygons	278
3-D Coordinate Transformations	280
Rotation	282
A Few More Vector Operations	283
Viewing a 3-D Scene	284
Transforming to View Coordinates	285
Perspective Projection	285
C++ Classes for 3-D Modeling	286
Defining the Primitive 3-D Classes	286
Defining the 3-D Scene	301
Loading a 3-D Scene from a File	311
Viewing a 3-D Scene	313
Summary	314
Further Reading	315

9 BLOCKADE—A Game of Modern Naval Simulation — 317

Playing BLOCKADE	318
Overview of BLOCKADE	318
Starting BLOCKADE	319
Terminology of BLOCKADE	320
Components of the BLOCKADE Screen	321
Views in BLOCKADE	321
Controlling Simulation Speed	324
Launching Weapons	325
Designing BLOCKADE	325
Simulating the Scenario	326
Viewing the Scenario	326
Game Definition Files	327
Implementing BLOCKADE	327

Taking Stock of the Source Files 328
　　The *Application* Class 331
　　BlockadeFrame Class 333
　　LogoWindow Class 353
　　DisplayWindow Classes 355
　　ToolWindow Classes 386
　　StatusWindow Class 402
　　InfoWindow Class 411
　　Scenario Class 427
　　Platform Class 450
　　Sensor Class 466
　　Weapon Class 472
　　Other Files 482
　　Building BLOCKADE 492
　Summary...493

Index   **495**

Preface

Computer games are by far the most popular type of software. The market for game software is huge—practically anyone with a PC can use games. If you are like me, you probably play your share of computer games and have your own favorite categories. And because you are a programmer, you might have thought of many ideas that could be the basis of a game—if only you knew how to get started on the project. As you will see after reading this book, writing a computer game is not as difficult as you might have imagined. In fact, once you see how a game is written, you have a number of well-defined steps that you can follow to create your own game. After you have had some fun writing your own game, it may even become a source of income for you.

The basic premise of *Programming Windows Games with Borland C++* is that whether entertaining or educational, all computer games have certain common elements: graphics, sound, and a mouse- or keyboard-based user interface. Thus, any programmer (with some imagination) who masters the basic techniques of manipulating images, generating sound, and controlling the mouse or keyboard can write a computer game. The best way to learn how to program games is to see working examples that illustrate how an imaginative idea can come alive in a computer game with graphics and sound.

Programming Windows Games with Borland C++ teaches intermediate to advanced level C++ programmers how to use object-oriented programming techniques to write computer games. Borland C++ offers exceptional support for Microsoft Windows programming, includes the ObjectWindows Library (OWL)—a comprehensive C function library—and provides a full set of programming tools such as MAKE, TLINK, TLIB, and the Turbo Debugger. The games presented in this book are meant to run under Microsoft Windows 3.1 because Windows offers a rich graphical user interface for the games and, more importantly, because there is a shortage of games that run under Windows.

Programming Windows Games with Borland C++ features the following:

- A quick overview of Windows programming with Borland C++ and ObjectWindows Library (OWL)
- C++ classes for image animation and sound generation
- Full source code for SPUZZLE, a spelling puzzle for young children
- Full source code for BLOCKADE, a game of strategy that simulates a naval blockade
- Disk with source and executable versions of SPUZZLE and BLOCKADE

Programming Windows Games with Borland C++ starts with an overview of Windows programming with Borland C++ and OWL followed by several chapters on graphics, image manipulation, and sound generation under Windows. Then the book presents SPUZZLE—an educational spelling puzzle for young children. This game teaches spelling through a simple jigsaw puzzle that has one or more letters associated with each piece of the puzzle. The child has to place the pieces of the puzzle in the right order (by dragging them around with the mouse) to complete an image, which spells the word and rewards the child with a musical tune. SPUZZLE illustrates the basic programming techniques for animating images and generating sound. This game makes use of a number of C++ classes that are designed to support image manipulation and sound generation. A significant aspect of image manipulation is the ability to read, interpret, and display image files of several common formats (PCX, BMP, and Truevision Targa). These techniques are described in the book.

The latter part of *Programming Windows Games with Borland C++* sketches the design and development of another more elaborate game called BLOCKADE, which is a modern naval simulation in which the player commands a combat ship as it enforces a naval blockade. As commander of the ship, the player relies on the ship's sensor systems to decide how to intercept, track, and stop "blockade runners."

Programming Windows Games with Borland C++ includes a bound-in disk that contains the complete source code for the games appearing in the book. This disk makes it easy for you to try out the games and even enhance them.

Acknowledgments

I am grateful to Stacy Hiquet for suggesting the idea of this exciting book concept—a book that shows the complete development of realistic computer games that run under Microsoft Windows. Thanks to Wayne Blankenbeckler for making the necessary arrangements to prepare the companion disk complete with a Windows installation utility.

Thanks to Nan Borreson of Borland International for keeping me supplied with the latest copies of the Borland C/C++ compiler and Application Framework.

As usual, the production team at Sams Publishing did an excellent job of turning my raw manuscript into this well-edited, beautifully packaged book. Thanks to all of you at Sams for doing your part with such dedication and perfection. In particular, thanks to Nancy Albright of Albright Communications for the thorough editing of the manuscript, and to Dean Miller at Sams for managing the development of the book.

Finally, my greatest thanks go to my wife, Leha, for her love and support and for taking care of everything while I went into hibernation with this book project. My daughters, Ivy, Emily, and Ashley, did more than simply encourage me during the project. This being a computer game book, Ivy and Emily were able to help me by testing the games and providing feedback while Ashley supervised the entire operation by roaming the halls with her no-nonsense attitude.

About the Author

Naba Barkakati, Ph.D., is an expert computer programmer and a successful author. He has written some of the most popular programming titles on the market, including *X Window System Programming; Object-Oriented Programming in C++; The Waite Group's Microsoft C Bible, Second Edition; The Waite Group's Turbo C++ Bible, Second Edition;* and *Microsoft C/C++ 7 Developer's Guide.*

Introduction

Programming Windows Games with Borland C++ is a book for intermediate-to-advanced C++ programmers that covers all aspects of writing computer games under Microsoft Windows. As the book's title implies, I used Borland C++ and the C++ classes in the ObjectWindows Library (OWL) to write the games that I describe in this book. Because graphics (especially image display and animation) and sound are at the heart of all computer games, I cover image display, animation, and sound generation in detail. In particular, I discuss how to read and interpret image files of several formats because you are likely to use scanned images or images drawn with a paint program as the graphics elements in a computer game.

I also developed C++ classes that provide the graphics and sound capabilities required by the games. Instead of many small games, I chose to develop two reasonably complex computer games:

- SPUZZLE, a spelling puzzle game for children
- BLOCKADE, a naval simulation game for kids of all ages

You will find ready-to-run copies of these games as well as their full source code in the companion disk.

What You Need

To make the best use of this book, you should have access to a system with Microsoft Windows 3.1 and the Borland C++ compiler. Then, you can test the example programs and run the games as you progress through the book. Additionally, you will want the following:

- A fast 80386/80486 system with a VGA or better display
- As much memory as possible (4MB or more)
- A reasonably large hard disk (100MB or more)

The system should be fast because the Windows environment puts a lot of demand on the processor. The extra memory helps, because Windows can use it with the 80386/80486 processor operating in what is known as the protected mode. The large hard disk is necessary because all software development tools seem to require a large amount of storage.

All examples in this book were tested with Borland C++ on an Intel 80386-based ISA (Industry Standard Architecture) PC with 8MB of memory, a 650MB hard disk, and a 640x480 resolution 16-color VGA display.

Conventions Used in This Book

Programming Windows Games with Borland C++ uses a simple notational style. All listings are typeset in a `monospace` font for ease of reading. All file names, function names, variable names, and keywords appearing in text are also in the same `monospace` font. The first occurrence of a new term or concept is in *italic*.

How to Use This Book

If you are a newcomer to Borland C++ and Windows programming, you should first get up to speed by using other resources such as Borland's manuals or one of the many books on Windows programming with Borland C++.

Once you are comfortable with Windows programming, you should browse through Chapters 1 through 3 to see how to use Borland C++ and the OWL classes. Chapter 1, in particular, provides an overview of the different types of games that are currently on the market.

If you are interested in reading and interpreting image files and animating images, you should consult Chapters 4 and 5. Chapter 6 gives a brief description of sound generation under Windows.

Introduction

Chapters 7 and 9 present sample games (SPUZZLE and BLOCKADE) with full source code. If you want to learn game programming from these chapters, start by installing and playing the games—they are on the companion disk. Once you have seen what the game does, you can go to the appropriate chapter to see how a specific feature is implemented.

How to Contact the Author

If you have any questions or suggestions, or if you want to report any errors, please feel free to contact me either by mail or through electronic mail. Here is how:

Write to LNB Software, Inc., 7 Welland Court, North Potomac, MD 20878-4847, USA.

- If you have access to an Internet node, send e-mail to:

  naba@grebyn.com

- If you use CompuServe, specify the following as SEND TO:

  >INTERNET:naba@grebyn.com

- From MCIMAIL, specify the following when sending mail:

  EMS: INTERNET

  MBX: naba@grebyn.com

Please do not phone, even if you happen to come across my telephone number. Instead, drop me a letter or send an e-mail message for a prompt reply.

PART I

Basics of Game Programming with Borland C++

Chapter 1

Game Programming for Windows

If you have browsed through the shelves in a software store recently, you know the tremendous variety of computer games available on the market. The offerings run the gamut from simple games such as Tic Tac Toe, pinball, and puzzles, to sophisticated simulations of real and make-believe worlds. Some of the latter include animated graphics with digitized voices and music generated by sound boards. Most of the games are designed to run under MS-DOS and only a few work under Windows. But this situation is bound to change as Windows gains popularity and game developers see the benefits of writing Windows versions of their games. In particular, with the multimedia extensions in Windows 3.1, game developers can begin using CD-ROM media and sound boards to bring a new level of sophistication to computer games.

The device-independent manner in which Windows allows an application to handle graphical output is another advantage of writing computer games for Windows. With minimal effort on your part, you can ensure that the same Windows game works properly on a 16-color EGA display as well as a 256-color Super VGA display and even the newer XGA display. This device independence comes at a price; animation under Windows is slower than that designed to work in a specific mode of a video adapter. For instance, most interactive DOS games display fast animated graphics scenes in a specific video mode of a display adapter, usually mode 13H of the VGA (the 256-color 320x200 resolution mode). The game programmer can exploit all nuances of the adapter, including the fact that a 256-color 320x200 image fits in exactly 64K—less than the maximum size of a single segment of memory in 80x86 processors—which makes image manipulation fast. You cannot use intimate knowledge of the display when programming a game for Windows, but the speed disadvantage is gradually disappearing as PCs and display adapters become faster.

This book looks to the future and, in anticipation of a large and profitable market for Windows games, shows you how to develop computer game applications designed to run under Microsoft Windows. There are three features common to all computer games:

- Two-dimensional (2-D) and three-dimensional (3-D) graphics
- Image manipulation
- Sound generation

Of course, you also have to come up with an idea for a game and design the game; these topics are illustrated through two complete sample games in Chapters 7 and 9.

Game Programming for Windows

This chapter starts with an overview of some popular computer games. These are mostly DOS games, but they should give you an idea of the types that are available on the market and even trigger some ideas for new games that you might want to write. The brief overview of computer games includes a classification of the current crop of games, the graphics and sound capabilities that each type of game uses, and the major steps in developing a game. Chapter 2 introduces the topic of Windows programming with Borland C++ and describes Windows graphics capabilities and how to use Windows Application Programming Interface (API) functions for the graphics needed in a game program. Chapters 3 through 6 cover the subjects of graphics, image manipulation, and sound generation—the features that are at the heart of any computer game.

An Overview of Computer Games

The following is a list of the current crop of computer games divided into seven categories:

- *Educational Games.* Slowly the line between educational and entertainment game software is getting blurred because developers realize that an entertaining educational game is a better teacher than a dull one. Some of the popular educational games are:

    Where in the World is Carmen Sandiego? and *Where in the U.S.A. is Carmen Sandiego?* from Broderbund Software, Inc., which teach geography through a game

    New Math Blaster Plus from Davidson & Associates, Inc., which teaches mathematical skills through simple games

    Learning Company's *Math Rabbit* and *Reader Rabbit,* which include a variety of activities to teach young children math and reading skills

- *Traditional Games.* These are the computerized versions of traditional games such as chess, card games (bridge, poker, solitaire), GO, mahjongg, and a variety of puzzles.

- *Arcade Games.* These are games offered in dedicated game machines that you see in places such as shopping center arcades. This category includes the PC versions of arcade games such as pinball, Tetris, Pac Man, and a variety of games where you shoot down space invaders. The games in this category use fast-paced animation of small images called *sprites*. They also include music and other sound effects.
- *Sports.* This category consists of software implementations of real sports such as golf, boxing, football, and baseball. These games include a moderate level of animation and sound. Some popular sports games are:

    Links 386 Pro golf game from Access Software, Inc.

    Jack Nicklaus Signature Edition Golf from Accolade

    NFL Pro League Football from Micro Sports
- *Adventure and Role Playing Games.* These are the "dungeons and dragons" games. You play the role of a character in a specific scenario (usually a dungeon), and move from level to level collecting weapons, potions, and spells. You encounter many nasty characters that you have to defeat using the weapons and spells. Some of the best known games of this genre are the Ultima series from Origin Systems, Inc. These games sport continuously moving 3-D graphics and realistic sounds, including digitized voice (on PCs equipped with special sound boards).
- *Real-Time Action Simulations.* These are the fast-paced simulations of airplanes, helicopters, and spaceships with reasonable renderings of 3-D scenarios. As you manipulate the controls of the craft (the airplane or the helicopter), the craft moves according to the current settings and the 3-D view reflects the motion. I classify these computer games as real-time action simulations because they simulate the behavior of the airplane or helicopter and the simulation reacts to the player's inputs as they are received (through keyboard, mouse, or joystick). These games are popular because the real-time feedback makes them exciting. Some of the games in this category are:

    Microsoft Flight Simulator from Microsoft Corporation, which simulates a number of airplanes

Game Programming for Windows

Wing Commander II from Origin, a space flight simulation game with very good graphics and sound effects

Gunship 2000 from MicroProse Software, Inc., a simulation of helicopter combat

- *Strategic Simulations*. These are simulations of large-scale systems such as cities, railroad systems, naval campaigns, and, in the case of a recent game called SimAnt, even ant colonies. In these simulations, you devise a strategy for the problem at hand and see the entire system evolve as time passes. Viewed from the perspective of time scales, real-time action simulations model systems that change fast—in seconds and minutes. In contrast, the strategic simulations are concerned with long-term reactions of a system, those occurring in hours or days— even years. In a strategic simulation game you do not get the thrill of immediate response to your actions, but you do get to think through problems and devise strategies. In fact, some of the war games have been used to train naval officers. Most of these games have 2-D graphics and minimal sound effects. Here are some of the popular titles in this category:

    SimCity for Windows from Maxis, which puts you in the role of a city planner

    Harpoon from Three-Sixty Pacific, Inc., a highly acclaimed naval war game

    Great Naval Battles, North Atlantic 1939-1943 from Strategic Simulation, Inc., which lets you command a battleship and participate in one of several naval battles of World War II

    Carriers at War from Strategic Studies Group, another simulation of World War II air and naval operations in the Pacific Ocean

    Railroad Tycoon from MicroProse Software, Inc., which lets you manage a railroad system

    SimAnt by Maxis, which lets you control an ant colony that has to fight for its survival in a suburban home's backyard

Common Themes in Computer Games

All computer games have two common elements: graphics and sound. Here is a quick look at some of the popular games from the real-time and strategy simulation categories. I selected games from these two categories because simulation games have some of the most demanding graphics, algorithmic, and sound requirements of all games. The details are omitted except for the basic idea and the graphics and sound elements of each game.

Microsoft Flight Simulator

Microsoft Flight Simulator is a best-selling, real-time game that simulates the flight of several types of aircraft from take-off to landing. The simulation takes into account a large number of aircraft characteristics, shows a standardized instrument panel, implements all necessary aircraft controls, and provides a number of 3-D views from different perspectives. As shown in Figure 1.1, the 3-D view is realistic enough to identify specific airports (from landmarks and runway layouts), yet fast enough to work on all Intel 80x86-based MS-DOS PCs with graphics adapters from CGA to VGA.

Microsoft Flight Simulator also provides sound effects to simulate the ambient noise inside a flying aircraft.

Figure 1.1. *View from the cockpit in Microsoft Flight Simulator.*

Game Programming for Windows

Gunship 2000

Gunship 2000 is a real-time simulation of helicopter combat from MicroProse Software, Inc. The version of this game designed for the VGA display adapter uses the 256-color 320x200 resolution mode of the VGA to display very realistic 3-D scenery as the helicopter flies. The game accepts input from the keyboard as well as a joystick. Also, Gunship 2000 can generate digitized sound using one of several popular sound boards, if your system has such a board. Otherwise, Gunship 2000 uses PC's internal speaker for sound effects.

As you can see from Gunship 2000's opening screen (Figure 1.2), the game emphasizes realistic 3-D graphics within the limits of a typical PC's display system. Although you cannot fly a real helicopter without extensive training, Gunship 2000 provides simplified controls to make flying easy. Once airborne, the helicopter flies within a few hundred feet from the ground or sea and you see a 3-D view of the terrain or water outside. As the at-sea view in Figure 1.3 shows, the 3-D rendering of the scene is reasonably realistic. Note the ship ahead of the helicopter in Figure 1.3.

Figure 1.2. *Opening screen of Gunship 2000, a helicopter combat simulation game.*

Figure 1.3. *View from the cockpit for an at-sea mission in Gunship 2000.*

SimCity for Windows

SimCity for Windows is a strategic simulation game—one of the few that runs under Microsoft Windows. Figure 1.4 shows the opening screen of the game. As you can see from the menu options listed on the sign, you can start a simulation of a new city, load an existing city's simulation into the game, or select to start with a predefined city's scenario. Figure 1.5 shows the windows after you load one of the predefined cities—Boston in the year 2010—and continue the simulation for a while.

In SimCity, you play as the planner for a city—you are responsible for setting up residential, commercial, and industrial zones. You also plan and build the roads, railroads, power plants, power lines, police stations, and fire stations. As you build these, money is expended from a budget. Once the infrastructure is in place, the city's simulation proceeds to build up population, traffic begins to flow on the roads, roads deteriorate, crimes and natural disasters happen. You have to tax the residents to raise money for the upkeep of the city. If you have excess revenues, you can spend the funds to help the city grow. As you might gather from this brief description, you have to attend to numerous details just to keep the infrastructure from collapsing. The game is fun, which is why it appears to be popular among strategy enthusiasts.

Game Programming for Windows

Chapter 1

Figure 1.4. *Opening screen of SimCity for Windows.*

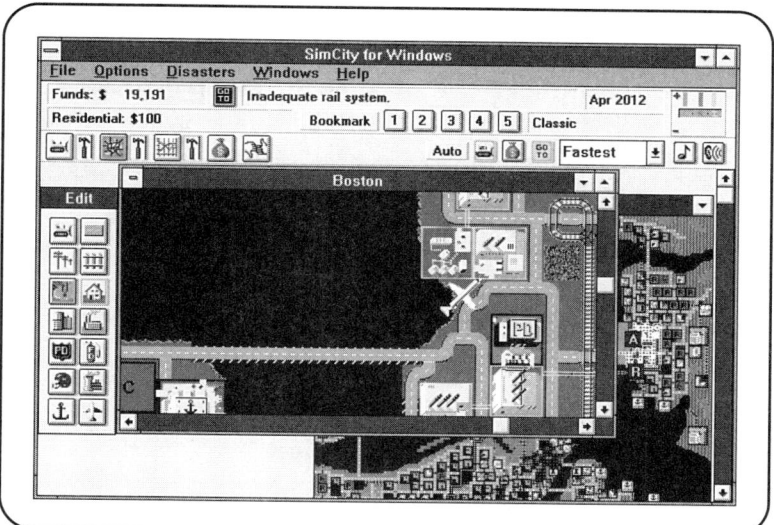

Figure 1.5. *View of Boston in SimCity for Windows.*

SimCity for Windows has good maplike views, but there are no demanding real-time 3-D graphics in the game. The only aspect of animation is the movement of some sprites representing vehicles such as cars, airplanes, and helicopters.

This game includes sound effects, but the sound is more of a distraction than an aid to the game.

Harpoon

Harpoon is another game of strategy that simulates naval war games. Harpoon's simulation of large-scale naval scenarios is accurate enough for evaluating naval strategies. As a player, you are given a geopolitical scenario with a need for naval intervention, and you get to command anything from a single ship to an entire group of ships with a specified mission. Figure 1.6 shows the main screen of Harpoon, where you play the game.

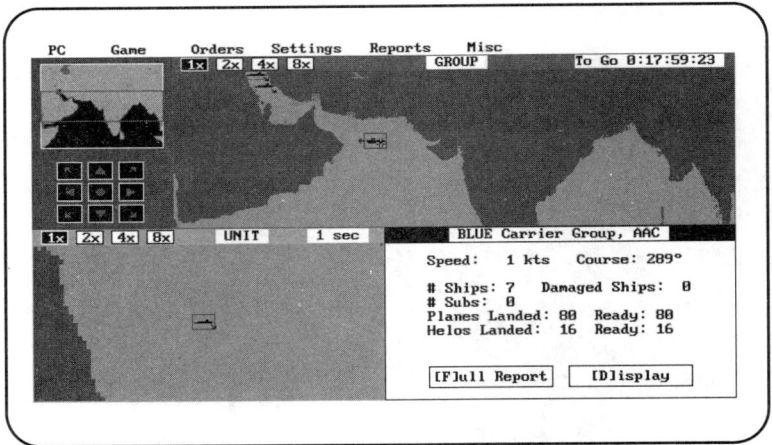

Figure 1.6. *Main screen of Harpoon.*

This game is the computer version of a naval war game by Larry Bond that appeared as a board game in 1980. Larry Bond's game gained fame when author Tom Clancy revealed that he used Harpoon as a source of information when writing the novel *The Hunt for Red October*. You use Harpoon's database of information on ships and aircraft to decide how to make the best use of the

Game Programming for Windows

naval and air units under your command. Figure 1.7 shows a typical screen that shows information on a specific class of ships, in this case, the Arleigh Burke class destroyer of the U.S. Navy. The player can get further information through the menu options at the bottom of the screen shown in Figure 1.7.

Harpoon includes sound effects for certain events such as missile warnings and ships taking hits from missiles.

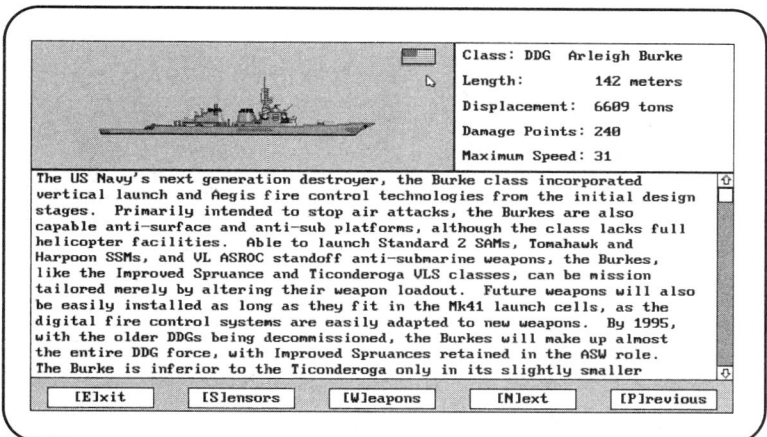

Figure 1.7. *Displaying information on a ship class in Harpoon.*

Great Naval Battles, North Atlantic 1939-1943

Great Naval Battles, North Atlantic 1939-1943 is a recent strategic simulation game depicting naval warfare during World War II, specifically the years 1939 through 1943. In contrast to Harpoon, this game emphasizes realistic graphics and sound as it offers a number of predefined encounters between British and German battleships. The scenarios are historically accurate except that, in the game, you get to command one of the sides and get a chance to change history by blasting the other side with your ship's guns and torpedoes. The game provides a number of 3-D views of the ships at sea, but there is no real-time animation as in a flight simulator or helicopter simulation. Figure 1.8 shows the opening screen of Great Naval Battles, North Atlantic 1939-1943; Figure 1.9 shows a view from the main gunnery station of one of the ships.

Figure 1.8. *Opening screen of Great Naval Battles, North Atlantic 1939-1943.*

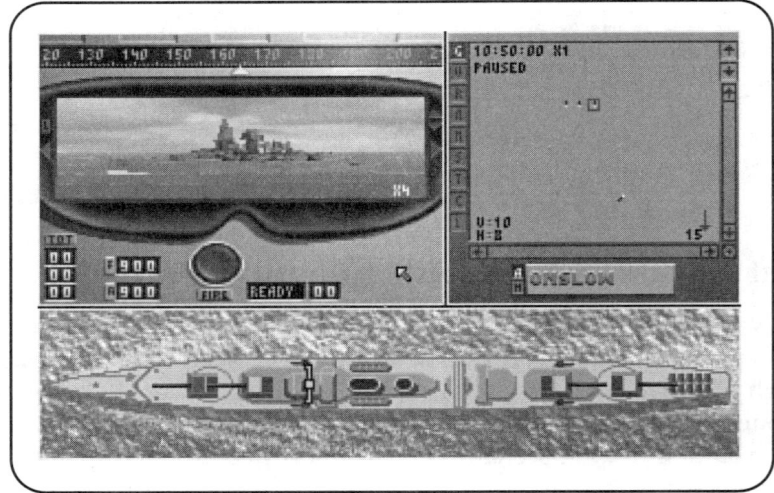

Figure 1.9. *View from the main gunnery station of a ship.*

Game Programming for Windows

Common Elements of Computer Games

From the brief overview of some of the current computer games, you can see the common features of these games: a central theme that tells us what the game does (for example, a naval war game or a helicopter combat simulation), 2-D and 3-D graphics, and sound effects to make the game seem realistic. Additionally, most games include some sort of copy protection scheme to deter unauthorized copying of the game software.

The game's main story line determines the types of programming you have to do to implement the game. For instance, realism in graphics and sound effects is very important in a role-playing game. A war game such as Harpoon, however, does not need much realism; a simplified display suffices in a game that emphasizes strategy over real-time simulation. Even with the differences in the exact requirements, the main story line, the graphics, and the sound effects are definitely the most important components of any game.

Story Line

Before you start developing a game, you must develop the story line, which dictates the details of the other programming requirements of the game. The game's story line should answer the following questions for the prospective player:

- *What is this game?* This clearly identifies the category of the game. Is it a role-playing adventure game? A real-time flight simulation with 3-D graphics? An educational game that teaches reading skills?

- *What is the goal of the game?* The answer tells the player what to do to succeed in the game. In an arcade game, the goal might be to shoot down as many space invaders as possible. In an educational game that teaches spelling, the goal is to correctly spell as many words as possible. For a helicopter combat simulation, the goal is to fly into enemy territory, destroy a specified target, and fly back without getting killed.

- *How does the game provide feedback on the player's performance?* This feature indicates how close the player is to achieving the game's goal. In an arcade game, a total score might indicate performance, whereas a flight simulator might provide feedback through a detailed 3-D view from the cockpit plus a view of the aircraft's instrumentation.

- *How does the game reward the player?* This tells the player what to expect once the game's goal is met. For a children's game, the reward might be an animation of some cartoon figures with an accompanying musical score. Arcade games maintain a list with names of the high-scoring players and their scores.

- *How is the game played?* This feature tells the player how to play the game. The story line does not have to provide the full details at this point, but the overall idea should be explained. For instance, in many arcade games, you basically point and shoot at targets with your weapons. In most flight simulators, you control the flight of the aircraft through the keyboard, and the instrument panel and outside view tell you whether you are controlling the aircraft properly.

Graphics

All computer games rely on the visual effects of graphics to establish the story line and provide the illusions needed to make the player feel like a part of the game. Computer games employ several different types of graphics techniques:

- *2-D Graphics.* This type includes points, lines, and outline and filled shapes such as rectangles, polygons, and ellipses—in a plane. Many simple games rely almost solely on 2-D figures. The Windows API provides functions for 2-D graphics.

- *3-D Graphics.* This type refers to the techniques used to display 2-D views of 3-D objects. One approach is to specify a 3-D object by many flat surfaces (defined by polygons) that represent the boundaries of the object. Mathematical algorithms are used to derive a 2-D view of the object for a given viewing location. The 2-D view is also a collection of color-filled polygons that are displayed using standard 2-D graphics primitives. Computer games often include many 3-D objects and require that these objects be redrawn many times a second, which may not be possible with a typical PC. Most commercially available games handle this requirement by using a limited number of 3-D objects and by representing each object with as few polygonal surfaces as possible.

- *Image Display and Manipulation.* An *image* is a 2-D array of points with each point drawn in a specific color and can represent a complex drawing. Images are useful because you can use a scanner to digitize detailed pictures and use them as graphical elements in your game's display screens. Image manipulation refers to the scaling and rotation

Game Programming for Windows

of images. Animation of images—moving one image over another without disturbing the background image—is another technique used in computer games. The Windows API includes functions to display and manipulate *bitmaps*—rectangular arrays of pixels.

Sound Effects

After graphics, sound is the element that makes a computer game come alive. Unfortunately, most MS-DOS PCs have very limited hardware support to generate sound. The speaker that is standard on most PCs can generate only a single tone at a time. Although programmers have found ways to generate complex sound with the PC's limited sound hardware, the Windows API supports the capability to generate only one tone at a time. However, most computer games can generate more complex sound (including digitized voice and music) using an optional sound board installed in the PC. These sound boards are plug-in cards that include hardware to generate more complex sound. Windows 3.1 also supports these additional sound boards. See Chapter 6 for more information about generating sound with the Windows API functions.

Copy Protection

Although copy protection has all but disappeared from mainstream applications such as word processors and spreadsheets, it is commonplace in computer games. One of these annoying techniques requires you to place the original diskette in the PC's drive even though you might have installed theprogram on your system's hard disk. A more palatable form of copy protection is based on the user's manual accompanying the game software. For instance, Great Naval Battles, North Atlantic 1939-1943 displays the dialog box shown in Figure 1.10, prompting you for a specific word from the user's manual. Once you type in the requested word, the game starts; otherwise the program terminates.

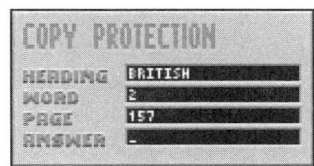

Figure 1.10. *Copy protection scheme that relies on the user's manual.*

Issues in Game Programming for Windows

One of the reasons most of the current crop of computer games do not run under Windows is that they existed before Windows became popular and they have not yet been ported to Windows. Another reason is that Windows adds a device-independent layer of functions that you must use to control the PC's hardware such as the display adapter, the keyboard and mouse, and the speaker. This device independence lets you write a single application that can run on many PCs with differing hardware configurations, but it also denies you access to the registers and ports on the display adapters. Many games are able to provide fast display only because they can manipulate the display adapter directly. It is difficult to port such games to Windows and achieve the same performance as under DOS. However, the speed disadvantage should gradually disappear as PC processors become faster and the display adapters are optimized for Windows.

Color

For striking graphics, a computer game needs to use color. In some ways, being able to display at least 256 colors is better than having high resolution. When the VGA display adapter was introduced for the IBM PC family of computers, the adapter came with enough memory to support, at most, 16 simultaneous colors at a 640x480 resolution. Although the 640x480 is an adequate resolution for the typical 13-inch or 14-inch monitor, the 16-color limit made it difficult to display good color images on a VGA display at its highest resolution. Only one mode of the VGA, mode 13H, provides more colors—256—but does so at a 320x200 resolution. Most DOS games use this VGA mode. The lower resolution is offset by the ability to display many shades of colors, which adds greatly to the realism of an image. The lower resolution also has an added advantage in this case. Because a byte is enough to hold any one of 256 colors, a 256-color 320x200 image can be stored in exactly 320x200 (64K). Because this image size is less than a 64K segment of memory addressable by the Intel 8086 processor, the processor can efficiently access and manipulate individual colored dots called *pixels* (picture elements) in the image.

Game Programming for Windows

Luckily for us, additional memory in the VGA cards soon provided many other video modes, including one at 640x480 with 256 colors and many others at varying combinations of resolution and colors. These so-called super VGA cards were difficult to support under DOS because the video modes were not standard, but Windows solved this problem in one fell swoop. Because Windows programs access the display adapter through a driver, Windows can use a super VGA card at any of its supported color-resolution combinations—as long as the VGA card's vendor provides a driver for the card. Thus, with Windows you should be able to write games that exploit, at a minimum, the 256-color 640x480 resolution of super VGA cards. In fact, many systems now sport other video adapters such as XGA and graphics accelerator chips that are designed to provide fast graphics output under Windows. Thanks to the device independence of Windows, your Windows games can support these advanced video cards as easily as the standard VGA adapters.

Multimedia Games for Windows

Starting with version 3.1, Windows supports *multimedia*—a collection of input and output capabilities including audio and video that go beyond the standard keyboard, mouse, and graphics display that have been part of PCs all along. Windows provides drivers for multimedia devices such as CD-ROM drive, sound board, image scanner, and videotape player, and an API for controlling any of these devices.

If you turn the pages of *Computer Shopper* magazine, you see a definite upsurge in advertisements for CD-ROM and sound boards such as the Sound Blaster or AdLib. Games such as Where in the World is Carmen Sandiego? and BattleChess are already beginning to take advantage of these multimedia devices to bring detailed images, interactive video, and digitized voices to their games. Although most of the games are still DOS-based, if you are planning a new multimedia game, you might want to write the game for Windows because the Windows API includes good support for multimedia programming.

Summary

Computer games are always popular and there are many computer games for the PC. You can organize the current crop of computer games into seven categories: educational, traditional, arcade, sports, adventures and role playing, real-time action simulations, and strategic simulations. All computer games use graphics and sound to create the special effects that make the games entertaining. If you have a good idea for a game, you can implement it by using a standard set of techniques for graphics and sound generation.

Most of the games run under MS-DOS and many games with good color graphics make use of the 256-color 320x200 resolution mode of the VGA display adapter. However, Microsoft Windows offers a unique opportunity to exploit advanced display adapters (with greater than 640x480 resolution and more than 256 colors) in a device-independent manner. Also, Windows supports devices such as CD-ROM and sound cards that you can use to enhance your computer game. The rest of this book focuses on illustrating how to develop games for Windows using Borland C++ and the Windows API.

Further Reading

Michael Young's book covers game programming with Microsoft Visual Basic. He describes and implements several traditional games such as Tic Tac Toe, a Fractal Puzzle, a Tetris-like game called TriPack, and a variation of Solitaire called Peg Solitaire.

To keep up with recent commercial computer game offerings and to learn more about the trends in popularity of different types of games, consult magazines such as *Computer Gaming World* (published monthly by Golden Empire Publications, Inc., Anaheim Hills, CA) and *PC Games* (published eight times a year by A+ Publishing, a subsidiary of Macworld Communications, Peterborough, NH).

 Young, Michael J. *Visual Basic—Game Programming for Windows.* Redmond, WA: Microsoft Press, 1992.

Chapter 2

Windows Programming with Borland C++

Programming Windows Games with Borland C++

Windows applications are easy to use and they have a rich graphical user interface; unfortunately for software developers, the ease of use comes at the expense of a complex *Application Programming Interface (API)*, the collection of functions that programmers use to write Windows applications. For example, the Windows API contains over 600 functions. Although you can get by with a small fraction of these, you are never quite sure if you are overlooking some function that does exactly what your application needs to do. In addition to the sheer volume of information, you have to follow an entirely different approach when you write Windows applications. Despite these drawbacks, writing games for Windows does offer several advantages:

- Windows offers *device independence*. The same Windows game should display its output on any monitor from EGA to VGA and print on any printer from dot-matrix to laser.
- For the developer, Windows offers a variety of predefined user-interface components such as pushbuttons, menus, dialog boxes, lists, and edit windows.
- Windows includes an extensive interface to any graphics device (called *Graphics Device Interface, GDI*) for drawing graphics and text. In particular, the GDI lets you draw in your own coordinate system.

Until now, C has been the programming language of choice for writing Windows applications. Meanwhile, C++ has been steadily gaining in popularity and many programmers are now interested in using it to write Windows applications. However, calling Windows functions from a C++ program is not as simple as calling, for instance, the functions from the standard C library. This is because the compiler has to generate special object code when calling Windows functions, and Windows uses a different method of passing arguments to its functions. In other words, the C++ compiler has to support the requirements imposed by Windows. Like most MS-DOS C++ compilers, Borland C++ supports Windows programming. In particular, Borland C++ comes with the *ObjectWindows Library (OWL)*, a library of C++ classes that makes it easier to write Windows applications.

This chapter is a quick introduction to writing Windows programs with Borland C++, OWL, and the utility class library often referred to as CLASSLIB, but it is not a complete tutorial. If you need further information on object-oriented programming or Windows programming, consult one of the books listed at the end of this chapter. Although the example program in this chapter is simple, it provides you with a complete framework for developing a Windows application with Borland C++.

Chapter 2

Windows Programming with Borland C++

Note that Borland C++ includes the full source code for the OWL and the class library. Therefore, if you want, you can always browse through the source code of the OWL classes to see exactly how the classes are defined and implemented.

> **Isn't Microsoft Windows Already Object-Oriented?**
>
> From the early years, books on Microsoft Windows have described its object-oriented architecture. Then why do programmers access the Windows environment through a layer of C++ classes such as those in the Borland's OWL? Because even though Windows supports the concept of certain objects, the data encapsulation and inheritance rely on the programmer's discipline. After all, when you write Windows programs in C, you can access and modify all parts of the structures that represent the "objects." Even if this were not an issue, anyone who has written a Windows program in C knows that the programmer has to attend to a myriad of details to get the application and its windows to "look" and "behave" properly. An object-oriented layer, in an object-oriented programming language such as C++, can help tremendously by hiding many unnecessary details. Basically, that's what you get when you use C++ classes that support Windows programming. You might say that the Windows environment has an underlying object-oriented architecture, but the Windows "programming interface" is procedural. By using a properly designed set of C++ classes, you are making the programming interface more object-oriented.

Microsoft Windows Programming with Borland C++ Classes

The primary purpose of the OWL classes is to provide a complete *application framework* for building Microsoft Windows applications. The collection of classes in OWL are referred to as a framework because they essentially provide all the components for skeletal programs that can be easily fleshed out into complete Windows applications.

Even though the Borland class libraries (CLASSLIB and OWL) include most classes necessary to build the user interface and represent various data types, it is easier to build an application if you follow a well-defined architecture (structural model) for the application. The *Model-View-Controller (MVC)* architecture prevalent in the Smalltalk-80 programming language is a good candidate for Windows applications.

Model-View-Controller (MVC) Architecture

The MVC architecture separates the application into three separate layers (see Figure 2.1):

- ■ *Model* refers to the *application layer* where all application-dependent objects reside. For example, in a drawing program, this is the layer that maintains the graphics objects.

- ■ *View* is the *presentation layer* which presents the application's data to the user. This layer extracts information from the model and displays the information in windows. In a drawing program, this layer gets the list of graphics objects from the model and renders them in a window. Also, the view provides the windows in the application's graphical user interface.

- ■ *Controller* is the *interaction layer* which provides the interface between the input devices (such as keyboard and mouse) and the View and Model layers.

The MVC architecture does an excellent job of separating the responsibilities of the objects in the system. The application-specific details are insulated from the user interface. Also, the user interface itself is broken down into two parts: the presentation is handled by the view and the interaction is handled by the controller.

When building Windows applications using OWL and CLASSLIB, you do not have to follow the MVC model strictly. For instance, when you use OWL classes, it is difficult to separate the view and controller layers. As shown in

Windows Programming with Borland C++

Figure 2.2, your application consists of a model and an associated view-controller pair. The figure also shows the usual interactions in Smalltalk-80's MVC architecture. The controller accepts the user's inputs and invokes the appropriate function from the model to perform the task requested by the user. When the work is done, the function in the model sends messages to the view and controller. The view updates the display in response to this message, accessing the model for further information if necessary. Thus, the model has a view and a controller, but it never directly accesses them. The view and controller, on the other hand, access the model's functions and data, when necessary.

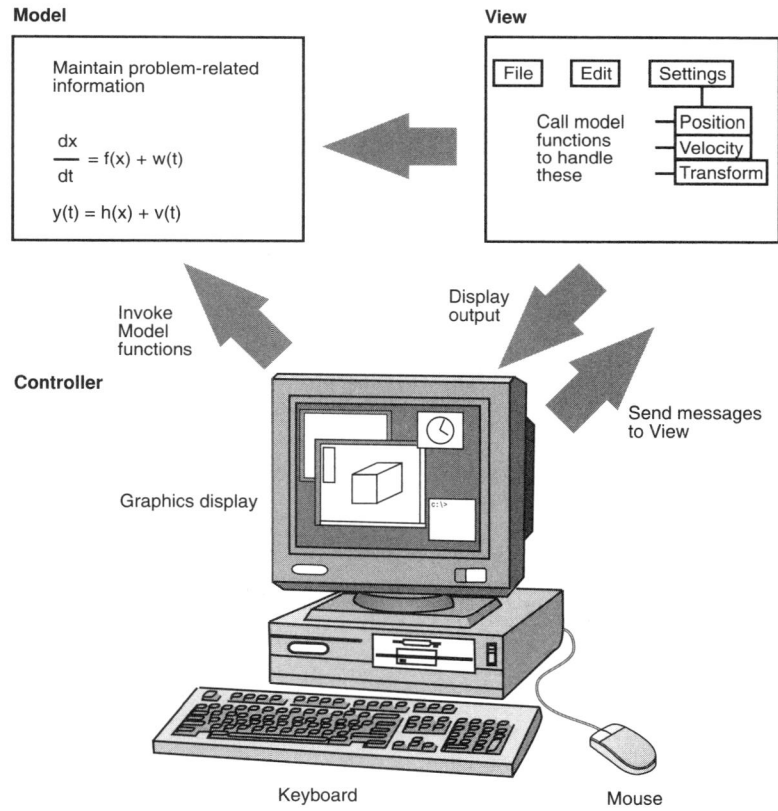

Figure 2.1. *Model-View-Controller (MVC) architecture of Smalltalk-80.*

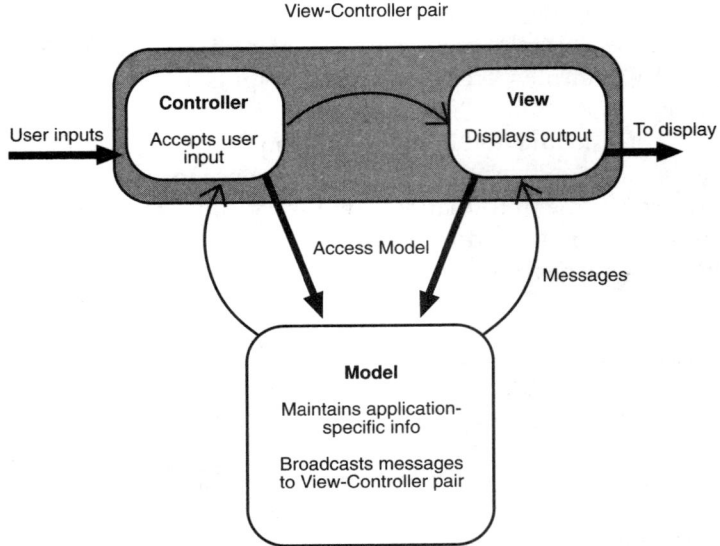

Figure 2.2. *Interactions among model, view, and controller in the MVC model.*

As you can see in the examples that follow, most of the OWL classes contribute to the view and controller pair. You typically use your own classes as well as the general-purpose classes such as strings, lists, and arrays in the application's model layer.

A Windows Application Using OWL and CLASSLIB

A simple example shows how to employ the MVC architecture to build a Windows application with the Borland C++ class libraries. This application uses OWL displaying `Hello, World!` in a window. Even with OWL, you have to attend to many details when writing a Microsoft Windows application. This simple example illustrates the steps, which you follow even when writing a more complex Windows application such as a game.

Windows Programming with Borland C++

HelloApp Class

As a consequence of the concept of an application framework, all OWL-based Microsoft Windows applications rely on a class derived from the `TApplication` class that models the entire application. Listing 2.1 shows the file `hello.cpp`. This implements the class `HelloApp` that models our sample application. In the `HelloApp` class, you define at least two member functions: `InitInstance` to initialize an instance of the application and `InitMainWindow` to initialize the main window of the application. When you use the MVC architecture, the basic steps for your application are

1. Create a model for the application. For this application, the model is a class named `HelloModel`, defined in the header file `hellomdl.h` (Listing 2.2). The model class holds all application-specific data—in this case, the data is a string to be displayed in a window.

2. Create a view and store a pointer to the model in the view. In this case, the view class is named `HelloView` and is declared in the header file `hellovw.h` (Listing 2.3).

3. Derive an application class from `TApplication`, and in the `InitMainWindow` function of the application class, create the model and the view.

4. Write a `WinMain` function. In that function create an instance of the application class and call the `Run` function to get the application going. Essentially, the application class, derived from `TApplication`, provides the functionality of the controller in the MVC architecture.

Listing 2.1. `hello.cpp` – The hello application based on the MVC architecture.

```
//-------------------------------------------------------------
//  File:   hello.cpp
//
//  A Windows application that uses the ObjectWindows Library
//-------------------------------------------------------------
#include "hellovw.h"
#include "hellomdl.h"

class HelloApp: public TApplication
{
```

continues

Listing 2.1. continued

```
public:
// Constructor that simply calls the base class constructor

    HelloApp(LPSTR name, HINSTANCE instance,
            HINSTANCE prev_instance, LPSTR  cmdline, int show) :

            TApplication(name, instance, prev_instance,
                        cmdline, show)   {}
    ~HelloApp() { delete m;}

// Define function to initialize application's main window
    void InitMainWindow();

// Define function to initialize an instance of this application
    void InitInstance();

private:
    HelloModel *m;
};
//----------------------------------------------------------------
// H e l l o A p p : : I n i t M a i n W i n d o w

void HelloApp::InitMainWindow()
{
    m = new HelloModel();
    MainWindow = new HelloView(m);
}
//----------------------------------------------------------------
// H e l l o A p p : : I n i t I n s t a n c e

void HelloApp::InitInstance()
{
   TApplication::InitInstance();
   HAccTable = LoadAccelerators(hInstance, "MainAccelTable");
}
//----------------------------------------------------------------
// W i n M a i n
//
// Create an instance of the application and "run" it.

int PASCAL WinMain(HINSTANCE instance, HINSTANCE prev_instance,
                LPSTR cmdline, int show)
```

Windows Programming with Borland C++

```
{
    HelloApp hello_world("Hello, World!", instance,
                    prev_instance, cmdline, show);

    hello_world.Run();

    return hello_world.Status;
}
```

HelloModel Class

An application's model is supposed to store data unique to the application. In this case, the application is simple enough that you can display the Hello, World! string directly from the view class. However, creating a model class illustrates how to build a realistic application using the MVC architecture. This application's model, the HelloModel class (Listing 2.2), contains the string to be displayed in the window. The string is stored in an instance of a String class (from Borland CLASSLIB) that is created in the constructor of the HelloModel class. The view class uses the member function named get_string to obtain a pointer to this String instance.

Listing 2.2. hellomdl.h—Definition of the HelloModel class.

```
//--------------------------------------------------------------
// File:  hellomdl.h
//
// The "model" for the "hello" application.  In this case,
// the model simply stores a string to be displayed in a window.

#if !defined(__HELLOMDL_H)
#define __HELLOMDL_H

#include <owl.h>
#include <strng.h>
#include <string.h>

class HelloModel
{
```

continues

29

Listing 2.2. continued

```
public:
    HelloModel() { p_str = new String("Hello, World!");}

    ~HelloModel() { delete p_str;}

    String* get_string() { return p_str;}
private:
    String *p_str;
};

#endif
```

HelloView Class

The HelloView class, declared in the file hellovw.h (Listing 2.3) and implemented in hellovw.cpp (Listing 2.4), provides the view for this application. The HelloView class is responsible for displaying in a window the message stored in the HelloModel class. HelloView is derived from the TWindow class which is designed to serve as the main window of an application. The view class stores a pointer to the model; through this pointer the view can access the model as needed.

The most important function of the HelloView class is called Paint. OWL automatically calls the Paint function for a window whenever the window needs repainting.

The About function is a Windows message response function as indicated by the way it is declared:

```
void About(RTMessage msg) = [CM_FIRST + IDM_ABOUT];
```

Notice the unusual [CM_FIRST + IDM_ABOUT] syntax. This is an extension to C++ indicating that About is a message response function that OWL calls to handle the Windows message identified by [CM_FIRST + IDM_ABOUT]. The constant CM_FIRST is defined in the header file <owldefs.h> and refers to the WM_COMMAND message. The constant IDM_ABOUT identifies this message as the one that Windows sends to your application's window when the user selects the About menu item in the Help menu. Note that you indicate the association between a menu item and a constant (such as IDM_ABOUT) in the resource file, in this case HELLO.RC (Listing 2.8).

Windows Programming with Borland C++

Chapter 2

As you can see in Listing 2.4, the `About` function displays a dialog box with information about the application.

> Microsoft Windows works by sending messages to the windows that constitute an application's user interface. OWL uses the idea of message response functions, each of which is associated with a specific Windows message. OWL automatically calls that response function when the corresponding Windows message occurs. Borland has extended the syntax of C++ function declaration to provide a way to associate a function with a Windows message. For example, to declare `WMTimer` as the function to be called in response to the `WM_TIMER` message, write
>
> `void WMTimer(RTMessage msg) = [WM_FIRST + WM_TIMER];`
>
> where `RTMessage` is a reference to a `TMessage` structure and the expression `[WM_FIRST + WM_TIMER]` evaluates to a message number that identifies the `WM_TIMER` message. You have to declare these message response functions in your application's window class, which is derived from the OWL class `TWindow`.

Listing 2.3. `hellovw.h`—Declaration of the `HelloView` class.

```
//------------------------------------------------------------
//  File:    hellovw.h
//
//  The "view" for the "hello" application. In this case,
//  the view is a window where the string from the model
//  is displayed.

#if !defined(__HELLOVW_H)
#define __HELLOVW_H

// Include necessary header files
#include <owl.h>
#include "hellores.h"   // Resource identifiers for application

class HelloModel;
```

continues

Listing 2.3. continued

```
class HelloView : public TWindow
{
public:
    HelloView(HelloModel *a_model);

// The following is needed to set up an icon for the application
    void GetWindowClass(WNDCLASS _FAR &wc);

// Declare functions for handling messages from Windows
    void Paint(HDC hdc, PAINTSTRUCT &ps);
    void About(RTMessage msg) = [CM_FIRST + IDM_ABOUT];

private:
    HelloModel *model;
};


#endif
```

Listing 2.4 shows the implementation of the `HelloView` class. In Listing 2.4, the `Paint` function contains the code that displays a message in the application's main window. In the `Paint` function, we get the message string from the model by calling the `get_string` function of the `HelloModel` class as follows:

```
void HelloView::Paint(HDC hdc, PAINTSTRUCT&)
{

// Get the message to be displayed
    String* p_string = model->get_string();

// Display the message ...
}
```

The actual rendering of the string is done by calling a text drawing function from the Windows API. Notice that the `Paint` function is called with a *handle*— an integer identifier— to a *device context (DC)* as an argument. The device context holds information that controls the appearance of drawings created by Windows drawing functions. In `Paint`, the device context is used as follows:

```
    SetTextAlign(hdc, TA_BASELINE | TA_CENTER);
    SetBkMode(hdc, TRANSPARENT);

//...
```

Windows Programming with Borland C++

```
// Draw the string
    TextOut(hdc, xpos, h/2, *p_string, len);
```

Graphics attributes such as alignment of text and the background mode are set by calling the Windows API functions `SetTextAlign` and `SetBkMode`, respectively.

The text string is displayed by calling the `TextOut` function. In the call to `TextOut`, xpos denotes the x-coordinate of the location in the window where the text output starts, h denotes the height of the window, and len is the number of characters in the text string being displayed. You can get the size (width and height) of the window and the length of a `String` object as follows:

```
// Get window size
    RECT r;
    GetClientRect(HWindow, &r);

    int w = r.right - r.left;
    int h = r.bottom - r.top;

// Get number of characters in string
    int len = strlen(*p_string);
```

If you want to draw other graphics in the window, you can call other drawing functions from the Windows API.

Listing 2.4. `hellovw.cpp`— Implementation of the `HelloView` class.

```
//--------------------------------------------------------------
// File:  hellovw.cpp
//
// The "view" layer for the "hello" application
//--------------------------------------------------------------
#include "hellovw.h"
#include "hellomdl.h"

//--------------------------------------------------------------
// H e l l o V i e w : : H e l l o V i e w
// Constructor for HelloView class
```

continues

Listing 2.4. continued

```
HelloView::HelloView(HelloModel* a_model) : model(a_model),
                    TWindow(NULL, "Hello")
{
    AssignMenu("MainMenu");
}
//-----------------------------------------------------------------
//    H e l l o V i e w : : G e t W i n d o w C l a s s
//    Set up icon for this application

void HelloView::GetWindowClass(WNDCLASS &wc)
{
// First call the GetWindowClass function of the base class
    TWindow::GetWindowClass(wc);

// Set up icon for this application
    wc.hIcon = LoadIcon(wc.hInstance, "HELLO_ICON");
}
//-----------------------------------------------------------------
//    H e l l o V i e w : : P a i n t
//    Draw contents of window

void HelloView::Paint(HDC hdc, PAINTSTRUCT&)
{
    SetTextAlign(hdc, TA_BASELINE | TA_CENTER);
    SetBkMode(hdc, TRANSPARENT);

// Get the message to be displayed
    String* p_string = model->get_string();

// Get window size
    RECT r;
    GetClientRect(HWindow, &r);

    int w = r.right - r.left;
    int h = r.bottom - r.top;

// Get number of characters in string
    int len = strlen(*p_string);

// Display string roughly at the center of window
    int xpos = w/2;
    if(xpos < 0) xpos = 0;
    TextOut(hdc, xpos, h/2, *p_string, len);
}
//-----------------------------------------------------------------
//    H e l l o A p p : : A b o u t
//    Display the "About..." box
```

Windows Programming with Borland C++

```
void HelloView::About(RTMessage)
{
    TDialog *p_about = new TDialog(this, "ABOUTHELLO");
    GetApplication()->ExecDialog(p_about);
}
```

Building the Application

Once you have the header files and source files ready, you have to compile and link them to create a Microsoft Windows application. I use the MAKE utility that comes with the Borland C++ compiler, but you can build the executable by defining a project within Borland's Windows-based development environment.

The input to the MAKE utility is called a *makefile*. For the hello application, the makefile (named MAKEFILE) is shown in Listing 2.5. Given the makefile of Listing 2.5, the following command builds the file HELLO.EXE:

```
make
```

Notice that the makefile shown in Listing 2.5 creates a configuration file, HELLO.CFG, with a list of options for the Borland C++ compiler. Nowadays the compiler options are so numerous and lengthy that if you were to run the Borland C++ compiler (bcc) by specifying the options on the command-line, the number of characters on the command-line exceeds 128—the maximum allowed by MS-DOS. The configuration file avoids this limitation because you only specify the name of the configuration file on the command-line that runs bcc.

You need a few more files to complete the process specified in the makefile:

- ■ HELLO.DEF *(Listing 2.6)*. This file is known as the *module definition* file and is needed to build Microsoft Windows applications.

- ■ HELLORES.H *(Listing 2.7)*. This file defines constants that identify resources such as menu item numbers.

- ■ HELLO.RC *(Listing 2.8)*. This file is known as the *resource file* and is a text file that specifies the layouts and contents of menus and dialog boxes. The Microsoft resource compiler (invoked by the RC command) compiles this file into a binary form and appends it to the executable file.

- **HELLO.DLG** *(Listing 2.9)*. This file contains the actual layout of the About Hello dialog box displayed by the HELLO application. The resource file, HELLO.RC, incorporates the contents of HELLO.DLG into HELLO.RC by using the rcinclude directive of the resource compiler.

- **HELLO.ICO**. This is a small image (32 pixels by 32 pixels) that you should prepare using the Resource Workshop application (WORKSHOP.EXE) that comes with the Borland C++ compiler. The icon file, HELLO.ICO, is referenced in the resource file HELLO.RC.

Listing 2.5. Makefile for building `HELLO.EXE`.

```
################################################################
# Makefile : Builds the Hello application
#
# Usage:        MAKE
#
# NOTE:         Change the INCLUDES and LIBS symbols so that the
#               pathnames are consistent with the drive and
#               directory where you installed Borland C++.
#

.AUTODEPEND
INCLUDES = e:\bc31\include;e:\bc31\classlib\include;e:\bc31\owl\include

LIBS = e:\bc31\lib;e:\bc31\owl\lib;e:\bc31\classlib\lib

CC = bcc +hello.cfg

LINK = tlink

OBJ = hello.obj hellovw.obj

# Explicit rule to build the executable file

hello.exe: $(OBJ) hello.def hello.res hello.cfg
    $(LINK)    /x/c/Twe/P-/C/L$(LIBS) @&&|
c0wl.obj+
$(OBJ)
hello
                        # no map file
owl.lib+
import.lib+
tclasdll.lib+
```

Windows Programming with Borland C++

```
  mathwl.lib+
  crtldll.lib+
  cwl.lib
  hello.def
¦
    rc hello.res hello.exe

# Other dependencies
hello.res: hello.rc hello.dlg hello.ico hello.cfg
    rc -r -I$(INCLUDES) -FO hello.res hello.rc

hello.obj: hello.cpp hellovw.h hellomdl.h hellores.h hello.cfg

hellovw.obj: hellovw.cpp hellovw.h hellomdl.h hellores.h hello.cfg

# Compiler configuration file
hello.cfg:   makefile
    copy &&¦
-ml
-2
-C
-d
-Fc
-WS
-vi
-H=HELLO.SYM
-DWIN31
-D_CLASSDLL
-I$(INCLUDES)
-L$(LIBS)
¦ hello.cfg
```

Listing 2.6. HELLO.DEF—Module definition file for HELLO.EXE.

```
NAME            Hello
DESCRIPTION     'Hello from ObjectWindows Library (OWL)'
EXETYPE         WINDOWS
STUB            'WINSTUB.EXE'

CODE            PRELOAD MOVEABLE DISCARDABLE
DATA            PRELOAD MOVEABLE MULTIPLE

HEAPSIZE        8192
STACKSIZE       8192
```

Listing 2.7. `hellores.h`—Resource identifiers for `HELLO.EXE`.

```
//-------------------------------------------------------------
//  File: hellores.h
//
//  Declare the resource IDs for the Hello application
//  In this case, we have only one.

#define IDM_ABOUT 100
```

Listing 2.8. `HELLO.RC`—Resource file for `HELLO.EXE`.

```
//-------------------------------------------------------------
//  File: hello.rc
//
//  Declare the resources for the Hello application
//-------------------------------------------------------------
#include <windows.h>
#include "hellores.h"

MainMenu MENU
{
    POPUP "&Help"
    {
        MENUITEM "&About Hello...\tF1", IDM_ABOUT
    }
}

MainAccelTable ACCELERATORS
{
    VK_F1,   IDM_ABOUT,   VIRTKEY
}

HELLO_ICON ICON hello.ico

rcinclude hello.dlg
```

Windows Programming with Borland C++

Listing 2.9. HELLO.DLG—
Definition of the dialogs used in HELLO.EXE.

```
//--------------------------------------------------------------
//   File: hello.dlg
//
//   Define the dialogs used in the Hello application.
//   In this case, we have only the "About Hello" dialog.

ABOUTHELLO DIALOG 22, 17, 144, 75
STYLE DS_MODALFRAME | WS_CAPTION | WS_SYSMENU
CAPTION "About Hello"
BEGIN
    CTEXT            "Hello, World! from", -1, 0, 2, 144, 8
    CTEXT            "ObjectWindows Library (OWL)", -1, 0, 12, 144, 8
    CTEXT            "Version 1.0", -1, 0, 22, 144, 8
    DEFPUSHBUTTON    "OK", IDOK, 56, 56, 32, 14, WS_GROUP
END
```

Testing *HELLO.EXE*

Once you successfully compile and link the sample application HELLO.EXE, you can run it under Microsoft Windows by typing the following command at the DOS prompt:

```
win hello
```

Or, if you are already running Windows, you can start HELLO.EXE from the **Run** option in the File menu of the Program Manager.

Figure 2.3 shows the output from the program. If you resize the window, Hello, World! should appear centered in the window. Note that a minimized version of a second copy of HELLO also appears in Figure 2.3.

Figure 2.3. `Hello, World!` from OWL-based `HELLO.EXE`.

Borland C++ Class Libraries

Now that you have seen an example of a Microsoft Windows application built using classes from CLASSLIB and OWL, here is an overview of the entire class hierarchy that accompanies Borland C++. You should know about the classes because your game application might need data types (strings, date, and time) as well as containers (arrays, lists, and queues) capable of holding a variety of objects. Of course, the OWL classes are useful for building the Windows interface for your game.

In addition to the CLASSLIB and OWL classes, Borland C++ 3.1 introduced another set of classes. These use class templates to define a variety of flexible container classes that can store anything from built-in C++ types, such as `int` and `float`, to your own class types. Class templates are class definitions parameterized by a data type. Borland calls these classes the Borland International Data Structures (BIDS). The BIDS classes are summarized later in this chapter. First let us look at the more conventional CLASSLIB and OWL classes.

Windows Programming with Borland C++

Breakdown of the CLASSLIB Classes

There are three categories of classes in CLASSLIB:

- *Container classes* that are meant to hold one or more objects (or pointers to objects)
- *Simple classes* that represent new data types such as string, date, and time
- *Iterator classes* that allow you to access the contents of a container, one after another

Container Class Hierarchy

Figure 2.4 shows the inheritance hierarchy of the container classes in CLASSLIB. As you can see, all classes in this category inherit from both the Object class and the TShouldDelete class. The Object class is an abstract base class, which means that you cannot create an instance of this class. The purpose of the Object class is to provide a common set of member functions for all the classes in the hierarchy.

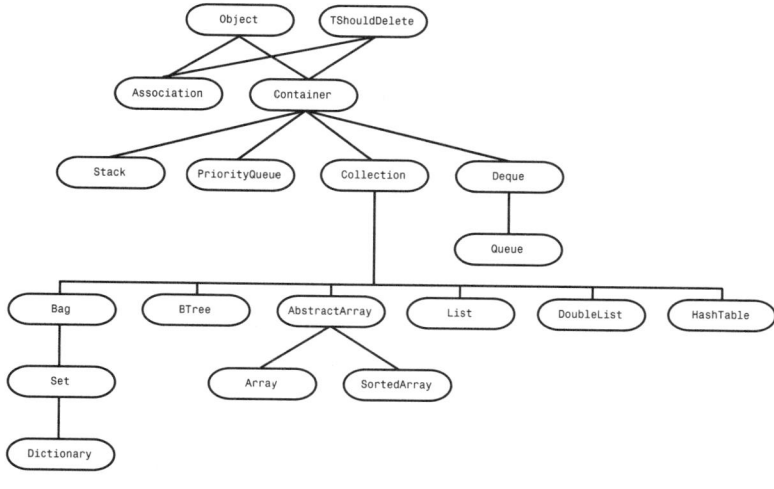

Figure 2.4. *Container class hierarchy in Borland CLASSLIB.*

The `TShouldDelete` class provides a mechanism for the programmer to indicate what should happen when you store pointers to objects in a container and the container is destroyed. By calling the `ownsElements` member function of the `TShouldDelete` class, you can indicate whether the container should delete the objects or leave them alone. By default, a container deletes the objects it contains. Table 2.1 summarizes the container classes in Borland CLASSLIB.

Table 2.1. Container classes in Borland CLASSLIB.

Class	Description
`AbstractArray`	An abstract class that represents an array
`Array`	An array that can grow at runtime
`Association`	A pair of objects (the first denotes a key, the second denotes the value associated with that key)
`Bag`	An unordered collection of objects that can have multiple instances of the same object
`BTree`	A B-Tree data structure
`Collection`	An abstract class representing a container that can keep track of the objects it holds
`Container`	An abstract class that models an object capable of holding many different types of objects
`Deque`	A variation of the well-known queue data structure allowing objects to be inserted and removed at both ends of the queue (a *double-ended queue*, pronounced "deck")
`Dictionary`	An unordered collection of association objects that provides a member function to look up associations using keys
`DoubleList`	A doubly-linked list data structure
`HashTable`	An unordered collection of objects that allows fast access through a hash function (the location of an object is computed directly from the data representing the object)

Windows Programming with Borland C++

`List`	A singly-linked list data structure
`PriorityQueue`	A queue that maintains objects in a specific order according to the priority assigned to each object (the order is determined by applying the < operator of the queued objects)
`Queue`	A FIFO (first-in first-out) data structure that allows you to insert objects at the tail of the queue and remove them from the head
`Set`	An unordered collection of objects in which only one occurrence of an object is allowed in the set
`SortedArray`	An array that keeps its contents sorted in ascending order (where the ascending order is defined by the operator < of the objects in the array)
`Stack`	A LIFO (last-in first-out) data structure

Simple Classes in CLASSLIB

Simple classes are the noncontainer classes that include the following:

- `BaseDate` An abstract class that provides the basic date manipulation functions.
- `BaseTime` An abstract class that provides the basic time manipulation functions.
- `Date` A class derived from `BaseDate` that provides the function used to print a date. This separation of responsibility between `BaseDate` and `Date` allows you to easily customize the way a date is displayed.
- `Error` A class that provides a mechanism to indicate error conditions that might occur in the library during memory allocations. There is a single instance of an `Error` object in a program and when memory allocation fails, the pointer returned by the `new` operator points to this global instance of the Error object. You can detect an error by comparing the pointer with the macro called `NOOBJECT` that is defined as a reference to the global `Error` object.

- **Sortable** An abstract class that encapsulates the property that objects can be compared. Classes derived from the Sortable class have to define the isEqual and isLessThan member functions.
- **String** An array of characters representing a C-style, null-terminated array of characters. The String class lets you define and manipulate strings without worrying about how the memory for the character array is managed.
- **Time** A class derived from BaseDate that provides the function used to print a time. This separation of responsibility between BaseTime and Time allows you to easily customize the way a time is displayed.

Figure 2.5 shows the class hierarchy of the simple classes in CLASSLIB.

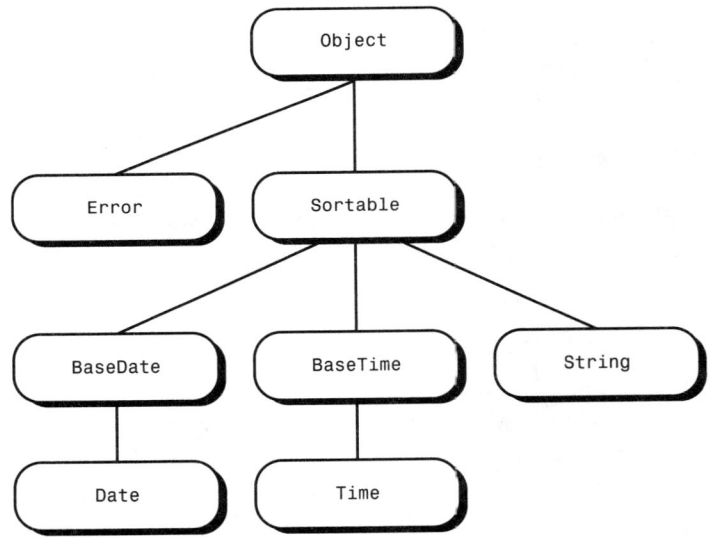

Figure 2.5. *Simple classes in CLASSLIB.*

Windows Programming with Borland C++

Iterator Classes in CLASSLIB

With the variety of containers available in CLASSLIB, you need a way to access the contents of a container. The iterator classes provide the ability to do this. As shown in Figure 2.6, the iterator classes form a simple hierarchy with the `ContainerIterator` class as the common base class. Here is a simple program that illustrates the use of the `ListIterator` to access each element in a list:

```
// Sample program that illustrates the use of iterators

#include <list.h>
#include <strng.h>
#include <iostream.h>

void main()
{
    List l;
    String *s1 = new String("One");
    String *s2 = new String("Two..");
    String *s3 = new String("Three...");

    l.add(*s1);
    l.add(*s2);
    l.add(*s3);

// Iterate over list
    ListIterator li(l);

    while(li)
    {
        cout << li++ << endl;
    }
}
```

When compiled and run, this program prints

```
Three...
Two..
One
```

These are all the `String` objects in the `List`. The printed order is the reverse of the order of insertion because the `add` member function of the `List` class adds an object to the head of the list.

45

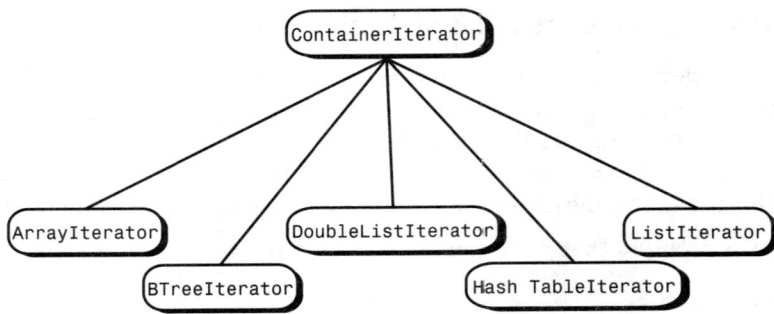

Figure 2.6. *Iterator classes in CLASSLIB.*

Template-Based Container Classes

One problem with the container classes in CLASSLIB (Figure 2.4) is that they can store only objects that are derived from the Object class. For instance, you cannot store any of the built-in data types such as float, int, or double in the CLASSLIB container classes. The template keyword that is part of AT&T C++ Release 3.0 provides a much better method of defining container classes that can hold any type of objects, including char, float, double, and int.

The BIDS classes offer two levels of abstraction:

■ Fundamental Data Structure (FDS)

■ Abstract Data Structure (ADT)

Consult the Borland C++ *Programmer's Guide* for more information on these template classes. The following is a brief description to refresh your memory.

Fundamental Data Structure (FDS)

FDSs are data structures at a lower-level of abstraction with close ties to the specific way they are implemented. The available FDSs are

■ Vectors

■ Singly-linked lists

■ Doubly-linked lists

Windows Programming with Borland C++

Borland calls this data structure an FDS because each implies a specific way of implementation: a vector is a contiguous sequence of memory locations and the lists are implemented as a collection of nodes connected by pointers. Table 2.2 lists the FDS class templates. Note that T denotes any type of object including built-in types such as `int` and `float` or your own class.

Table 2.2. Fundamental Data Structure FDS) container classes in Borland C++.

Class Template	Description
`BI_VectorImp<T>`	A vector of objects of type T
`BI_VectorIteratorImp<T>`	An iterator for `BI_VectorImp<T>`
`BI_CVectorImp<T>`	A counted vector of objects of type T
`BI_SVectorImp<T>`	A sorted vector of objects of type T
`BI_IVectorImp<T>`	A vector of pointers to objects of type T
`BI_IVectorIteratorImp<T>`	An iterator for a vector of pointers to type T
`BI_ICVectorImp<T>`	A counted vector of pointers to objects of type T
`BI_ISVectorImp<T>`	A sorted vector of pointers to objects of type T
`BI_ListImp<T>`	A list of objects of type T
`BI_SListImp<T>`	A sorted list of objects of type T
`BI_IListImp<T>`	A list of pointers to objects of type T
`BI_ISListImp<T>`	A sorted list of pointers to objects of type T
`BI_DoubleListImp<T>`	A doubly-linked list of objects of type T
`BI_SDoubleListImp<T>`	A sorted doubly-linked list of objects of type T

continues

Table 2.2. continued

Class Template	Description
`BI_IDoubleListImp<T>`	A doubly-linked list of pointers to objects of type T
`BI_ISDoubleListImp<T>`	A sorted doubly-linked list of pointers to objects of type T

Abstract Data Type (ADT)

To distinguish from the fundamental data structures, Borland uses the term ADT to denote containers at a higher level of abstraction. The ADT containers include

- `Array`
- `Bag`
- `Deque`
- `Queue`
- `Set`
- `Sorted Array`
- `Stack`

Note that these ADT containers provide the same functionality as the `Object`-based container classes in CLASSLIB. Each is implemented using one or more of the FDSs. For instance, a stack can be implemented as a vector or a singly-linked list. The names of ADT container class templates listed in Table 2.3 indicate which FDS each ADT class uses for its implementation.

Windows Programming with Borland C++

Table 2.3. Abstract Data Type (ADT) container classes in Borland C++.

Class Template	Description
`BI_StackAsVector<T>`	A stack implemented as a vector
`BI_QueueAsVector<T>`	A queue implemented as a vector
`BI_DequeAsVector<T>`	A deque (double-ended queue) implemented as a vector
`BI_BagAsVector<T>`	A bag implemented as a vector
`BI_SetAsVector<T>`	A set implemented as a vector
`BI_ArrayAsVector<T>`	An array implemented as a vector
`BI_SArrayAsVector<T>`	A sorted array implemented as a vector
`BI_IStackAsVector<T>`	A stack of pointers to T implemented as a vector
`BI_IQueueAsVector<T>`	A queue of pointers to T implemented as a vector
`BI_StackAsList<T>`	A stack implemented as a list
`BI_IStackAsList<T>`	A stack of pointers to T implemented as a list
`BI_QueueAsDoubleList<T>`	A stack implemented as a doubly-linked list
`BI_DequeAsDoubleList<T>`	A deque (double-ended queue) implemented as a doubly-linked list
`BI_IQueueAsDoubleList<T>`	A stack of pointers to T implemented as a doubly-linked list
`BI_IDequeAsDoubleList<T>`	A deque (double-ended queue) of pointers to T implemented as a doubly-linked list

OWL Classes

The sample Windows application presented in the early part of this chapter uses a number of OWL classes, including TApplication which provides the framework for a complete Windows program. Figure 2.7 shows the OWL class hierarchy. As you can see, like the CLASSLIB hierarchy, all classes in the OWL hierarchy are derived from the Object class. The TApplication class is used to represent the full application and the TWindowsObject classes provide the user-interface objects—windows, dialog boxes, and controls.

Window Classes

The classes TWindow, TEditWindow, and TFileWindow represent different types of windows. TWindow is a general-purpose window that can be the main, pop-up, or child window of an application—the main window of OWL applications is typically derived from the TWindow class. A TEditWindow is a specialized TWindow that allows text editing in the window. TFileWindow behaves like TEditWindow, but also allows loading text from and saving text to a file.

Dialog Classes

Dialogs are used to solicit input from the user. A dialog window displays a collection of controls such as buttons, list boxes, and scroll bars. The dialog classes make it very easy to display and use a dialog. For instance, with the TDialog class, here is what you have to write to display the About box in the sample application shown earlier in this chapter:

```
TDialog *p_about = new TDialog(this, "ABOUTHELLO");
GetApplication()->ExecDialog(p_about);
```

ABOUTHELLO is the name of the dialog box, as defined in the application's resource file.

The dialog classes in OWL include TDialog, TFileDialog, and TInput Dialog. As you have noticed from the sample usage above, TDialog represents a generic dialog. TFileDialog provides a dialog box that allows the user to choose a file from a directory listing. The TInputDialog class represents a dialog box that prompts the user for a single text item.

Chapter 2

Windows Programming with Borland C++

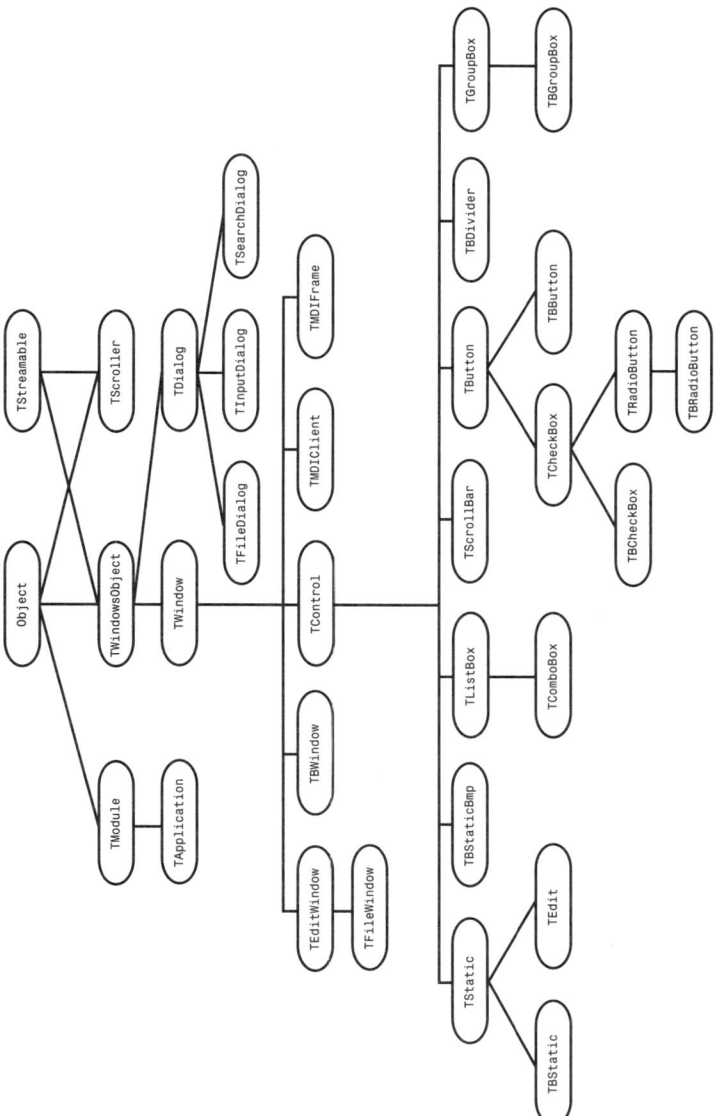

Figure 2.7. *OWL class hierarchy.*

> *Borland Windows Custom Controls (BWCC)* are a set of controls with a sophisticated 3-D look that accompanies Borland C++. You can conveniently create the BWCC controls by using the OWL classes: `TBButton`, `TBCheckBox`, `TBDivider`, `TBGroupBox`, `TBRadioBox`, `TBStatic`, and `TBStaticBmp`.

Control Classes

Controls refer to user-interface items such as buttons and scroll bars that the user manipulates with the mouse to supply input to the application. The sixteen control classes in OWL are derived from the abstract base class `TControl`:

`TBButton`	A pushbutton with the look and feel of BWCC
`TButton`	A Windows pushbutton
`TBCheckBox`	A box that can display check marks depending on the value of an internal variable (the style conforms to that of BWCC)
`TBDivider`	A class that displays a horizontal or vertical divider—a straight line
`TBGroupBox`	A class that behaves like `TGroupBox` but uses the BWCC style
`TBRadioButton`	A class that behaves like a `TRadioButton` but uses the BWCC style
`TBStatic`	A class that, like the TStatic class, displays a text string in a window using the BWCC style
`TBStaticBmp`	A class that behaves like the `TStatic` class, but displays a bitmap instead of a text string
`TCheckBox`	A box that displays a check mark if an internal variable is set
`TComboBox`	A Windows combo box control, which consists of an edit control with a drop-down list box for making selections

- **TEdit** — A Windows edit control with extensive text editing capabilities
- **TGroupBox** — A class that, like a Windows group box, draws a frame around a set of radio buttons or check boxes (unlike a Windows group box, a TGroupBox also manages the group of controls that it contains)
- **TListBox** — A Windows list box that displays a scrolling list of text strings in a window
- **TRadioButton** — A Windows radio button that the user can turn on or off
- **TScrollBar** — A Windows scroll bar control
- **TStatic** — A Windows static control that displays a text string (cannot be edited by user) in a window

Multiple Document Interface (MDI)

There are two more important classes in the TWindow hierarchy—TMDIClient and TMDIFrame—that are meant to support the Windows *multiple document interface (MDI)*. MDI refers to the technique of managing several child windows by an outer frame window. For example, the Windows Program Manager uses MDI to display the program groups in various child windows.

The TMDIFrame class, derived from TWindow, represents the frame window that serves as the main window in an application that uses MDI. The TMDIFrame class provides member functions, such as TileChildren and CloseChildren, that manipulate MDI child windows.

TMDIClient is also derived from TWindow. The TMDIClient class represents the client window that manages the child windows in an MDI frame.

TScroller Class

The TScroller class in OWL provides an automated way to scroll the contents of a window. A TScroller can scroll windows that are created with one or both of these styles: WS_HSCROLL and WS_VSCROLL. Additionally, a TScroller object can scroll its associated window even if the window does not have any scroll bars.

Summary

Windows programming is difficult because of the large number of functions (over 600) in the Windows API and because you have to attend to a myriad of details to get a Windows application up and running. C++ class libraries such as Borland's OWL help you manage the complexity by encapsulating many details of the user interface in a set of C++ classes. Note, however, that even when you use C++ and class libraries such as OWL, you have to use Windows API functions for graphics output and define other C++ classes that may be required by your application.

Although class libraries such as OWL provide the building blocks for your application, you also need an overall structure. For this you can use the Model-View-Controller (MVC) architecture of Smalltalk-80. In MVC, the classes are grouped by specific and well-defined tasks with the application-specific data encapsulated in a model class. The next chapter focuses on graphics programming with the Windows API functions.

Further Reading

If you are beginning to learn object-oriented programming (OOP) and C++, this author's recent book, *Object-Oriented Programming in C++*, is useful. It explains how C++ supports data abstraction, inheritance, and polymorphism, the major features of OOP. The list of references in that book guides you to other resources that teach C++ and OOP.

For more information on B-Trees, mentioned in Table 2.1, see Donald E. Knuth's classic book.

There are a host of books on Windows programming with Borland C++. Ted Faison's book covers programming with OWL and CLASSLIB in detail. Peter Norton and Paul Yao focus exclusively on Windows programming with OWL.

Barkakati, Nabajyoti. *Object-Oriented Programming in C++*. Carmel, IN: SAMS Publishing, 1991.

Faison, Ted. *Borland C++ 3.1 Object-Oriented Programming, Second Edition*. Carmel, IN: SAMS Publishing, 1992.

Knuth, Donald E. *The Art of Computer Programming, Volume 3: Sorting and Searching*. Reading, MA: Addison-Wesley Publishing, 1973.

Norton, Peter, and Paul Yao. *Borland C++ Programming for Windows*. New York: Bantam, 1992.

Chapter 3

Graphics Programming with the Windows API

The OWL and CLASSLIB classes provide the framework to build the application and define any internal data structures. In a Windows game, however, you have to display graphics in your application's window and for this you use functions from the Windows Graphics Device Interface (GDI). This chapter briefly describes the GDI functions for drawing graphics and text. Chapters 4 and 5 cover specific techniques for displaying images, and Chapter 8 describes how to render views of 3-D objects.

Windows Graphics Device Interface

GDI refers to the graphics output functions of Windows, and is designed to isolate a Windows program from the physical output device such as the display or the printer. The basic idea is that you call GDI functions for all graphics output and they access specific device drivers. In addition to producing output on physical devices, GDI also supports output to two pseudodevices: bitmaps and *metafiles* (stored collections of GDI function calls). Bitmaps are useful for displaying and animating images—tasks that are commonly needed in computer games. Therefore, a Windows game typically needs to draw in bitmaps and manipulate them. See Chapters 4 and 5 for further information about bitmaps.

Many GDI functions are important when writing game software. In particular, you need the following categories:

■ Vector drawing functions that can draw graphical objects such as lines, rectangles, and ellipses

■ Bitmap manipulation functions to display and manipulate images

■ Text output functions to display text in a window

■ Palette management functions to exploit the colors supported by a display adapter

Palette management functions are useful in systems with super VGA or better display adapters that support more than the 16 colors supported by standard VGA. The next sections provide an overview of these functions, but before you proceed, you have to understand the device context.

Graphics Programming with the Windows API

Chapter 3

Device Context

Recall that the device context (DC) is the key to the GDI's support for device-independent graphics in Windows. All GDI functions require a handle to a DC as an argument. You can think of the DC as a generalized model of a graphics output device. In reality, the DC is a data structure that holds all information needed to generate graphics output. In particular, the DC contains graphics attributes, such as background color, pen, fill style, and font, that control the appearance of graphics and text.

Because the DC represents a graphics device, you have to treat it as a shared resource. When using a DC for graphics output, you first call an appropriate GDI function to access the DC, use that DC to draw, and immediately release the DC. Note that Windows allows, at most, five DCs to be open at any one time—that's five DCs for the entire Windows system, not per application. This is not a limitation because at any instant only one process is displaying graphics output on a device. The only important point is that the process must release the DC as soon as it is done.

Contents of a DC

The DC contains drawing objects, such as brush, pen, and bitmap, and drawing attributes, such as background color, text color, and font. Table 3.1 summarizes the contents of the DC and provides the default value of each item in it. Note that the constants appearing in the default values column are defined in the include file `windows.h`.

Table 3.1. Contents of a DC and their default values.

Item	Default Value	Comments
Background color	White	
Background mode	OPAQUE	Background areas in drawings are filled with the background color as opposed to being left untouched

continues

Table 3.1. continued

Item	Default Value	Comments
Bitmap	No default	Used when selecting a bitmap into a memory device context
Brush	`WHITE_BRUSH`	Defines a fill style
Brush origin	(0,0)	
Clipping region	Entire client area	Drawing operations affect the area within the clipping region only
Color palette	`DEFAULT_PALETTE`	
Current pen position	(0,0)	
Device origin	Upper left corner	
Drawing mode	`R2_COPYPEN`	Specifies how to combine the pen's color with the color that already exists on the drawing surface
Font	`SYSTEM_FONT`	
Intercharacter spacing	0	
Mapping mode	`MM_TEXT`	One logical unit equals one pixel
Pen	`BLACK_PEN`	
Polygon fill mode	`ALTERNATE`	
Stretching mode	`BLACKONWHITE`	Used by `StretchBlt` when copying bitmaps from one device to another
Text alignment	`TA_LEFT, TA_TOP,` and `TA_NOUPDATECP`	

Graphics Programming with the Windows API

Item	Default Value	Comments
Text color	Black	
Viewport extent	(1,1)	Viewport refers to a rectangle in the device coordinate system
Viewport origin	(0,0)	
Window extent	(1,1)	Window refers to a rectangle in the logical coordinate system (the mapping mode maps the window to the viewport)
Window origin	(0,0)	

Getting a DC

Your Windows game application probably will acquire a DC in response to the WM_PAINT message because that's when an application's window has to be redrawn. If you use OWL classes and you derive your application's main window from the TWindow class, you can handle all graphics output in a member function named Paint, which has the following prototype:

```
void Paint(HDC hdc, PAINTSTRUCT& ps);
```

OWL calls the Paint function whenever Windows sends a message to the window. As you can see, the function is called with a valid DC as an argument, so you do not have to explicitly get a DC. The second argument is a reference to a PAINTSTRUCT structure that contains information about the area of the screen that needs to be redrawn.

There is, however, another way to handle graphics in an OWL-based application. In your window class you can define a message-handler for the WM_PAINT function like this:

```
void draw_window(RTMessage msg) = [WM_FIRST + WM_PAINT];
```

In this case, you have to first get a DC in the `draw_window` function. Use the `BeginPaint` function to get a DC that you can use to draw in your window and after you are done, call `EndPaint` to release the DC.

Both of the approaches mentioned so far require that you get a DC when Windows sends a `WM_PAINT` message to your application's window. If you need to update the window as soon as possible without waiting for a `WM_PAINT` message, you can call the `GetDC` function to get a DC. The corresponding function to release the DC is `ReleaseDC`. By the way, you can also force an immediate `WM_PAINT` event by calling the `UpdateWindow` function.

Persistent DC

When you get the handle to a DC and make changes to the attributes, these changes are lost as soon as you release the DC. There is a way to create a private DC for a window so that the contents of the DC persist until the window is destroyed. To do this in a window class `MyWindow` derived from the OWL class `TWindow`, override the `GetWindowClass` function and add the `CS_OWNDC` flag to the class—the Windows class representing the type of a window that is not a C++ class—style as follows:

```
// Assume that MyWindow: public TWindow

void MyWindow::GetWindowClass(WNDCLASS& wclass)
{
    TWindow::GetWindowClass(wclass);
    wclass.style |= CS_OWNDC;
}
```

Now the window associated with each instance of `MyWindow` class has its own private DC that exists until the window is destroyed. You still have to call `GetDC` (or `BeginPaint`) to get a handle to this DC, but you do not have to call `ReleaseDC` (or `EndPaint`) to release it. The penalty you pay for this convenience is about 800 bytes of storage for the DC for each window with the `CS_OWNDC` style.

If you need to store a DC temporarily (perhaps to change some attributes, do some drawing with the changed attributes, and revert back to the original attributes), you can do so by calling `SaveDC` like this:

```
    int saved_DC_id;
    saved_DC_id = SaveDC(hdc);
// Make changes to DC and use it...
// After you are through using the changed DC, restore the DC
    RestoreDC(hdc, saved_DC_id);
```

Graphics Programming with the Windows API

If you simply want to revert a DC back to the state that existed before the last call to SaveDC, call

```
RestoreDC(hdc, -1); // No need for exact ID
```

Using a DC for Graphics Output

The primary use of a DC is to draw graphics output. In fact, each GDI function expects the handle to a DC as the first argument of the function. Here is the typical sequence you follow when using a DC for graphics output:

1. Get the DC.
2. Set up the graphics attributes.
3. Call GDI drawing functions.
4. Release the DC.

Setting up the graphics attributes involves selecting one of the six DC drawing objects into the DC:

- *Pen* controls the appearance of lines and borders of rectangles, ellipses, and polygons.
- *Brush* provides a fill pattern used to draw filled figures.
- *Font* specifies the shape and size of textual output.
- *Palette* is an array of colors—the array index identifies each color. For display adapters that can display more than 16 colors, Windows uses a palette to pick the current selection of displayable colors out of the millions of colors that a display can represent.
- *Bitmap* is used to draw images.
- *Region* is a combination of rectangles, ellipses, and polygons that you can use for drawing or clipping.

At any time, the DC can have one copy of each type of graphics object. Use the SelectObject function to select a graphics object into a DC. For instance, to draw a rectangle filled with a specific fill pattern, you might write

```
// Draw a filled rectangle with specific pen and brush
    HPEN old_pen = SelectObject(hdc, GetStockObject(WHITE_PEN));
    HBRUSH hatch_brush = CreateHatchBrush(HS_DIAGCROSS,
                                RGB(0, 255, 255));
```

```
    HBRUSH old_brush = SelectObject(hdc, hatch_brush);
    Rectangle(hdc, 20, 10, 80, 50);

    SelectObject(hdc, old_pen);

// Reset the brush and delete the newly-created brush
    SelectObject(hdc, old_brush);
    DeleteObject(hatch_brush);
```

Notice how the first call to SelectObject selects a stock pen, one of the pre-defined graphics objects that are always available. The brush, hatch_brush, is created by calling CreateHatchBrush. Once you are finished using the graphics objects, you have to delete the objects that you created. In this example, the brush is deleted by calling DeleteObject. Note that you should not delete an object while it is selected in a DC and you must not delete a stock object.

Determining Device Capabilities with a DC

In addition to drawing with a DC, you can also determine the capabilities of a device through the DC. Specifically, you can call the GetDeviceCaps function to get a value for a specified capability code. For instance, to determine the number of color planes available in the display device, call GetDeviceCaps with the handle to a display DC:

```
int nplanes = GetDeviceCaps(hdc, PLANES);
```

PLANES denotes the capability that you are querying.

You can also use GetDeviceCaps to determine if a device supports enough colors or specific types of graphic operations—copying bitmaps, for instance, or drawing curves such as circles and ellipses. For example, in a Windows game you might want to use as many colors as the display adapter supports. If a display adapter supports 256 colors, the DC supports a logical palette. To determine this, write

```
    if(GetDeviceCaps(hdc, RASTERCAPS) & RC_PALETTE)
    {
// Yes, device supports logical palette
//...
    }
```

Graphics Programming with the Windows API

You can even test if the device driver associated with a DC is written for Windows 3.0 or later:

```
    if(GetDeviceCaps(hdc, DRIVERVERSION) >= 0x300)
    {
// Yes, device driver is for Windows 3.0 or later.
//...
    }
```

GDI Coordinate Systems

The GDI supports the notion of two coordinate systems: physical and logical. The physical or device coordinate system is fixed for a device. For a window on the display screen, the physical coordinate system's origin is at the upper left corner of a window's client area with positive x-axis extending to the right and positive y-axis going down.

The logical coordinate system can be one of several, and Windows maps each logical coordinate system onto the physical one before displaying any graphics output. All GDI drawing functions accept logical coordinates as arguments. The mapping mode—the way a logical coordinate system is scaled to the physical one—identifies the types of logical coordinate systems that Windows supports. Table 3.2 lists the mapping modes available in Windows GDI.

Table 3.2. Mapping modes in Windows GDI.

Mapping Mode Identifier	Description
MM_ANISOTROPIC	Logical units along x- and y-axes can be set independently. Use `SetViewportExt` (set viewport extent) and `SetWindowExt` (set window extent) to set up the x- and y-ratios of logical-to-physical units. (A viewport is a rectangular area in physical coordinate space and a window is a rectangle in logical coordinates.) The viewport extent is the width and height

continues

Table 3.2. continued

Mapping Mode Identifier	Description
	of the viewport. The scaling along x- and y-axes are set so that the specified window in logical coordinates is mapped to the viewport in physical coordinates.
MM_HIENGLISH	Each logical unit is 0.001 inch, with the positive x-axis extending to the right and positive y-axis going up.
MM_HIMETRIC	Each logical unit is 0.01 millimeter; the x-axis increases to the right and the positive y-axis extends upward.
MM_ISOTROPIC	This is like MM_ANISOTROPIC except that the x- and y-scalings must be the same.
MM_LOENGLISH	This is like MM_HIENGLISH but each logical unit is 0.01 inch.
MM_LOMETRIC	This is like MM_HIMETRIC but each logical unit is 0.1 millimeter.
MM_TEXT	This is the default mapping mode where the logical coordinate system is the same as the physical one—each logical unit is one pixel with the x-axis increasing to the right and the y-axis increasing downward.
MM_TWIPS	Each logical unit is 1/20 of a point, where a point is 1/72 inch. Thus, each logical unit is 1/1440 inch. The positive x-axis extends to the right and the y-axis increases upward.

Chapter 3

Graphics Programming with the Windows API

Setting a Mapping Mode

Use the `SetMapMode` function to set a mapping mode. At any time, you can get the current mapping mode with `GetMapMode`. For example, to set the mapping mode to `MM_TWIPS`, write

```
int old_mapmode = SetMapMode(hdc, MM_TWIPS);
```

Specifying the mapping mode may not be enough to draw in a window. After setting a mapping mode such as `MM_TWIPS`, you have the situation shown in Figure 3.1. A portion of the lower right quadrant from the logical coordinate space is mapped to the display screen (or the device's work area, in case of devices other than the display). This means that drawings with positive x- and negative y-coordinates are the only ones that get displayed because the logical frame's y-axis increases upward and the physical frame's y-axis increases downward. This is true for all mapping modes except `MM_TEXT`.

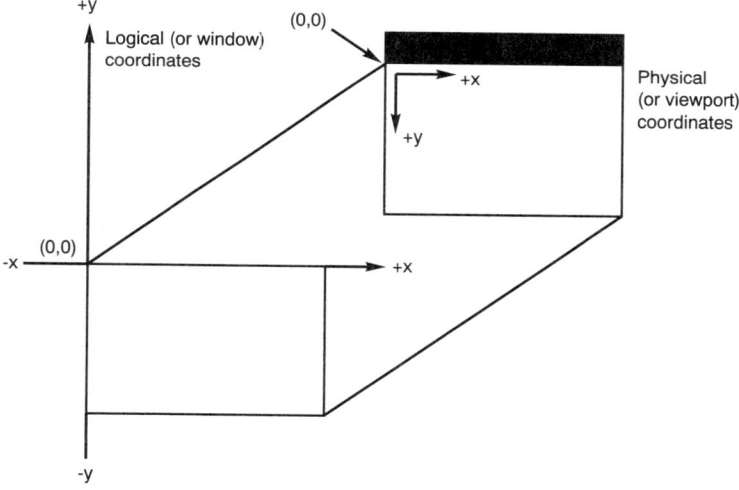

Figure 3.1. *Default mapping from logical to physical coordinates.*

If you want to work with positive logical coordinates, you have to move the origin of the logical coordinate frame to an appropriate location in the physical space so that the positive quadrant (the quadrant where both x- and y-coordinates are positive) of the logical frame is mapped to the visible quadrant of the physical coordinate frame. You can use the SetViewportOrg to relocate the origin of the logical frame. Figure 3.2 illustrates the effect of changing the origin of the logical coordinate axes.

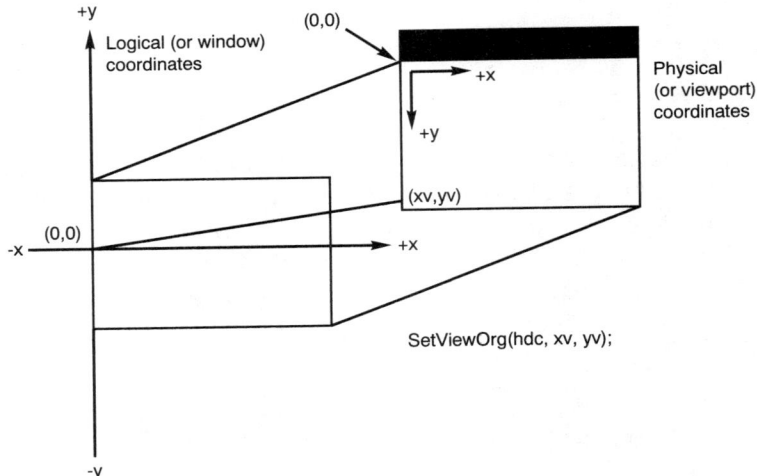

Figure 3.2. *Effect of aligning the window origin with a point in the viewport.*

Note that you have to follow these steps whenever you are using one of the device-independent modes: MM_HIENGLISH, MM_HIMETRIC, MM_LOENGLISH, MM_LOMETRIC, or MM_TWIPS. They are device-independent because they express the logical units in absolute measurements such as millimeters and inches.

Drawing with GDI Functions

The GDI provides a large number of drawing functions, including functions to draw individual pixels, lines, rectangles and polygons, and ellipses.

Graphics Programming with the Windows API

Drawing Points

You can draw a single point in a specified color with the `SetPixel` function, which you would call as follows:

```
COLORREF actual_RGB = SetPixel(hdc, x, y, color);
```

This paints the point at the logical coordinates (x,y) with the specified color. The color argument to the `SetPixel` function is a 32-bit value whose least significant 3 bytes represent the red (R), green (G), and blue (B) components of a color. You can specify the color using the RGB macro as follows:

```
SetPixel(hdc, x, y, RGB(r, g, b));
```

where *r*, *g*, and *b* are integers between 0 and 255 representing the intensity of red, green, and blue components, respectively. Windows uses the nearest available color and paints the pixel with that color. `SetPixel` returns the RGB value of the actual color used by Windows.

Although `SetPixel` can be used to draw an image directly on the display screen, you should use the bitmap manipulation functions to display images in Windows because the bitmap functions are much faster than `SetPixel`.

Drawing Lines

The GDI functions `MoveTo` and `LineTo` are meant for drawing lines. To draw a line from the logical point (x1, y1) to (x2, y2), write the following:

```
MoveTo(hdc, x1, y1);
LineTo(hdc, x2, y2);
```

Windows draws all the pixels starting at (x1, y1) up to, but not including, (x2, y2). The `MoveTo` and `LineTo` functions draw lines with the currently selected pen. The `MoveTo` function moves the pen to a new location without drawing anything and `LineTo` draws a line to a specified point with the pen. The pen determines the appearance of the line being drawn. You can either call `SelectObject` to select a predefined pen into the device context or call `CreatePen` to create a new pen with a specific style, color, and width. To use the pen, you have to select it into the DC and, when you no longer need the pen, you must destroy it by calling `DeleteObject` with the handle to the pen as an argument.

69

To draw multiple line segments, you should use the `Polyline` function, storing the end points of all the line segments in an array. For example, to join the points (x1, y1), (x2, y2), and (x3, y3) with line segments, write

```
POINT points[3] = {x1, y1, x2, y2, x3, y3};
Polyline(hdc, points, 3);
```

Note that to draw a closed polygon using `Polyline`, you have to explicitly close the figure by specifying the same coordinates for the first and the last point in the array of points.

In addition to straight lines, the GDI includes the `Arc` function to draw a curved line that is part of an ellipse. `Arc` requires four sets of x-y coordinates as its arguments:

```
// Prototype of Arc
BOOL Arc(
    HDC    hdc,              // Handle to device context
    short  x1, short y1,     // Upper left corner of bounding box
    short  x2, short y2,     // Lower right corner of bounding box
    short  xs, short ys,     // Defines start point of arc
    short  xe, short ye);    // Defines end point of arc
```

The points (x1, y1) and (x2, y2) are the opposite corners of a rectangle that encloses the ellipse to which the arc belongs. The starting point of the arc is where a line joining the center of the ellipse and (xs, ys) intersects the ellipse's boundary. The end point is defined similarly by the line joining the ellipse's center and (xe, ye). The arc is drawn counterclockwise from the starting point up to, but not including, the end point.

Drawing Closed Figures

The GDI provides the following functions to draw closed figures:

- `Rectangle(HDC hdc, int x1, int y1, int x2, int y2);` draws a rectangle whose upper left corner is (x1, y1) and lower right corner is (x2, y2). Note that the right and bottom edges of the rectangle are one pixel less than the corner (x2, y2).

- `RoundRect(HDC hdc, int x1, int y1, int x2, int y2, int x_ellipse, int y_ellipse);` draws a rectangle with rounded corners. The rectangle's bounding box is specified by the upper left corner (x1, y1)

Graphics Programming with the Windows API

Chapter 3

and lower right corner (x2, y2). Each corner is rounded by drawing a small ellipse whose width and height are x_ellipse and y_ellipse, respectively.

- ■ `Ellipse(HDC hdc, int x1, int y1, int x2, int y2);` draws an ellipse bounded by the rectangle whose opposite corners are (x1, y1) and (x2, y2).

- ■ `Pie(HDC hdc, int x1, int y1, int x2, int y2, int x_start, int y_start, int x_end, int y_end);` draws a pie-shaped wedge whose curved edge is a segment of the ellipse bounded by the rectangle defined by the corners (x1, y1) and (x2, y2). The two straight edges of the pie are defined by the line joining the center of the ellipse and the points (x_start, y_start) and (x_end, y_end). The pie slice starts at the point where the line from the center to (x_start, y_start) intersects the ellipse and continues counterclockwise to the point where the line from the center to (x_end, y_end) cuts the ellipse.

- ■ `Chord(HDC hdc, int x1, int y1, int x2, int y2, int x_start, int y_start, int x_end, int y_end);` draws a segment of an ellipse as `Pie` does, but unlike `Pie`, `Chord` joins the end points of the arc with a straight line.

- ■ `Polygon(HDC hdc, LPPOINT pt, int numpt);` draws a polygon by joining the points in the array `pt`. `Polygon` automatically joins the first and last points in the array to form a closed figure.

Note that all drawing functions expect logical coordinates. For each of these closed figures, the Windows GDI draws the outline with the current pen style and fills the inside of the figures with the current brush. There are seven stock brush objects, which you can use by creating an instance of the brush. Call `GetStockObject` with one of the following as argument:

BLACK_BRUSH

DKGRAY_BRUSH

GRAY_BRUSH

HOLLOW_BRUSH

LTGRAY_BRUSH

NULL_BRUSH

WHITE_BRUSH

You can create your own brush objects by using one of these functions:

```
CreateBrushIndirect
CreateDIBPatternBrush
CreateHatchBrush
CreatePatternBrush
CreateSolidBrush
```

`CreateSolidBrush` is particularly useful for creating a brush of a specified color:

```
HBRUSH red_brush = CreateSolidBrush(RGB(255, 0, 0));
```

The color is specified by an RGB triplet. If you specify a color that is not supported by hardware, Windows uses *dithering*—the process of combining neighboring pixels of different colors to create unique shades—to produce a close approximation to the requested color.

Manipulating Rectangles

Rectangles play an important part in the GDI. Accordingly, the GDI includes several functions that manipulate rectangles. You have already seen the functions `Rectangle` and `RoundRect` meant for drawing rectangles. Table 3.3 lists several other rectangle functions. Most of these use the RECT structure, which is defined in the header file <windows.h> as

```
typedef struct tagRECT
{
    int left;    // Upper left corner of rectangle
    int top;
    int right;   // Lower right corner of rectangle
    int bottom;
} RECT;
```

Graphics Programming with the Windows API

Chapter 3

Table 3.3. GDI functions that manipulate rectangles.

Name	Description
CopyRect	Copy from one RECT structure to another: `CopyRect(&dest_rect, &src_rect);`
EqualRect	Returns TRUE if two RECT structures are equal: `if(EqualRect(&rect1, &rect2)) { /* Rectangles are equal */ }`
FillRect	Fills a rectangle, up to but not including the right and bottom coordinates, with the specified brush: `FillRect(hdc, &rect, hbrush);`
FrameRect	Uses the current brush (not the pen) to draw a rectangular frame: `FrameRect(hdc, &rect, hbrush);`
InflateRect	Increases or decreases the size of a rectangle: `InflateRect(&rect, x, y);`
InvertRect	Inverts all the pixels in a rectangle: `InvertRect(hdc, &rect);`
OffsetRect	Moves a rectangle along x- and y-axes: `MoveRect(&rect, x, y);`
PtInRect	Returns TRUE if a point is in a rectangle: `if(PtInRect(&rect, point)) { /* Point is in rectangle */ }`
SetRect	Sets the fields of a RECT structure: `SetRect(&rect, left, top, right, bottom);`
SetRectEmpty	Sets the fields in a RECT structure to zero: `SetRectEmpty(&rect);`
UnionRect	Sets the fields of a RECT structure to be the union of two other rectangles: `UnionRect(&result_rect, &rect1, &rect2);`

Regions

Regions are areas of the drawing surface. The GDI allows you to define a region as a combination of rectangles, polygons, and ellipses. You can use a region to draw—by filling the region with the current brush—or use it as the clipping region—the area where the drawing appears. Table 3.4 lists the GDI functions meant for defining and using regions. Note that to use a region, you must have a handle to it. Also, when using a region as a clipping region, you have to call `SetClipRgn` to select the region into the device context.

Table 3.4 GDI functions that manipulate regions.

Name	Description
`CreateRectRgn`	Creates a rectangular region using specified coordinates for the opposite corners of the rectangle: `CreateRectRgn(left, top, right, bottom);`
`CreateRectRgnIndirect`	Creates a rectangular region using the fields of a `RECT` structure: `CreateRectRgnIndirect(&rect);`
`CreateRoundRectRgn`	Creates a rectangular region with rounded corners, specified the same way as the `RoundRect` function
`CreateEllipticRgn`	Creates an elliptic region: `CreateEllipticRgn(left, top, right, bottom);`
`CreateEllipticRgnIndirect`	Creates an elliptic region using the fields in a `RECT` structure: `CreateEllipticRgnIndirect(&rect);`
`CreatePolygonRgn`	Creates a polygon region: `CreatePolygonRgn(points, npoints, fill_mode);` where `fill_mode` is `ALTERNATE` or `WINDING`
`CreatePolyPolygonRgn`	Creates a region out of multiple polygons

Graphics Programming with the Windows API

Name	Description
CombineRgn	Combines two regions into one according to a specified combining mode which can be one of the following: RGN_AND, RGN_COPY, RGN_DIFF, RGN_OR, RGN_XOR: CombineRgn(hresult_rgn, hrgn1, hrgn2, combine_flag);
EqualRgn	Returns TRUE if two regions are equal: if(EqualRgn(hrgn1, hrgn2)) { /* regions are equal */}
FillRgn	Fills a region with the current brush: FillRgn(hdc, hrgn, hbrush);
FrameRgn	Draws a frame around a region with the current brush: FrameRgn(hdc, hrgn, hbrush, xframe, yframe);
GetRgnBox	Returns the bounding box (largest rectangle enclosing the region) of a region: GetRgnBox(hrgn, &rect);
InvalidateRgn	Marks the specified region for repainting: InvalidateRgn(hwnd, hrgn, erase_flag);
InvertRgn	Inverts the pixels in a region: InvertRgn(hdc, hrgn);
OffsetRgn	Moves a region by specified x- and y-offsets: OffsetRgn(hrgn, x, y);
PaintRgn	Fills the region with the current brush: PaintRgn(hdc, hrgn);
SelectClipRgn	Uses the specified region as the clipping region: SelectClipRgn(hdc, hrgn);
ValidateRgn	Removes the region from the area to be repainted: ValidateRgn(hwnd, hrgn);

Drawing Mode

When drawing lines and filled figures, the drawing mode controls the way the pen color is combined with the existing colors. This is referred to as a *raster operation*, or *ROP* for short. The GDI defines sixteen ROPs identified by symbols that start with the R2 prefix. The default ROP is R2_COPYPEN, which means that the pen simply overwrites whatever exists on the drawing surface. Table 3.5 lists the names of the ROP codes that apply when drawing with the GDI functions. Note that there is another set of ROP codes that apply when copying a bitmap to a device context.

Table 3.5. Drawing modes in Windows GDI.

Mode	Boolean Operation	Comments
R2_BLACK	all bits zero	Draws in black, ignoring pen color and existing color
R2_COPYPEN	pen	Draws with the pen color (the default drawing mode)
R2_MASKNOTPEN	(NOT pen) AND dest	Inverts the bits in the pen color and performs a bitwise-AND with existing color
R2_MASKPEN	pen AND dest	Performs bitwise-AND of pen color and existing color
R2_MASKPENNOT	pen AND (NOT dest)	Inverts existing color and performs bitwise-AND with pen color
R2_MERGENOTPEN	(NOT pen) OR dest	Inverts pen color and performs bitwise-OR with existing color
R2_MERGEPEN	pen OR dest	Performs bitwise-OR of pen color and existing color
R2_MERGEPENNOT	pen OR (NOT dest)	Inverts existing color and performs bitwise-OR with pen color

Chapter 3

Graphics Programming with the Windows API

Mode	Boolean Operation	Comments
R2_NOP	dest	Leaves existing color unchanged (hence the name NOP for "no operation")
R2_NOT	NOT dest	Inverts existing color
R2_NOTCOPYPEN	NOT pen	Draws with inverted pen color
R2_NOTMASKPEN	NOT (pen AND dest)	Performs bitwise-AND of pen and existing color and inverts the result
R2_NOTMERGEPEN	NOT (pen OR dest)	Performs bitwise-OR of pen and existing color and inverts the result
R2_NOTXORPEN	NOT (pen XOR dest)	Performs bitwise exclusive-OR of pen and existing color and inverts the result
R2_WHITE	all bits 1	Draws in white color
R2_XORPEN	pen XOR dest	Performs bitwise exclusive-OR of pen color and existing color

Use the SetROP2 function to specify a new drawing mode:

```
int previous_ROP = SetROP2(hdc, R2_XORPEN);
```

In this case, SetROP2 sets the ROP code to R2_XORPEN and returns the old ROP code, which is stored in the variable named previous_ROP.

Text Output

The Windows GDI provides several functions for displaying text. Here are the three prominent text output functions:

- `DrawText(hdc, str, nchars, &rect, format_flag);` displays `nchars` characters from the text string `str` inside the rectangle defined by a `RECT` structure specified by `rect`. The `format_flag` indicates the positioning and formatting of the string.
- `TabbedTextOut(hdc, x, y, str, nchars, ntabs, tabpos, tab_origin);` displays `nchars` characters from the string `str` at the logical coordinates (x, y). Embedded tabs (`'\t'`) in the string are interpreted according to the tab positions specified (in terms of pixels) in the array of integers `tabpos` with `ntabs` entries. The `tab_origin` argument is the logical x-coordinate where the tabs begin. This function returns a 32-bit value (`DWORD`) whose low-order word holds the width of the string in pixels and the high-order word the height.
- `TextOut(hdc, x, y, str, nchars);` displays `nchars` characters from the text string `str` at the logical coordinate (x, y). The positioning of the characters with respect to (x, y) depends on the current text alignment specified by the `SetTextAlign` function.

You specify the text alignment by calling the `SetTextAlign` function:

`SetTextAlign(hdc, TA_BOTTOM | TA_LEFT);`

The second argument is a bitwise-OR of flags indicating the location of the text string with respect to the output position. In this case, the text output position is at the top left corner of the string. The vertical alignment can be one of the following:

TA_BASELINE	Baseline of text is aligned with the y-coordinate of the output position
TA_BOTTOM	Bottom of text is aligned with the y-coordinate of the output position
TA_TOP	Top of text is aligned with the y-coordinate of the output position

The horizontal alignment can be one of the following:

TA_CENTER	Horizontal center of text is aligned with the x-coordinate of the output position
TA_LEFT	Left side of text is aligned with the x-coordinate of the output position

Graphics Programming with the Windows API

TA_RIGHT   Right side of text is aligned with the x-coordinate of
                the output position

The default alignment is TA_TOP ¦ TA_LEFT. Also, by default, TextOut does not update the current position after the text output. If you want the current position updated, include the TA_UPDATECP flag with a bitwise-OR operator in the call to SetTextAlign.

In addition to the text alignment, several other attributes in the DC affect text output. By default, the text color is black, but you can set it to any RGB value:

```
SetTextColor(hdc, RGB(255, 0, 0));  // Set text color to red.
```

The background mode determines whether the spaces between the characters are filled in with the current background color. By default, the background mode is OPAQUE, which means Windows uses the background color to fill in the spaces between the character strokes. You can set the background mode to TRANSPARENT and display the characters without affecting the pixels in between:

```
SetBkMode(hdc, TRANSPARENT);
```

The font is another important attribute that determines the appearance (shape and size) of the text output. By default, Windows displays the text in the system font, but you can create and use a new font. Here is an example that displays a text string in bold Helvetica font with characters 60 logical units tall (thus font size depends on the mapping mode):

```
HFONT hfont = CreateFont(
            60,                   // height (logical units)
            0,                    // width (0 means
                                  // Windows chooses width)
            0,                    // escapement
            0,                    // orientation
            FW_BOLD,              // weight
            0,                    // italic - off
            0,                    // underline - off
            0,                    // strikeout - off
            ANSI_CHARSET,         // character set
            OUT_DEFAULT_PRECIS,   // output precision
            CLIP_DEFAULT_PRECIS,  // clipping precision
            PROOF_QUALITY,
            VARIABLE_PITCH,       // pitch and family
            "Helv");              // name of font face
```

```
// Select the font into the DC (save old font handle).
HFONT oldfont = SelectObject(hdc, hfont);

// Now display the text string using the selected font.
TextOut(hdc, 100, 100, "Test", strlen("Test"));

// Reset font in DC and delete the font
SelectObject(hdc, oldfont);
DeleteObject(hfont);
```

This brief overview of the Windows text output functions should be enough to display any needed text in a Windows game. For more details on text output and fonts, consult the Windows API Reference Guides that accompany Borland C++ 3.1.

Handling Color

Prior to Windows 3.0, the only way to represent a color was to express it in terms of the red (R), green (G), and blue (B) intensities of the color. To represent the RGB value, the Windows API defines the COLORREF type, which is a 32-bit integer value with the red, green, and blue intensities stored in the low-order bytes (see Figure 3.3). The most significant byte of the COLORREF type indicates whether to interpret the value as a color or a palette entry—a topic that is discussed in the next section.

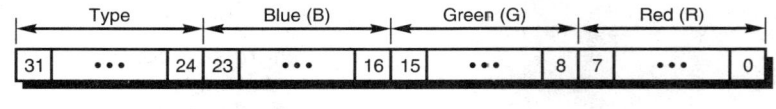

Type = 0 explicit RGB color
       1 logical palette index
       2 RGB from palette

Figure 3.3. *Interpreting the contents of a COLORREF value.*

You can use the RGB macro to represent an RGB color. For instance, RGB(255, 0, 0) denotes a full-intensity red color. Because each intensity is an 8-bit value, the intensity can range from 0 to 255.

Note that if Windows uses dithering to display colors, it may not be supported by the display hardware. Because dithering requires a collection of pixels

Graphics Programming with the Windows API

to work, Windows uses dithering only when filling an area, not when drawing points, lines, and text.

System Palette

Display adapters such as VGA, XGA, and 8514/A can generate the necessary signals to display a large number of colors on a color display, but only a small number of these colors are available at any one time. The number of colors that can be displayed at a time is determined by the number of bits of storage allocated for each pixel. In a standard VGA in 640x480 mode, each pixel has 4 bits of storage—this means the standard VGA can display $2^4 = 16$ simultaneous colors. On the other hand, a super VGA adapter with enough memory may support a mode where each pixel can have an 8-bit value. In this case, the display adapter can show $2^8=256$ simultaneous colors.

Although the number of simultaneous colors is limited, the display adapter represents each color in terms of the red (R), green (G), and blue (B) intensities of the color and uses several bits to represent the R, G, and B components. For instance, a VGA display adapter that uses 6 bits per R, G, and B component allows up to $2^6 \times 2^6 \times 2^6 = 262,144$ distinct colors from which you can display any 16 colors if the display adapter supports 4 bits per pixel. It displays 256 colors if the adapter supports 8 bits per pixel. The display adapter converts each pixel's contents into a color by interpreting the pixel's value as an index into a table. This table is known as the *color palette* and its entries are RGB values.

In keeping with the hardware palette in display adapters, Windows also defines a palette called the *system palette* that has 16 predefined colors for EGA and VGA displays and 20 predefined colors on displays that support 256 colors or more.

Logical Palette

Starting with Version 3.0, Windows supports the notion of a logical palette that allows applications to take advantage of the large number of colors available in a system. Provided the display hardware supports more that 20 colors, Windows provides an extended system palette that mimics the hardware palette. Windows automatically sets aside 20 entries in the extended system palette—the 20 default colors. When you define a logical palette (a table of RGB colors), Windows maps it to the extended system palette as follows:

1. If a color in the logical palette already exists in the system palette, that color is mapped to the matching color index in the system palette.
2. A logical palette color with no match in the system palette is added to the system palette, provided there is room.
3. When the system palette becomes full, a logical palette color is mapped to the closest matching color in the system palette.

When there are several applications with logical palettes, Windows maps the logical palette of the topmost window into the system palette.

If you write a Windows game and want to use all 256 colors in a super VGA adapter, you have to use a logical palette; otherwise you can use only the 20 default colors in the system palette.

Creating and Using Logical Palettes

Like a hardware palette, a logical palette is simply a table of RGB colors. Each entry in the table is a PALETTEENTRY structure, defined in <windows.h> as

```
typedef struct tagPALETTEENTRY
{
    BYTE     peRed;
    BYTE     peGreen;
    BYTE     peBlue;
    BYTE     peFlags;
} PALETTEENTRY;
```

The logical palette itself is a LOGPALETTE structure, declared in <windows.h> as

```
typedef struct tagLOGPALETTE
{
    WORD          palVersion;      // Windows version
    WORD          palNumEntries;   // Number of palette entries
    PALETTEENTRY  palPalEntry[1];  // Array of palette entries
} LOGPALETTE;
```

Here are the steps to creating and using a logical palette:

1. Check if the display driver supports logical palettes:

    ```
    if((GetDeviceCaps(hdc, RASTERCAPS) & RC_PALETTE) &&
       (GetDeviceCaps(hdc, DRIVERVERSION) >= 0x0300))
    ```

Graphics Programming with the Windows API

Chapter 3

```
{
// Supports logical palettes.
}
else
{
// Does not support logical palettes.
}
```

2. Allocate room for a palette and define the palette entries. For example, here is the C++ code to allocate a logical palette with 16 entries (defined to be shades of red):

```
const int ncolors = 16;
LPLOGPALETTE lpal = (LPLOGPALETTE) new char[sizeof(LOGPALETTE) +
                                (ncolors - 1) *
sizeof(PALETTEENTRY)];

lpal->palVersion = 0x030a;    // Windows 3.10
lpal->palNumEntries = ncolors;

int i;
for(i = 0; i < ncolors; i++)
{
    lpal->palPalEntry[i].peRed   = 16*i;
    lpal->palPalEntry[i].peGreen = 0;
    lpal->palPalEntry[i].peBlue  = 0;
    lpal->palPalEntry[i].peFlags = 0;
}
```

The `peFlags` field in each palette entry can be one of the following:

Value	Meaning
0	The entry is a normal palette entry.
PC_EXPLICIT	Treat the low-order 16-bit word as an index to the hardware palette.
PC_NOCOLLAPSE	Do not map this entry to any existing color in the system palette.
PC_RESERVED	This entry will be used for palette animation (the entry will be changed often). Do not map colors from other logical palettes with this entry.

3. Call `CreatePalette` with a pointer to the `LOGPALETTE` structure to get a handle to a logical palette:

```
HPALETTE hpal = CreatePalette(lpal);
```

4. Call `SelectPalette` to select the new palette into the device context:

   ```
   HPALETTE old_pal = SelectPalette(hdc, hpal, 0);
   ```

   Note that a zero for the last argument to `SelectPalette` specifies that the palette is to be used as a foreground palette; otherwise the palette is used for background. `SelectPalette` returns the handle of the previously selected palette.

5. Before using the colors in the palette, call `RealizePalette` to install the logical palette into the system palette and make the colors available:

   ```
   RealizePalette(hdc);
   ```

6. Specify colors from the palette using the `PALETTEINDEX` or `PALETTERGB` macros. For example, `PALETTEINDEX(10)` evaluates to a `COLORREF` value that matches the color at index 10 of the logical palette (as defined by you in step 1). `PALETTERGB` is similar to the RGB macro, except that it defines a `COLORREF` value representing a color from the logical palette.

7. Before exiting the program, call `delete` to free the memory allocated for the logical palette and discard the palette by calling `DeleteObject`:

   ```
   delete lpal;
   DeleteObject(hpal);
   ```

   You may want to do this cleanup in the handler for the `WM_DESTROY` event that Windows sends when a window is being closed.

Manipulating Logical Palettes

The Windows GDI provides a number of functions for manipulating logical and system palettes. Table 3.6 summarizes these functions.

Table 3.6. Windows functions that manipulate palettes.

Name	Description
`AnimatePalette`	Changes entries in a logical palette, resulting in instant changes to colors on the display

Chapter 3: Graphics Programming with the Windows API

Name	Description
CreatePalette	Creates a logical palette and returns a handle to the palette
GetNearestPaletteIndex	Returns index of palette entry that most closely matches a specified RGB color
GetPaletteEntries	Retrieves the color values for a specified number of entries in a logical palette
GetSystemPaletteEntries	Retrieves the color values for a specified number of entries in the system palette
GetSystemPaletteUse	Returns a flag indicating whether an application can change the system palette
RealizePalette	Maps the entries of the currently selected logical palette into the system palette
ResizePalette	Enlarges or reduces the size of a logical palette after it has been created (by calling CreatePalette)
SelectPalette	Selects a logical palette into a device context
SetPaletteEntries	Changes the color values of a specified number of entries in the logical palette
SetSysColors	Sets one or more colors in the system palette, identified by constants such as COLOR_ACTIVEBORDER, COLOR_MENU, and COLOR_WINDOW
SetSystemPaletteUse	Allows the currently active application to change the entries in the system palette
UpdateColors	Updates the color of the pixels in the client area of a window to reflect the current entries in the system palette

Bitmaps

Recall that a bitmap is a rectangular array of bits that represents an image. Each pixel in the image corresponds to one or more bits in the bitmap. In a monochrome bitmap, corresponding to a black-and-white image, each bit in the bitmap represents a pixel in the image. For color images, each pixel requires more than one bit in the bitmap to indicate the color of the pixel. Additionally, the mapping of the bits in a pixel to a specific color depends on a color map.

Prior to version 3.0, Windows supported a single bitmap format, the *Device Dependent Bitmap (DDB)*, that made certain assumptions about the display device. Windows 3.0 introduced a new version, the *Device Independent Bitmap (DIB)*, that stores the bitmap information in a device-independent manner—primarily by adding a color table (a palette) to the old DDB format.

You can think of a bitmap as a canvas in memory where you can draw images. The Windows GDI includes functions such as `BitBlt` and `StretchBlt` that can quickly copy a bitmap to the display device. Bitmaps are very useful in games that require animating images. For instance, if you have to move a small image around on the display screen, you can store that image in a bitmap and use `BitBlt` to copy the image to the display screen as needed. See Chapters 4 and 5 for further information about interpreting image file formats and animating images.

Device-Dependent Bitmaps

You can derive the bitmap of a monochrome image directly from the image by assigning a 1 to each white pixel and 0 to the black ones. Figure 3.4 shows how to write the hexadecimal values representing an 8x8 image. Note that Windows requires that the width (in pixels) of each row of the image be a multiple of 16—each row must have an even number of bytes. Thus, in the example of Figure 3.4, each row is padded with a null byte.

Graphics Programming with the Windows API

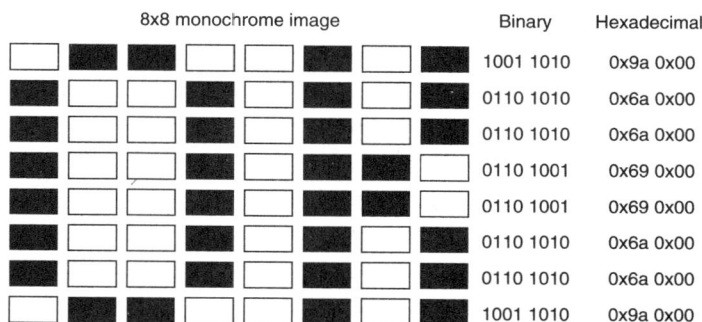

Figure 3.4. *Monochrome bitmap format.*

Displaying a Bitmap

Once you have the bitmap data, you can display it by following these steps:

1. Define an array of bytes with the bitmap data—simply write down the hexadecimal values row by row:

   ```
   static BYTE image1[] = // This is the image from Figure 3.4
   {
       0x9a, 0x00,  // Pad with zeros to get an even
       0x6a, 0x00,  // number of bytes per row of image
       0x6a, 0x00,
       0x69, 0x00,
       0x69, 0x00,
       0x6a, 0x00,
       0x6a, 0x00,
       0x9a, 0x00
   };
   ```

2. Create a monochrome bitmap from the bitmap data:

   ```
   // Create the bitmap from the image data
       HBITMAP hbm = CreateBitmap(
   ```

87

```
                    8,        // Width of bitmap (in pixels)
                    8,        // Width of bitmap (in pixels)
                    1,        // Number of planes
                    1,        // Bits per pixel
                    image1);  // Bitmap data
```

3. Create a memory device context that is compatible with the device where you plan to display the bitmap, and select the bitmap into the memory DC:

```
// Create a memory device context compatible with
// the display device context (whose handle is assumed
// to be hdc)
    HDC hmemdc = CreateCompatibleDC(hdc);
// Select bitmap into memory device context
    SelectObject(hmemdc, hbm);
```

4. Transfer the bitmap from the memory DC to the display device context by calling `BitBlt`:

```
// Copy bitmap into the display device context
BitBlt(
    hdc,      // Copy to this device context (destination)
    10, 10,   // Copy to this logical x,y coordinate
    8, 8,     // Width, height of destination rectangle
    hmemdc,   // Copy from this device context (source)
    0, 0,     // Copy from this logical x,y coordinate
    SRCCOPY   // One of 256 raster operation codes
    );
```

5. Delete the memory device context:

```
DeleteDC(hmemdc);
```

If you are going to use a bitmap throughout your program, you should create the bitmap at the beginning (in response to the `WM_CREATE` message) and delete it before exiting (in response to the `WM_DESTROY` message). To delete the bitmap, call `DeleteObject` as follows:

```
DeleteObject(hbm); // hbm is the handle to the bitmap
                   // that you can derive directly from
                   // the image
```

Chapter 3: Graphics Programming with the Windows API

Stretching a Bitmap

The `BitBlt` function copies a bitmap from one device context to an identically sized rectangle in another DC. The `StretchBlt` function is another block transfer function that can shrink or stretch a bitmap to fit a specified rectangle in the destination DC. For example, if you want to stretch the 8x8 bitmap of Figure 3.4 to 64x64, you can do so with the following call to StretchBlt:

```
StretchBlt(
    hdc,    // Copy to this device context (destination)
    10, 10, // Copy to this logical x,y coordinate
    64, 64, // Width, height of destination rectangle
    hmemdc, // Copy from this device context (source)
    0, 0,   // Copy from this logical x,y coordinate
    8, 8,   // Width and size of source rectangle
    SRCCOPY // One of 256 raster operation codes
    );
```

Drawing on a Bitmap

Sometimes you want to prepare a drawing in memory before copying it to a device for displaying or printing. One good place to use this technique is when you are repeatedly drawing the same figure over and over. Keeping the drawing in memory and copying it to the device with a call to `BitBlt` is much faster than drawing everything directly on the device. This technique is useful for animation as well—the animation looks smoother when you prepare the animated drawing offscreen in memory and copy the drawing to the display.

To prepare a drawing in memory, you have to create a bitmap of specified size, select it into a memory DC, and draw using that memory DC. The bitmap must be compatible with the device where you plan to display it. Here are the steps to follow:

1. Create a bitmap compatible with the display device context. You have to specify the size of the bitmap:

    ```
    HBITMAP hbm1 = CreateCompatibleBitmap(
                    hdc,     // compatible with this DC
                    64, 64); // width and height in pixels
    ```

2. Select the bitmap into a memory DC that is compatible with the display DC:

    ```
    SelectObject(hmemdc, hbm1);
    ```

89

3. Fill the bitmap with a background color (otherwise the bitmap will have a random bit pattern):

```
// Fill the bitmap with white color
    HBRUSH holdbr = SelectObject(hmemdc,
                    GetStockObject(WHITE_BRUSH));

    PatBlt(
        hmemdc,    // Copy pattern to this DC
        0, 0,      // Copy to this logical x,y coordinate
        64, 64,    // Width and height of rectangle to
                   // be filled with pattern
        PATCOPY); //

    SelectObject(hmemdc, holdbr); // Reset the brush
```

4. Draw in the bitmap using GDI drawing functions:

```
// Draw in the bitmap with GDI drawing functions
    Rectangle(hmemdc, 4, 4, 40, 20);
    TextOut(hmemdc, 10, 40, "Hello", 5);
```

5. Display the bitmap by calling `BitBlt` as shown in earlier sections.

Because bitmaps use memory, you should call `DeleteObject` to delete the bitmap when no longer needed.

ROP Codes

The last argument to the block transfer functions, `BitBlt`, `StretchBlt`, and `PatBlt`, is an ROP code that specifies how the source bitmap is combined with the brush pattern and the destination pixels. There are 256 possible ROP codes, of which the 15 most common ones have names as shown in Table 3.7. In these, the logical operations between the source (S), destination (D), and pattern (P) are expressed using the C++ bitwise logical operators: invert(~), AND(&), OR(|), XOR (^).

Graphics Programming with the Windows API

Table 3.7. Some raster operation codes used by the block transfer functions.

Constant	Operation	Meaning
BLACKNESS	0	Sets all destination pixels to zero (black)
DSTINVERT	~D	Inverts the destination pixels
MERGECOPY	P&S	Performs bitwise-AND of source bitmap and brush pattern
MERGEPAINT	~S¦D	Performs bitwise-OR of the inverted source bitmap and the destination pixels
NOTSRCCOPY	~S	Copies the inverted source bitmap to the destination
NOTSRCERASE	~(S¦D)	Inverts the result of bitwise-OR of the source and destination
PATCOPY	P	Copies the brush pattern to the destination
PATINVERT	P^D	Performs exclusive-OR of the pattern and the destination
PATPAINT	P¦(~S)¦D	Inverts the source bitmap and performs bitwise-OR of the result with the pattern and the destination
SRCAND	S&D	Performs bitwise-AND of source bitmap and destination
SRCCOPY	S	Copies the source bitmap to the destination
SRCERASE	S&(~D)	Performs bitwise-OR of the source and the inverted destination
SRCINVERT	S^D	Performs exclusive-OR of the source and the destination
SRCPAINT	S¦D	Performs bitwise-OR of the source and the destination
WHITENESS	1	Sets all bits of the destination pixels to 1 (white)

The *BITMAP* Structure

Device-dependent bitmaps are represented in memory by a BITMAP structure, which is defined in <windows.h> as

```
typedef struct tagBITMAP
{
    int       bmType;       // Always set to zero
    int       bmWidth;      // Width of bitmap (in pixels)
    int       bmHeight;     // Height of bitmap (in pixels)
    int       bmWidthBytes; // Bytes per row of bitmap data
                            //     (must be even)
    BYTE      bmPlanes;     // Number of bit planes
    BYTE      bmBitsPixel;  // Number of bits per pixel
    void FAR* bmBits;       // Array of bitmap data
} BITMAP;
```

For color bitmaps, each pixel requires multiple bits of data, which may be stored as a number of planes or as groups of bits per pixel. The fields `bmPlanes` and `bmBitsPixel` determine how the bitmap data `bmBits` is interpreted.

When the data is organized as planes, `bmBitsPixel` is set to 1 and the `bmPlanes` field has the number of planes. The `bmBits` array starts with the first line of the image: all the bits of the first plane for the first line followed by the bits for that line from the second plane, and so on.

On the other hand, if the bitmap is meant for a device that stores all bits for a pixel contiguously, the `bmPlanes` field of the BITMAP structure is 1, but the `bmBitsPixel` is set to the number of bits used for each pixel. The `bmBits` array then stores the data for the image line by line, with each group of `bmBitsPixel` bits representing the color of consecutive pixels on a line.

The exact storage format for color bitmaps depends on the type of device where the bitmap is to be displayed. Apart from the device-dependent manner of storing the image data, the BITMAP structure has no provision for indicating how the pixel values are mapped to actual colors. The DIB format, described next, corrects this shortcoming of the DDB format.

Device-Independent Bitmap (DIB) Format

DIB format solves some of the device dependencies of the old-style bitmap format. Here are the specific differences:

- The internal representation of bitmap data is standardized—color bitmaps are stored as multiple bits per pixel with only one plane per pixel. The number of bits per pixel can be one of the following:

    1 for monochrome bitmaps

    4 for 16-color bitmaps

    8 for 256-color bitmaps

    24 for 16,777,216 or 16 million color bitmaps

- The array of bits stores the image data from the bottom row to the top (in DDB format, the data starts from the top row).
- The DIB format includes information about the resolution of the image.
- The bitmap data for 16- and 256-color bitmaps may be compressed using a run-length encoding (RLE) algorithm.

The DIB format is useful for storing images in files. The Windows PaintBrush application can store bitmaps in DIB format (with the .BMP file extension).

Summary

The C++ classes in OWL and CLASSLIB provide the framework for a Windows application, but you have to use the Windows Graphical Device Interface (GDI) for displaying graphics, text, and images in your application's windows. The device context, DC, is the key to device-independent graphics in Windows. The DC holds drawing tools and attributes such as pen, brush, background color, and font that affect all graphics and text output.

The Windows GDI also supports drawing to bitmaps. You can define a memory DC with an associated bitmap and load images or draw in the bitmap with GDI drawing functions. The GDI includes several block transfer functions such as `BitBlt` and `StretchBlt` that can efficiently copy bitmaps from memory to a device.

There are two types of bitmaps: the device-dependent bitmaps (DDB) from Windows versions prior to 3.0, and device-independent bitmaps (DIB) introduced in Windows 3.0. The DIB format is used to store images in files—the

.BMP files created by Windows PaintBrush use the DIB format. The next chapter describes how to interpret and display image files of various formats, including the DIB format.

Further Reading

Loren Heiny's book shows examples of graphics programming for Windows using Borland C++ and OWL. Brian Myers and Chris Doner provide very good tutorial coverage of graphics programming with the Windows API and Microsoft C. Although Myers and Doner do not cover Windows programming with Borland C++, you can readily adapt the information from their book for use in your Borland C++ programs.

For reference information on Windows API functions, James Conger's recent book is handy. And last but not least, there is Charles Petzold's classic book on Windows programming. Petzold's book is another good tutorial on programming in C with the Windows API.

Conger, James L. *The Waite Group's Windows API Bible*. Corte Madera, CA: Waite Group Press, 1992.

Heiny, Loren. *Windows Graphics Programming with Borland C++*. New York: Wiley, 1992.

Myers, Brian, and Chris Doner. *Programmer's Introduction to Windows 3.1*. Alameda, CA: SYBEX, 1992.

Petzold, Charles. *Programming Windows*. Redmond, WA: Microsoft Press, 1992.

Chapter 4

Understanding Image File Formats

Computer games need images. Almost all games use images in their opening screen and as integral elements of a game. Arcade games might use an image as a background on which sprites—other smaller images—are animated. Role-playing games use many images to provide realistic settings and get the player into the mood of the game. Educational games use images extensively to capture the child's attention and achieve the game's goal of teaching something.

To use an image, you need it in an electronic form. Many commercial game publishers employ professional artists who draw the images for a game— either directly on a computer or on paper. For conventional hard copy drawings, you have to use a scanner to convert the images into electronic form. Whether drawn with a paint program or scanned from a hard copy, the image is stored in a disk file with its file contents interpreted before you use it in your game. This chapter introduces a number of common image file formats that describe the layout of the pixels in the file, and also presents a number of C++ classes that can read image files and display images in Windows. The chapter ends with a Windows application, `ImageView`, that lets you open image files and view them.

Image File Formats

Recall that an image is a 2-D array of pixels, often called a raster. Each horizontal line is called a *scan line* or a *raster line*. In the computer, the color of each pixel is represented in one of the following ways:

- If the image is monochrome, the color of each pixel is expressed as a 1-bit value: a 1 or a 0.

- For a true color image, each pixel's color is expressed in terms of red (R), green (G), and blue (B) intensities that make up the color. Typically, each component of the color is represented by a byte—thus providing 256 levels for each color component. This approach requires 3 bytes for each pixel and allows up to 256x256x256 = 16,777,216 or nearly 17 million distinct combinations of RGB values (colors).

- For a palette-based image, each pixel's value is interpreted as an index to a table of RGB values known as a color palette or colormap. For each pixel, you are supposed to display the RGB value corresponding to

Chapter 4

Understanding Image File Formats

that pixel's contents. The number of bits needed to store each pixel's value depends on the number of colors in the color palette. The common sizes of color palettes are 16 (needs 4 bits per pixel) and 256 (needs 8 bits per pixel).

Figure 4.1 shows some of the components of an image. The width and height are expressed in terms of number of pixels along the horizontal and vertical directions, respectively.

Figure 4.1. *Elements of an image.*

Common Characteristics of Image Files

When storing an image in a file, you have to make sure that you can later interpret and display the image. Thus, the image file must contain the following information:

- The dimensions of the image—the width and the height
- The number of bits per pixel
- The type of image—whether pixel values should be interpreted as RGB colors or indexes to a color palette
- The color palette, or colormap, if the image uses a color palette
- The image data, which is the array of pixel values

Almost all image files contain this information, but each specific file format organizes it in a different way. Figure 4.2 shows the layout of a typical image file. The file starts with a short header—anywhere from a few to 128 or so bytes. The header contains any information besides the image data and the color palette. Next comes a color palette—if the pixel values in the image require one. The image data—the array of pixel values—appear after the palette. Usually, the pixel array is stored line by line.

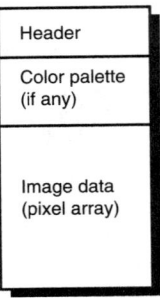

Figure 4.2. *Typical image file format.*

The array of pixels constitutes the bulk of the image file. For instance, a 256-color 640x480 image requires 640x480 = 307,200 bytes of storage because each pixel's value occupies 1 byte. Of course, the storage requirements of the image data can be reduced by compressing the data, either by run-length encoding or some other compression scheme.

Note that even though most image files have a layout similar to the one shown in Figure 4.2, there is still room for many possible variations:

- The order of information in the header can vary from one file format to another.
- Some display-dependent image file formats skip the color palette entirely and store only the pixel array.
- The pixel array might be stored from top to bottom or bottom to top.
- If the pixel values are RGB components, the order of red, green, and blue may vary.

Chapter 4

Understanding Image File Formats

- The pixel values may be stored in packed format or as bit planes. In the packed format, all bits belonging to a pixel are stored contiguously. When the image is stored according to bit planes, the bits for each pixel are split according to the bit position; the least significant bits of all pixels are stored line by line, then come the bits for the next bit position, and so on.

Some Common Formats

As you can see, there are a variety of ways to store an image in a file, which is why you find so many different types of image file formats. Here are some of the popular ones:

- PCX format, originally used by ZSoft's PC PaintBrush, is a popular image file format that many drawing programs and scanners support. PCX files use a run-length encoding (RLE) scheme to store the image in a compressed form.

- The Windows BMP format stores an image as a Device Independent Bitmap (DIB), a format introduced in Microsoft Windows 3.0. As described briefly in Chapter 3, the DIB format includes a color palette and stores the image data in a standard manner to make the image file device-independent. The Windows BMP format can store images with 1 (monochrome), 4 (16-color), 8 (256-color), or 24 (16 million-color) bits per pixel. The BMP format is not as efficient as PCX and other formats, but it is relatively easy to interpret a BMP file.

- The 24-bit Truevision Targa file format originated with Truevision's high-performance display adapters for PCs. There are several different types of Targa files; the most popular one is the 24-bit/pixel version that uses 8 bits for each of the R, G, and B components. This format can store image files with up to 16 million colors. However, the file size for a 24-bit image is very large—a 640x480 24-bit image requires 3x640x480 = 921,600 bytes or almost 1M.

- TIFF or Tagged Image File Format was developed jointly by Microsoft Corporation and Aldus Corporation as a flexible, system-independent file format to store monochrome through 24-bit color images. Most desktop publishing and word processing software can read and use TIFF images. Additionally, all scanners provide control software that can save images in TIFF.

99

- GIF (pronounced "jif") or Graphics Interchange Format was developed by CompuServe for compact storage of images with up to 256 colors. GIF files store images using LZW (Lempel-Ziv and Welsh) compression schemes.

C++ Classes for Handling Image Files

Because all images have a common set of information, the starting point of the C++ class hierarchy is an abstract base class named Image. The Image class stores the image in a standard internal format and provides pure virtual functions write and read to transfer an image to and from disk files. Note that a pure virtual function refers to a virtual function that is set equal to zero:

```
// Functions to load and save images
    virtual int read(const char* filename) = 0;
    virtual int write(const char* filename) = 0;
```

The C++ compiler does not allow you to create instances of a class with pure virtual functions. Thus, to actually use the Image class, you have to first derive a class from Image and define the read and write functions in that class. My idea for this design is that each class responsible for handling a specific image type is derived from Image. For instance, a 24-bit Truevision Targa image file (which usually has a .TGA file extension) is handled by the TGAImage class, which includes concrete implementations of the read and write member functions to load and save a Targa image. Similarly, classes such as PCXImage and BMPImage can handle PCX and Windows BMP images, respectively. Figure 4.3 shows the Image class hierarchy for the classes needed to handle Targa, PCX, and Windows BMP images.

I have also decided to make the Image class dependent on Microsoft Windows by selecting the Windows DIB format for the internal representation of an image in the Image class. This makes it easy to display the image because the Image class itself can include a member function that: accepts a device context as an argument, converts the internal DIB into a device-dependent bitmap, and displays the bitmap by calling Windows API functions. (Details are explained in subsequent sections.)

Understanding Image File Formats

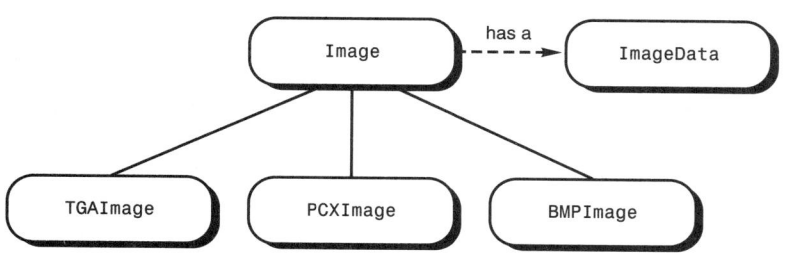

Figure 4.3. *Image class hierarchy to handle Targa, PCX, and BMP images.*

Another important design decision is to use an `ImageData` class to encapsulate the image's pixel array and then use a pointer to an `ImageData` object in each `Image` class (see Figure 4.3). Here is why I made this decision. The DIB format, used for internal representation of images, requires a considerable amount of memory for any reasonably sized color image. When equating one image to another, I do not want to make a complete copy of the image's pixel array. Instead, I want to copy a pointer to the pixel array and keep a count of how many `Image` class instances are sharing a specific pixel array. When an `Image` is destroyed, the destructor decrements the pixel array's count and destroys the array only when the count is zero, which indicates that the pixel array is not referenced by any `Image` object. This scheme is known as *reference counting*.

ImageData Class

The `ImageData` class represents all data necessary to represent an image—the pixel array as well as other pertinent information about the image. Because I am using a Windows DIB format to represent the image, the definition of the `ImageData` class (Listing 4.1) is very simple. The most important data in `ImageData` is the pointer (declared with the type `LPVOID`) `p_dib`. This is a pointer to a Windows DIB—a block of memory that has the layout shown in Figure 4.4. The `BITMAPINFOHEADER`, a structure at the beginning of the DIB, contains all relevant information, such as image dimensions and number of bits per pixel, that you need to interpret the image's pixel array. You see more about the fields of the `BITMAPINFOHEADER` in the `PCXImage` class. In this class, the `read` member function initializes the fields after reading an image in the PCX format and converting it to the internal DIB format.

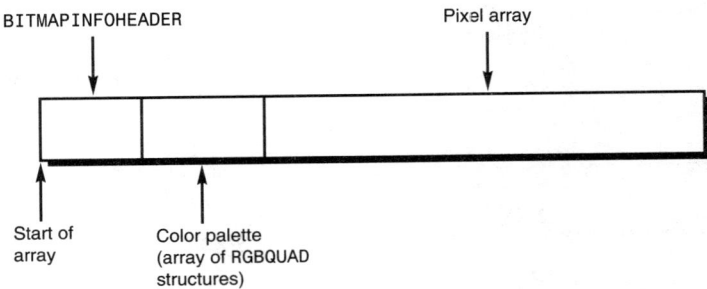

Figure 4.4. *Layout of a DIB in memory.*

Listing 4.1. `image.h`—
Header file for the `ImageData` and `Image` classes.

```
//----------------------------------------------------------------
// File: image.h
//
// Defines the Image class.
//
//----------------------------------------------------------------
#if !defined(__IMAGE_H)
#define __IMAGE_H

#include <windowsx.h>

// This class represents the data for an image
class ImageData
{
friend Image;
friend TGAImage;
friend BMPImage;
friend PCXImage;
friend TIFImage;

protected:
    ImageData() : p_dib(0), count(1), hpal(0), hbm_ddb(0),
                  bytes_per_line(0), w(0), h(0) {}

    ~ImageData();

protected:
```

Understanding Image File Formats

```cpp
// This points to a BITMAPINFOHEADER followed by the
// image data.
    LPVOID          p_dib;    // Device independent bitmap
    HPALETTE        hpal;     // Color palette
    HBITMAP         hbm_ddb;  // Device dependent bitmap

    unsigned short w, h;      // Width and height
    unsigned short bytes_per_line;

    unsigned short count;
};

// Abstract base class for all images
class Image
{
public:
// Constructors
    Image()
    {
        imdata = new ImageData;
    }
    Image(HBITMAP hbm, unsigned short w, unsigned short h)
    {
        imdata = new ImageData;
        imdata->hbm_ddb = hbm;
        imdata->w = w;
        imdata->h = h;
    }

    Image(HDC hdc, Image *img, short x, short y,
          unsigned short w, unsigned short h);

// Copy Constructor
    Image(const Image& img);

    virtual ~Image()
    {
        if(--imdata->count <= 0) delete imdata;
    }

// Operators
    Image& operator=(const Image& img);

// Copy the imdata pointer from another image
    void image_data(const Image* img);
```

continues

Listing 4.1. continued

```
// Functions to load and save images
    virtual int read(const char* filename){ return 0;};
    virtual int write(const char* filename){ return 0;};

// Returns pointer to the Windows Device Independent
// Bitmap (DIB).
    LPVOID get_dib() { return imdata->p_dib;}

// Function to return the handle to the device dependent
// bitmap.
    HBITMAP get_ddb() { return imdata->hbm_ddb;}

    unsigned short width()
    {
        if(imdata->p_dib != 0)
          return((LPBITMAPINFOHEADER)imdata->p_dib)->biWidth;
        return imdata->w;
    }
    unsigned short height()
    {
        if(imdata->p_dib != 0)
          return ((LPBITMAPINFOHEADER)imdata->p_dib)->biHeight;
        return imdata->h;
    }

    int image_loaded()
    {
        if(imdata->p_dib == 0) return 0;
        else return 1;
    }

    void detach()
    {
        if(--imdata->count == 0) delete imdata;
        imdata = new ImageData;
    }

// Functions to make palette and convert to DDB
    void make_palette();
    void DIBtoDDB(HDC hdc);

// Function that displays the DIB on a Windows device
// specified by a device context.
    void show(HDC hdc, short xfrom = 0, short yfrom = 0,
```

Understanding Image File Formats

Chapter 4

```
                       short xto = 0,    short yto = 0,
                       short width = 0,  short height = 0,
                       DWORD ropcode = SRCCOPY);

    unsigned int numcolors();

protected:
    ImageData* imdata;
};

#endif
```

The `ImageData` class also includes two important member variables:

- `HPALETTE hpal;` is a handle to a Windows color palette—an array of `PALETTEENTRY` structures (defined in <windows.h>) that associates an index with an RGB color. The `make_palette` member function of the `Image` class creates the palette.

- `HBITMAP hbm_ddb;` is the handle to the Device Dependent Bitmap (DDB) corresponding to the DIB. The `DIBtoDDB` member function of the `Image` class creates the DDB (for a specified device) from the DIB.

Encapsulating the image's data in the `ImageData` class allows sharing of the data between images, but I do not want to give up the ability to directly access and manipulate the image's pixel array from other image classes. One way to provide this access is to declare as `friend` all classes that have to manipulate the private and protected member variables of `ImageData`. In this case, the `Image` and its derived classes such as `PCXImage`, `BMPImage`, and `TGAImage` are declared with the `friend` keyword in the `ImageData` class.

Image Class

The `Image` class, declared in the file `image.h` (Listing 4.1), is an abstract base class that encapsulates the common features of all images. Because all images are internally maintained in the Windows DIB format, the `Image` class can take care of displaying the image instead of delegating that responsibility to the derived classes. The `show` member function of `Image` displays the image on a device specified by a DC. The Windows API provides a function, `SetDIBitsToDevice`, that lets you directly display a DIB on a device, but this function is comparatively slow. A faster approach is to convert the DIB into a DDB and use the `BitBlt` function to display the DDB. The drawback is that creating the DDB requires memory. Consult the listing of the `show` function (Listing 4.2) for complete details of how to display a DIB. The general steps to convert the DIB to a DDB and display the DDB are as follows:

1. Set up a color palette if the image needs one. DIBs with 1, 4, or 8 bits per pixel use color palettes. The `make_palette` function in Listing 4.2 illustrates how to create a palette. Before converting a DIB to a DDB, you have to realize the color palette.

2. Call the `CreateDIBitmap` function to get back a handle to a DDB created from the DIB for a specified device. The `DIBtoDDB` function performs this task by calling `CreateDIBitmap` as follows:

```
// Note: imdata is a pointer to an ImageData object
//       hbm_ddb is a handle to a bitmap (HBITMAP)
   imdata->hbm_ddb = CreateDIBitmap(
                    hdc,            // Device context handle
                    p_bminfo,       // Pointer to BITMAPINFOHEADER
                    CBM_INIT,       // Initialize DDB from DIB
                    p_image,        // Pointer to image data
                    (LPBITMAPINFO)p_bminfo, // Pointer to
                                    // a BITMAPINFO structure
                    DIB_RGB_COLORS); // Interpret palette
                                    // entries as RGB colors
```

As indicated by the comments, the DIB is specified by three pointers: a pointer to the `BITMAPINFOHEADER`, a pointer to the image's pixel array, and a pointer to a `BITMAPINFO` structure with the color palette. In this case, the `BITMAPINFO` and `BITMAPINFOHEADER` structures overlap and the image data follows the `BITMAPINFOHEADER`.

3. Call `CreateCompatibleDC` to get back a handle to a memory device context (DC) compatible with a specified DC.

4. If the compatible DC is created successfully (the handle is nonzero), select the DDB into the DC by calling the Windows API function named `SelectBitmap`.

5. Call `BitBlt` to copy the bitmap from the memory DC to the actual device. The sample call

Understanding Image File Formats

```
        BitBlt(hdc, xto, yto, wdth, hght,
              memdc, xfrom, yfrom, ropcode);
```

copies from the `memdc` device context to `hdc`. The `wdth` and `hght` represent the width and height of the bitmap being copied to the screen.

6. Clean up by deleting the memory DC. The DDB should be deleted also—this is done by the destructor of the `ImageData` class when the image is no longer needed.

Listing 4.2. `image.cpp`—Member functions of the `Image` class.

```cpp
//-------------------------------------------------------------
// File: image.cpp
//
// Image manipulation functions
//-------------------------------------------------------------
#include <fstream.h>
#include "image.h"

//-------------------------------------------------------------
// I m a g e D a t a : : ~ I m a g e D a t a
// Destructor for an Image.

ImageData::~ImageData()
{
// If a DIB exists, delete it.
    if(p_dib != 0) GlobalFreePtr(p_dib);

// If a palette exists, free it also.
    if(hpal != 0) DeletePalette(hpal);

// If a DDB exists, destroy it.
    if(hbm_ddb != 0) DeleteBitmap(hbm_ddb);
}
//-------------------------------------------------------------
// I m a g e : : I m a g e
// Copy constructor

Image::Image(const Image& img)
{
    img.imdata->count++;
    if(--imdata->count <= 0) delete imdata;
    imdata = img.imdata;
}
```

continues

Listing 4.2. continued

```
//------------------------------------------------------------
// Image::image_data
// Copy the ImageData pointer from another image

void Image::image_data(const Image* img)
{
    img->imdata->count++;
    if(--imdata->count <= 0) delete imdata;
    imdata = img->imdata;
}
//------------------------------------------------------------
// Image::operator=
// Assignment operator

Image& Image::operator=(const Image& img)
{
    img.imdata->count++;
    if(--imdata->count <= 0) delete imdata;
    imdata = img.imdata;
    return *this;
}
//------------------------------------------------------------
// Image::numcolors
// Returns the number of colors used. Returns 0 if image uses
// 24-bit pixels.

unsigned int Image::numcolors()
{
    if(imdata->p_dib == 0) return 0;
    LPBITMAPINFOHEADER p_bminfo =
                (LPBITMAPINFOHEADER)(imdata->p_dib);

// If the biClrUsed field is nonzero, use that as the number of
// colors
    if(p_bminfo->biClrUsed != 0)
        return (unsigned int)p_bminfo->biClrUsed;

// Otherwise, the number of colors depends on the bits per pixel
    switch(p_bminfo->biBitCount)
    {
        case 1: return 2;
        case 4: return 16;
        case 8: return 256;
        default: return 0; // Must be 24-bit/pixel image
    }
}
```

Chapter 4

Understanding Image File Formats

```
//----------------------------------------------------------------
// Image::make_palette
// Create a color palette using information in the DIB

void Image::make_palette()
{
// Set up a pointer to the DIB
    LPBITMAPINFOHEADER p_bminfo =
                        (LPBITMAPINFOHEADER)(imdata->p_dib);
    if(p_bminfo == 0) return;

// Free any existing palette
    if(imdata->hpal != 0) DeletePalette(imdata->hpal);

// Set up the palette, if needed
    if(numcolors() > 0)
    {
        LPLOGPALETTE p_pal = (LPLOGPALETTE) GlobalAllocPtr(GHND,
                                        sizeof(LOGPALETTE) +
                            numcolors() * sizeof(PALETTEENTRY));

        if(p_pal)
        {
            p_pal->palVersion = 0x030a;
            p_pal->palNumEntries = numcolors();

// Set up palette entries from DIB
            LPBITMAPINFO p_bi = (LPBITMAPINFO)p_bminfo;
            int i;
            for(i = 0; i < numcolors(); i++)
            {
                p_pal->palPalEntry[i].peRed =
                        p_bi->bmiColors[i].rgbRed;
                p_pal->palPalEntry[i].peGreen =
                        p_bi->bmiColors[i].rgbGreen;
                p_pal->palPalEntry[i].peBlue =
                        p_bi->bmiColors[i].rgbBlue;
                p_pal->palPalEntry[i].peFlags = 0;
            }
            imdata->hpal = CreatePalette(p_pal);
            GlobalFreePtr(p_pal);
        }
    }
}
//----------------------------------------------------------------
// Image::DIBtoDDB
// Create a device dependent bitmap from the DIB
```

continues

Listing 4.2. continued

```
void Image::DIBtoDDB(HDC hdc)
{
// Set up a pointer to the DIB
    LPBITMAPINFOHEADER p_bminfo =
                            (LPBITMAPINFOHEADER)(imdata->p_dib);
    if(p_bminfo == 0) return;

// If a DDB exists, destroy it first.
    if(imdata->hbm_ddb != 0) DeleteBitmap(imdata->hbm_ddb);

// Build the device dependent bitmap.

// Set up pointer to the image data (skip over BITMAPINFOHEADER
// and palette).
    LPSTR p_image = (LPSTR)p_bminfo +
                    sizeof(BITMAPINFOHEADER) +
                    numcolors() * sizeof(RGBQUAD);

// Realize palette, if there is one. Note that this does not do
// anything on the standard 16-color VGA driver because that
// driver does not allow changing the palette, but the new palette
// should work on Super VGA displays.

    HPALETTE hpalold = NULL;
    if(imdata->hpal)
    {
        hpalold = SelectPalette(hdc, imdata->hpal, FALSE);
        RealizePalette(hdc);
    }

// Convert the DIB into a DDB (device dependent bitmap) and
// block transfer (blt) it to the device context.
    HBITMAP hbm_old;
    imdata->hbm_ddb = CreateDIBitmap(hdc,
                                p_bminfo,
                                CBM_INIT,
                                p_image,
                                (LPBITMAPINFO)p_bminfo,
                                DIB_RGB_COLORS);

// Don't need the palette once the bitmap is converted to DDB
// format.
    if(hpalold)
        SelectPalette(hdc, hpalold, FALSE);
}
```

Understanding Image File Formats

Chapter 4

```
//--------------------------------------------------------------
// I m a g e : : s h o w
// Display a DIB on a Windows device specified by a
// device context

void Image::show(HDC hdc, short xfrom, short yfrom,
                          short xto,   short yto,
                          short wdth,  short hght,
                          DWORD ropcode)
{
// Set up a pointer to the DIB
    LPBITMAPINFOHEADER p_bminfo =
                        (LPBITMAPINFOHEADER)(imdata->p_dib);
    if(p_bminfo != NULL)
    {
// Set up the palette, if needed
        if(imdata->hpal == 0 && numcolors() > 0) make_palette();

// Convert to DDB, if necessary
        if(imdata->hbm_ddb == 0) DIBtoDDB(hdc);
    }

// "Blit" the DDB to hdc
    if(imdata->hbm_ddb != 0)
    {
        HDC memdc = CreateCompatibleDC(hdc);
        if(memdc != 0)
        {
            HBITMAP hbm_old = SelectBitmap(memdc,
                                           imdata->hbm_ddb);
// If width or height is zero, use corresponding dimension
// from the image.
            if(wdth == 0) wdth = width();
            if(hght == 0) hght = height();

            BitBlt(hdc, xto, yto, wdth, hght,
                   memdc, xfrom, yfrom, ropcode);
            SelectBitmap(memdc, hbm_old);
            DeleteDC(memdc);
        }
    }
}
//--------------------------------------------------------------
// Image::I m a g e
// Construct an image by copying a portion of the bitmap from
// another image
```

continues

111

Listing 4.2. continued

```cpp
Image::Image(HDC hdc, Image *img, short x, short y,
             unsigned short w, unsigned short h)
{
    imdata = new ImageData;
    if(img == NULL) return;

    unsigned short iw = img->width();
    unsigned short ih = img->height();

    if(x < 0) x = 0;
    if(y < 0) y = 0;

// If width or height is 0, adjust them
    if(w == 0) w = iw;
    if(h == 0) h = ih;

// Make sure width and height are not too large
    if((w+x) > iw) w = iw - x;
    if((h+y) > ih) h = ih - y;

// Save width and height
    imdata->w = w;
    imdata->h = h;

// Create a new bitmap for the new image
    imdata->hbm_ddb = CreateCompatibleBitmap(hdc, w, h);
    if(imdata->hbm_ddb != 0)
    {
        HDC memdcn = CreateCompatibleDC(hdc);
        HDC memdco = CreateCompatibleDC(hdc);
        if(memdcn != 0 && memdco != 0)
        {
            HBITMAP ohbm = SelectBitmap(memdco, img->get_ddb());
            HBITMAP nhbm = SelectBitmap(memdcn, imdata->hbm_ddb);
            BitBlt(memdcn, 0, 0, w, h, memdco, x, y, SRCCOPY);
            SelectBitmap(memdco, ohbm);
                SelectBitmap(memdcn, nhbm);
            DeleteDC(memdco);
            DeleteDC(memdcn);
        }
    }
}
```

Understanding Image File Formats

BMPImage Class

The BMPImage class handles Windows DIB images. These are usually stored in files with the .BMP file extension and thus go by the name of BMP images. A BMP image file is the same as the in-memory representation of a DIB, shown in Figure 4.4, with a file header prefix added to the DIB. The header is represented by a BITMAPFILEHEADER structure defined in <windows.h> as follows:

```
typedef struct tagBITMAPFILEHEADER
{
    UINT     bfType;      // File type. Should be 'BM'
    DWORD    bfSize;      // Size of file in bytes
    UINT     bfReserved1; // 0
    UINT     bfReserved2; // 0
    DWORD    bfOffBits;   // Offset to the start of image data
} BITMAPFILEHEADER;
```

A BITMAPINFOHEADER structure follows the file header. The color palette, if any, and the image's pixel array come after the BITMAPINFOHEADER.

Listing 4.3 shows the declaration of the BMPImage class. As you can see, the BMPImage class provides the read and write member functions and defines one additional member variable. BITMAPFILEHEADER bmphdr; is an instance of a BITMAPFILEHEADER structure that is used when reading or writing a BMP image file.

Listing 4.3. `bmpimage.h`—Declaration of the **BMPImage** class.

```
//---------------------------------------------------------------
// File: bmpimage.h
//
// Defines the BMPImage class representing a Windows BMP image.
//
//---------------------------------------------------------------
#if !defined(__BMPIMAGE_H)
#define __BMPIMAGE_H

#include "image.h"

class BMPImage: public Image
{
public:
    BMPImage() {}
```

continues

113

Listing 4.3. continued

```
    ~BMPImage() {}

    int read(const char* filename);
    int write(const char* filename);
private:
    BITMAPFILEHEADER bmphdr;
};

#endif
```

Reading a BMP Image

Listing 4.4 shows the file `bmpimage.cpp` that implements the member functions, `read` and `write`, of the `BMPImage` class. Reading a BMP image into a `BMPImage` object is straightforward because the internal data format of the `Image` class hierarchy is the DIB and because a BMP image file is a file header followed by a DIB. As you can see from the `read` function, reading the BMP image file requires the following steps:

1. Read the file header into the `bmphdr` member of the `BMPImage` class. If `ifs` represents the input file stream, you can read the header as follows:

   ```
   // Read the file header
      ifs.read((unsigned char*)&bmphdr,
               sizeof(BITMAPFILEHEADER));
   ```

2. Check that the `bfType` field of the header contains the characters `BM`, which indicates that this is a BMP image.

3. Determine the number of bytes remaining in the file—these are the bytes that make up the DIB stored in the BMP image file. You can position the file pointer at the end of the file and read the byte offset to determine the file size. Subtracting the size of the file header from the length of the file gives you the number of bytes in the DIB that you want to read. Here is how:

Understanding Image File Formats

```
    // Determine size of DIB to read
    // (that's file length - size of BITMAPFILEHEADER)
        ifs.seekg(0, ios::end);
        long bmpsize = ifs.tellg() - sizeof(BITMAPFILEHEADER);

    // Reset file pointer...
        ifs.seekg(sizeof(BITMAPFILEHEADER), ios::beg);
```

4. Allocate memory for the DIB by calling the `GlobalAlloc` function:

```
    // Allocate space for the bitmap
        imdata->p_dib = GlobalAllocPtr(GHND, bmpsize);
```

5. Read the bytes from the file into this memory. For efficient file I/O, you should read from the file in large chunks. The `BMPImage::read` function reads the image in blocks that are up to 30K in size as defined by the constant `maxread` declared at the beginning of the `bmpimage.cpp` file (Listing 4.4).

Note that I had to use an intermediate buffer when reading the image because the read function of the `ifstream` class (from the C++ iostream library) did not work properly with the pointer `imdata->p_dib` that was returned by `GlobalAlloc`.

Listing 4.4. bmpimage.cpp—
Member functions of the BMPImage class.

```
//------------------------------------------------------------
//  File: bmpimage.cpp
//
//  Image manipulation functions for Windows BMP images.
//------------------------------------------------------------
#include <fstream.h>
#include <limits.h>
#include "bmpimage.h"

const size_t maxread  = 30*1024; // Read 30K at a time
const size_t maxwrite = 30*1024; // Write 30K at a time
//------------------------------------------------------------
//  B M P I m a g e : : r e a d
//  Read and interpret a Windows .BMP image (Device Independent
//  Bitmap).
```

continues

Listing 4.4. continued

```
int BMPImage::read(const char* filename)
{
// If there is an existing image, detach the image data
// before reading a new image
    if(imdata->p_dib != 0) detach();

// Open file for reading
    ifstream ifs(filename, ios::in | ios::binary);
    if(!ifs)
    {
// Error reading file. Return 0.
        return 0;
    }

// Read the file header
    ifs.read((unsigned char*)&bmphdr, sizeof(BITMAPFILEHEADER));

// Check if image file format is acceptable (the type
// must be 'BM'
    if(bmphdr.bfType != (('M' << 8) | 'B')) return 0;

// Determine size of DIB to read (that's file length - size of
// BITMAPFILEHEADER)
    ifs.seekg(0, ios::end);
    long bmpsize = ifs.tellg() - sizeof(BITMAPFILEHEADER);

// Reset file pointer...
    ifs.seekg(sizeof(BITMAPFILEHEADER), ios::beg);

// Allocate space for the bitmap
    imdata->p_dib = GlobalAllocPtr(GHND, bmpsize);

// If memory allocation fails, return 0
    if(imdata->p_dib == 0) return 0;

// Load the file in big chunks. We don't have to interpret
// because our internal format is also BMP.

// Allocate a large buffer to read from file
    unsigned char *rbuf = new unsigned char[maxread];
    if(rbuf == NULL)
    {
        detach();
        return 0;
    }
```

Understanding Image File Formats

```
        unsigned char huge *data = 
                    (unsigned char huge*)imdata->p_dib;
        unsigned int chunksize;
        unsigned int i;

        while(bmpsize > 0)
        {
            if(bmpsize > maxread)
                chunksize = maxread;
            else
                chunksize = bmpsize;
            ifs.read(rbuf, chunksize);

// Copy into DIB
            for(i = 0; i < chunksize; i++) data[i] = rbuf[i];
            bmpsize -= chunksize;
            data += chunksize;
        }
        delete rbuf;

        return 1;
}
//------------------------------------------------------------
// B M P I m a g e : : w r i t e
// Write a Windows .BMP image to a file (in Device Independent
// Bitmap format)

int BMPImage::write(const char* filename)
{
// If there is no image, return without doing anything
    if(imdata->p_dib == 0) return 0;

// Open file for binary write operations.
    ofstream ofs(filename, ios::out | ios::binary);
    if(!ofs) return 0;

// Set up BMP file header
    bmphdr.bfType = ('M' << 8) | 'B';
    bmphdr.bfReserved1 = 0;
    bmphdr.bfReserved2 = 0;
    bmphdr.bfOffBits = sizeof(BITMAPFILEHEADER) +
                       sizeof(BITMAPINFOHEADER) +
                       numcolors() * sizeof(RGBQUAD);
    bmphdr.bfSize = (long) height() *
                    (long) imdata->bytes_per_line +
                                bmphdr.bfOffBits;
```

continues

Listing 4.4. continued

```
// Write the file header to the file
    ofs.write((unsigned char*)&bmphdr, sizeof(BITMAPFILEHEADER));

// Save the file in big chunks.

// Allocate a large buffer to be used when transferring
// data to the file

    unsigned char *wbuf = new unsigned char[maxwrite];
    if(wbuf == NULL) return 0;

    unsigned char huge *data =
                (unsigned char huge*)imdata->p_dib;
    unsigned int chunksize;
    long bmpsize = bmphdr.bfSize - sizeof(BITMAPFILEHEADER);

    unsigned int i;

    while(bmpsize > 0)
    {
        if(bmpsize > maxwrite)
            chunksize = maxwrite;
        else
            chunksize = bmpsize;
// Copy image from DIB to buffer
        for(i = 0; i < chunksize; i++) wbuf[i] = data[i];
        ofs.write(wbuf, chunksize);
        bmpsize -= chunksize;
        data += chunksize;
    }
    delete wbuf;
    return 1;
}
```

Writing a BMP Image

To save a DIB in a BMP format image file, you must first prepare a header by initializing the fields of the bmphdr member variable, which is a BITMAPFILEHEADER structure. As shown in the write function in Listing 4.4, you can initialize the file header as follows:

Understanding Image File Formats

```
// Set up BMP file header
    bmphdr.bfType = ('M' << 8) | 'B';
    bmphdr.bfReserved1 = 0;
    bmphdr.bfReserved2 = 0;
    bmphdr.bfOffBits = sizeof(BITMAPFILEHEADER) +
                       sizeof(BITMAPINFOHEADER) +
                       numcolors() * sizeof(RGBQUAD);
    bmphdr.bfSize = (long) height() *
                    (long) imdata->bytes_per_line +
                          bmphdr.bfOffBits;
```

Once the file header is set up, save the header in this file:

```
// Write the file header to the file
    ofs.write((unsigned char*)&bmphdr, sizeof(BITMAPFILEHEADER));
```

Then you can write the entire DIB to the file in large chunks from imdata->p_dib.

TGAImage Class

The Truevision Targa file format originated with Truevision's display hardware—one of the first video adapters capable of displaying 24-bit RGB color. Although the Targa file format can store images with 1, 8, 16, or 24 bits per pixel, I focus on the 24-bit format because it is the most commonly used 24-bit color format for IBM-compatible PCs. Almost any application that deals with 24-bit RGB colors supports the 24-bit Targa file format. For instance, the Targa format is the output format of choice among the popular ray-tracing software such as DKBTrace by David Buck and Aaron Collins.

Listing 4.5 shows the declaration of the TGAImage class representing a Targa 24-bit color image. Most Targa files are stored with the .TGA file extension; hence the class name TGAImage. Note that the TGAImage class defines the read member function only. The read function reads a Targa 24-bit RGB image and converts it into a Windows DIB. I did not develop a write function because I did not need that function to write computer games. But the write function may be important if you are contemplating converting images from other formats to the Targa format.

Like the BMPImage class, the TGAImage class includes a new member variable, hdr—an instance of a TARGAHeader structure—which is defined in Listing 4.5 as follows:

```
struct TARGAHeader
{
    char           offset;
    char           cmap_type;
    char           image_type;
    unsigned short cmap_start;
    unsigned short cmap_length;
    char           cmap_bits;
    unsigned short hoffset;
    unsigned short voffset;
    unsigned short width;
    unsigned short height;
    char           bits_per_pixel;
    char           flags;
};
```

This structure represents the header of a Targa image file. The meanings of the fields of `TARGAHeader` are

- `char offset;` specifies the number of bytes to skip after reading the header. Usually this field is zero.

- `char cmap_type;` indicates the type of colormap being used. For 24-bit color images, this field should be zero.

- `char image_type;` defines the way the image's data is stored (whether it is uncompressed or run-length encoded). A value of 2 indicates an uncompressed RGB color image, which is the only image type that the `TGAImage` class can handle.

- `unsigned short cmap_start, cmap_length; char cmap_bits;` specify the colormap, if there is one. There is no colormap for 24-bit RGB color images.

- `unsigned short hoffset, voffset;` specifies the offset between the upper left corner of the screen and the upper left corner of the image to be displayed. These fields are usually zero.

- `unsigned short width, height;` are the width and height of the image in pixel.

- `char bits_per_pixel;` indicates the number of bits used to represent the color of each pixel. For 24-bit color images, this field is 24.

- `char flags;` specifies how to interpret the image's data. The `TGAImage` class handles the case when `flags` is 0x20, which implies that the image is stored in a top-down format starting with the first scan line.

Understanding Image File Formats

Listing 4.5. tgaimage.h—Declaration of the TGAImage class.

```
//----------------------------------------------------------------
// File: tgaimage.h
//
// Defines the TGAImage class representing Targa True
// Color images (handles only 24-bit color formats).
//
//----------------------------------------------------------------
#if !defined(__TGAIMAGE_H)
#define __TGAIMAGE_H

#include "image.h"

class TGAImage: public Image
{
public:
    TGAImage() {}
    TGAImage(Image& img) : Image(img) {}

    ~TGAImage() {}

    int read(const char* filename);
    int write(const char* filename)
    { return 1;} // Do nothing for now

private:
// A structure for the file header
    struct TARGAHeader
    {
        char           offset;
        char           cmap_type;
        char           image_type;
        unsigned short cmap_start;
        unsigned short cmap_length;
        char           cmap_bits;
        unsigned short hoffset;
        unsigned short voffset;
        unsigned short width;
        unsigned short height;
        char           bits_per_pixel;
        char           flags;
    };
    TARGAHeader hdr;
};

#endif
```

121

After the file header comes the image's pixels, one scan line after another. For 24-bit RGB color images, each pixel's color is stored in 3 bytes: first a byte for the blue (B) component, then the green (G), then the red (R). (Yes, it is opposite of the red-green-blue RGB order that you might have expected.)

The read function in Listing 4.6 shows how to load a Targa 24-bit RGB color image into a DIB. The first task is to read the header of the Targa file and initialize the fields of a BITMAPINFOHEADER structure. Reading the actual image data is straightforward because Windows 24-bit DIBs use the same layout for image data as the 24-bit Targa format except that DIBs expect the image data bottom-to-top with the pixels of the last scan line appearing first. Another important point to note is that the number of bytes in each scan line of a DIB must be a multiple of 4. Thus, you may have to pad the scan lines of the Targa image to meet this requirement.

Listing 4.6. `tgaimage.cpp`— Implementation of the `TGAImage` class.

```
//---------------------------------------------------------------
//   File: tgaimage.cpp
//
//   Image manipulation functions for 24-bit Targa TrueColor
//   images.
//---------------------------------------------------------------
#include <fstream.h>
#include "tgaimage.h"
//---------------------------------------------------------------
//   T G A I m a g e : : r e a d
//   Read a Targa image (only 24-bit TrueColor images handled)

int TGAImage::read(const char* filename)
{
// If there is an existing image, detach the image data
// before reading a new image
    if(imdata->p_dib != 0) detach();

// Open file for reading
    ifstream ifs(filename, ios::in | ios::binary);
    if(!ifs)
    {
// Error reading file. Return 0.
        return 0;
    }
```

Understanding Image File Formats

```
// Read TARGA header
    ifs.read((unsigned char*)&hdr, sizeof(TARGAHeader));

// Check if image file format is acceptable
    if(hdr.cmap_type) return 0;    // We don't handle colormaps

// Allocate memory for the device independent bitmap (DIB)
// Note that the number of bytes in each line of a DIB image
// must be a multiple of 4.
    imdata->bytes_per_line = 3 * hdr.width;
    if(imdata->bytes_per_line % 4)
        imdata->bytes_per_line = 4 *
                    (imdata->bytes_per_line/4 + 1);

    imdata->p_dib = GlobalAllocPtr(GHND,
                        sizeof(BITMAPINFOHEADER) +
                (long) imdata->bytes_per_line *
                            (long) hdr.height);

// If memory allocation fails, return 0
    if(imdata->p_dib == 0) return 0;

// Set up bitmap info header
    LPBITMAPINFOHEADER p_bminfo = (LPBITMAPINFOHEADER)imdata->p_dib;
    p_bminfo->biSize = sizeof(BITMAPINFOHEADER);
    p_bminfo->biWidth = hdr.width;
    p_bminfo->biHeight = hdr.height;
    p_bminfo->biPlanes = 1;
    p_bminfo->biBitCount = hdr.bits_per_pixel;
    p_bminfo->biCompression = BI_RGB;
    p_bminfo->biSizeImage = (long)hdr.height *
                            (long)imdata->bytes_per_line;
    p_bminfo->biXPelsPerMeter = 0;
    p_bminfo->biYPelsPerMeter = 0;
    p_bminfo->biClrUsed = 0;
    p_bminfo->biClrImportant = 0;

// Skip "offset" bytes from current position to find image
// data. Usually, offset is zero, in which case this call
// to seekg does nothing.

    ifs.seekg(hdr.offset, ios::cur);

// Load image data into the DIB. Note the DIB image must be
// stored "bottom-to-top" line order. That's why we position
// data at the end of the array so that the image can be
// stored backwards--from the last line to the first.
```

continues

Listing 4.6. continued

```
    unsigned char huge *data =
            (unsigned char huge*)imdata->p_dib +
                    sizeof(BITMAPINFOHEADER) +
                (unsigned long)(hdr.height - 1) *
        (unsigned long)(imdata->bytes_per_line);

// Need a buffer to read each line because the read function of
// the ifstream class does not work with huge pointers

    unsigned char *rbuf = new unsigned char[imdata->bytes_per_line];
    if(rbuf == NULL)
    {
        detach();
        return 0;
    }

    int i, j;
    unsigned short actual_bytes_per_line = 3*hdr.width;

// Pad part of rbuf beyond actual_bytes_per_line with zeros
    if(actual_bytes_per_line < imdata->bytes_per_line)
    {
        for(i = actual_bytes_per_line;
            i < imdata->bytes_per_line;
            i++) rbuf[i] = 0;
    }

// Now read the image data...
    for(i = 0; i < hdr.height; i++, data -= imdata->bytes_per_line)
    {
// Read a line of image data into the buffer
        ifs.read(rbuf, actual_bytes_per_line);

// Copy from buffer into DIB's image data area
        for(j = 0; j < actual_bytes_per_line; j++)
            data[j] = rbuf[j];
    }
    delete rbuf;
// Success!
    return 1;
}
```

Understanding Image File Formats

PCXImage Class

The PCX file format was developed by ZSoft to store images created by the PC PaintBrush paint program. The name PCX comes from the file extension .PCX used for PC PaintBrush files. The PCX file format is as follows:

- The file starts with a 128-byte header (described later). The header is followed by encoded scan lines of the image.

- Each scan line in the PCX file is created by first laying out the scan lines of individual bit planes one after another. Then the entire line is encoded using a run-length encoding scheme that works like this: if the two highest order bits of a byte are set, the low-order six bits indicate how many times the following byte must be repeated. If the two highest order bits are not both 1, the byte represents the bitmap data.

Examine the read function (Listing 4.8) of the PCXImage class to understand this better.

PCX File Header

As you can see from the declaration of the PCXImage class in Listing 4.7, the PCX file's header is represented by the following PCXHeader structure:

```
struct PCXHeader
{
    unsigned char   manufacturer;
    unsigned char   version;
    unsigned char   encoding;
    unsigned char   bits_per_pixel_per_plane;
    short           xmin;
    short           ymin;
    short           xmax;
    short           ymax;
    unsigned short  hresolution;
    unsigned short  vresolution;
    unsigned char   colormap[48];
    unsigned char   reserved;
    unsigned char   nplanes;
    unsigned short  bytes_per_line;
    short           palette_info;
    unsigned char   filler[58];    // Header is 128 bytes
};
```

Here are the meanings of some of the important fields of the PCX file header:

- `unsigned char manufacturer;` is always set to 0x0a for a valid PCX file. You can use this information to verify that a file contains a PCX format image.
- `unsigned char version;` indicates the version of PC PaintBrush that created the image file. Note that if `version` is greater than 5 and `bits per pixel per plane*nplanes` is 8, the file has a 256-entry color palette (consisting of 256 RGB bytes occupying 256x3 = 768 bytes) appended at the end of the image.
- `unsigned char encoding;` should always be 1 to indicate that the image is stored using run-length encoding.
- `unsigned char bits_per_pixel_per_plane;` is the number of bits for each pixel in each bit plane. For instance, a 256-color image would have 1 bit plane with 8 bits per pixel per plane.
- `short xmin, ymin, xmax, ymax;` specifies the dimensions of the image. The width is (`xmax` - `xmin` + 1) and the height is (`ymax` - `ymin` + 1).
- `unsigned char colormap[48];` is a 16-entry colormap with a 3-byte RGB value per entry. This colormap is valid if `bits_per_pixel_per_plane*nplanes` is less than or equal to 4.
- `unsigned char nplanes;` is the number of bit planes.

Note that the PCX file header is always 128 bytes long, so you have to pad the structure with enough bytes to make the total size.

Listing 4.7. `pcximage.h`—Declaration of the `PCXImage` class.

```
//-------------------------------------------------------------
//  File: pcximage.h
//
//  Defines the PCXImage class representing PCX images.
//
//-------------------------------------------------------------
#if !defined(__PCXIMAGE_H)
#define __PCXIMAGE_H

#include "image.h"
```

Understanding Image File Formats

```
class PCXImage: public Image
{
public:
    PCXImage() {}
    PCXImage(Image& img) : Image(img) {}

    ~PCXImage() {}

    int read(const char* filename);
    int write(const char* filename)
    { return 1;} // Do nothing for now
private:
// A structure for the file header
    struct PCXHeader
    {
        unsigned char   manufacturer;
        unsigned char   version;
        unsigned char   encoding;
        unsigned char   bits_per_pixel_per_plane;
        short           xmin;
        short           ymin;
        short           xmax;
        short           ymax;
        unsigned short  hresolution;
        unsigned short  vresolution;
        unsigned char   colormap[48];
        unsigned char   reserved;
        unsigned char   nplanes;
        unsigned short  bytes_per_line;
        short           palette_info;
        unsigned char   filler[58];    // Header is 128 bytes
    };
    PCXHeader hdr;

};

#endif
```

Reading a PCX File

Conceptually, reading the PCX file is simple—you simply read one byte at a time and repeat the byte a specified number of bytes when the byte indicates run-length encoding. The early part of the read function in Listing 4.8 shows the loop that unpacks the PCX image by undoing the effect of run-length encoding. Written in C++-like pseudocode, the loop looks like this:

```
while (file has not ended)
{
    read a byte
    if(byte & 0xc0) // Are 2 high bits set?
    {
        count = byte & 0x3f;
        copy the byte count number of times
    }
    else
        copy the byte once
}
```

Decoding the run-length encoding is the easy part of reading a PCX image. Because of the design of our Image class hierarchy, you also have to convert the PCX image from its bit plane oriented structure to a packed format Windows DIB. The code to this conversion is somewhat messy because to store as a DIB, you have to combine bits from each bit plane of the PCX image into a packed format representing a pixel's value. Figure 4.5 illustrates the process of converting a PCX image into a Windows DIB format.

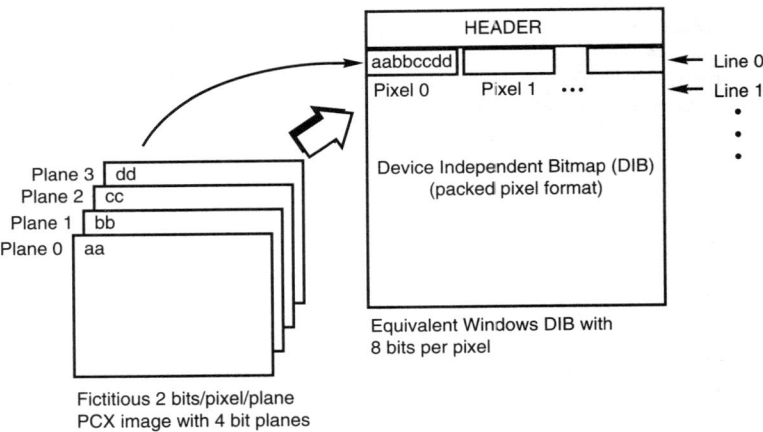

Figure 4.5. *Converting a PCX image into a Windows DIB.*

The first step in converting the image to a DIB is to initialize the BITMAPINFOHEADER that precedes the image in a DIB. The BITMAPINFOHEADER structure is defined in <windows.h> as

Understanding Image File Formats

```
typedef struct tagBITMAPINFOHEADER
{
    DWORD    biSize;            // Size of this structure
    LONG     biWidth;           // Width in pixels
    LONG     biHeight;          // Height in pixels
    WORD     biPlanes;          // Number of planes (always 1)
    WORD     biBitCount;        // Bits per pixel
    DWORD    biCompression;     // One of: BI_RGB, BI_RLE4 or
                                //         BI_RLE8
    DWORD    biSizeImage;       // Number of bytes in image
    LONG     biXPelsPerMeter;   // Horizontal resolution
    LONG     biYPelsPerMeter;   // Vertical resolution
    DWORD    biClrUsed;         // Number of colors used
    DWORD    biClrImportant;    // How many colors important?
} BITMAPINFOHEADER;
typedef BITMAPINFOHEADER*        PBITMAPINFOHEADER;
typedef BITMAPINFOHEADER FAR*    LPBITMAPINFOHEADER;
```

The `read` function of the `PCXImage` class intializes these fields of the `BITMAPINFOHEADER` with information derived from the header of the PCX file.

After setting the `BITMAPINFOHEADER`, the `read` function initializes the color palette that follows the `BITMAPINFOHEADER` in a DIB. The color palette consists of an array of `RGBQUAD` structures, each with the following fields:

```
typedef struct tagRGBQUAD
{
    BYTE    rgbBlue;      // Intensity of blue component (0-255)
    BYTE    rgbGreen;     // Intensity of green component (0-255)
    BYTE    rgbRed;       // Intensity of red component (0-255)
    BYTE    rgbReserved;  // Reserved (set to zero)
} RGBQUAD;
```

Each `RGBQUAD` structure defines an RGB color for an entry in the color palette.

Once the color palette is initialized, the `read` function proceeds to convert the PCX bit planes into a packed pixel format image representing a DIB. The pseudocode for this operation looks like this (*mask* refers to a black silhouette of the image):

```
Create a mask with the high-order
    "bits_per_pixel_per_plane" bits set
Loop over (all lines in the PCX image)
{
    Loop over (all bytes in each plane)
    {
        Loop over ("8/bits_per_pixel_per_plane" times)
        {
```

```
        Loop over (all planes)
        {
            Pack bits from each plane into a byte
            If all 8bits are filled, copy byte to
            appropriate location in DIB
        }
        Shift mask to right by
    "bits_per_pixel_per_plane" bits
    }
  }
}
```

To understand this operation, you should carefully study the corresponding loops in the read function shown in Listing 4.8. As you can see from the sample programs in the companion disk, the conversion from the PCX format to DIB works perfectly for monochrome, 4-, 8-, and even 24-bit color images.

Listing 4.8. pcximage.cpp—Implementation of the PCXImage class.

```
//-----------------------------------------------------------------
//  File: pcximage.cpp
//
//  Image manipulation functions for PCX format images.
//-----------------------------------------------------------------
#include <fstream.h>
#include "pcximage.h"
//-----------------------------------------------------------------
//  P C X I m a g e : : r e a d
//  Read a PCX image.

int PCXImage::read(const char* filename)
{
// If there is an existing image, detach the image data
// before reading a new image
    if(imdata->p_dib != 0) detach();

// Open file for reading
    ifstream ifs(filename, ios::in | ios::binary);
    if(!ifs)
    {
// Error reading file. Return 0.
        return 0;
    }

// Read PCX header
    ifs.read((unsigned char*)&hdr, sizeof(FCXHeader));
```

Understanding Image File Formats

```
// Check if image file format is acceptable
    if(hdr.manufacturer != 0x0a) return 0;

// We only handle 1, 4, 8, or 24-bit images
    int bits_per_pixel = hdr.nplanes *
                         hdr.bits_per_pixel_per_plane;

    if(bits_per_pixel != 1 &&
       bits_per_pixel != 4 &&
       bits_per_pixel != 8 &&
       bits_per_pixel != 24) return 0;

    unsigned short image_width = hdr.xmax - hdr.xmin + 1;
    unsigned short image_height = hdr.ymax - hdr.ymin + 1;

// Allocate space where the PCX image will be unpacked.
// Read in PCX image into this area.
    long pcx_image_size = (long) hdr.nplanes *
                          (long) image_height *
                          (long) hdr.bytes_per_line;
    unsigned char huge *image = new unsigned char huge
                          [pcx_image_size];
    if(image == NULL) return 0;

// Decode run-length encoded image data

    int i, byte, count;
    unsigned long pos = 0L;

    while((byte = ifs.get()) != EOF)
    {
        if((byte & 0xc0) == 0xc0)
        {
            count = byte & 0x3f;
            if((byte = ifs.get()) != EOF)
            {
                for(i = 0; i < count; i++)
                {
                    if(pos >= pcx_image_size) break;
                    image[pos] = byte;
                    pos++;
                }
            }
        }
        else
        {
            if(pos >= pcx_image_size) break;
            image[pos] = byte;
```

continues

Listing 4.8. continued

```
            pos++;
        }
    }

// Allocate memory for the device-independent bitmap (DIB)
// Note that the number of bytes in each line of a DIB image
// must be a multiple of 4.
    unsigned short bytes_per_line_per_plane = (image_width *
                        hdr.bits_per_pixel_per_plane + 7) / 8;

    unsigned short actual_bytes_per_line = (image_width *
                                                    hdr.nplanes *
                        hdr.bits_per_pixel_per_plane + 7) / 8;
    imdata->bytes_per_line = actual_bytes_per_line;

    if(imdata->bytes_per_line % 4)
        imdata->bytes_per_line = 4 *
                        (imdata->bytes_per_line/4 + 1);

// Make room for a palette
    int palettesize = 16;
    if(bits_per_pixel == 1) palettesize = 2;
    if(hdr.version >= 5 && bits_per_pixel > 4)
    {
// Go back 769 bytes from the end of the file
        ifs.seekg(-769L, ios::end);
        if(ifs.get() == 12)
        {
// There is a 256-color palette following this byte
            palettesize = 256;
        }
    }
// If image has more than 256 colors then there is no palette
    if(bits_per_pixel > 8) palettesize = 0;

    imdata->p_dib = GlobalAllocPtr(GHND,
                        sizeof(BITMAPINFOHEADER) +
                    palettesize * sizeof(RGBQUAD) +
                    (long) imdata->bytes_per_line *
                                (long) image_height);

// If memory allocation fails, return 0
    if(imdata->p_dib == 0) return 0;
```

Understanding Image File Formats

```
// Set up bitmap info header
    LPBITMAPINFOHEADER p_bminfo = (LPBITMAPINFOHEADER)imdata->p_dib;
    p_bminfo->biSize = sizeof(BITMAPINFOHEADER);
    p_bminfo->biWidth = image_width;
    p_bminfo->biHeight = image_height;
    p_bminfo->biPlanes = 1;
    p_bminfo->biBitCount = hdr.bits_per_pixel_per_plane *
                           hdr.nplanes;
    p_bminfo->biCompression = BI_RGB;
    p_bminfo->biSizeImage = (long)image_height *
                            (long)imdata->bytes_per_line;
    p_bminfo->biXPelsPerMeter = 0;
    p_bminfo->biYPelsPerMeter = 0;
    p_bminfo->biClrUsed       = 0;
    p_bminfo->biClrImportant  = 0;

// Set up the color palette
    if(palettesize > 0)
    {
        RGBQUAD *palette = (RGBQUAD*) ((LPSTR)imdata->p_dib
                            + sizeof(BITMAPINFOHEADER));

        int palindex;
        for(palindex = 0; palindex < palettesize; palindex++)
        {
            if(palettesize == 256)
            {
// Read palette from file
                palette[palindex].rgbRed      = ifs.get();
                palette[palindex].rgbGreen    = ifs.get();
                palette[palindex].rgbBlue     = ifs.get();
                palette[palindex].rgbReserved = 0;
            }
            if(palettesize == 16)
            {
// 16-color palette from PCX header
                palette[palindex].rgbRed =
                                hdr.colormap[3*palindex];
                palette[palindex].rgbGreen =
                                hdr.colormap[3*palindex+1];
                palette[palindex].rgbBlue =
                                hdr.colormap[3*palindex+2];
                palette[palindex].rgbReserved = 0;
            }
            if(palettesize == 2)
            {
// Set up palette for black-and-white images
                palette[palindex].rgbRed =
                                palindex * 255;
```

continues

Listing 4.8. continued

```
                palette[palindex].rgbGreen =
                                palindex * 255;
                palette[palindex].rgbBlue =
                                palindex * 255;
                palette[palindex].rgbReserved  = 0;
        }
    }
}

// Load image data into the DIB. Note the DIB image must be
// stored in "bottom-to-top" line order. That's why we position
// data at the end of the array so that the image can be
// stored backwards--from the last line to the first.
    unsigned char huge *data =
            (unsigned char huge*)imdata->p_dib +
                    sizeof(BITMAPINFOHEADER) +
                palettesize * sizeof(RGBQUAD) +
                (unsigned long)(image_height - 1) *
            (unsigned long)(imdata->bytes_per_line);

// Define a macro to access bytes in the PCX image according
// to specified line and plane index.

    int lineindex, byteindex, planeindex;

#define bytepos(lineindex,planeindex,byteindex)  \
            ((long)(lineindex)*(long)hdr.bytes_per_line* \
            (long)hdr.nplanes + \
            (long)(planeindex)*(long)hdr.bytes_per_line + \
            (long)(byteindex))

// Construct packed pixels out of decoded PCX image.

    unsigned short onebyte, bits_copied, loc, few_bits, m,
            k, bbpb = 8/hdr.bits_per_pixel_per_plane;

// Build a mask to pick out bits from each byte of the PCX image
    unsigned short himask = 0x80, mask;
    if(hdr.bits_per_pixel_per_plane > 1)
            for(i = 0; i < hdr.bits_per_pixel_per_plane - 1;
            i++) himask = 0x80 | (himask >> 1);

    for(lineindex = 0; lineindex < image_height;
        lineindex++, data -= imdata->bytes_per_line)
    {
        if(actual_bytes_per_line < imdata->bytes_per_line)
            for(loc = actual_bytes_per_line;
```

Understanding Image File Formats

```
                    loc < imdata->bytes_per_line; loc++)
                                        data[loc] = 0;
        loc = 0;
        onebyte = 0;
        bits_copied = 0;
        for(byteindex = 0;
            byteindex < bytes_per_line_per_plane;
            byteindex++)
        {
            for(k = 0, mask = himask; k < bbpb;
                k++, mask >>= hdr.bits_per_pixel_per_plane)
            {
// Go through all scan lines for all planes and copy bits into
// the data array
                for(planeindex = 0; planeindex < hdr.nplanes;
                    planeindex++)
                {
                    few_bits = image[bytepos(lineindex,
                            planeindex, byteindex)] & mask;

// Shift the selcted bits to the most significant position
                    if(k > 0) few_bits <<=
                                (k*hdr.bits_per_pixel_per_plane);

// OR the bits with current pixel after shifting them right
                    if(bits_copied > 0)
                            few_bits >>= bits_copied;

                    onebyte |= few_bits;
                    bits_copied += hdr.bits_per_pixel_per_plane;

                    if(bits_copied >= 8)
                    {
                        data[loc] = onebyte;
                        loc++;
                        bits_copied = 0;
                        onebyte = 0;
                    }
                }
            }
        }
    }
    delete image;
// Success!
    return 1;
}
```

ImageView—A Windows Image Viewer

Now that you have seen an `Image` class hierarchy for handling BMP, PCX, and Targa image files, it's time for an application that uses these classes. The remainder of this chapter presents `ImageView`, a Windows application with a multiple-document interface (MDI) that allows the user to open one or more image files for viewing. `ImageView` uses the `Image` class hierarchy developed earlier in this chapter. You can view PCX, BMP, 24-bit Targa files with `ImageView`.

This book's companion disk includes the complete source code for `ImageView` together with necessary auxiliary files such as the module definition file (`IMAGEVW.DEF`) and the resource file (`IMAGEVW.RES`). Before reading any more about `ImageView`, you should run the program and see how it works. Then you can read the following descriptions and study the source listings to understand how the program is implemented.

Running ImageView

If you have added a new program item for the `ImageView` application in Windows Program Manager, you can start the program by double-clicking on its icon. Otherwise, you have to start the program by selecting **R**un from the File menu in the Program Manager and specifying the application's name (`IMAGEVW.EXE`). To view an image, select Open from `ImageView`'s File menu. Select an image file from the file selection dialog box. Each image appears in its own window inside `ImageView`'s main window. Figure 4.6 shows the basic features of `ImageView` including a number of images, the About dialog box, and one minimized window.

ImageViewApp Class

The `ImageView` application is built from Borland's OWL classes. As you can see from Listing 4.9, the main source file `imagevw.cpp` (the one with the `WinMain` function) looks very much like the main source file of any OWL-based application.

Chapter 4

Understanding Image File Formats

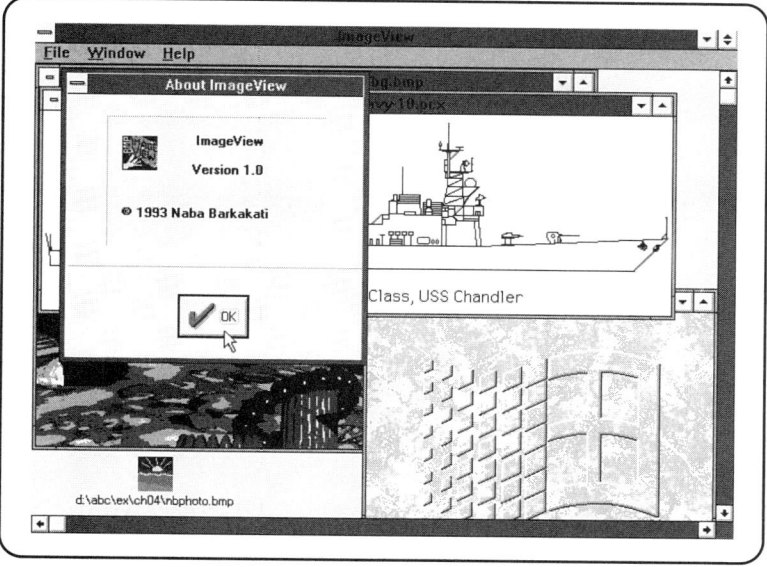

Figure 4.6. *Viewing images with ImageView.*

The ImageViewApp class, derived from TApplication, models the ImageView application. Its InitMainWindow function creates an instance of an ImageViewFrame class, which is the main window of the ImageView application. The images are displayed in child windows of ImageViewFrame. The actual image display is done in an instance of the ImageViewWindow class that is created as a child window of an ImageViewFrame class.

Listing 4.9. imagevw.cpp—Main source file of ImageView.

```
//----------------------------------------------------------------
// File:   imagevw.cpp
//
// A Windows application for viewing images in a variety of
// formats such as Windows bitmap (.BMP), PC PaintBrush (.PCX),
// and Targa (.TGA).
//----------------------------------------------------------------
#include "imvwwin.h"
```

continues

Listing 4.9. continued

```
class ImageViewApp: public TApplication
{
public:
// Constructor that simply calls the base class constructor

    ImageViewApp(LPSTR name, HINSTANCE instance,
            HINSTANCE prev_instance, LPSTR  cmdline, int show) :

            TApplication(name, instance, prev_instance,
                        cmdline, show)   {}

// Define function to initialize application's main window
    void InitMainWindow();

// Define function to initialize an instance of this application
    void InitInstance();
};
//-------------------------------------------------------------
//   I m a g e V i e w A p p : : I n i t M a i n W i n d o w

void ImageViewApp::InitMainWindow()
{
    MainWindow = new ImageViewFrame("ImageView", "MainMenu");
}
//-------------------------------------------------------------
//   I m a g e V i e w A p p : : I n i t I n s t a n c e

void ImageViewApp::InitInstance()
{
   TApplication::InitInstance();
   HAccTable = LoadAccelerators(hInstance, "MainAccelTable");
}
//-------------------------------------------------------------
//   W i n M a i n
//
//   Create an instance of the application and "run" it.

int PASCAL WinMain(HINSTANCE instance, HINSTANCE prev_instance,
                LPSTR cmdline, int show)
{
    ImageViewApp ImageView("ImageView", instance,
                        prev_instance, cmdline, show);

    ImageView.Run();

    return ImageView.Status;
}
```

Chapter 4
Understanding Image File Formats

ImageViewFrame and *ImageViewWindow* Classes

Listing 4.10 shows the declarations of the `ImageViewWindow` and `ImageViewFrame` classes. The `ImageViewWindow` class has a member variable, `image`, which is a pointer to the `Image` object that it displays. The `ImageViewFrame` class represents the frame window inside which one or more `ImageViewWindow` objects display images. As such, the `ImageViewFrame` class does not have any member variables—it only provides member functions such as `OpenFile` and `About` that handle menu messages.

**Listing 4.10. `imvwwin.h`—
Declaration of the window classes in `ImageView`.**

```
//-------------------------------------------------------------
// File: imvwwin.h
//
// Classes for an OWL application that lets you open an image
// file and view the image in a window.
//-------------------------------------------------------------
#if !defined(__IMVWWIN_H)
#define __IMVWWIN_H

#include <owl.h>
#include <mdi.h>
#include <strng.h>
#include "imvwres.h"   // Resource identifiers for the application
#include "image.h"

class ImageViewWindow : public TWindow
{
public:
    ImageViewWindow(PTWindowsObject parent, LPSTR title,
                    LPSTR fname);

    ~ImageViewWindow()
    {
        if(filename != NULL) delete filename;
        if(image != NULL) delete image;
    }

    void GetWindowClass(WNDCLASS _FAR &wc);
    void Paint(HDC hdc, PAINTSTRUCT &ps);
```

continues

Listing 4.10. continued

```
    void SaveFile(RTMessage msg) = [CM_FIRST + CM_FILESAVE];
private:
    String  *filename;
    Image   *image;
};

class ImageViewFrame: public TMDIFrame
{
public:
    ImageViewFrame(LPSTR title, LPSTR menu) :
        TMDIFrame(title, menu)
    {
// Append list of open child windows to the menu at this
// position (0 = first menu, 1 = second, and so on).
        ChildMenuPos = 1;
    }

// The following is needed to set up an icon for the application
    void GetWindowClass(WNDCLASS _FAR &wc);

// Declare functions for handling messages from Windows
    void OpenFile(RTMessage msg) = [CM_FIRST + CM_MDIFILEOPEN];
    void SaveAsFile(RTMessage msg) = [CM_FIRST + CM_FILESAVEAS];
    void About(RTMessage msg) = [CM_FIRST + IDM_ABOUT];
};

#endif
```

The file imvwres.h, which is included in imvwwin.h (Listing 4.10), defines certain resource identifiers used in the ImageView application. Listing 4.11 shows the header file imvwres.h. In this case there is only one identifier—the ID for the About menu item in ImageView.

Listing 4.11. imvwres.h—Resource identifiers in ImageView.

```
//-------------------------------------------------------------
// File: imvwres.h
// Resource identifiers for the ImageView application
//-------------------------------------------------------------
#if !defined(__IMVWRES_H)
```

Chapter 4

Understanding Image File Formats

```
#define __IMVWRES_H

#include <owlrc.h>   // For definitions of OWL IDs

#define IDM_ABOUT 200

#endif
```

Remember, the `ImageViewWindow` class contains information about the image it is displaying—in the form of a pointer to an `Image` object as a member variable. The `ImageViewWindow` constructor expects as an argument the name of an image file, which it uses to create and intialize the image. Remember, the image file's extension is used to decide which type of image is created: .BMP implies a Windows DIB file, .PCX means PC PaintBrush files, and .TGA refers to a 24-bit Truevision Targa image. Consult Listing 4.12 for further details of the `ImageViewWindow` constructor.

You should note that the image is displayed in the window by the `Paint` function of the `ImageViewWindow` class. Listing 4.12 shows the simplicity of the `ImageViewWindow::Paint` function—it simply calls the `show` member function of the image object. This shows the benefits of developing a C++ class hierarchy to handle a specific task such as managing and displaying images. (You can see the benefits even more clearly with the image animation program in Chapter 5, "Animating Images.")

Listing 4.12. `imvwwin.cpp`—
Implementation of the window classes in `ImageView`.

```
//-------------------------------------------------------------
// File: imvwwin.cpp
//
// Member functions of the ImageViewFrame and ImageViewWindow
// classes.
//-------------------------------------------------------------
#include <strstrea.h>
#include <string.h>
#include <filedial.h>
#include "imvwwin.h"
#include "bmpimage.h"
#include "pcximage.h"
#include "tgaimage.h"
```

continues

Listing 4.12. continued

```
//--------------------------------------------------------------
// I m a g e V i e w W i n d o w
// Constructor for the ImageViewWindow class

ImageViewWindow::ImageViewWindow(PTWindowsObject parent,
    LPSTR title, LPSTR fname) : TWindow(parent, title)
{
    image = NULL;
    filename = NULL;

// Open the image file. We will decide the file type from
// the file extension:
//    .BMP  = Windows bitmap file
//    .PCX  = PC PaintBrush file
//    .TGA  = 24-bit true color Targa file

// Convert filename to uppercase
    strupr(fname);
    char *ext = strrchr(fname, '.');
    filename = new String(fname);

// Change to an hourglass cursor
    SetCapture(HWindow);
    SetCursor(LoadCursor(NULL, IDC_WAIT));

// Load file
    if(strcmp(ext, ".BMP") == 0)
    {
        image = new BMPImage;
        image->read(fname);
    }

    if(strcmp(ext, ".PCX") == 0)
    {
        image = new PCXImage;
        image->read(fname);
    }

    if(strcmp(ext, ".TGA") == 0)
    {
        image = new TGAImage;
        image->read(fname);
    }
// Reset cursor to arrow
    SetCursor(LoadCursor(NULL, IDC_ARROW));
    ReleaseCapture();
```

Understanding Image File Formats

```
// Display a message if image format is unknown
    if(image == NULL)
    {
     MessageBox(HWindow, "Unknown image format!",
            "ImageView",
                MB_OK | MB_ICONEXCLAMATION);
    }
}
//----------------------------------------------------------------
//  ImageViewWindow:: P a i n t
//  Draw image in the window

void ImageViewWindow::Paint(HDC hdc, PAINTSTRUCT&)
{
    if(image != NULL) image->show(hdc);
}
//----------------------------------------------------------------
//  ImageViewWindow:: G e t W i n d o w C l a s s
//  Set up icon for each image window

void ImageViewWindow::GetWindowClass(WNDCLASS _FAR &wc)
{
// First call the GetWindowClass function of the base class
    TWindow::GetWindowClass(wc);

// Set up icon for this image window
    wc.hIcon = LoadIcon(wc.hInstance, "IMAGEVIEWWIN_ICON");
}
//----------------------------------------------------------------
//  ImageViewFrame:: G e t W i n d o w C l a s s
//  Set up icon for the application

void ImageViewFrame::GetWindowClass(WNDCLASS _FAR &wc)
{
// First call the GetWindowClass function of the base class
    TMDIFrame::GetWindowClass(wc);

// Set up icon for this application
    wc.hIcon = LoadIcon(wc.hInstance, "IMAGEVIEWAPP_ICON");
}
//----------------------------------------------------------------
//  ImageViewFrame:: A b o u t
//  Display the "About..." box

void ImageViewFrame::About(RTMessage)
{
    TDialog *p_about = new TDialog(this, "ABOUTIMAGEVIEW");
```

continues

Listing 4.12. continued

```
    PTApplication app = GetApplication();
    app->ExecDialog(p_about);
}
//-----------------------------------------------------------------
// ImageViewFrame:: O p e n  F i l e
// Display file dialog and open requested image file

void ImageViewFrame::OpenFile(RTMessage)
{
    char name[80] = "*.bmp";

    TFileDialog *p_fd = new TFileDialog(this,
                                    SD_FILEOPEN, name);
    int status = GetApplication()->ExecDialog(p_fd);

    if (status == IDOK)
    {
     ImageViewWindow* p_iw = new ImageViewWindow(this,
                           name, name);
        GetApplication()->MakeWindow(p_iw);
    }
}

//-----------------------------------------------------------------
// ImageViewWindow:: S a v e  F i l e
// Display file dialog and save image in .BMP format in a file
// with the same name as the original, except for a .BMP
// extension.

void ImageViewWindow::SaveFile(RTMessage)
{
    char *ext = strrchr(*filename, '.');
    if(strcmp(ext, ".BMP") != 0)
    {
// Change to an hourglass cursor
        SetCapture(HWindow);
        SetCursor(LoadCursor(NULL, IDC_WAIT));

    char bmpfilename[128];
    strcpy(bmpfilename, *filename);
    ext = strrchr(bmpfilename, '.');
        strcpy(ext, ".BMP");
        BMPImage ibmp;
        ibmp.image_data(image);
```

Understanding Image File Formats

```
       ibmp.write(bmpfilename);
// Reset cursor to arrow
       SetCursor(LoadCursor(NULL, IDC_ARROW));
       ReleaseCapture();
    }
}
void ImageViewFrame::SaveAsFile(RTMessage){}
```

Building ImageView

The Windows-based development environment of Borland C++ is used to build the ImageView application. The companion disk has the project file (IMAGEVW.PRJ) that lists the files necessary to build the application. The disk also includes all files needed to build the executable, IMAGEVW.EXE. There are a few items in the project file that reflect the name of the drive and directory where I installed Borland C++ in my system. Here are the changes you have to make before using the project file in your system:

1. Open the project file IMAGEVW.PRJ by selecting Open Project... from the Project menu of Borland C++ for Windows.

2. In the list of items shown in the project window, bwcc.lib is listed with a specific drive and directory name. Select that line and get rid of the line by selecting Delete Item... from the menu.

3. Select Add Item... from the Project menu. In the file selection dialog box that appears, go to the directory where you have installed Borland C++ and select bwcc.lib (in the LIB subdirectory). Click on the Add button to add the library to the project. Click on Done to close the dialog box.

4. Select the Directories item from the Option menu in Borland C++ for Windows. Edit the pathnames to reflect the drive and directory names where you have installed Borland C++.

After making these changes, you should be able to build IMAGEVW.EXE by selecting Make from the Compile menu. Once the program is successfully built, you can add it to Windows Program Manager by selecting New... from the Program Manager's File menu.

One of the files that you need to build a Windows program is a resource file. For the `ImageView` application, the resource file, `IMAGEVW.RES`, is included in the companion disk. I prepared the resource file using the Resource Workshop program included with Borland C++.

Summary

Images are an integral part of games and you need lots of images to create an exciting game. Whether you draw images in a paint program or scan from a hard copy, the images are ultimately stored in image files that you have to interpret and use. The basic information in an image file is the same—the dimensions of the image and the pixel array that makes up the image—but there are many ways to organize this information in a file, including popular image file formats such as PCX, TIFF, Windows BMP, and Truevision Targa. The next chapter uses the image classes to define sprites that can be animated—moved smoothly—over a background image.

Further Reading

For information on displaying and manipulating Windows DIB files (the ones commonly known as the BMP files), consult the book by Brian Myers and Chris Doner.

Steve Rimmer has written several books that explain many popular file formats such as MacPaint, PCX, GIF, TIFF, Truevision Targa, and Microsoft Windows BMP formats. Rimmer's books include source code in C and 80x86 assembly language to interpret image files. He also provides code to display images on display adapters such as EGA, VGA, and super VGA.

David Kay and John Levine have recently written a book on graphics file formats. Their book describes a large number of image file formats including PCX, TIFF, Windows DIB, Truevision Targa, GIF, MacPaint, and Macintosh PICT. This is the book to consult if you have questions about any of the image file formats described in this chapter.

Understanding Image File Formats

Craig Lindley's books also cover a number of image file formats, most notably, PCX, TIFF, and GIF. Additionally, one of his books, *Practical Ray Tracing in C*, describes the public domain ray-tracing program, DKBTrace, which you can use to create computer-generated imagery.

Kay, David C., and John R. Levine. *Graphics File Formats*. Blue Ridge Summit, PA: Windcrest/McGraw-Hill, 1992.

Lindley, Craig A. *Practical Image Processing in C*. New York: Wiley, 1991.

Lindley, Craig. *Practical Ray Tracing in C*. New York: Wiley, 1992.

Myers, Brian, and Chris Doner. *Programmer's Introduction to Windows 3.1*. Alameda, CA: SYBEX, 1992.

Rimmer, Steve. *Bit-Mapped Graphics*. Blue Ridge Summit, PA: Windcrest/McGraw-Hill, 1990.

Rimmer, Steve. *Supercharged Bit-Mapped Graphics*. Blue Ridge Summit, PA: Windcrest/McGraw-Hill, 1992.

Chapter 5

Animating Images

Animation is the process of bringing an image to life. We usually associate animation with movement of images and the good examples pioneered by The Walt Disney Company. This chapter includes several C++ classes to model and animate the small images known as sprites. These sprite animation classes rely on the Image classes developed in Chapter 4. This chapter ends with a Windows program that animates a number of sprites on a background image.

Animation Techniques

The Disney movies use a traditional approach to animation in which each frame of the movie has to be prepared individually. This style is commonly known as *frame animation* or *cel animation*. (Cel refers to the sheets of acetate on which the images are drawn.) Cel animation is a discipline by itself and is not covered in this book.

Sprite Animation

Sprites are used in interactive video games to represent characters and fixtures that are part of the game. When the player moves an input device, such as a joystick, trackball, or mouse, the sprite moves over a background. Essentially, the player plays the video game by manipulating the sprites. Video game machines usually have graphics hardware with built-in support for sprites. In IBM-compatible PCs, the display hardware does not support sprites, so you have to rely on software techniques.

Erase and Redraw Technique

The obvious way to move an image is to erase it at the old location and redraw it at the new location. In a Windows program, you can use the `BitBlt` function for this. If you erase-and-redraw repeatedly, the image appears to move across the screen. However, a major drawback of this approach is that the display flickers as the image is erased and redrawn.

Animating Images

Chapter 5

One way to avoid flickers in erase-and-redraw animation is to use video page flipping, provided the display hardware supports more than one video page. With multiple video pages, you draw the entire screen in the hidden video page while the active page is being displayed. Then, you swap the active and hidden video pages to display the updated image. To continue the animation, you simply repeat this process in a loop. Many high-end graphics workstations (Silicon Graphics workstations, for instance) support animation through page flipping—or *buffer swapping* as the technique is known in the workstation world.

Unfortunately, most PC display adapters do not support multiple video pages in the high-resolution video modes. More importantly, Microsoft Windows does not support multiple video pages. So, you need some other approach to create flicker-free animation in Windows.

Offscreen Bitmap Technique

Screen flickers occur with the erase-and-redraw animation because all screen drawing operations are visible. As an image is erased, you see it vanish from the screen. Then the image appears again at a new location. When two video pages are used, the flicker goes away because the screen updates are always done in the hidden page. The fully updated screen appears instantaneously when the video pages are swapped. By this logic, you should be able to avoid the flicker as long as the images are prepared offscreen and the updated screen is redrawn quickly. Luckily, Windows supports drawing on an offscreen bitmap, which can serve as an ideal canvas for preparing the display screen. Then a single call to `BitBlt` can quickly transfer the updated images to the display screen. Of course, you have to attend to a myriad of details to prepare the image properly in the offscreen bitmap, but this basic idea works remarkably well for image animation under Windows.

To see how well the offscreen bitmap animation works, all you need to do is run the ANIMATE application (ANIMATE.EXE) from the CH05 directory of the companion disk. The ANIMATE program performs well under Windows even on a lowly 1984-vintage IBM PC-AT (6MHz 80286) equipped with the original IBM EGA display adapter.

C++ Classes for Sprite Animation

To support a Windows application that animates sprites using an offscreen bitmap, you need C++ classes to represent the sprites and to animate them. The animation consists of a fixed background image and zero or more sprites that can be moved around on the background. In the following sections, a Sprite class is defined to model a sprite and a SpriteAnimation class is defined to maintain the sprites and the background image.

Sprite Class

Listing 5.1 shows the declaration of the Sprite class. A Sprite has two Image objects:

- The Sprite's image in a black background
- A black silhouette of the Sprite's image in a white background (a mask)

As you can see in the animate function of the SpriteAnimation class, both the image and the mask are needed to allow drawing the Sprite's outline without affecting the background on which the Sprite is drawn. In addition to the image and the mask, a Sprite has an x- and y-position and several other variables to keep track of its motion on the background.

A Sprite class also has a *display priority* associated with it. This is an integer, stored in the member variable disp_priority, that determines the order in which overlapping sprites are drawn—a Sprite with a higher priority is drawn over one with a lower priority.

Another interesting member variable is dproc of type DRAWPROC, which is declared with this typedef statement:

```
typedef void (_FAR PASCAL *DRAWPROC)(HDC hdc, short x, short y,
                                     LPVOID data);
```

As you can see, dproc is a pointer to a function. The function specified by dproc is called whenever the Sprite's image needs to be drawn. You can draw objects—such as a line, a rectangle, an ellipse, or text—so that a sprite can have

Chapter 5 — Animating Images

much more than a bitmapped image. The moving text in the sample application ANIMATE (in the companion disk) is displayed using this feature of a Sprite.

A *Sprite* Is a *Sortable*

I derived the Sprite class from the Sortable class of the Borland class library (CLASSLIB) because I plan to store Sprite objects in a SortedArray (another class from Borland's CLASSLIB), and only Sortable objects can reside in a SortedArray. As a consequence of deriving from Sortable, the Sprite class must define the following member functions:

```
classType isA() const;

char _FAR *nameOf() const;

hashValueType hashValue() const;

void printOn(ostream _FAR& os);
```

You can see from Listing 5.1 that these four functions are defined in a straightforward manner. The isA function returns a unique integer identifier for the Sprite class while nameOf returns the string "Sprite" as the name of the class.

Additionally, to properly sort Sprite objects, the Sprite class must include these member functions:

```
int isLessThan(const Object _FAR& ob) const;

int isEqual(const Object _FAR& ob) const;
```

The isLessThan function is used to test if one Sprite is "less than" another. As defined in Listing 5.1, isLessThan compares the display priority of the Sprites to determine which Sprite is "smaller."

Listing 5.1. `sprite.h`—Declaration of the Sprite class.

```
//--------------------------------------------------------------
// File: sprite.h
//
// Declares a Sprite class representing a small image that
// can be animated.
//--------------------------------------------------------------
```

continues

Listing 5.1. continued

```cpp
#if !defined(__SPRITE_H)
#define __SPRITE_H

#include <sortable.h>   // So that we can sort the Sprites
#include <strng.h>      // For the String class
#include "image.h"

const unsigned short SPRITE_ACTIVE    = 1;
const unsigned short SPRITE_UPDATE    = 2;
const unsigned short SPRITE_OVERLAP   = 4;
const unsigned short SPRITE_ERASE     = 8;


typedef void (_FAR PASCAL *DRAWPROC)(HDC hdc, short x, short y,
                                     LPVOID data);

class Sprite : public Sortable
{
public:
    Sprite() : image(NULL), mask(NULL), disp_priority(1),
               dproc(NULL), dpdata(NULL), status(0), sid(-1),
               image_filename(NULL), mask_filename(NULL)
    {
       curpos.x = curpos.y = 0;
       lastpos.x = lastpos.y = 0;
    }

    Sprite(HDC hdc, LPSTR imagefilename,
           LPSTR maskfilename, short priority = 1);

    Sprite(Image *img, Image *msk, short priority = 1);

    ~Sprite();

// Read in an image and a mask
    void load_images(HDC hdc, LPSTR imagefilename,
                     LPSTR maskfilename);

// The next four functions are required because Sprite is
// derived from the Sortable class.

    classType isA() const { return SpriteClass;}

    char _FAR *nameOf() const { return "Sprite";}

    hashValueType hashValue() const { return 0;}
```

Chapter 5

Animating Images

```cpp
void printOn(ostream _FAR& os) const
{
    os << "Sprite : " << *image_filename << endl;
}

short priority() { return disp_priority;}
void priority(short dp) { disp_priority = dp;}

unsigned short width() { return w;}
unsigned short height() { return h;}
void width(unsigned wdth) { w = wdth;}
void height(unsigned hght) { h = hght;}

short xpos() { return curpos.x;}
short ypos() { return curpos.y;}
void xpos(short x)
{
    lastpos.x = curpos.x;
    curpos.x = x;
}
void ypos(short y)
{
    lastpos.y = curpos.y;
    curpos.y = y;
}
void newpos(short x, short y)
{
    lastpos.x = curpos.x;
    lastpos.y = curpos.y;
    curpos.x = x;
    curpos.y = y;
    reset_moves();
}

short lastxpos() { return lastpos.x;}
short lastypos() { return lastpos.y;}

void reset_moves()
{
    xdelta = ydelta = 0;
}
short xmove() { return xdelta;}
short ymove() { return ydelta;}

void move(short x, short y)
{
    xdelta += x;
    ydelta += y;
```

continues

Listing 5.1. continued

```
// Mark sprite for update
        status |= SPRITE_UPDATE;
    }

// Functions to manipulate the status of a sprite
    unsigned short needs_update()
    { return status & SPRITE_UPDATE;}
    unsigned short is_active()
    { return status & SPRITE_ACTIVE;}
    unsigned short is_overlapping()
    { return status & SPRITE_OVERLAP;}
    unsigned short to_be_erased()
    { return status & SPRITE_ERASE;}
    void active() { status |= SPRITE_ACTIVE | SPRITE_UPDATE;}
    void update() { status |= SPRITE_UPDATE;}
    void erase() { status |= SPRITE_ERASE;}
    void overlaps(){ status |= SPRITE_OVERLAP;}
    void update_done(){ status &= ~SPRITE_UPDATE;}
    void unerase() { status &= ~SPRITE_ERASE;}
    void inactive() { status &= ~SPRITE_ACTIVE;}
    void no_overlap() { status &= ~SPRITE_OVERLAP;}

// Convert the device independent bitmaps to device
// dependent bitmaps
    void make_ddb(HDC hdc)
    {
        if(image != NULL) image->DIBtoDDB(hdc);
        if(mask != NULL) mask->DIBtoDDB(hdc);
    }

// The following function is needed to sort the Sprites
// according to display priority.
    int isLessThan(const Object _FAR& ob) const
    { return disp_priority < ((Sprite&)ob).disp_priority;}

    int isEqual(const Object _FAR& ob) const
    { return disp_priority == ((Sprite&)ob).disp_priority;}

    void drawproc(DRAWPROC dp, LPVOID data)
    {
        dproc = dp;
        dpdata = data;
    }
    DRAWPROC drawproc() { return dproc;}
    LPVOID data() { return dpdata;}
```

Chapter 5

Animating Images

```cpp
    HBITMAP hbm_image()
    {
        if(image != NULL) return image->get_ddb();
        else return NULL;
    }
    HBITMAP hbm_mask()
    {
        if(mask != NULL) return mask->get_ddb();
        else return NULL;
    }

    Image* sprite_image() { return image;}
    Image* sprite_mask()  { return mask;}

    void id(short _id) { sid = _id;}
    short id() { return sid;}

    static Image* init_image(LPSTR fname);

protected:
    Image           *image;   // The sprite's image
    Image           *mask;    // The mask: a silhouette of image
    unsigned short  w, h;     // Width and height of sprite
    short           disp_priority;
    POINT           curpos;
    POINT           lastpos;
    short           xdelta;
    short           ydelta;
    unsigned short  status;
    DRAWPROC        dproc;    // Pointer to user-supplied
                              // function to draw
    LPVOID          dpdata;   // Argument for drawproc
    String          *image_filename;
    String          *mask_filename;

    short           sid; // Normally unused, but may be
                         // used to identify Sprite

    enum { SpriteClass = __firstUserClass + 1};
};

#endif
```

Initializing a *Sprite*

Listing 5.2 shows the file `sprite.cpp` with several member functions of the `Sprite` class. A typical way to create and initialize a `Sprite` is to use the constructor that accepts the names of image and mask files as arguments:

```
Sprite::Sprite(HDC hdc, LPSTR imagefilename,
               LPSTR maskfilename, short priority);
```

This constructor calls the `init_image` function to load the bitmaps corresponding to the image and the mask. The constructor also requires the handle to a DC because the image and mask bitmaps are converted to a device-dependent format and this step needs a DC.

The `init_image` function (Listing 5.2) loads an image from a file. It uses the file name extension to determine the type of image. The extensions it accepts are

- .BMP for Windows DIB files
- .PCX for PC PaintBrush files
- .TGA for 24-bit Truevision Targa files

Listing 5.2. `sprite.cpp`—Implementation of the `Sprite` class.

```
//-------------------------------------------------------------
// File: sprite.cpp
// Member functions of the Sprite class.
//
//-------------------------------------------------------------
#include <string.h>
#include "sprite.h"
#include "bmpimage.h"
#include "pcximage.h"
#include "tgaimage.h"
#include <stdio.h>  //NBNBNB
//-------------------------------------------------------------
// S p r i t e : : S p r i t e
// Constructor for a Sprite

Sprite::Sprite(HDC hdc, LPSTR imagefilename,
               LPSTR maskfilename, short priority):
    disp_priority(priority)
{
    image_filename = mask_filename = NULL;
```

Chapter 5

Animating Images

```cpp
// Read the image and the mask bitmaps
    image = init_image(imagefilename);
    if(image != NULL)
    {
        w = image->width();
        h = image->height();
        image_filename = new String(imagefilename);
    }

    mask = init_image(maskfilename);
    if(mask != NULL) mask_filename = new String(maskfilename);

// Convert the image and the mask into device dependent bitmaps
    make_ddb(hdc);

// Initialize other member variables
    curpos.x = curpos.y = 0;
    lastpos.x = lastpos.y = 0;
    dproc = NULL;
    dpdata = NULL;
    status = SPRITE_UPDATE | SPRITE_ACTIVE;
}
//-------------------------------------------------------------
// Sprite::S p r i t e ( I m a g e * , I m a g e * ...)
// Construct a Sprite from an image and a mask.

Sprite::Sprite(Image *img, Image *msk, short priority):
    disp_priority(priority)
{
    image_filename = mask_filename = NULL;

    image = img;
    if(image != NULL)
    {
        w = image->width();
        h = image->height();
    }
    mask = msk;

// Initialize other member variables
    curpos.x = curpos.y = 0;
    lastpos.x = lastpos.y = 0;
    dproc = NULL;
    dpdata = NULL;
    status = SPRITE_UPDATE | SPRITE_ACTIVE;
}
//-------------------------------------------------------------
```

continues

Listing 5.2. continued

```cpp
// S p r i t e : : ~ S p r i t e
// Destructor for a Sprite

Sprite::~Sprite()
{
    if(image_filename != NULL) delete image_filename;
    if(mask_filename != NULL) delete mask_filename;
    if(image != NULL) delete image;
    if(mask != NULL) delete mask;
}
//------------------------------------------------------------
// S p r i t e : : l o a d _ i m a g e s
// Read in image and mask from files

void Sprite::load_images(HDC hdc, LPSTR imagefilename,
                         LPSTR maskfilename)
{
// Read the image and the mask bitmaps
    image = init_image(imagefilename);
    if(image != NULL)
    {
        w = image->width();
        h = image->height();
        image_filename = new String(imagefilename);
    }

    mask = init_image(maskfilename);
    if(mask != NULL) mask_filename = new String(maskfilename);

// Convert the image and the mask into device dependent bitmaps
    make_ddb(hdc);

// Mark sprite as active and in need of update
    status = SPRITE_UPDATE | SPRITE_ACTIVE;
}
//------------------------------------------------------------
// S p r i t e : : i n i t _ i m a g e
// Read an image from a file

Image* Sprite::init_image(LPSTR fname)
{
    Image *img = NULL;
    if(fname == NULL) return img;
```

Chapter 5

Animating Images

```cpp
    // Read the image file. We will decide the file type from
    // the file extension:
    //   .BMP = Windows bitmap file
    //   .PCX = PC PaintBrush file
    //   .TGA = 24-bit true color Targa file

    // Locate file name extension
        char *ext = strrchr(fname, '.');
        if(ext == NULL) return img;

    // Load file
        if(strnicmp(ext, ".BMP", 4) == 0)
        {
            img = new BMPImage;

            if(!img->read(fname))
            {
                delete img;
                img = NULL;
            }
        }

        if(strnicmp(ext, ".PCX", 4) == 0)
        {
            img = new PCXImage;
            if(!img->read(fname))
            {
                delete img;
                img = NULL;
            }
        }

        if(strnicmp(ext, ".TGA", 4) == 0)
        {
            img = new TGAImage;
            if(!img->read(fname))
            {
                delete img;
                img = NULL;
            }
        }
        return img;
}
```

SpriteAnimation Class

The `SpriteAnimation` class, declared in the file `spranim.h` (Listing 5.3), manages a number of sprites and a background and also provides the capability to animate the sprites. The following are its main data members:

- `SortedArray *sprites;` is an array of pointers to sprites that are part of the animation.
- `Image *background;` is the background image that serves as the canvas on which the sprites are animated.
- `HBITMAP hbm_bg;` is the DDB of the background image.
- `HBITMAP hbm_scratch;` is a bitmap that serves as the scratch area where images are prepared before copying to the onscreen window (to be described later).

Additionally, there are a number of handles to DCs that are kept ready for copying bitmaps to and from various components of the animation.

**Listing 5.3. `spranim.h`—
Declaration of the `SpriteAnimation` class.**

```
//-------------------------------------------------------------
// File: spranim.h
//
// Classes for animating sprites.
//-------------------------------------------------------------
#if !defined(__SPRANIM_H)
#define __SPRANIM_H

#include <sortarry.h>   // For the SortedArray class
#include "sprite.h"

// A class that manages the animation
class SpriteAnimation
{
public:
    SpriteAnimation(HDC hdc, unsigned short w,
                    unsigned short h,
                    LPSTR filename);
    SpriteAnimation(HDC hdc, unsigned short w,
                    unsigned short h, Image* bg);
```

Animating Images

```
    ~SpriteAnimation();

// Add a sprite to the animation
    void add(Sprite* s)
    {
        if(sprites != NULL && s != NULL)
            sprites->add(*s);
    }

// Animate the images
    void animate(HDC hdc, short x, short y);

    void draw_bg(HDC hdc, short x, short y);

    void redisplay_all(HDC hdc, short x, short y);

    void set_refresh(BOOL flag) { refresh = flag;}

// Utility functions
    BOOL rects_overlap(short x1, short y1, short w1, short h1,
                       short x2, short y2, short w2, short h2)
    {
        if((x2 - x1) > w1) return FALSE;
        if((x1 - x2) > w2) return FALSE;
        if((y2 - y1) > h1) return FALSE;
        if((y1 - y2) > h2) return FALSE;
        return TRUE;
    }

    void set_priority(Sprite* s, short prio)
    {
        if(sprites != NULL && s != NULL)
        {
            if(prio != s->priority())
            {
                sprites->detach(*s);
                s->priority(prio);
                sprites->add(*s);
            }
        }
    }
// Returns sprite of highest priority that encloses point (x,y)
    Sprite* sprite_at(short x, short y);

    Image* bgimage() { return background;}
    HBITMAP bg_bitmap() { return hbm_bg;}
```

continues

Listing 5.3. continued

```
//Function to scroll the bitmap by changing top and left
    void xbmp_origin(short x) { left = x;}
    void ybmp_origin(short y) { top = y;}
    short xbmp_origin() { return left;}
    short ybmp_origin() { return top;}

// Functions that draw on the background bitmap
    void bg_rect(short x1, short y1, short x2, short y2)
    { Rectangle(hdc_bg, x1, y1, x2, y2);}
    void bg_line(short x1, short y1, short x2, short y2)
    {
        MoveTo(hdc_bg, x1, y1);
        LineTo(hdc_bg, x2, y2);
    }

protected:
    SortedArray     *sprites;
    Image           *background;    // The background image
    HBITMAP         hbm_bg;         // Bitmap from "background"
    HBITMAP         hbm_scratch;    // Images prepared here before
                                    // copying to window
    short           top, left;      // Top left corner and
    short           width;          // dimensions of background
    short           height;         // being displayed
    short           ws, hs;         // Dimensions of scratch
                                    // bitmap
    short           bg_image;
    HBITMAP         hbm_sprite;
    HDC             hdc_bg;
    HDC             hdc_sprite;
    HDC             hdc_scratch;
    HBITMAP         old_hbm_bg;
    HBITMAP         old_hbm_sprite;
    HBITMAP         old_hbm_scratch;
    BOOL            refresh;
};

#endif
```

Setting Up a *SpriteAnimation* Object

A SpriteAnimation object is designed to manage animation of a number of sprites on a background image. To use SpriteAnimation, you have to use this constructor:

Animating Images

```
SpriteAnimation::SpriteAnimation(HDC hdc,
                                 unsigned short w,
                                 unsigned short h,
                                 LPSTR filename);
```

The constructor expects a DC, the width and height of the scratch bitmap, and the name of an image file to be used as the background of the animation. It loads the background image, sets up a number of bitmaps and DCs, and creates a `SortedArray` to hold the `Sprite` objects.

Once the `SpriteAnimation` object is created, you can add `Sprites` to the animation by calling the `add` member function of the `SpriteAnimation` class. You have to move the `Sprites` by calling the `move` function of each `Sprite`. To update the display, call the `animate` function of the `SpriteAnimation` class. A sample application that uses the `SpriteAnimation` class appears later in this chapter.

Animating the Sprites

The `animate` member function of the `SpriteAnimation` class is at the heart of animating sprites on a background image. Before looking into the problem of updating the screen image in an efficient way, consider the problem of redrawing the entire window. If you look at the beginning of the `animate` function in Listing 5.4, you see this line:

```
if(refresh) redisplay_all(hdc, x, y);
```

When the `refresh` flag is set, the `animate` function calls `redisplay_all` to update the entire window. The next section describes how the sprites are drawn on the background.

Updating the Entire Window

In Listing 5.4 (presented in the next section), you find the source code for the function `redisplay_all` that draws the background and sprites. In a C++-like pseudocode notation, the steps involved in updating the animation are as follows:

```
Copy designated portion of background into scratch bitmap
    using BitBlt.

for(all Sprite objects in the animation)
{
    Copy the Sprite's mask to the scratch bitmap using
        BitBlt in the SRCAND mode.
```

165

```
        Copy the Sprite's image to the scratch bitmap using
            BitBlt in the SRCPAINT mode.

        if(Sprite has a dproc)
            Call dproc.
    }

    Copy the scratch bitmap into the window using BitBlt
        in the SRCCOPY mode.
```

Thus the basic idea is to copy the background into a scratch bitmap and draw all the sprites on the background. Because `SpriteAnimation` class stores the sprites ordered by display priority, this step draws the sprites in the correct order.

Figure 5.1 illustrates the process of drawing a sprite on a background. The steps are

1. Combine the sprite's mask bitmap with the background image using a bitwise-AND operation. Remember that the mask is a silhouette of the sprite's image—it is black (all bits 0) on a white (all bits 1) background. This step essentially punches a hole the shape of the sprite in the background image.

2. Combine the sprite's image with the modified background image using a bitwise-OR operation. Because the image is on a white (all bits 1) background, this step fills the hole created in the previous step.

Efficient Animation of Overlapping Sprites

When the whole window does not need to be updated, the `animate` function draws the sprites using an algorithm that updates the window in an efficient manner. The basic algorithm for efficient updates is

1. For a sprite S that needs updating, determine all other sprites that touch sprite S and are also in need of update. Determine the smallest rectangle that encloses all sprites that satisfy these conditions.

2. Find all stationary sprites that also touch the rectangle and mark them as overlapping.

3. Copy from the background image to the scratch bitmap an area corresponding to the rectangle determined in step 1.

4. Draw all overlapping sprites in the scratch bitmap. Set the status of the sprites as updated so that they are not included again.

Animating Images

5. Copy the rectangle from the scratch bitmap to the window.
6. Repeat steps 1 through 5 for all sprites.

These steps are implemented in the `animate` function in Listing 5.4. Figure 5.2 depicts the update process for sprite animation.

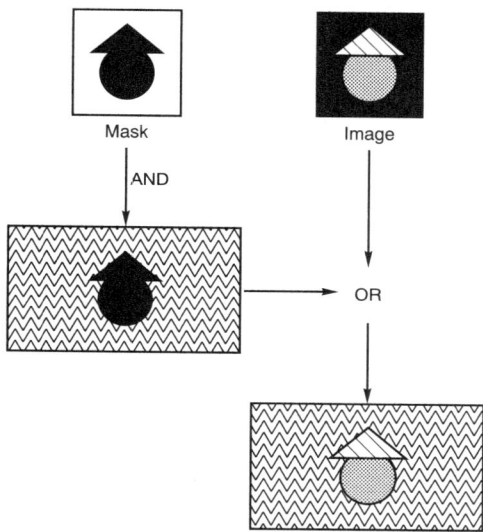

Figure 5.1. *Drawing a sprite on a background.*

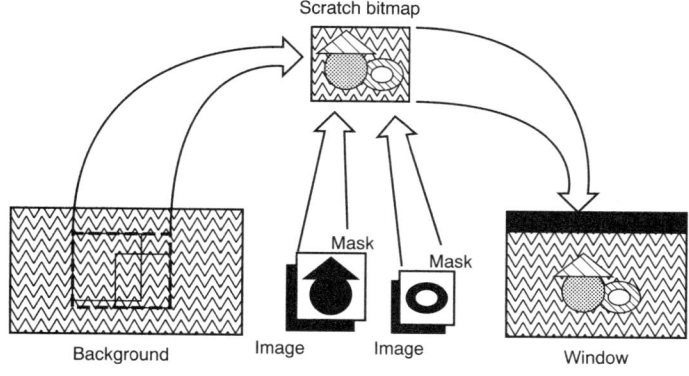

Figure 5.2. *Updating the display to animate sprites.*

167

Listing 5.4. spranim.cpp— Implementation of the SpriteAnimation class.

```cpp
//---------------------------------------------------------------
// File: spranim.cpp
//
// Member functions of the sprite animation classes.
//---------------------------------------------------------------
#include <stdlib.h>
#include "spranim.h"

inline short min(short x, short y)
{
    return (((x) < (y)) ? (x) : (y));
}
inline short max(short x, short y)
{
    return (((x) > (y)) ? (x) : (y));
}
//---------------------------------------------------------------
// S p r i t e A n i m a t i o n
// Constructor for the SpriteAnimation class

SpriteAnimation::SpriteAnimation(HDC hdc,
                                 unsigned short w,
                                 unsigned short h,
                                 LPSTR filename)
{
// Set up coordinates of rectangle to be displayed
    top = left = 0;
    width = w;
    height = h;
    ws = w;
    hs = h;
    refresh = TRUE;

// Initialize all handles to zero
    sprites = NULL;
    hbm_bg = 0;
    hbm_scratch = 0;
    hbm_sprite = 0;
    old_hbm_bg = 0;
    old_hbm_sprite = 0;
    old_hbm_scratch = 0;
    hdc_bg = 0;
    hdc_sprite = 0;
    hdc_scratch = 0;
```

Animating Images

Chapter 5

```cpp
// Load the background image from the specified file
    background = Sprite::init_image(filename);
    if(background != NULL)
    {
        background->DIBtoDDB(hdc);
        hbm_bg = background->get_ddb();
        bg_image = 1;
    }
    else
    {
// Create a blank bitmap that's used as the background
        hbm_bg = CreateCompatibleBitmap(hdc, w, h);
        bg_image = 0;
    }

// Memory device context for the background image
    hdc_bg = CreateCompatibleDC(hdc);
    if(hbm_bg != 0 && hdc_bg != 0)
        old_hbm_bg = SelectBitmap(hdc_bg, hbm_bg);

// Initialize the background bitmap, if it did not come
// from an image.
    if(!bg_image && hbm_bg != 0 && hdc_bg != 0)
    {
        HBRUSH hbrbg = CreateSolidBrush(
                            GetSysColor(COLOR_WINDOW));
        HBRUSH oldbr = SelectBrush(hdc_bg, hbrbg);
        PatBlt(hdc_bg, 0, 0, w, h, PATCOPY);
        SelectBrush(hdc, oldbr);
        DeleteBrush(hbrbg);
    }

// Create a scratch bitmap of size w x h
    hbm_scratch = CreateCompatibleBitmap(hdc, w, h);

// Memory device context for the scratch bitmap
    hdc_scratch = CreateCompatibleDC(hdc);
    if(hbm_scratch != 0 && hdc_scratch != 0)
        old_hbm_scratch = SelectBitmap(hdc_scratch, hbm_scratch);

// Create a number of other memory device contexts for use
// during the animation. Select a 1x1 bitmap into each
// device context and save the old bitmaps (to be restored
// in the destructor).
    HBITMAP hbm_sprite = CreateCompatibleBitmap(hdc, 1, 1);

    hdc_sprite = CreateCompatibleDC(hdc);
    if(hdc_sprite != 0 && hbm_sprite != 0)
        old_hbm_sprite = SelectBitmap(hdc_sprite, hbm_sprite);
```

continues

Listing 5.4. continued

```
// Create a "sorted array" for the sprites.
// Start with 64 sprites; allow growth 16 sprites at a time.
    sprites = new SortedArray(64, 0, 16);
}
//--------------------------------------------------------------
// S p r i t e A n i m a t i o n
// Constructor for the SpriteAnimation class

SpriteAnimation::SpriteAnimation(HDC hdc,
                                 unsigned short w,
                                 unsigned short h,
                                 Image *bg)
{
// Set up coordinates of rectangle to be displayed
    top = left = 0;
    width = w;
    height = h;
    ws = w;
    hs = h;
    refresh = TRUE;

// Initialize all handles to zero
    sprites = NULL;
    hbm_bg = 0;
    hbm_scratch = 0;
    hbm_sprite = 0;
    old_hbm_bg = 0;
    old_hbm_sprite = 0;
    old_hbm_scratch = 0;
    hdc_bg = 0;
    hdc_sprite = 0;
    hdc_scratch = 0;

// Load the background image from the specified file
    background = bg;
    if(background != NULL)
    {
        background->DIBtoDDB(hdc);
        hbm_bg = background->get_ddb();
        bg_image = 1;
    }
    else
    {
// Create a blank bitmap that's used as the background
        hbm_bg = CreateCompatibleBitmap(hdc, w, h);
        bg_image = 0;
```

Animating Images

Chapter 5

```
    }
// Memory device context for the background image
    hdc_bg = CreateCompatibleDC(hdc);
    if(hbm_bg != 0 && hdc_bg != 0)
        old_hbm_bg = SelectBitmap(hdc_bg, hbm_bg);

// Initialize the background bitmap, if it did not come
// from an image.
    if(!bg_image && hbm_bg != 0 && hdc_bg != 0)
    {
        HBRUSH hbrbg = CreateSolidBrush(
                            GetSysColor(COLOR_WINDOW));
        HBRUSH oldbr = SelectBrush(hdc_bg, hbrbg);
        PatBlt(hdc_bg, 0, 0, w, h, PATCOPY);
        SelectBrush(hdc, oldbr);
        DeleteBrush(hbrbg);
    }

// Create a scratch bitmap of size w x h
    hbm_scratch = CreateCompatibleBitmap(hdc, w, h);

// Memory device context for the scratch bitmap
    hdc_scratch = CreateCompatibleDC(hdc);
    if(hbm_scratch != 0 && hdc_scratch != 0)
        old_hbm_scratch = SelectBitmap(hdc_scratch, hbm_scratch);

// Create a number of other memory device contexts for use
// during the animation. Select a 1x1 bitmap into each
// device context and save the old bitmaps (to be restored
// in the destructor).
    HBITMAP hbm_sprite = CreateCompatibleBitmap(hdc, 1, 1);

    hdc_sprite = CreateCompatibleDC(hdc);
    if(hdc_sprite != 0 && hbm_sprite != 0)
        old_hbm_sprite = SelectBitmap(hdc, hbm_sprite);

// Create a "sorted array" for the sprites.
// Start with 64 sprites; allow growth 16 sprites at a time.
    sprites = new SortedArray(64, 0, 16);
}
//-------------------------------------------------------------
// ~ S p r i t e A n i m a t i o n
// Destructor for the SpriteAnimation class

SpriteAnimation::~SpriteAnimation()
{
```

continues

Listing 5.4. continued

```
// Deselect the bitmaps and destroy them. Also delete
// the DCs.
    if(hdc_scratch != 0 && old_hbm_scratch != 0)
        SelectBitmap(hdc_scratch, old_hbm_scratch);
    if(hbm_scratch != 0) DeleteBitmap(hbm_scratch);
    if(hdc_scratch != 0) DeleteDC(hdc_scratch);

    if(hdc_bg != 0 && old_hbm_bg != 0)
        SelectBitmap(hdc_bg, old_hbm_bg);
    if(hdc_bg != 0) DeleteDC(hdc_bg);

    if(background != NULL) delete background;
    if(!bg_image) DeleteBitmap(hbm_bg);

    if(hdc_sprite != 0 && old_hbm_sprite != 0)
        SelectBitmap(hdc_sprite, old_hbm_sprite);
    if(hdc_sprite != 0) DeleteDC(hdc_sprite);

    if(hbm_sprite != 0) DeleteBitmap(hbm_sprite);

// Delete the sorted array of sprites--this also deletes the
// sprites currently in the array.
    if(sprites != NULL) delete sprites;
}
//----------------------------------------------------------------
// S p r i t e A n i m a t i o n : : a n i m a t e
// Function that animates the sprites. The selected portion
// of the background is displayed at (x,y) in the window.

void SpriteAnimation::animate(HDC hdc, short x, short y)
{
    if(refresh) redisplay_all(hdc, x, y);

    int i, j, numsprites = sprites->getItemsInContainer();
    for(i = 0; i < numsprites; i++)
    {
        Sprite& spr = (Sprite&)(*sprites)[i];
        if(spr.needs_update())
        {
            short xdel = spr.xmove();
            short ydel = spr.ymove();
            short w = spr.width() + abs(xdel);
            short h = spr.height() + abs(ydel);
            short xold = spr.xpos();
            short xnew = xold + xdel;
            short yold = spr.ypos();
```

Animating Images

```
            short ynew = yold + ydel;
            short xfrom = min(xold, xnew);
            short yfrom = min(yold, ynew);
// Mark this sprite as the lone overlapping sprite
            spr.overlaps();

// Find other moving sprites that intersect this sprite
            for(j = 0; j < numsprites; j++)
            {
                Sprite& spr2 = (Sprite&)(*sprites)[j];
                if(!spr2.is_overlapping() &&
                spr2.needs_update())
                {
                    short xdel2 = spr2.xmove();
                    short ydel2 = spr2.ymove();
                    short w2 = spr2.width() + abs(xdel2);
                    short h2 = spr2.height() + abs(ydel2);
                    short xold2 = spr2.xpos();
                    short xnew2 = xold2 + xdel2;
                    short yold2 = spr2.ypos();
                    short ynew2 = yold2 + ydel2;
                    short xfrom2 = min(xold2, xnew2);
                    short yfrom2 = min(yold2, ynew2);

                    if(rects_overlap(xfrom, yfrom, w, h,
                        xfrom2, yfrom2, w2, h2))
                    {
// Adjust dimensions of rectangle to be copied
                        short oldw = w;
                        w = max(xfrom2+w2,xfrom+w) -
                            min(xfrom,xfrom2);
                        if(w != oldw) j = 0;
                        short oldh = h;
                        h = max(yfrom2+h2,yfrom+h) -
                            min(yfrom,yfrom2);
                        if(h != oldh) j = 0;
                        if(xfrom2 < xfrom) xfrom = xfrom2;
                        if(yfrom2 < yfrom) yfrom = yfrom2;
                        spr2.overlaps();
                    }
                }
            }
// Adjust xfrom, yfrom, w, and h by comparing with the region
// of background (top, left, width, height) that is currently
// being displayed
            if(rects_overlap(xfrom, yfrom, w, h,
                            left, top, width, height))
```

continues

Listing 5.4. continued

```
            {
                w = min(xfrom+w,left+width) -
                    max(xfrom,left);
                h = min(yfrom+h,top+height) -
                    max(yfrom,top);
                xfrom = max(xfrom,left);
                yfrom = max(yfrom,top);
            }
            else
                continue;
// Check for intersection of the rectangle xfrom, yfrom, w, h
// with stationary sprites.
            for(j = 0; j < numsprites; j++)
            {
                Sprite& spr2 = (Sprite&)(*sprites)[j];
                if((!spr2.needs_update() ||
                    !spr2.is_overlapping()) && spr2.is_active())
                {
                    short w2 = spr2.width();
                    short h2 = spr2.height();
                    short xfrom2 = spr2.xpos();
                    short yfrom2 = spr2.ypos();

                    if(rects_overlap(xfrom, yfrom, w, h,
                                    xfrom2, yfrom2, w2, h2))
                        spr2.overlaps();
                }
            }

// Get a piece of the background into the scratch bitmap

            BitBlt(hdc_scratch, 0, 0, w, h, hdc_bg,
                   xfrom, yfrom, SRCCOPY);
// Loop through all sprites and draw the ones that overlap
            for(j = 0; j < numsprites; j++)
            {
                Sprite& spr2 = (Sprite&)(*sprites)[j];
                if(!spr2.is_overlapping()) continue;
                short xdel2 = spr2.xmove();
                short ydel2 = spr2.ymove();
                short w2 = spr2.width() + abs(xdel2);
                short h2 = spr2.height() + abs(ydel2);
                short xold2 = spr2.xpos();
                short xnew2 = xold2 + xdel2;
                short yold2 = spr2.ypos();
```

Chapter 5

Animating Images

```
                short ynew2 = yold2 + ydel2;
                short xto2 = xnew2 - xfrom;
                short yto2 = ynew2 - yfrom;

// AND sprite's mask onto the scratch bitmap
                HBITMAP hbm = spr2.hbm_mask();
                if(hbm != NULL)
                {
                    SelectBitmap(hdc_sprite, spr2.hbm_mask());
                    BitBlt(hdc_scratch, xto2, yto2, w2, h2,
                        hdc_sprite, 0, 0, SRCAND);

// Now OR sprite's image onto the scratch bitmap
                    SelectBitmap(hdc_sprite, spr2.hbm_image());
                    BitBlt(hdc_scratch, xto2, yto2, w2, h2,
                        hdc_sprite, 0, 0, SRCPAINT);
                }
                else
                {
// Copy the image if there is no mask...
                    if(spr2.hbm_image() != NULL)
                    {
                        SelectBitmap(hdc_sprite,
                                spr2.hbm_image());
                        BitBlt(hdc_scratch, xto2, yto2, w2, h2,
                            hdc_sprite, 0, 0, SRCCOPY);
                    }
                }
// Call the "draw" function, if any
                if(spr2.is_active() && spr2.drawproc() != NULL)
                    (*(spr2.drawproc()))(hdc_scratch, xto2, yto2,
                        spr2.data());

// Update the sprite's position and change its status bits
                spr2.newpos(xnew2, ynew2);
                spr2.update_done();
                spr2.no_overlap();
            }

// BitBlt the scratch area onto the window
            BitBlt(hdc, x+xfrom-left, y+yfrom-top, w, h,
                hdc_scratch, 0, 0, SRCCOPY);
        }
    }
}
//---------------------------------------------------------------
// SpriteAnimation:: r e d i s p l a y _ a l l
// Redisplay the background plus all sprites
```

continues

Listing 5.4. continued

```
void SpriteAnimation::redisplay_all(HDC hdc, short x, short y)
{
// Copy designated portion of background into scratch bitmap
    SelectBitmap(hdc_scratch, hbm_scratch);
    BitBlt(hdc_scratch, 0, 0, ws, hs, hdc_bg, left, top,
        SRCCOPY);

// Draw the active sprites on the scratch bitmap
    int i, numsprites = sprites->getItemsInContainer();
    for(i = 0; i < numsprites; i++)
    {
        Sprite& spr = (Sprite&)(*sprites)[i];
        short xs = spr.xpos() - left;
        short ys = spr.ypos() - top;

        HBITMAP hbm = spr.hbm_mask();
        if(spr.is_active() && hbm != NULL)
            {
// AND the mask
            SelectBitmap(hdc_sprite, spr.hbm_mask());
            BitBlt(hdc_scratch, xs, ys,
                spr.width(), spr.height(), hdc_sprite,
            0, 0, SRCAND);
// OR the image
            SelectBitmap(hdc_sprite, spr.hbm_image());
            BitBlt(hdc_scratch, xs, ys,
                spr.width(), spr.height(), hdc_sprite,
                0, 0, SRCPAINT);
        }
        if(spr.is_active() && hbm == NULL &&
            spr.hbm_image() != NULL)
        {
// Simply copy the image of the sprite
            SelectBitmap(hdc_sprite, spr.hbm_image());
            BitBlt(hdc_scratch, xs, ys,
                spr.width(), spr.height(), hdc_sprite,
                0, 0, SRCCOPY);
        }
        if(spr.is_active() && spr.drawproc() != NULL)
            (*(spr.drawproc()))(hdc_scratch, xs, ys,
                spr.data());
        spr.update_done();
        spr.no_overlap();
    }
```

Animating Images — Chapter 5

```
    // Copy the scratch bitmap into the window
    BitBlt(hdc, x, y, ws, hs,
            hdc_scratch, 0, 0, SRCCOPY);

    refresh = FALSE;
}
//----------------------------------------------------------------
// SpriteAnimation::draw_bg
// Draw the background bitmap

void SpriteAnimation::draw_bg(HDC hdc, short x, short y)
{
    BitBlt(hdc, x, y, width, height, hdc_bg, left, top,
            SRCCOPY);
}
//----------------------------------------------------------------
// SpriteAnimation::sprite_at
// Returns pointer to Sprite that encloses point (x,y)

Sprite* SpriteAnimation::sprite_at(short x, short y)
{
    int i, numsprites = sprites->getItemsInContainer();
    Sprite* rs = NULL;

    for(i = numsprites - 1; i >= 0; i--)
    {
        Sprite& spr = (Sprite&)(*sprites)[i];
        if(!spr.is_active()) continue;
        short xs = spr.xpos();
        short ys = spr.ypos();
        if(x < xs) continue;
        if(y < ys) continue;

        short ws = spr.width();
        short hs = spr.height();
        if(x > (xs + ws - 1)) continue;
        if(y > (ys + hs - 1)) continue;

        rs = &spr;
        break;
    }
    return rs;
}
```

A Sample Animation Program

This section describes a sample OWL-based Windows program that makes use of the Sprite and SpriteAnimation classes to animate a number of sprites on a background image. You can find the program in the companion directory—it should be in the CH05 directory after you install the code on your system. When you run the ANIMATE application, you see a number of sprites, including one with a text message animated on a complex background image. Figure 5.3 shows a sample output of the program (after you select the About item from the Help menu).

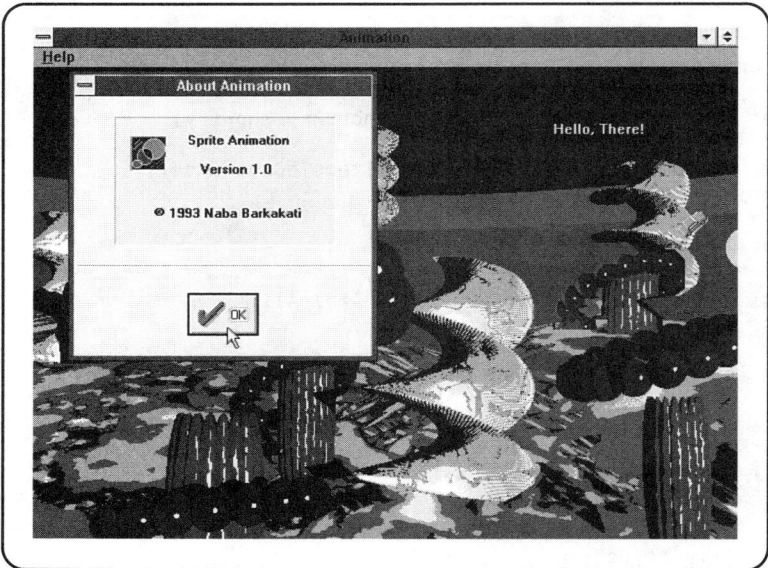

Figure 5.3. *Output of the sample animation program.*

AnimationWindow Class

The ANIMATE program uses an AnimationWindow class as its main window. Listing 5.5 shows the declaration of the AnimationWindow class, which is derived from TWindow.

Animating Images

Chapter 5

AnimationWindow has a pointer to the SpriteAnimation object that manages the animation for the application. The SpriteAnimation object is created and initialized in the WM_CREATE message-handler of the AnimationWindow class. An array of pointers to the Sprite objects is also maintained in AnimationWindow because we have to manipulate the Sprite objects using these pointers.

Listing 5.5. animwin.h— Declaration of the AnimationWindow class.

```
//---------------------------------------------------------------
// File: animwin.h
//
// Window classes for a sprite animation application.
//---------------------------------------------------------------
#if !defined(__ANIMWIN_H)
#define __ANIMWIN_H
#include <owl.h>
#include <strng.h>
#include "animres.h"   // Resource identifiers for the application
#include "spranim.h"   // Sprite animation class

#define SPRITE_ANIMATE 1 // ID of timer for moving and
                         // drawing sprites

const short AnimBGWidth  = 640;
const short AnimBGHeight = 480;

class AnimationWindow : public TWindow
{
public:
    AnimationWindow(PTWindowsObject parent, LPSTR title,
                    LPSTR menu): TWindow(parent, title),
                anim(0), top(0), left(0),
                width(AnimBGWidth), height(AnimBGHeight)
    {
        AssignMenu(menu);
    }


    ~AnimationWindow();

    void GetWindowClass(WNDCLASS _FAR &wc);
    void Paint(HDC hdc, PAINTSTRUCT &ps);
```

continues

Listing 5.5. continued

```
    void WMCreate(RTMessage msg) = [WM_FIRST + WM_CREATE];
    void WMTimer(RTMessage msg) = [WM_FIRST + WM_TIMER];
    void About(RTMessage msg) = [CM_FIRST + IDM_ABOUT];

private:
    SpriteAnimation     *anim;
    Sprite              **s;
    short               top;    // The point where the background
    short               left;   // is displayed
    short               width;
    short               height;

    void move_sprites();
};

#endif
```

The resource identifiers for the animation program are declared in the header file animres.h shown in Listing 5.6.

Listing 5.6. animres.h—
Resource identifiers for the animation example.

```
//--------------------------------------------------------------
// File: animres.h
// Resource identifiers for the Sprite Animation application
//--------------------------------------------------------------
#if !defined(__ANIMRES_H)
#define __ANIMRES_H

#include <owlrc.h>   // For definitions of OWL IDs

#define IDM_ABOUT 200

#endif
```

Animating Images

Chapter 5

Sprites in the Sample Animation

For this sample application, the file `animwin.cpp` (Listing 5.7) includes the definition of the sprites. I have defined a `SpriteInfo` structure to hold the information needed to define a `Sprite`. A static array of `SpriteInfo` structures, called `sprite_data`, defines all the sprites for this application. Notice that the last `SpriteInfo` structure in the `sprite_data` array does not provide any file names for the image and mask bitmaps. This `Sprite` is used to illustrate the use of a drawing procedure (the `dproc` member variable of a `Sprite`). I use the function `draw_text` (Listing 5.4) to display a text message that can be animated like a bitmapped sprite.

Initializing the Animation

The entire animation is set up in the `WMCreate` function (Listing 5.4). This function handles the `WM_CREATE` message sent by Windows to the `AnimationWindow` when the window is created. The initialization involves creating a `SpriteAnimation` object and an array of `Sprite` objects and adding each `Sprite` object to the `SpriteAnimation`.

Animation Strategy

My strategy for this animation is to use a Windows timer event to move the sprites and update the display. Thus, I call `SetTimer` to set up a 50-millisecond timer in the `WMCreate` function. Note, however, that Windows delivers at most 18.2 timer events per second or a timer event every 55 milliseconds.

The `WM_TIMER` events are handled by the `WMTimer` function (Listing 5.4). `WMTimer` first checks to ensure that the timer ID matches the one used when the timer was started. Then the sprites are moved. Finally, the display is updated by calling the animate function of the `SpriteAnimation` object that manages this animation.

In Listing 5.7, the sprites simply bounce back and forth within the confines of the animation's background. Listing 5.4, the `move_sprites` function, handles the details of the movement algorithm.

Listing 5.7. `animwin.cpp`—
Implementation of the `AnimationWindow` class.

```cpp
//--------------------------------------------------------------
// File: animwin.cpp
//
// Member functions for the AnimationWindow class.
//--------------------------------------------------------------
#include <stdlib.h>
#include <string.h>
#include "animwin.h"

struct SpriteInfo
{
    SpriteInfo(char* imgfname, char* mskfname,
               short xp, short yp, short xv, short yv,
               short prio) :
               imagefilename(imgfname), maskfilename(mskfname),
               xpos(xp), ypos(yp), xvel(xv), yvel(yv),
               priority(prio) {}

    char*  imagefilename;
    char*  maskfilename;
    short  xpos, ypos;     // Initial x-y position
    short  xvel, yvel;     // Initial x- and y-velocity
    short  priority;
};
// Declare an array of sprites to be loaded from image files
static SpriteInfo sprite_data[] =
{
    SpriteInfo("face1.bmp",  "face1m.bmp", 10, 10, 3, 2, 4),
    SpriteInfo("ring.bmp",   "ringm.bmp", 200, 10, -3, 2, 5),
    SpriteInfo("car.bmp",    "carm.bmp",  10, 200, -1, -1, 2),
    SpriteInfo("strange.bmp","strangem.bmp",100, 100, 1, 1, 1),
    SpriteInfo(NULL, NULL, 100, 50, 1, 0, 99)
};
// Total number of sprites
static int numsprites = sizeof(sprite_data) /
                        sizeof(sprite_data[0]);

void _FAR PASCAL _export draw_text(HDC hdc, short x, short y,
                                   LPVOID data);

struct TEXT_DATA
{
    LPSTR   text;
    size_t  numchars;
};
```

Animating Images

```
static TEXT_DATA dt;
static LPSTR msg = "Hello, There!";
//--------------------------------------------------------------
// Animation::WMCreate
// Initialize everything for the animation

void AnimationWindow::WMCreate(RTMessage)
{
// Get a DC for this window
    HDC hdc = GetDC(HWindow);

// Set timers for moving sprites and displaying them
    SetTimer(HWindow, SPRITE_ANIMATE, 50, NULL);

// Create an instance of the SpriteAnimation class and
// load the images (background plus the sprites)

    anim = new SpriteAnimation(hdc, width, height, "animbg.bmp");

// Create the array of sprites
    s = new Sprite*[numsprites];
    int i;
    for(i = 0; i < numsprites; i++)
    {
        s[i] = new Sprite(hdc, sprite_data[i].imagefilename,
                          sprite_data[i].maskfilename);
        s[i]->priority(sprite_data[i].priority);
        s[i]->newpos(sprite_data[i].xpos, sprite_data[i].ypos);
// Add sprite to animation
        anim->add(s[i]);
    }

// The last sprite is used to display a text string
    s[numsprites-1]->width(100);
    s[numsprites-1]->height(16);
    dt.text = msg;
    dt.numchars = strlen(msg);
    DRAWPROC proc = (DRAWPROC) MakeProcInstance(
                                    (FARPROC) draw_text,
                                    GetApplication()->hInstance);
    s[numsprites-1]->drawproc(proc, &dt);
    s[numsprites-1]->active();
    s[numsprites-1]->update();

// Release the DC
    ReleaseDC(HWindow, hdc);
```

continues

Listing 5.7. continued

```
// Initialize the random number generator with a random seed.
    randomize();
}
//---------------------------------------------------------------
// ~AnimationWindow
// Destructor for the animation window.

AnimationWindow::~AnimationWindow()
{
    if(anim != NULL) delete anim;
    if(s != NULL) delete s;
    KillTimer(HWindow, SPRITE_ANIMATE);
}
//---------------------------------------------------------------
// AnimationWindow::WMTimer
// Handle WM_TIMER events

void AnimationWindow::WMTimer(RTMessage msg)
{
    switch(msg.WParam)
    {
        case SPRITE_ANIMATE:
            HDC hdc = GetDC(HWindow);
// Move the sprites
            move_sprites();
            anim->animate(hdc, top, left);
            ReleaseDC(HWindow, hdc);
            break;

        default:
            break;
    }
}
//---------------------------------------------------------------
// AnimationWindow:: Paint
// Draw everything in the window

void AnimationWindow::Paint(HDC hdc, PAINTSTRUCT&)
{
    if(anim != NULL)
    {
        anim->set_refresh(TRUE);
        anim->animate(hdc, top, left);
    }
}
//---------------------------------------------------------------
// AnimationWindow:: GetWindowClass
```

Chapter 5

Animating Images

```cpp
//   Set up icon for each image window

void AnimationWindow::GetWindowClass(WNDCLASS _FAR &wc)
{
// First call the GetWindowClass function of the base class
    TWindow::GetWindowClass(wc);

// Set up icon for this image window
    wc.hIcon = LoadIcon(wc.hInstance, "ANIMATION_ICON");
}
//---------------------------------------------------------------
//   A n i m a t i o n W i n d o w :: A b o u t
//   Display the "About..." box

void AnimationWindow::About(RTMessage)
{
    TDialog *p_about = new TDialog(this, "ABOUTANIMATION");
    PTApplication app = GetApplication();
    app->ExecDialog(p_about);
}
//---------------------------------------------------------------
// m o v e _ s p r i t e s
// Move the sprites

void AnimationWindow::move_sprites()
{
    int i;
    for(i = 0; i < numsprites; i++)
    {
        if(s[i]->xpos() <= 0 || s[i]->xpos() >= width)
            sprite_data[i].xvel = -sprite_data[i].xvel;

        if(s[i]->ypos() <= 0 || s[i]->ypos() >= height)
            sprite_data[i].yvel = -sprite_data[i].yvel;

        s[i]->move(sprite_data[i].xvel, sprite_data[i].yvel);
    }
}
//---------------------------------------------------------------
void _FAR PASCAL _export draw_text(HDC hdc, short x, short y,
                                   LPVOID data)
{
    TEXT_DATA *td = (TEXT_DATA*)data;
    SetBkMode(hdc, TRANSPARENT);

    SetTextColor(hdc, RGB(255,255,0));
    TextOut(hdc, x, y, td->text, td->numchars);
}
```

The *ANIMATE* Application

Listing 5.8 shows the main program of the ANIMATE application. Like all OWL-based Windows programs, the ANIMATE application creates an instance of its main window, an AnimationWindow object, and starts an event-handling loop by calling the Run member function of the application class AnimationApp. All application-specific work is done in the AnimationWindow class, described in previous sections.

Listing 5.8. `animate.cpp`—
Main program of the animation application.

```cpp
//-----------------------------------------------------------
//  File:   animate.cpp
//
//  A Windows application that animates a number of sprites
//  over a background image. Also allows user to move an
//  image around using the mouse.
//-----------------------------------------------------------
#include "animwin.h"

//-----------------------------------------------------------
class AnimationApp: public TApplication
{
public:
// Constructor that simply calls the base class constructor

    AnimationApp(LPSTR name, HINSTANCE instance,
            HINSTANCE prev_instance, LPSTR  cmdline, int show) :

            TApplication(name, instance, prev_instance,
                        cmdline, show) {}

// Define function to initialize application's main window
    void InitMainWindow();

// Define function to initialize an instance of this application
    void InitInstance();
};
//-----------------------------------------------------------
//   A n i m a t i o n A p p : : I n i t M a i n W i n d o w

void AnimationApp::InitMainWindow()
{
    MainWindow = new AnimationWindow(NULL, "Animation",
                                    "MainMenu");
```

Chapter 5

Animating Images

```
}
//---------------------------------------------------------------
// AnimationApp::InitInstance

void AnimationApp::InitInstance()
{
    TApplication::InitInstance();
    HAccTable = LoadAccelerators(hInstance, "MainAccelTable");
}
//---------------------------------------------------------------
// WinMain
//
// Create an instance of the application and "run" it.

int PASCAL WinMain(HINSTANCE instance, HINSTANCE prev_instance,
                   LPSTR cmdline, int show)
{
    AnimationApp Animation("Sprite Animation", instance,
                           prev_instance, cmdline, show);

    Animation.Run();

    return Animation.Status;
}
```

Building *ANIMATE.EXE*

Borland C++ for Windows is used to build the ANIMATE application. The companion disk has all the files needed to build the executable, ANIMATE.EXE. In particular, the project file ANIMATE.PRJ lists the source files and library necessary to build the application. There are a few items in the project file that reflect the name of the drive and directory where I installed Borland C++ in my system. Make the same changes to the project file as the ones suggested in Chapter 4 for building the ImageView application.

After making the necessary changes, you should be able to build ANIMATE.EXE by selecting Make from the Compile menu. Once the program is successfully built, you can add it to Windows Program Manager by selecting New... from the Program Manager's File menu.

One of the files that you need to build ANIMATE.EXE is the resource file ANIMATE.RES, which is included in the companion disk. I prepared the resource file using the Resource Workshop program included with Borland C++.

Summary

Images used in a computer game are usually animated in some way to support the interactive nature of the game. One of the common tasks in many games is to animate (move) small images known as sprites over a background image. The obvious approach of erasing and redrawing a sprite produces an undesirable flicker. One way to get around this problem is to draw the images on an offscreen bitmap and copy the final image to the screen using the Windows API function `BitBlt`. This chapter shows the `Sprite` and `SpriteAnimation` classes that allow you to animate sprites over a background image using the offscreen bitmap technique. A sample application, ANIMATE, illustrates how to use the sprite animation classes. The next chapter uses the sprite classes in an educational game.

Further Reading

If you are interested in cel animation, you might want to try out the animation studio software from The Walt Disney Company. It runs under DOS and includes the tools necessary to create the cels for an animation.

For a general discussion of animation, consult Chapter 21 of the classic graphics textbook by Foley, van Dam, Feiner, and Hughes.

The books by Loren Heiny and Myers and Doner cover simple animations under Windows. However, unlike this book, their books do not describe any technique to animate several moving sprites without any flickers.

The Animation Studio. Burbank, CA: Walt Disney Computer Software, Inc., 1991.

Foley, James D., Andries van Dam, Steven K. Feiner, and John F. Hughes. *Computer Graphics Principles and Practice, Second Edition*. Reading, MA: Addison-Wesley Publishing, 1990.

Heiny, Loren. *Windows Graphics Programming with Borland C++*. New York: Wiley, 1992.

Myers, Brian, and Chris Doner. *Programmer's Introduction to Windows 3.1*. Alameda, CA: SYBEX, 1992.

Chapter 6

Generating Sound

In addition to image manipulation, the generation of *sound* (a string of notes) is a common feature of most games, whether they are designed to run under MS-DOS or Microsoft Windows. The previous chapters covered image manipulation under Windows. This chapter describes how to play musical notes using a number of Windows API functions.

Sound under Windows

Compared to the Apple Macintosh, the sound generation capabilities of the IBM-compatible PCs are rather limited. Essentially, all you can do with the PC's speaker is play single notes—you cannot even vary the *volume* (loudness).

One way to improve the sound output under Windows (and DOS) is to install a sound card that can synthesize a wide range of sounds. Some of the popular sound cards are Sound Blaster, Media Vision, and Microsoft Windows Sound System. These cards convert the *analog* (continuously varying) sound waves into 8-bit or 16-bit numbers, sampling the wave at rates from 4 to 44KHz (22,000 times a second). Higher sampling rates and higher number of bits (16-bit) provide better quality, but you need more disk space to store high-quality sound.

Programming for Sound

Like any other device, the sound cards are controlled through drivers. The sound driver provides a standard programming interface for all sound boards. If you look at the SYSTEM.INI file in your system's Windows directory, you might find this line:

```
sound.drv=sound.drv
```

This tells Microsoft Windows that the sound output is to be performed through the driver named sound.drv, which is the default driver for the PC's built-in speaker. The right side of the line is different if you have a sound card installed in your system—it is the name of the driver that Windows uses to control that sound card.

Chapter 6

Generating Sound

Once the sound driver is installed, you can use a small set of Windows functions to generate sound. Windows 3.1 includes another simpler API, called the multimedia API, for sound cards and other multimedia devices such as the CD-ROM drive and video output device. The multimedia API relies on a *dynamic link library (DLL)* MMSYSTEM, which provides a high-level set of commands called *Media Control Interface (MCI)*. As a programmer, you can control a multimedia device by sending commands using the `mciSendCommand` function. See the "Further Reading" section at the end of this chapter for sources of information on the MCI functions.

This chapter covers sound generation under Windows with the PC's built-in speaker or a sound board with a driver that responds to the Windows sound functions. Although Microsoft recommends that programmers use the MCI functions for controlling sound devices, using the old API functions is the only way to guarantee that sound output will work in all PCs—whether they have a sound card or they rely on the PC's built-in speaker.

Windows Sound Model

Whenever a device is controlled through a driver, the driver presents an abstract model of the device to the programmer. The Windows sound drivers model each sound as a *voice*. You can think of each voice as a queue with a number of notes that are to be played in sequence (see Figure 6.1). At any instant of time, the sound card plays notes from all the voices simultaneously. The PC's speaker can handle only one voice, but most sound cards can handle from 8 to 16 voices.

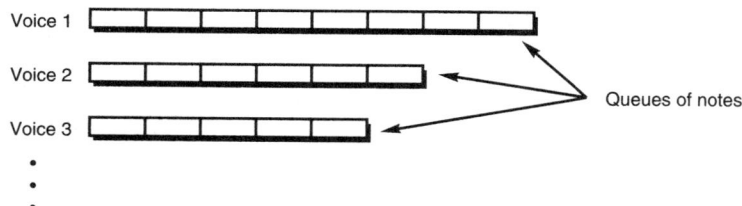

Figure 6.1. *Voices in Windows.*

To generate sound, you have to follow these steps:

1. Open the sound driver by calling `OpenSound`. If the sound device is not being used by another application, `OpenSound` returns the number of voices available. Otherwise, it returns a negative number. Thus, you start the sound generation code with

   ```
   if(OpenSound() > 0)
   {
   // Sound driver successfully opened. OK to proceed
   }
   ```

2. Call `SetVoiceQueueSize` to set the size of queues for each voice. You have to specify the size in number of bytes. Each note requires 6 bytes of memory. To make room for n notes in the first voice's queue, use

   ```
   SetVoiceQueueSize(1, 6*n);
   ```

3. Call `SetVoiceAccent` to set the tempo, volume, and mode (legato, normal, or staccato) of the notes in a voice.

4. Call `SetVoiceNote` to add notes to a voice queue. For each note, you can specify the following characteristics:

   - The note number (between 1 and 84)
   - Duration of the note (1 for a whole note, 2 for a half-note, 4 for a quarter-note, and so on)
   - The number of quarter-note durations to add to the note's duration

5. Call `StartSound` to begin the sound output.

6. You can proceed with other programming tasks while the sound plays. At any time, you can call `CountVoiceNotes` to check how many notes remain in a voice's queue. Once the queue is empty, you should call `StopSound` followed by `CloseSound` to release the sound device for use by other processes.

C++ Structures for Sound under Windows

For use in C++ programs, it makes sense to define a number of object types to help with sound output. Listing 6.1 shows the header file `sounds.h` that defines

Generating Sound

the structures Note and Music. Note represents a single note and Music represents a voice. An important feature of Music is the ability to load a simple piece of music from a file into a Music object.

Listing 6.1. sounds.h—
Declaration of Note and Music structures.

```
//--------------------------------------------------------------
// File: sounds.h
// Defines arrays of notes for use in Windows programs.
//--------------------------------------------------------------

#if !defined __SOUNDS_H
#define __SOUNDS_H

#include <windows.h>

struct Note
{
    Note() : number(1), duration(1), dots(0) {}
    Note(short n, short d, short dt) :
        number(n), duration(d), dots(dt) {}

    short number;    // Note number (range: 1 to 84)
    short duration;  // Note duration (1 = whole note,
                     // 2 = half note, 4 = quarter note)
    short dots;      // Number of beats to add to duration
};

struct Music
{
    Music() : tempo(120), volume(128), mode(S_NORMAL),
              pitch(0), numnotes(0), notes(NULL) {}

    Music(short tmpo, short vol, short m, short po,
          short nn, Note *nt) : tempo(tmpo), volume(vol),
     mode(m), pitch(po), numnotes(nn), notes(nt) {}

    ~Music()
    {
        if(notes != NULL) delete notes;
    }

    short read(char *filename); // Read music from a file
```

continues

Listing 6.1. continued

```
    short tempo;    // Beats (quarter notes) per minute
                    // (default is 120)
    short volume;   // From 0 to 255 (ignored by PC speaker)
    short mode;     // Legato, Normal, Staccato (ignored by
                    // PC speaker)
    short pitch;    // Pitch offset to add to notes
    short numnotes; // Number of notes
    Note  *notes;   // Array of notes
};

#endif
```

Music File Format

To store the music in a file, I adopted a simple text file format. You can decipher the format by reading the source code of the Music::read function shown in Listing 6.2. Before making some comments about the format, let me show you the contents of a sample music file:

```
SPUZZLE.MUSIC       This tune is "Mary Had a Little Lamb"
1                   Version
NUMBER_DURATION_DOT Format
100         Tempo
128         Volume
NORMAL      Mode
0           Pitch offset
11          Number of notes in this music
43 8 0      First note (Note number, duration, beats to add)
41 8 0      Second note
39 8 0      and so on...
42 8 0
43 8 0
43 8 0
43 8 0
0  8 0
41 8 0
41 8 0
41 8 0
```

I had developed this format for the SPUZZLE game (described in Chapter 7), which is why I added an identifying comment referring to SPUZZLE on the

Generating Sound

first line. The second and third lines specify a version number and the file format. Next comes the characteristics of the music: tempo, volume, and mode. Finally, there is a number of notes followed by the individual notes.

Listing 6.2. `sounds.cpp`—
Implementation of `Music`'s member function.

```
//-------------------------------------------------------------
// File: sounds.cpp
// Member functions of the Music class
//-------------------------------------------------------------
#include <string.h>
#include <stdlib.h>
#include "sounds.h"
#include "fstream.h"


//-------------------------------------------------------------
// M u s i c : : r e a d
// Read music from a file

short Music::read(char * filename)
{
// Open file for reading
    ifstream ifs(filename, ios::in);
    if(!ifs)
    {
// Error reading file. Return 0.
        return 0;
    }

// Read and interpret the contents of the file
    char line[81];

// First line should have the string SPUZZLE.MUSIC
    ifs.getline(line, sizeof(line));
    strupr(line);
    if(strnicmp(line, "SPUZZLE.MUSIC",
            strlen("SPUZZLE.MUSIC")) != 0) return 0;

// Second line has a version number--just in case the
// contents have to change in the future
    ifs.getline(line, sizeof(line));
    short version = atoi(line);
    if(version != 1) return 0;
```

continues

Listing 6.2. continued

```
// Third line has the format type--it's a string.
// Right now I interpret the "NUMBER_DURATION_DOT" format
    ifs.getline(line, sizeof(line));
    strupr(line);
    if(strnicmp(line, "NUMBER_DURATION_DOT",
        strlen("NUMBER_DURATION_DOT")) != 0) return 0;

// Next few lines...
// Tempo (between 32 to 255)
// Volume (between 0 and 255)
// Mode (a string: NORMAL, LEGATO, or STACCATO)
// Pitch Offset (between 0 and 83)
    ifs.getline(line, sizeof(line));
    tempo = atoi(line);

    ifs.getline(line, sizeof(line));
    volume = atoi(line);

    ifs.getline(line, sizeof(line));
    strupr(line);
    if(strncmp(line, "NORMAL", strlen("NORMAL")))
        mode = S_NORMAL;
    if(strncmp(line, "LEGATO", strlen("LEGATO")))
        mode = S_LEGATO;
    if(strncmp(line, "STACCATO", strlen("STACCATO")))
        mode = S_STACCATO;

    ifs.getline(line, sizeof(line));
    pitch = atoi(line);

// Next comes the number of notes in this piece of music
    ifs.getline(line, sizeof(line));
    numnotes = atoi(line);

// Allocate an array of Note structures
    Note *new_notes = new Note[numnotes];
    if(new_notes == NULL) return 0;

// At this point we have an array of Note structures
// allocated. If there is an existing Note array,
// delete it before loading new value
    if(notes != NULL) delete notes;
    notes = new_notes;

// From this point on each line in the file has the following
// form:
```

Generating Sound

```
//         Note #(0-83)  Duration (1, 2, 4, 8, ...) Dots (beats)
// example:
//         42     8      0
//         41     8      0
//         39     4      0
// and so on.
    short i;
    char *token;
    for(i = 0; i < numnotes; i++)
    {
        if(ifs.eof())
        {
            numnotes = i;
            break;
        }
        ifs.getline(line, sizeof(line));
// Parse the line...first token
        token = strtok(line, " ");
        notes[i].number = atoi(token);
// Second token
        token = strtok(NULL, " ");
        notes[i].duration = atoi(token);
// Third token
        token = strtok(NULL, " ");
        notes[i].dots = atoi(token);
    }
    return 1;
}
```

A Sample Program

Listing 6.3 shows the file `playsnd.cpp` that implements a simple application to let the user open a sound file and play the notes in that file. All the work of the application is done in the `InitMainWindow` function by using the standard file open dialog (identified by the resource ID `SD_FILEOPEN`) that comes with Borland C++. Once the user selects a file from the list of files displayed in this dialog and clicks on the OK pushbutton, `InitMainWindow` calls the `playmusic` function to open the selected file, interpret the notes, and play them. Then the dialog is displayed again. The user has to press the Cancel button to exit the application. Figure 6.2 shows the single dialog box that constitutes the user interface of the `playsnd.exe` program.

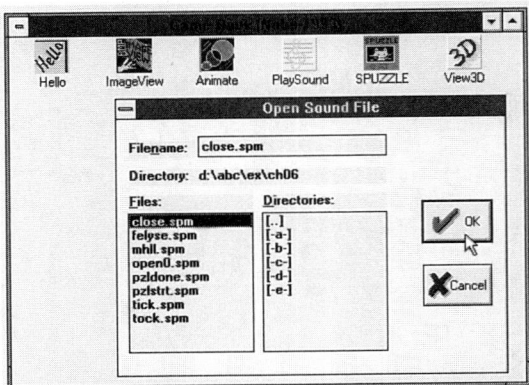

Figure 6.2. *Main dialog box of the* `playsnd.exe` *application.*

All the files needed to build `playsnd.exe` are in the companion disk. Open the project file, `playsnd.prj`, in Borland C++ for Windows and select the Make option from the Compile menu to build the program. You have to change the directories for include files and libraries to match your installation of Borland C++. To do this, select the Directories item from the Options menu in Borland C++.

Listing 6.3. `playsnd.cpp`—
Program that plays notes from a sound file.

```
//-------------------------------------------------------------
//  File:   playsnd.cpp
//
//  A simple program that plays musical notes from files.
//
//-------------------------------------------------------------
#include <filedial.h>
#include <owl.h>
#include <windobj.h>
#include <owlrc.h>
#include "sounds.h"

static Music m;
static short sound_playing = 0;
void playmusic(Music& m, short wait_till_done);
```

Generating Sound

Chapter 6

```
//------------------------------------------------------------
class PlaySoundApp: public TApplication
{
public:
// Constructor that simply calls the base class constructor

    PlaySoundApp(LPSTR name, HINSTANCE instance,
        HINSTANCE prev_instance, LPSTR  cmdline, int show) :

        TApplication(name, instance, prev_instance,
                    cmdline, show) {}

// Define function to initialize application's main window

    void InitMainWindow();

// Define function to initialize an instance of this application
    void InitInstance();
};
//------------------------------------------------------------
// P l a y S o u n d A p p : : I n i t M a i n W i n d o w
// Everything happens in this function. We display a dialog
// box and play the music from the selected file.

void PlaySoundApp::InitMainWindow()
{
    char name[80] = "*.*";
    int status = IDOK;

    while(status == IDOK)
    {
// Create and display file selection dialog...
        TFileDialog *p_fd = new TFileDialog(NULL, SD_FILEOPEN, name);
        status = ExecDialog(p_fd);

 // Load selected music and play
        if(status == IDOK)
        {
            if(m.read(name)) playmusic(m, 0);
        }
    }
// Quit ...
    PostQuitMessage(0);
}
//------------------------------------------------------------
// P l a y S o u n d A p p : : I n i t I n s t a n c e
```

continues

Listing 6.3. continued

```
void PlaySoundApp::InitInstance()
{
    TApplication::InitInstance();
}
//-----------------------------------------------------------------
// WinMain
//
// Create an instance of the application and "run" it.

int PASCAL WinMain(HINSTANCE instance, HINSTANCE prev_instance,
                   LPSTR cmdline, int show)
{
    PlaySoundApp PlaySound("PlaySound", instance,
                           prev_instance, cmdline, show);

    PlaySound.Run();
    return 0;
}
//-----------------------------------------------------------------
// playmusic
// Play the notes specified in a Music structure

void playmusic(Music& m, short wait_till_done)
{
    if((m.notes == NULL) || (m.numnotes == 0)) return;

// Wait if something is already playing...
    if(!wait_till_done && sound_playing)
    {
        while(CountVoiceNotes(1) > 0);
        sound_playing = 0;
    }

// Turn off anything that might be playing now...
    StopSound();
    CloseSound();

// Open sound driver and play the notes...
    if(OpenSound() > 0)
    {
     SetVoiceQueueSize(1, 6*m.numnotes);
        SetVoiceAccent(1, m.tempo, m.volume,
                       m.mode, m.pitch);
        short i;
        for(i = 0; i < m.numnotes; i++)
```

Generating Sound

```
            SetVoiceNote(1, m.notes[i].number,
                        m.notes[i].duration,
                        m.notes[i].dots);
        StartSound();
        sound_playing = 1;
// Wait till music is done (if wait_till_done is TRUE)
        if(wait_till_done)
        {
            while(CountVoiceNotes(1) > 0);
            StopSound();
            CloseSound();
        }
    }
}
```

Summary

Sound is an integral part of computer games. Until recently, games for IBM-Compatible PCs had to rely on the simple speaker built into every PC. Nowadays many PC owners install sound cards capable of generating musical quality sounds, and many games exploit this capability. Windows provides a device-independent interface to the sound cards through device drivers. Windows 3.1 makes programming the sound cards easier through the Multimedia Control Interface (MCI) of the MMSYSTEM dynamic link library. This chapter describes how to generate sound using a number of Windows API functions. Two C++ classes, Note and Music, are used to illustrate how musical notes can be stored in a file, interpreted, and played.

Further Reading

Popular programming journals are a good source of information on programming with Windows Multimedia Control Interface (MCI). Chapter 15 of the book by Brian Myers and Chris Doner shows a sample application, written in C, that plays sound waves using the MCI commands of the MMSYSTEM DLL.

James Conger's book includes a concise description of the Windows API functions for generating sound.

> Conger, James L. *The Waite Group's Windows API Bible*. Corte Madera, CA: Waite Group Press, 1992.

> Myers, Brian, and Chris Doner. *Programmer's Introduction to Windows 3.1*. Alameda, CA: SYBEX, 1992.

PART II

Sample Games

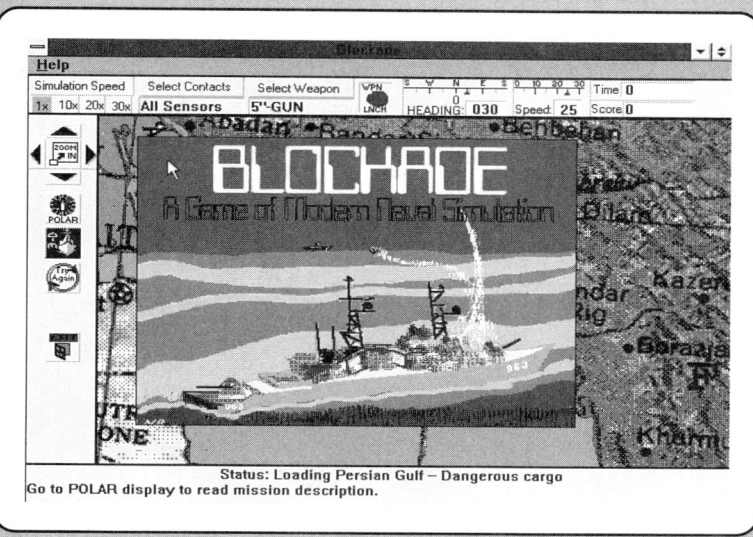

Chapter 7

SPUZZLE— A Spelling Puzzle

Programming Windows Games with Borland C++

The previous chapters discuss a number of techniques for image animation and sound generation. This chapter turns to the practical and shows a working game that I call SPUZZLE, for Spelling Puzzle. As you might guess, it is meant to teach children spelling through a jigsaw puzzle. This chapter starts with a description of the game followed by the game's design. Finally, the chapter covers the C++ classes that are used to build SPUZZLE: Borland's OWL and CLASSLIB classes and classes shown in Chapters 4, 5, and 6.

After reading this chapter, you can use your own imagination to improve SPUZZLE or build other new games that rely on image animation techniques.

Playing SPUZZLE

Before reading the description of SPUZZLE, install the contents of the companion disk so that you can follow my description of the game. If you have any trouble playing SPUZZLE, you can get on-line help from the Help menu or by pressing the F1 function key. Figure 7.1 shows a help screen for SPUZZLE with instructions for playing the game.

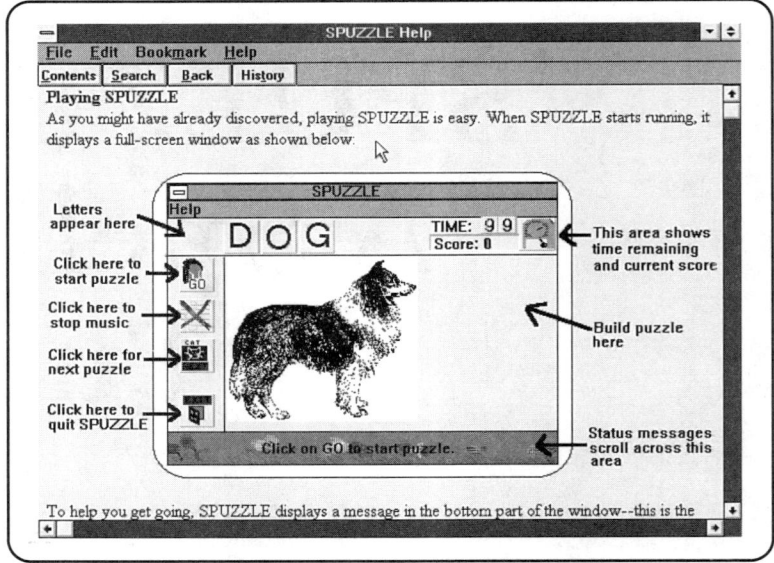

Figure 7.1. *A help screen for SPUZZLE.*

Chapter 7

SPUZZLE—A Spelling Puzzle

Starting SPUZZLE

When you first start SPUZZLE, it displays a full-screen main window with four distinct child windows (see the layout in Figure 7.2):

- A large child window in the middle where the player builds the puzzle
- A tool window with a number of pushbuttons to the left of the puzzle window
- A child window along the top edge where the letters of the word appear and the score is displayed
- A status window along the bottom edge where some status information is displayed

Figure 7.2. *Main screen of SPUZZLE.*

Building a Puzzle

The initial display shows a picture in the puzzle window and the corresponding word above the picture. To play the game, you click on the button labeled GO, which is the first pushbutton in the tool window. The picture is sliced into as many pieces as there are letters in the corresponding word. The puzzle pieces and the letters are scrambled and shown in random order (see Figure 7.3). You drag the puzzle pieces and place them next to each other in correct order. As you move a piece, the corresponding letter also moves in the top window. Thus, once the puzzle pieces are in correct order, the spelling of the word should be complete.

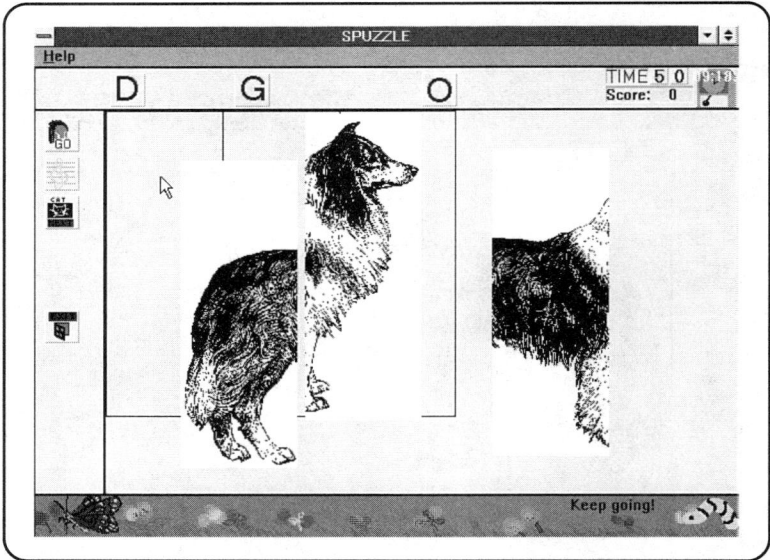

Figure 7.3. *Scrambled puzzle pieces and letters in SPUZZLE.*

After you complete a puzzle you can go on to another puzzle by clicking on the button labeled NEXT.

SPUZZLE—A Spelling Puzzle

Keeping Score

In the right corner of SPUZZLE's display, you can see a clock, a time counter, and the current score. Initially, the score is zero and the time counter is set to 99. When you click on the GO pushbutton, the timer begins to count down. Your score for a puzzle is the sum of the clock count at the time of finishing the puzzle and the number of letters in the word that you spelled. Thus you get a higher score if you finish faster. Also, your score for spelling a longer word is more than that for spelling a shorter word.

Like many other games, SPUZZLE maintains a high scores file. If your score is one of the 30 best scores thus far, SPUZZLE displays a dialog box when you exit the game. The dialog prompts for your name and a quotation. When you click on the OK button, SPUZZLE saves your name, score, and the quotation in the high scores file.

Controlling Sound Output

By default, SPUZZLE plays some musical notes at certain times in the game: when you start a new puzzle, when you complete the puzzle, and when you exit. Also, the clock makes a tick-tock sound all the time. You can turn all this sound off by clicking on the pushbutton with the picture of a musical note. That button acts as a toggle—clicking on that button again turns the sound on.

SPUZZLE loads the musical scores from text files that list the notes. For instance, when a puzzle is completed, SPUZZLE plays the notes listed in the file PZLDONE.SPM. Here is a typical PZLDONE.SPM file:

```
SPUZZLE.MUSIC        Play after a puzzle is done
1           Version
NUMBER_DURATION_DOT   Format
120         Tempo (between 32 and 255)
128         Volume (between 0 and 255)
NORMAL      Mode (NORMAL, STACCATO, or LEGATO)
0           Pitch offset
6           Number of notes in this music
36 8 0      Note # 1 (Note number, Duration, Dots)
36 8 0
36 8 0
35 8 0
38 8 0
41 8 0
```

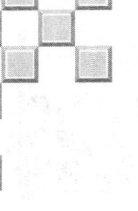

The file specifies a tempo (quarter-notes per minute), volume (between 0 and 255), mode (NORMAL, STACCATO, or LEGATO), and the number of notes in the musical score, followed by a list of the notes. Each note has a note number (between 1 and 84), a duration in quarter-notes, and the number of beats to add to the note's duration. Chapter 6 describes the format of the music files.

To change the music, you can experiment by changing the notes. To specify the notes from scratch, you have to be knowledgeable about music as well as the way sound is played in Windows. Here are the sound files used by SPUZZLE (the corresponding sound is not played if a file does not exist):

OPEN.SPM	Music played when SPUZZLE first starts up
PZLDONE.SPM	Music to be played after a puzzle is complete
PZLSTRT.SPM	Music played at the start of each puzzle
CLOSE.SPM	Music to be played when SPUZZLE exits
TICK.SPM	The clock tick (should be a single note)
TOCK.SPM	The other note of the clock's tick-tock sound

Adding a New Word

SPUZZLE is designed to be *extensible*—you can add new words easily. To add a word, you need a picture to go along with it. SPUZZLE sets up the puzzles by reading the text file SPUZZLE.CFG at start-up. Here is the listing of a sample SPUZZLE.CFG file:

```
SPUZZLE.CFG
1              The version number
24             Number of puzzles in file
eagle          eagle.bmp
cat            cat.bmp
elephant       eleph1.bmp
chess          chess1.bmp
dog            dog.bmp
zebra          zebra.bmp
horse          horse.bmp
mule           mule.bmp
panda          panda.bmp
kitten         kitty.bmp
```

SPUZZLE—A Spelling Puzzle

```
tiger       tiger.bmp
leopard     leop2.bmp
bird        bird.bmp
owl         owl.bmp
deer        deer.bmp
dinosaur    dino.bmp
apple       apple.bmp
cherry      cherry.bmp
rose        rose2.bmp
eagle       eagle2.bmp
computer    compu2.bmp
goat        goat.bmp
train       train.bmp
ram         goat.bmp
```

As you can see, each word and its related picture are specified on a separate line in the format:

```
word       imagefile.ext
```

The extension of the image file determines the type of image. The .BMP extension implies a Windows BITMAP file (the DIB format). SPUZZLE also accepts .PCX (PC PaintBrush format) and .TGA (24-bit Truevision Targa format) image files.

To add a new word to SPUZZLE, you need an image file for the word. You can either draw a picture in PC PaintBrush and save as a .BMP or .PCX file or use a scanner to convert a paper image to digital form. Once you have a picture, use your favorite text editor to add a line at the end of the SPUZZLE.CFG file listing the word and the image file's name. Then change the number of puzzles shown in the third line of the SPUZZLE.CFG file.

If you have both .BMP and .PCX format images, specify the .BMP image file name in SPUZZLE.CFG. SPUZZLE can load the .BMP files much faster than it loads .PCX files.

Designing SPUZZLE

By playing the game and reading the description in previous chapters, you already know most of the features of SPUZZLE. In the following sections, I go over some of the issues in designing SPUZZLE. The latter part of this chapter describes the C++ classes that implement the game.

Window Hierarchy

I started SPUZZLE's design by selecting a hierarchy of windows suitable for the user interface. I sketched out a layout that made sense to me. Like many drawing programs, I wanted a work area surrounded by smaller windows that provide a palette of tools or display status messages. For SPUZZLE, I selected a work area for the puzzle, a tool window for the bitmap buttons used to initiate actions, an area for status messages, and a window to display the letters of the word being spelled. Thus, I decided to divide the client area of the main window into four different areas, each managed by a child window. When designing specific features, I always have in mind at least a vague notion of how to implement the feature. In this case, I intended to derive each of these child windows as well as the main window from the OWL class TWindow. You can see SPUZZLE's window hierarchy in Figure 7.4, which also shows the correspondence between the screen layout and the windows.

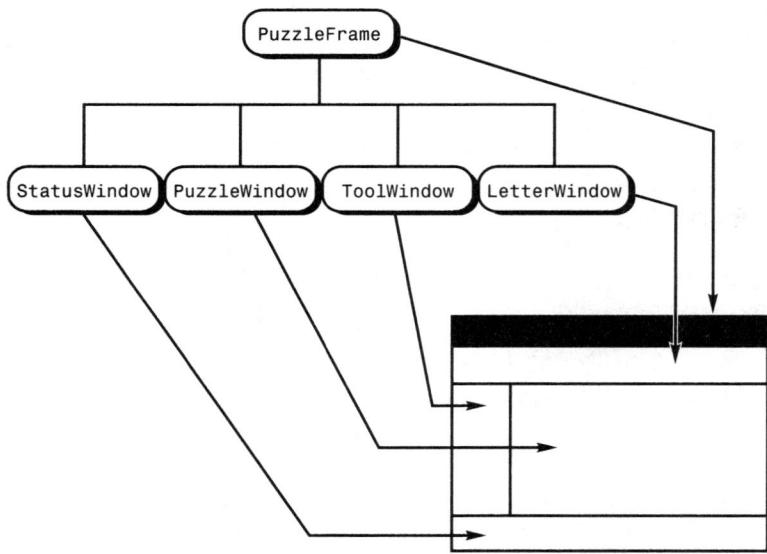

Figure 7.4. *Window hierarchy in SPUZZLE.*

SPUZZLE—A Spelling Puzzle

Assigning the Responsibilities

After settling on the window classes, I assigned specific responsibilities to each class. Here are the nominal responsibilities of the five window classes in SPUZZLE (see Figure 7.4):

- `PuzzleFrame` is the main window of the application. All other windows are contained in `PuzzleFrame`. The `PuzzleFrame` class maintains information about the current set of puzzles and processes `WM_TIMER` events to keep all the child windows animated.

- `PuzzleWindow` class represents the area where the player prepares the puzzle. This window maintains the puzzle pieces, handles mouse inputs, and moves the puzzle pieces when the user drags the mouse with the (left) button pressed down. `PuzzleWindow` uses the services of the `SpriteAnimation` class (see Chapter 5) to animate the puzzle pieces.

- `ToolWindow` class manages a number of bitmap buttons that initiate actions such as start a puzzle, turn the sound on or off, go to the next puzzle, and exit SPUZZLE.

- `LetterWindow` class displays the letters of the word being spelled. It also shows the current score and the current clock count. `LetterWindow` uses the `SpriteAnimation` class to move a number of sprites representing the letters and the clock count.

- `StatusWindow` class displays a status message animated on an interesting background. It uses an instance of the `SpriteAnimation` class to manage the animation.

Maintaining Information about the Puzzles

SPUZZLE is fun to play only when it offers a large number of words to spell. For this to happen, I had to ensure that new puzzles could be added with minimal effort. To support this goal, I decided to load the puzzles from a file named `SPUZZLE.CFG`. The `PuzzleFrame` class is responsible for reading the `SPUZZLE.CFG` file and loading the information into internal data structures. I decided to use an array of `PuzzleInfo` structures to hold the information about all the available puzzles.

From the available puzzles, `PuzzleFrame` picks a small subset for the current game. `PuzzleFrame` uses an array of `PuzzlePick` structures to hold information about the puzzles that are picked. Finally, each puzzle piece also has a lot of information, such as the sprite representing the puzzle piece, the letter corresponding to the piece, and a sprite for that letter. The `PuzzlePiece` structure holds this sort of information for each puzzle piece.

Implementing SPUZZLE

Although SPUZZLE is conceptually simple, implementing it requires attention to many details. I started implementing SPUZZLE by defining the classes outlined in the design phase. My implementation strategy is to get a bare bones framework up and running. By framework I mean a working prototype with just enough code to compile and link without errors. For SPUZZLE, building the framework required defining the five window classes, `PuzzleFrame`, `PuzzleWindow`, `ToolWindow`, `StatusWindow`, and `LetterWindow`—with a minimal set of member functions. Most functionality is missing from the framework, but I have found that having a working prototype lets me build the full application iteratively a block at a time without being deluged with many issues (and bugs) at once.

Although the following sections do not focus on the iterative process when describing the building blocks of SPUZZLE, what you see are the final steps of an iterative process.

SpuzzleApp Class

Because SPUZZLE is based on Borland's OWL classes, the application itself is a class named `SpuzzleApp`, which is derived from the OWL class `TApplication`. Listing 7.1 shows the file `spuzzle.cpp` that defines the `SpuzzleApp` class and provides the `WinMain` function necessary for any OWL-based application. The `WinMain` function creates an instance of `SpuzzleApp` and calls the `Run` member function to begin processing events. SPUZZLE's main window is displayed when the `Run` calls the `InitMainWindow` function. `InitMainWindow` creates an instance of `PuzzleFrame` and this, in turn, displays all the child windows in SPUZZLE.

SPUZZLE—A Spelling Puzzle

Listing 7.1. `spuzzle.cpp`—Definition of the `SpuzzleApp` class.

```cpp
//--------------------------------------------------------------
//  File:   spuzzle.cpp
//
//  An educational game that teaches spelling through puzzles.
//
//--------------------------------------------------------------
#include "pzlframe.h"

//--------------------------------------------------------------
class SpuzzleApp: public TApplication
{
public:
// Constructor that simply calls the base class constructor

    SpuzzleApp(LPSTR name, HINSTANCE instance,
        HINSTANCE prev_instance, LPSTR  cmdline, int show) :

        TApplication(name, instance, prev_instance,
                    cmdline, show) {}

// Define function to initialize application's main window
    void InitMainWindow();

// Define function to initialize an instance of this application
    void InitInstance();
};
//--------------------------------------------------------------
//    S p u z z l e A p p : : I n i t M a i n W i n d o w

void SpuzzleApp::InitMainWindow()
{
    MainWindow = new PuzzleFrame(NULL, "SPUZZLE", "MainMenu");
}
//--------------------------------------------------------------
//    S p u z z l e A p p : : I n i t I n s t a n c e

void SpuzzleApp::InitInstance()
{
   TApplication::InitInstance();
   HAccTable = LoadAccelerators(hInstance, "MainAccelTable");
}
//--------------------------------------------------------------
//    W i n M a i n
//
//  Create an instance of the application and "run" it.
```

continues

Listing 7.1. continued

```
int PASCAL WinMain(HINSTANCE instance, HINSTANCE prev_instance,
                   LPSTR cmdline, int show)
{
    SpuzzleApp Spuzzle("SPUZZLE", instance,
                       prev_instance, cmdline, show);

    Spuzzle.nCmdShow = SW_SHOWMAXIMIZED;
    Spuzzle.Run();

    return Spuzzle.Status;
}
```

PuzzleFrame Class

The `PuzzleFrame` class is responsible for creating and initializing the child windows that constitute the user interface of the SPUZZLE game. As you can see from the header file `pzlframe.h` (Listing 7.2), The `PuzzleFrame` keeps track of a large set of static variables representing global data for the application. `PuzzleFrame` stores pointers to all its child windows so that it can control them.

Listing 7.2. `pzlframe.h`—Declaration of the `PuzzleFrame` class.

```
//-----------------------------------------------------------
// File: pzlframe.h
//
// Declares the PuzzleFrame class that represents the main
// window of the SPUZZLE application.
//-----------------------------------------------------------
#if !defined(__PZLFRAME_H)
#define __PZLFRAME_H

#include <owl.h>
#include "pzlwin.h"
#include "toolwin.h"
#include "ltrwin.h"
#include "statwin.h"
#include "spzlres.h"
#include "pzlinfo.h"
#include "sounds.h"
```

SPUZZLE—A Spelling Puzzle

Chapter 7

```cpp
#define DISPLAY_TIMER    1
#define DISP_MILLISECONDS 60

const short maxpzls = 10;
const short bmpheight = 40;
const short toolwidth = 64;

class PuzzleFrame: public TWindow
{
public:
    PuzzleFrame(PTWindowsObject parent, LPSTR title,
                LPSTR menu): TWindow(parent, title),
                puzzle(NULL), letters(NULL),
                status(NULL), tools(NULL)
    {
        AssignMenu(menu);
    }

    ~PuzzleFrame();

    PuzzleWindow* puzzle_window() { return puzzle;}
    LetterWindow* letter_window() { return letters;}
    StatusWindow* status_window() { return status;}
    ToolWindow* tool_window() { return tools;}

    short pzl_wmax() { return wpzl;}
    short pzl_hmax() { return hpzl;}
    short ltr_wmax() { return wltr;}
    short ltr_hmax() { return hltr;}
    short sts_wmax() { return wsts;}
    short sts_hmax() { return hsts;}

    int load_puzzles(const char* filename);
    void load_music();

    void hi_scores(const char* filename);

    void GetWindowClass(WNDCLASS _FAR &wc);
    void WMCreate(RTMessage msg) = [WM_FIRST + WM_CREATE];
    void WMSize(RTMessage msg) = [WM_FIRST + WM_SIZE];
    void WMTimer(RTMessage msg) = [WM_FIRST + WM_TIMER];
    void About(RTMessage msg) = [CM_FIRST + IDM_ABOUT];
    void Help(RTMessage msg) = [CM_FIRST + IDM_HELP]
    {
        WinHelp(HWindow, "SPZLHLP.HLP", HELP_INDEX, 0);
    }
```

continues

Listing 7.2. continued

```
    static PuzzleInfo  *puzzle_data;
    static PuzzleInfo  *cur_puzzle;
    static PuzzlePiece *pzlpcs;
    static PuzzlePick  pzl_todo[maxpzls];
    static short       numpuzzles;
    static short       numpzl_todo;
    static short       numpzl_done;
    static short       score;
    static short       done_curpzl;
    static short       ticks_curpzl;
    static short       start_curpzl;
    static short       sound_on;
    static short       sound_playing;
    static short       init_in_progress;

    static Music       opening_music;
    static Music       puzzle_done_music;
    static Music       puzzle_start_music;
    static Music       closing_music;
    static Music       tick_music;
    static Music       tock_music;

    static PuzzleInfo* next_puzzle();
    static void pick_puzzles();
    static short playmusic(Music& m, short wait_till_done);
private:
    PuzzleWindow   *puzzle;
    LetterWindow   *letters;
    StatusWindow   *status;
    ToolWindow     *tools;
    unsigned short wmax, hmax; // PuzzleFrame's dimensions
    unsigned short wpzl, hpzl; // Puzzle window's dimensions
    unsigned short wltr, hltr; // Letter window's dimensions
    unsigned short wsts, hsts; // Status window's dimensions
    short          timer_id;
};

#endif
```

Creating and Initializing Child Windows

Listing 7.3 shows the file pzlframe.cpp, which implements the member functions and initializes a host of static variables of the PuzzleFrame class. One of

SPUZZLE—A Spelling Puzzle

the first tasks of the `PuzzleFrame` class is to create the child windows and position them properly. The child windows are created in `WMCreate`, which handles the `WM_CREATE` message that Windows sends when creating the `PuzzleFrame` window.

The sizes and positions of the child windows cannot be determined until the size of `PuzzleFrame` is known. Because Windows sends a `WM_SIZE` message when the `PuzzleFrame` window is moved or resized, I handle the resizing and positioning of the child windows in the `WMSize` function. Note that in `spuzzle.cpp` (Listing 7.1), the SPUZZLE application is started with the `nCmdShow` parameter set to `SW_SHOWMAXIMIZED`, which means SPUZZLE's main window appears full-screen. This ensures that all available screen area is used by SPUZZLE.

Managing the Puzzles

`PuzzleFrame`'s `load_puzzles` function opens the file `SPUZZLE.CFG` and initializes an array of `PuzzleInfo` structures (`puzzle_data`) with information about all available puzzles. The `pick_puzzles` function selects a subset of the puzzles and stores them in the static array `pzl_todo`.

A static function, `next_puzzle`, returns a pointer to the next puzzle to be done. Here are a few other static member variables that manage information about the puzzles:

- `static short numpuzzles;` is the total number of available puzzles.
- `static short numpzl_done;` is the total number of puzzles that have been done.
- `static short numpzl_todo;` is the total number of puzzles to be done.
- `static PuzzleInfo *cur_puzzle;` is a pointer to the current puzzle.
- `static PuzzlePiece *pzlpcs;` is an array of `PuzzlePiece` structures with information about the current puzzle pieces.
- `static short done_curpzl;` is nonzero if the current puzzle is done.
- `static short ticks_curpzl;` is the number of clock ticks remaining (remember, the clock starts counting down from 99).
- `static short start_curpzl;` is nonzero if the current puzzle should be started (set when the player presses on the GO button).

Playing Music

`PuzzleFrame` provides the static function `playmusic` for playing musical tunes. The `load_music` function loads the music into a number of static `Music` structures. A static variable named `sound_on` indicates whether music should be played or not. As the name indicates, when `sound_on` is nonzero, SPUZZLE plays music.

Animating the Child Windows

In SPUZZLE, I animate the images in all the windows by using the strategy demonstrated in Chapter 5. A timer is set up and the images are moved in the `WMTimer` function, which handles the `WM_TIMER` events. `PuzzleFrame`'s `WMTimer` function animates the display by calling the `update` function of the child windows, `PuzzleWindow`, `LetterWindow`, and `StatusWindow`.

Listing 7.3. `pzlframe.cpp`— Implementation of the `PuzzleFrame` class.

```
//-------------------------------------------------------------
// File: pzlframe.cpp
//
// Implementation of the PuzzleFrame class--the main window of
// the SPUZZLE game.
//-------------------------------------------------------------
#include <string.h>
#include <fstream.h>
#include <strng.h>
#include "pzlframe.h"
#include "pzlinfo.h"
#include "hscdial.h"

// Information about the available spelling puzzles
// This is initialized in the load_puzzles function
PuzzleInfo* PuzzleFrame::puzzle_data = NULL;
PuzzleInfo* PuzzleFrame::cur_puzzle = NULL;
PuzzlePiece* PuzzleFrame::pzlpcs = NULL;

PuzzlePick PuzzleFrame::pzl_todo[maxpzls] = { PuzzlePick(0,0) };

short PuzzleFrame::numpuzzles = 0;
short PuzzleFrame::numpzl_todo = 0;
```

SPUZZLE—A Spelling Puzzle

Chapter 7

```cpp
    short PuzzleFrame::numpzl_done = 0;
    short PuzzleFrame::score = 0;
    short PuzzleFrame::done_curpzl = 0;
    short PuzzleFrame::start_curpzl = 0;
    short PuzzleFrame::ticks_curpzl = 0;

    Music PuzzleFrame::opening_music;
    Music PuzzleFrame::puzzle_done_music;
    Music PuzzleFrame::puzzle_start_music;
    Music PuzzleFrame::closing_music;
    Music PuzzleFrame::tick_music;
    Music PuzzleFrame::tock_music;

    short PuzzleFrame::sound_on = 1;
    short PuzzleFrame::sound_playing = 0;
    short PuzzleFrame::init_in_progress = 0;

static short first_time = 1;
//-------------------------------------------------------------
// P u z z l e F r a m e : : W M C r e a t e
// Initializes everything for the SPUZZLE game

void PuzzleFrame:: WMCreate(RTMessage)
{
// Load music
    load_music();

// Start playing the opening tune...
    playmusic(opening_music, 0);

// Initialize random number generator with a random seed
    randomize();

// Read the list of puzzles from the SPUZZLE.CFG file
    load_puzzles("SPUZZLE.CFG");
    pick_puzzles();
    cur_puzzle = next_puzzle();

// Create the other windows
    puzzle = new PuzzleWindow(this, this);
    GetApplication()->MakeWindow(puzzle);

    letters = new LetterWindow(this, this);
    GetApplication()->MakeWindow(letters);

    status = new StatusWindow(this, this);
    GetApplication()->MakeWindow(status);
```

continues

Listing 7.3. continued

```
    tools = new ToolWindow(this, this);
    GetApplication()->MakeWindow(tools);
}
//--------------------------------------------------------------
// P u z z l e F r a m e : : l o a d _ p u z z l e s
// Initialize an array of PuzzleInfo by reading from a file

int PuzzleFrame::load_puzzles(const char* filename)
{
// Open file for reading
    ifstream ifs(filename, ios::in);
    if(!ifs)
    {
// Error reading file. Return 0.
        return 0;
    }

// Read and interpret the contents of the file
    char line[81];

// First line should have the string SPUZZLE.CFG
    ifs.getline(line, sizeof(line));
    strupr(line);
    if(strnicmp(line, "SPUZZLE.CFG",
                strlen("SPUZZLE.CFG")) != 0) return 0;

// Second line has a version number--just in case the
// contents have to change in the future
    ifs.getline(line, sizeof(line));
    short version = atoi(line);
    if(version != 1) return 0;

// Third line has the number of puzzles in this file.
    ifs.getline(line, sizeof(line));
    numpuzzles= atoi(line);

// Allocate an array of PuzzleInfo structures
    PuzzleInfo *new_puzzles = new PuzzleInfo[numpuzzles];
    if(new_puzzles == NULL) return 0;

// At this point we have an array of PuzzleInfo structures
// allocated. If there is an existing PuzzleInfo array,
// delete it before loading new values
    if(puzzle_data != NULL) delete puzzle_data;
    puzzle_data = new_puzzles;
```

Chapter 7

SPUZZLE—A Spelling Puzzle

```cpp
// From this point on each line in the file has the following
// form:
//          word       image_file_name
// example:
//          CAT cat.pcx
//          HOUSE house.bmp
// and so on.
    short i;
    char *token;
    for(i = 0; i < numpuzzles; i++)
    {
        ifs.getline(line, sizeof(line));
// Parse the line...first token
        token = strtok(line, " ");
        strupr(token);
        puzzle_data[i].numchars = strlen(token);
        puzzle_data[i].word = new char[puzzle_data[i].numchars+1];
        strcpy(puzzle_data[i].word, token);
// Second token
        token = strtok(NULL, " ");
        size_t nc = strlen(token);
        puzzle_data[i].imgfname = new char[nc+1];
        strcpy(puzzle_data[i].imgfname, token);
    }
    return 1;
}
//--------------------------------------------------------------
// PuzzleFrame:: ~ P u z z l e F r a m e
// Destructor for a PuzzleFrame

PuzzleFrame::~PuzzleFrame()
{
// Delete the puzzle, letters, and status windows
    if(puzzle != NULL) delete puzzle;
    if(letters != NULL) delete letters;
    if(status != NULL) delete status;
    if(tools != NULL) delete tools;
    if(puzzle_data != NULL) delete puzzle_data;

// Kill the timer
    if(timer_id) KillTimer(HWindow, timer_id);

// Clean up sound driver...
    StopSound();
    CloseSound();
}
//--------------------------------------------------------------
// PuzzleFrame:: G e t W i n d o w C l a s s
```

continues

Listing 7.3. continued

```
//  Set up icon for the Application

void PuzzleFrame::GetWindowClass(WNDCLASS _FAR &wc)
{
// First call the GetWindowClass function of the base class
    TWindow::GetWindowClass(wc);

// Set up icon for this application
    wc.hIcon = LoadIcon(wc.hInstance, "SPUZZLE_ICON");
}
//--------------------------------------------------------------
// PuzzleFrame:: A b o u t
// Display the "About..." box

void PuzzleFrame::About(RTMessage)
{
    TDialog *p_about = new TDialog(this, "ABOUTSPUZZLE");
    PTApplication app = GetApplication();
    app->ExecDialog(p_about);
}
//--------------------------------------------------------------
// PuzzleFrame:: W M S i z e
// Resize/Reposition all child windows when frame changes size

void PuzzleFrame::WMSize(RTMessage)
{
// Get the size of this window
    RECT r;
    GetClientRect(HWindow, &r);

    unsigned short w = r.right - r.left + 1;
    unsigned short h = r.bottom - r.top + 1;

// Resize and reposition child windows
// The letters window is across the top
    if(letters != NULL)
    {
        MoveWindow(letters->HWindow, 0, 0, w, bmpheight, TRUE);
        letters->width(w);
        letters->height(bmpheight);
    }

// The status window is at the bottom
    if(status != NULL)
    {
        MoveWindow(status->HWindow, 0, h - bmpheight, w,
                    bmpheight, TRUE);
```

SPUZZLE—A Spelling Puzzle

```
            status->width(w);
            status->height(bmpheight);
        }
// The tools window is at the left
        short htool = h - 2*bmpheight;
        if(tools != NULL)
        {
            MoveWindow(tools->HWindow, 0, bmpheight, toolwidth,
                    htool, TRUE);
        }

// Puzzle window is the large one in the middle to the right
        if(puzzle != NULL)
        {
            MoveWindow(puzzle->HWindow, toolwidth, bmpheight,
                    w - toolwidth, htool, TRUE);
            puzzle->width(w-toolwidth);
            puzzle->height(htool);
        }

        if(first_time)
        {
            first_time = 0;

// Save the maximum dimensions of some windows...
            wmax = w;
            hmax = h;
            wpzl = w-toolwidth;
            hpzl = htool;
            wltr = w;
            hltr = bmpheight;
            wsts = w;
            hsts = bmpheight;

// Initialize the puzzle, letters, and the status windows
            if(numpuzzles > 0 && puzzle != NULL) puzzle->init();
            if(numpuzzles > 0 && letters != NULL) letters->init();
            status->init();

// Set up a timer to update the display and manage the game
            timer_id = SetTimer(HWindow, DISPLAY_TIMER,
                    DISP_MILLISECONDS, NULL);
            if(!timer_id)
                MessageBox(HWindow, "Failed to start Timer!",
                        "SPUZZLE: PuzzleFrame",
                        MB_ICONEXCLAMATION | MB_OK);
        }
```

continues

225

Listing 7.3. continued

```cpp
}
//------------------------------------------------------------
// PuzzleFrame:: p i c k _ p u z z l e s
// Pick a set of new puzzles to do

void PuzzleFrame::pick_puzzles()
{
// How many puzzles to do...
    numpzl_todo = maxpzls;
    if(numpuzzles <= maxpzls) numpzl_todo = numpuzzles;

// Generate randomized indexes from 0 to (numpzl_todo - 1)
    short i, j, index;
    for(i = 0; i < numpzl_todo; i++)
    {
        while(1)
        {
            index = random(numpuzzles);
// Make sure index is not already in pzl_todo array
            for(j = 0; j < i; j++)
                if(pzl_todo[j].index == index) break;
            if(j == i) break;
        }
        pzl_todo[i].index = index;
        pzl_todo[i].done = 0;
    }
}
//------------------------------------------------------------
// PuzzleFrame:: n e x t _ p u z z l e
// Return next puzzle to do

PuzzleInfo* PuzzleFrame::next_puzzle()
{
    if(cur_puzzle == NULL)
        return &puzzle_data[pzl_todo[0].index];

    if(numpzl_done < numpzl_todo)
    {
// Return the next puzzle that's not yet done
        short i, j;
// First find the index of the current puzzle
        for(i = 0; i < numpzl_done+numpzl_todo; i++)
        {
            if(cur_puzzle == &puzzle_data[pzl_todo[i].index])
            {
// Set current puzzle's done flag, if puzzle's done
                if(done_curpzl)
```

Chapter 7

SPUZZLE—A Spelling Puzzle

```
                {
                    pzl_todo[i].done = 1;
                    done_curpzl = 0;
                }
                break;
            }
        }
// Find next puzzle that's not done yet
        for(j = i+1; j < numpzl_done+numpzl_todo; j++)
        {
            if(!pzl_todo[j].done)
                return &puzzle_data[pzl_todo[j].index];
        }
    }
// Pick some more puzzles...
    pick_puzzles();
    numpzl_done = 0;
    return next_puzzle();
}
//----------------------------------------------------------
// PuzzleFrame::  W M T i m e r
// Handle WM_TIMER events

void PuzzleFrame::WMTimer(RTMessage msg)
{
    switch(msg.WParam)
    {
        case DISPLAY_TIMER:
// Call the update function of the two windows...
// (puzzles and letters)
            if(!init_in_progress)
            {
                if(puzzle != NULL) puzzle->update();
                if(letters != NULL) letters->update();
            }
            if(status != NULL) status->update();

// Check if it's time to turn off sound...
            if(sound_playing && CountVoiceNotes(1) < 1)
            {
                StopSound();
                CloseSound();
                sound_playing = 0;
            }

            break;

        default:
```

continues

Listing 7.3. continued

```
            break;
    }
}
//---------------------------------------------------------------
// PuzzleFrame:: p l a y m u s i c
// Play music

short PuzzleFrame::playmusic(Music& m, short wait_till_done)
{
    if((m.notes == NULL) || (m.numnotes == 0)) return 0;

// Do nothing if something is already playing...
    if(!wait_till_done &&
        sound_playing) return wait_till_done;

// Turn off anything that might be playing now...
    StopSound();
    CloseSound();

// Check if sound is allowed, then play.
    if(PuzzleFrame::sound_on && OpenSound() > 0)
    {
        SetVoiceQueueSize(1, 6*m.numnotes);
        SetVoiceAccent(1, m.tempo, m.volume,
                        m.mode, m.pitch);
        short i;
        for(i = 0; i < m.numnotes; i++)
            SetVoiceNote(1, m.notes[i].number,
                            m.notes[i].duration,
                            m.notes[i].dots);
        StartSound();
        sound_playing = 1;

// Wait till music is done (if wait_till_done is TRUE)
        if(wait_till_done)
        {
            while(CountVoiceNotes(1) > 0);
            StopSound();
            CloseSound();
        }
    }
    return wait_till_done;
}
//---------------------------------------------------------------
// PuzzleFrame:: l o a d _ m u s i c
// Load some pieces of music used in the game
```

SPUZZLE—A Spelling Puzzle

```
void PuzzleFrame::load_music()
{
// Now set up each piece of music
    opening_music.read("open.spm");
    puzzle_done_music.read("pzldone.spm");
    puzzle_start_music.read("pzlstrt.spm");
    closing_music.read("close.spm");
    tick_music.read("tick.spm");
    tock_music.read("tock.spm");
}
//-------------------------------------------------------------
// PuzzleFrame::  h i _ s c o r e s
// Display the high scores and enter current score into the
// table (only if the current score is greater than the
// 20 highest scores in the "high score" file).

void PuzzleFrame::hi_scores(const char *filename)
{
// Load the current hi score table from the file
// Open file for reading
    ifstream ifs(filename, ios::in);
    if(!ifs)
    {
// Create a file with a single entry
        ofstream ofs(filename, ios::out);
        if(!ofs) return;
        ofs << "SPUZZLE.HISCORES" << endl;
        ofs << 1 << endl;
        ofs << 1 << endl;
        ofs << "Naba Barkakati" << endl;
        ofs << 999 << endl;
        ofs << "Hope you like SPUZZLE!" << endl;
        ofs.close();
// Reopen it for reading
        ifs.open(filename, ios::in);
        if(!ifs) return;
    }

// Read and interpret the contents of the file
    char line[81];

// First line should have the string SPUZZLE.HISCORES
    ifs.getline(line, sizeof(line));
    strupr(line);
    if(strnicmp(line, "SPUZZLE.HISCORES",
            strlen("SPUZZLE.HISCORES")) != 0) return;
```

continues

Listing 7.3. continued

```
// Second line has a version number--just in case the
// contents have to change in the future
    ifs.getline(line, sizeof(line));
    short version = atoi(line);
    if(version != 1) return;

// Third line has the number of entries in the file
    ifs.getline(line, sizeof(line));
    short numentries = atoi(line);

// Read all the entries into a SortedArray
    SortedArray* hiscores = new SortedArray(32, 0, 8);
    if(hiscores == NULL) return;
    short i;

    for(i = 0; i < numentries; i++)
    {
        HiScore *s = new HiScore;
        if(s == NULL)
        {
            delete hiscores;
            return;
        }
        if(ifs.eof())
        {
            numentries = i;
        }
        ifs.getline(line, sizeof(line));
        s->name = new char[strlen(line) +1];
        strcpy(s->name, line);

        ifs.getline(line, sizeof(line));
        s->score = atoi(line);

    ifs.getline(line, sizeof(line));
        s->quote = new char[strlen(line) +1];
        strcpy(s->quote, line);

// Add the score to the array
        hiscores->add(*s);
    }

// Check if current score is greater than the top 30 scores
    short lastindex = 29;
    if(lastindex > numentries) lastindex = numentries - 1;
    HiScore& last_hi = (HiScore&)(*hiscores)[lastindex];
    if(((lastindex == numentries - 1) && (score > 0)) ||
        (score > last_hi.score))
    {
```

```
// Display the dialog box HISCORES
        HiscoreDialog *p_hiscores = new HiscoreDialog(this,
                        "HISCORES", hiscores, lastindex+1);
        PTApplication app = GetApplication();
        short r = app->ExecDialog(p_hiscores);

        if(r == IDOK)
        {
            HiScore *s = p_hiscores->hi_score();
            s->score = score;
// Add this score to the hiscores array
            hiscores->add(*s);

// Now save the top 30 scores back in the file
            ifs.close();
// Open file for reading
            ofstream ofs(filename, ios::out);
            if(!ofs)
            {
// Error opening file. Return.
                return;
            }
            ofs << "SPUZZLE.HISCORES" << endl;
            ofs << 1 << endl;
            short n = hiscores->getItemsInContainer();
            if(n > 30) n = 30;
            ofs << n << endl;
            for(i = 0; i < n; i++)
            {
                HiScore& hi = (HiScore&)(*hiscores)[i];
                ofs << hi;
            }
        }
    }
// Delete the SortedArray hiscores
    delete hiscores;
}
```

Displaying the High Scores Dialog

The PuzzleFrame class includes the hi_scores function for displaying the high scores dialog box. As you can see from Listing 7.3, hi_scores gets the top 30 scores from a file and displays them in a list box inside the high scores dialog

box, which is an instance of the `HiscoreDialog` class (described later). The `hi_scores` function is called from the `ToolWindow` class when the player clicks on the EXIT button.

PuzzleWindow Class

The `PuzzleWindow` class represents the child window where the puzzle's picture appears and where the player manipulates the puzzle pieces to play the game. Listing 7.4 shows the header file `pzlwin.h` that declares the `PuzzleWindow` class and defines a number of inline functions.

The `PuzzleWindow` class uses an instance of the `SpriteAnimation` class to animate the puzzle pieces, and it provides member functions such as `init`, `update`, `shuffle`, and `reposition` to initialize and manipulate the animation of the puzzle pieces.

Listing 7.4. `pzlwin.h`—Declaration of the `PuzzleWindow` class.

```
//-------------------------------------------------------------
// File: pzlwin.h
//
// Declares the PuzzleWindow class that represents the window
// where the player puts together the puzzle in the SPUZZLE game.
//-------------------------------------------------------------
#if !defined(__PZLWIN_H)
#define __PZLWIN_H

#include <owl.h>
#include "spranim.h"
#include "pzlinfo.h"

const short xyerror = 8; // Tolerate this many pixels of error
                         // in aligning puzzle pieces

class PuzzleFrame;

class PuzzleWindow: public TWindow
{
public:
    PuzzleWindow(PTWindowsObject parent, PuzzleFrame *pzlf) :
        TWindow(parent, NULL), pf(pzlf),
        top(0), left(0), mouse_captured(0), w(1), h(1),
```

SPUZZLE—A Spelling Puzzle

```
        anim(NULL), fullpzl(NULL), spr_current(NULL),
        sound_playing(0)
        {
            Attr.Style = WS_CHILD | WS_BORDER | WS_VISIBLE |
                         WS_CLIPSIBLINGS;
        }

        ~PuzzleWindow();

        void update();       // Display puzzle pieces
        void init();         // Initialize puzzle
        void shuffle();      // Shuffle the puzzle pieces
        short check_puzzle();// Check if puzzle is complete
        void reposition();   // Reposition puzzle pieces and letters

        void Paint(HDC hdc, PAINTSTRUCT& ps);
        void WMSize(RTMessage msg) = [WM_FIRST + WM_SIZE];
        void WMLButtonDown(RTMessage msg) = [WM_FIRST + WM_LBUTTONDOWN];
        void WMLButtonUp(RTMessage msg) = [WM_FIRST + WM_LBUTTONUP];
        void WMMouseMove(RTMessage msg) = [WM_FIRST + WM_MOUSEMOVE];

        unsigned short width() { return w;}
        unsigned short height() { return h;}
        void width(unsigned short _w) { w = _w;}
        void height(unsigned short _h) { h = _h;}
private:
        PuzzleFrame     *pf;
        short           top, left;
        unsigned short  w, h; // Size of client area
        SpriteAnimation *anim;
        Sprite          *fullpzl;
        short           numpieces;
        short           iw, ih;
        short           wslice;
        short           hslice;
        short           mouse_captured;
        Sprite          *spr_current;
        short           xoff;
        short           yoff;
        short           xlast;
        short           ylast;
        short           sound_playing;
};

#endif
```

Initializing the Current Puzzle

Listing 7.5 shows the file pzlwin.cpp, which implements the member functions of the PuzzleWindow class. The main responsibility of PuzzleWindow is to prepare the puzzle and let the player manipulate the puzzle pieces. The init member function initializes the currently selected puzzle, which is indicated by the PuzzleFrame::cur_pzl pointer. Here are the major initialization steps that init performs:

1. If this is the first call to init (indicated by a nonzero firsttime variable), load a number of strings from the STRINGTABLE resource. These strings are the status messages that appear in the StatusWindow.
2. Delete any existing puzzle.
3. Load the current puzzle's picture into a Sprite object.
4. Create the SpriteAnimation object that will manage the puzzle pieces.
5. Slice up the puzzle's picture into as many pieces as there are letters in the corresponding word, create a Sprite for each piece, and add these Sprites to the SpriteAnimation.

Once the SpriteAnimation is set up with the Sprite objects corresponding to the puzzle pieces, the SpriteAnimation will display the puzzle pieces at the next WM_TIMER event.

Manipulating the Puzzle Pieces

The player moves a puzzle piece by placing the mouse cursor on the piece, pressing down the left mouse button, and moving the mouse. As the player drags the mouse around, the puzzle piece should move also. To support this type of direct manipulation, I defined the member functions WMLButtonDown, WMMouseMove, and WMLButtonUp, which handle the Windows messages WM_LBUTTONDOWN, WM_LBUTTONUP, and WM_MOUSEMOVE, respectively. You can see the details of these functions in Listing 7.5, but the basic idea is to change the position of the sprite corresponding to the selected puzzle piece as the mouse moves; the SpriteAnimation object anim takes care of updating the display. Note that the functions WMMouseMove and WMLButtonUp also must move the sprite of the letter corresponding to the selected puzzle piece.

SPUZZLE—A Spelling Puzzle

Listing 7.5. `pzlwin.cpp`— Implementation of the `PuzzleWindow` class.

```cpp
//-------------------------------------------------------------
// File: pzlwin.cpp
//
// Implementation of the PuzzleWindow class. This is the window
// where the player constructs the puzzle in the SPUZZLE game.
//-------------------------------------------------------------
#include <stdlib.h>
#include "pzlframe.h"
#include "sounds.h"

static char press_go[41];
static short npgo;
static char keep_going[41];
static short nkg;
static char ucandoit[41];
static short nucan;
static char wow[41];
static short nwow;
static char good_job[41];
static ngj;
static char times_up[41];
static short ntu;
static char press_next[41];
static short npn;

static char *curmsg;
static short curlen;

static short firsttime = 1;
static short done_since = 0;
//-------------------------------------------------------------
// ~ P u z z l e W i n d o w
//   Destructor for the puzzle window.

PuzzleWindow::~PuzzleWindow()
{
    if(anim != NULL) delete anim;
    if(fullpzl != NULL) delete fullpzl;
    if(PuzzleFrame::pzlpcs != NULL) delete PuzzleFrame::pzlpcs;
}
//-------------------------------------------------------------
// PuzzleWindow::  P a i n t
//   Draw everything in the window
```

continues

235

Listing 7.5. continued

```
void PuzzleWindow::Paint(HDC hdc, PAINTSTRUCT&)
{
    if(anim != NULL)
    {
        anim->set_refresh(TRUE);
        anim->animate(hdc, top, left);
    }
}
//--------------------------------------------------------------
// PuzzleWindow:: u p d a t e
// Animate the sprites in the puzzle window

void PuzzleWindow::update()
{
    if(anim != NULL)
    {
        HDC hdc = GetDC(HWindow);
        anim->animate(hdc, top, left);
        ReleaseDC(HWindow, hdc);
    }

    if(done_since++ < 600) return;

    if(PuzzleFrame::start_curpzl)
    {
        done_since = 0;
        if(curmsg == press_go)
        {
            curmsg = keep_going;
            curlen = nkg;
            pf->status_window()->set_text(curmsg, curlen);
        }
        else
        {
            if(curmsg == keep_going &&
               PuzzleFrame::ticks_curpzl < 75)
            {
                curmsg = ucandoit;
                curlen = nucan;
                pf->status_window()->set_text(curmsg, curlen);
            }
        }
        if(PuzzleFrame::ticks_curpzl < 1)
        {
            curmsg = times_up;
            curlen = ntu;
```

SPUZZLE—A Spelling Puzzle

```
                pf->status_window()->set_text(curmsg, curlen);
            }
        }
        else
        {
            if(PuzzleFrame::done_curpzl && curmsg != press_next)
            {
                curmsg = press_next;
                curlen = npn;
                pf->status_window()->set_text(curmsg, curlen);
            }
        }
    }
    //----------------------------------------------------------------
    // PuzzleWindow:: i n i t
    // Clean up after the last puzzle and initialize the next puzzle

    void PuzzleWindow::init()
    {
        if(firsttime)
        {
            firsttime = 0;
    // Load message strings from the STRINGTABLE resource
            HINSTANCE hinst = GetApplication()->hInstance;

            LoadString(hinst, IDS_PRESSGO, press_go,
                        sizeof(press_go));
            npgo = strlen(press_go);

            LoadString(hinst, IDS_KEEPGOING, keep_going,
                        sizeof(keep_going));
            nkg = strlen(keep_going);

            LoadString(hinst, IDS_UCANDOIT, ucandoit,
                        sizeof(ucandoit));
            nucan = strlen(ucandoit);

            LoadString(hinst, IDS_GOODJOB, good_job,
                        sizeof(good_job));
            ngj = strlen(good_job);

            LoadString(hinst, IDS_WOW, wow, sizeof(wow));
            nwow = strlen(wow);

            LoadString(hinst, IDS_PRESSNEXT, press_next,
                        sizeof(press_next));
            npn = strlen(press_next);
```

continues

Listing 7.5. continued

```
        LoadString(hinst, IDS_TIMESUP, times_up,
                sizeof(times_up));
        ntu = strlen(times_up);
    }

// Do nothing if the current puzzle is not valid
    PuzzleInfo* pzl = PuzzleFrame::cur_puzzle;
    if(pzl == NULL) return;

// Change the cursor to an hourglass
    SetCapture(HWindow);
    SetCursor(LoadCursor(NULL, IDC_WAIT));

// Clean up existing puzzle, if any
    if(anim != NULL) delete anim;

    if(PuzzleFrame::pzlpcs != NULL) delete PuzzleFrame::pzlpcs;

    if(fullpzl != NULL) delete fullpzl;

// Get a DC for this window
    HDC hdc = GetDC(HWindow);

// Build puzzle from specified image
    if(pzl != NULL)
    {
        Image *fimg = NULL;

        while(fimg == NULL)
        {
            numpieces = pzl->numchars;
            fullpzl = new Sprite(hdc, pzl->imgfname, NULL);
            fimg = fullpzl->sprite_image();

            if(fimg == NULL)
            {
// Get another puzzle
                PuzzleFrame::cur_puzzle = pf->next_puzzle();
                pzl = PuzzleFrame::cur_puzzle;
                if(pzl == NULL) return;
            }
        }

        iw = fimg->width();
        ih = fimg->height();
        wslice = iw / pzl->numchars;
        hslice = ih;
```

Chapter 7

SPUZZLE—A Spelling Puzzle

```
// Construct a SpriteAnimation with background for the puzzle
        anim = new SpriteAnimation(hdc, pf->pzl_wmax(),
                            pf->pzl_hmax(), "spuzzle.bmp");
        if(anim == NULL) return;

// Draw a grid in which the puzzle is to be constructed

        if(anim->bg_bitmap() != 0)
        {
            anim->bg_rect(0, 0, iw, ih);
            short i;
            for(i = 1; i < numpieces; i++)
            anim->bg_line(i*wslice, 0, i*wslice, ih);
        }

        Image *img;
        short i, x = 0, y = 0;
// Create the array of sprites
        PuzzleFrame::pzlpcs = new PuzzlePiece[numpieces];
        for(i = 0; i < pzl->numchars-1; i++)
        {
            PuzzleFrame::pzlpcs[i].x = x;
            PuzzleFrame::pzlpcs[i].y = y;
            PuzzleFrame::pzlpcs[i].c = pzl->word[i];
            img = new Image(hdc, fimg, x, y, wslice, ih);
            PuzzleFrame::pzlpcs[i].sprite = new
                                Sprite(img, NULL, 1);

// Store index of sprite as the Sprite's id. We need this to
// relate the puzzle pieces to images of the letters
            PuzzleFrame::pzlpcs[i].sprite->id(i);

            PuzzleFrame::pzlpcs[i].sprite->newpos(x, y);
// Add sprite to animation
            anim->add(PuzzleFrame::pzlpcs[i].sprite);
            x += wslice;
        }
// Add the last slice
        img = new Image(hdc, fimg, x, y,
                        iw-(pzl->numchars-1)*wslice, ih);
        PuzzleFrame::pzlpcs[i].sprite = new
                            Sprite(img, NULL, 1);
        PuzzleFrame::pzlpcs[i].x = x;
        PuzzleFrame::pzlpcs[i].y = y;
        PuzzleFrame::pzlpcs[i].sprite->id(i);
        PuzzleFrame::pzlpcs[i].sprite->newpos(x, y);
        anim->add(PuzzleFrame::pzlpcs[i].sprite);
    }
```

continues

Listing 7.5. continued

```
// Set the text for the status window
    pf->status_window()->set_text(press_go, npgo);
    curmsg = press_go;
    curlen = npgo;

// Remember to release the DC
    ReleaseDC(HWindow, hdc);

// Reset cursor to arrow
    SetCursor(LoadCursor(NULL, IDC_ARROW));
    ReleaseCapture();
}
//----------------------------------------------------------------
// PuzzleWindow:: W M S i z e
// Save the location and size of the window

void PuzzleWindow::WMSize(RTMessage)
{
    RECT r;
    GetClientRect(HWindow, &r);
    w = r.left - r.right + 1;
    h = r.bottom - r.top + 1;
}
//----------------------------------------------------------------
void PuzzleWindow::WMLButtonDown(RTMessage msg)
{
    if(!PuzzleFrame::start_curpzl) return;

    short x = msg.LP.Lo;
    short y = msg.LP.Hi;
    spr_current = anim->sprite_at(x, y);
    if(spr_current != NULL)
    {
        spr_current->active();
        xlast = x;
        ylast = y;
        SetCapture(HWindow);
        mouse_captured = 1;
    }
}
//----------------------------------------------------------------
void PuzzleWindow::WMMouseMove(RTMessage msg)
{
    if(!mouse_captured) return;

    short x = msg.LP.Lo;
    short y = msg.LP.Hi;
```

SPUZZLE—A Spelling Puzzle

Chapter 7

```cpp
// Don't let the image move out of the window...
    short xs = spr_current->xpos();
    short ys = spr_current->ypos();
    short xdel = x - xlast;
    short ydel = y - ylast;
    if(xs + xdel <= 0) xdel = 0;
    if(xs + xdel >= w-wslice) xdel = 0;
    if(ys + ydel <= 0) ydel = 0;
    if(ys + ydel >= h-hslice) ydel = 0;

// Move sprite
    spr_current->move(xdel, ydel);

    xlast = xlast + xdel;
    ylast = ylast + ydel;

// Move the letters also...
    PuzzleFrame::pzlpcs[spr_current->id()].ltr_sprite->
                                        move(xdel, 0);
}
//-------------------------------------------------------------
void PuzzleWindow::WMLButtonUp(RTMessage msg)
{
    if(!mouse_captured) return;

    short x = msg.LP.Lo;
    short y = msg.LP.Hi;

// Don't let the image move out of the window...
    short xs = spr_current->xpos();
    short ys = spr_current->ypos();

    short xdel = x - xlast;
    short ydel = y - ylast;

    if((xs + xdel >= 0) && (xs + xdel <= w-wslice) &&
       (ys + ydel >= 0) && (ys + ydel <= h-hslice))
    {
// Move sprite representing puzzle piece
        spr_current->move(xdel, ydel);
        xlast = x;
        ylast = y;

// Move corresponding letter
        PuzzleFrame::pzlpcs[spr_current->id()].ltr_sprite->
                                        move(xdel, 0);
    }
```

continues

Listing 7.5. continued

```cpp
// Check if puzzle is complete...
    check_puzzle();

// De-select the Sprite...and release the mouse
    spr_current = NULL;
    ReleaseCapture();
    mouse_captured = 0;
}
//----------------------------------------------------------------
// PuzzleWindow:: s h u f f l e
// Shuffle the puzzle pieces...

void PuzzleWindow::shuffle()
{
    short xrange = width() - wslice;
    if(xrange < 0) xrange = wslice/2;

    short yrange = height() - hslice;
    if(yrange < 0) yrange = hslice/2;

// Now position the puzzle pieces randomly...and the letters too
    short i;
    for(i = 0; i < numpieces; i++)
    {
        short xrnd = random(xrange);
        short xmov = xrnd -
                PuzzleFrame::pzlpcs[i].sprite->xpos();

        short yrnd = random(yrange);
        short ymov = yrnd -
        PuzzleFrame::pzlpcs[i].sprite->ypos();

        PuzzleFrame::pzlpcs[i].sprite->move(xmov, ymov);

// Move the letters to random positions also
        xmov = xrnd -
                PuzzleFrame::pzlpcs[i].ltr_sprite->xpos();

        PuzzleFrame::pzlpcs[i].ltr_sprite->move(xmov, 0);
    }

// Make some sound...
    PuzzleFrame::playmusic(PuzzleFrame::puzzle_start_music, 0);
}
//----------------------------------------------------------------
// PuzzleWindow:: c h e c k _ p u z z l e
```

SPUZZLE—A Spelling Puzzle

Chapter 7

```cpp
// Set appropriate flags if puzzle is done. Return 1 if done,
// zero otherwise.

short PuzzleWindow::check_puzzle()
{
    short i;
    short xpli = PuzzleFrame::pzlpcs[0].sprite->xpos();
    short ypli = PuzzleFrame::pzlpcs[0].sprite->ypos();
    short xplip1, yplip1;

    for(i = 1; i < numpieces; i++)
    {
        xplip1 = PuzzleFrame::pzlpcs[i].sprite->xpos();
        if(abs(xpli + wslice - xplip1) > xyerror) return 0;

        yplip1 = PuzzleFrame::pzlpcs[i].sprite->ypos();
        if(abs(ypli - yplip1) > xyerror) return 0;

// Remember this piece's position
        xpli = xplip1;
        ypli = yplip1;
    }

// If here, all pieces met the positioning requirements
// Puzzle is done. Reposition puzzle pieces to show
// complete puzzle and the letters in correct order
    if(PuzzleFrame::ticks_curpzl > 70)
    {
        curmsg = wow;
        curlen = nwow;
    }
    else
    {
        if(PuzzleFrame::ticks_curpzl > 20)
         {
            curmsg = good_job;
            curlen = ngj;
        }
    }
    pf->status_window()->set_text(curmsg, curlen);

    reposition();
    PuzzleFrame::done_curpzl = 1;
    PuzzleFrame::start_curpzl = 0;
    PuzzleFrame::numpzl_done++;
    PuzzleFrame::numpzl_todo--;
```

continues

Listing 7.5. continued

```
// This puzzle's done...make some happy sounds
    PuzzleFrame::playmusic(PuzzleFrame::puzzle_done_music, 0);

// Update the score
    PuzzleFrame::score += PuzzleFrame::ticks_curpzl;
    PuzzleFrame::score += numpieces;
    pf->letter_window()->set_score(PuzzleFrame::score);

    return 1;
}
//----------------------------------------------------------------
// PuzzleWindow::  r e p o s i t i o n
// Repositions the puzzle pieces and letters

void PuzzleWindow::reposition()
{
    short i;

    for(i = 0; i < numpieces; i++)
    {
// First position the puzzle pieces
        short xs = PuzzleFrame::pzlpcs[i].sprite->xpos();
        short ys = PuzzleFrame::pzlpcs[i].sprite->ypos();
        PuzzleFrame::pzlpcs[i].sprite->move(
                PuzzleFrame::pzlpcs[i].x - xs,
                PuzzleFrame::pzlpcs[i].y - ys);

// Now the letter sprites
        xs = PuzzleFrame::pzlpcs[i].ltr_sprite->xpos();
        ys = PuzzleFrame::pzlpcs[i].ltr_sprite->ypos();
        PuzzleFrame::pzlpcs[i].ltr_sprite->move(
                PuzzleFrame::pzlpcs[i].lx - xs,
                PuzzleFrame::pzlpcs[i].ly - ys);
    }
}
```

Checking for Puzzle Completion

Whenever the player moves a puzzle piece and releases the mouse button, Windows sends a WM_LBUTTONUP message that invokes the WMLButtonUp function. The WMLButtonUp function calls the check_puzzle function to see if the puzzle is done. The puzzle is considered done if all the pieces are in sequence and

SPUZZLE—A Spelling Puzzle

neighboring pieces are no more than a specified number of pixels apart (determined by the constant xyerror in pzlwin.h). If the puzzle is considered done, check_puzzle sets the appropriate flags, places all the puzzle pieces in proper position, updates the score, and plays some music.

LetterWindow Class

Recall from the description of SPUZZLE that LetterWindow is the narrow strip of a window above the PuzzleWindow. The primary purpose of LetterWindow is to display the letters that make up the word corresponding to the current puzzle. Additionally, LetterWindow also displays the following items:

- A clock with an oscillating pendulum
- A text string that shows the time of day superimposed on the clock
- The two digits of the clock ticks to count down after the puzzle starts
- The current score

Listing 7.6 shows the header file ltrwin.h that declares the LetterWindow class. As you can see from the member variables, LetterWindow uses a SpriteAnimation object to manage the contents of the window.

Listing 7.6. ltrwin.h—Declaration of the LetterWindow class.

```
//--------------------------------------------------------------
// File: ltrwin.h
//
// Declares the LetterWindow class that represents the window
// where the letters appear in the SPUZZLE game.
//--------------------------------------------------------------
#if !defined(__LTRWIN_H)
#define __LTRWIN_H

#include <owl.h>
#include "spranim.h"
#include "pzlinfo.h"
#include "sounds.h"

const short lbmpwidth = 32;
const short lystart = 4;
```

continues

245

Listing 7.6. continued

```cpp
class PuzzleFrame;

class LetterWindow: public TWindow
{
public:
    LetterWindow(PTWindowsObject parent, PuzzleFrame* pzlf);

    ~LetterWindow();

    void update();
    void init();
    void set_score(short s);

    void Paint(HDC hdc, PAINTSTRUCT& ps);

    unsigned short width() { return w;}
    unsigned short height() { return h;}
    void width(unsigned short _w) { w = _w;}
    void height(unsigned short _h) { h = _h;}

private:
    PuzzleFrame     *pf;

// SpriteAnimation with letters of the word being spelled
    SpriteAnimation *anim;
    Sprite          *clock[2];
    Sprite          *time;          // time of day display
    Sprite          *ticklabel;     // Label for time display
    Sprite          *tickpos0[10];  // These sprites are used
    Sprite          *tickpos1[10];  // to display time
    short           pos0, pos1;
    short           curclock;

    Sprite          *score; // To display the current score

    short           top, left;
    unsigned short  w, h; // Size of client area

    short           sound_playing;
    Music           *ticktock[2];
};

#endif
```

Chapter 7

SPUZZLE—A Spelling Puzzle

Listing 7.7 shows the implementation of the `LetterWindow` class. As in `PuzzleWindow`, the `init` is the most important member function in `LetterWindow`. The `init` function creates the `SpriteAnimation` and adds to it a `Sprite` object for each letter of the current puzzle word. All the other sprites, the clocks, the digits for the clock ticks, and the score are also added to the `SpriteAnimation` (described in Chapter 5).

Listing 7.7. ltrwin.cpp—
Implementation of the `LetterWindow` class.

```cpp
//-------------------------------------------------------------
// File: ltrwin.cpp
//
// Implementation of the LetterWindow class.
//-------------------------------------------------------------
#include "pzlframe.h"
#include <time.h>
#include <stdio.h>

static char lfname[] = "?.BMP"; // Filename of letter images

const short tpsec = 1000 / DISP_MILLISECONDS;
const short htpsec = tpsec / 2;
static short tcount = 0;

void _FAR PASCAL _export disp_score(HDC hdc, short x, short y,
                                    LPVOID data);

void _FAR PASCAL _export disp_time(HDC hdc, short x, short y,
                                   LPVOID data);

struct TEXT_DATA
{
    LPSTR   text;
    size_t  numchars;
};

static TEXT_DATA dt;
static char msg[16] = "Score:     0";
//-------------------------------------------------------------
// LetterWindow:: L e t t e r W i n d o w

LetterWindow::LetterWindow(PTWindowsObject parent,
                           PuzzleFrame* pzlf) :
```

continues

Listing 7.7. continued

```cpp
        TWindow(parent, NULL), pf(pzlf),
        top(0), left(0), w(1), h(1), anim(NULL),
        sound_playing(0), curclock(0), pos0(0), pos1(0)
{
    Attr.Style = WS_CHILD | WS_BORDER | WS_VISIBLE |
                 WS_CLIPSIBLINGS;
    ticktock[0] = &PuzzleFrame::tick_music;
    ticktock[1] = &PuzzleFrame::tock_music;
}
//----------------------------------------------------------------
// LetterWindow:: ~ L e t t e r W i n d o w
// Destructor for the LetterWindow class

LetterWindow::~LetterWindow()
{
    if(anim != NULL) delete anim;
}
//----------------------------------------------------------------
//  LetterWindow:: P a i n t
//  Draw everything in the window

void LetterWindow::Paint(HDC hdc, PAINTSTRUCT&)
{
    if(anim != NULL)
    {
        anim->set_refresh(TRUE);
        anim->animate(hdc, top, left);
    }
}
//----------------------------------------------------------------
//  LetterWindow:: u p d a t e
//  Animate the sprites in the puzzle window

void LetterWindow::update()
{
    if(tcount++ > htpsec)
    {
        tcount = 0;
        clock[curclock]->inactive();
        curclock = 1 - curclock;
        clock[curclock]->active();
        PuzzleFrame::playmusic(*ticktock[curclock], 0);
        if(PuzzleFrame::start_curpzl &&
           PuzzleFrame::ticks_curpzl > 0)
        {
```

SPUZZLE—A Spelling Puzzle

Chapter 7

```
// Show updated count
            tickpos0[pos0]->inactive();
            tickpos1[pos1]->inactive();
            PuzzleFrame::ticks_curpzl--;
            pos1 = PuzzleFrame::ticks_curpzl / 10;
            pos0 = PuzzleFrame::ticks_curpzl - 10*pos1;
            tickpos0[pos0]->active();
            tickpos1[pos1]->active();
        }
        score->move(0, 0);
        time->move(0, 0);
    }
    if(anim != NULL)
    {
        HDC hdc = GetDC(HWindow);
        anim->animate(hdc, top, left);
        ReleaseDC(HWindow, hdc);
    }
}
//----------------------------------------------------------------
// LetterWindow:: i n i t
// Initialize the animation for this window

void LetterWindow::init()
{
// Do nothing if the current puzzle is not valid
    PuzzleInfo* pzl = PuzzleFrame::cur_puzzle;
    if(pzl == NULL) return;

// Change the cursor to an hourglass
    SetCapture(HWindow);
    SetCursor(LoadCursor(NULL, IDC_WAIT));

// Clean up existing puzzle, if any
    if(anim != NULL) delete anim;

// Get a DC for this window
    HDC hdc = GetDC(HWindow);


// Assuming that PuzzleWindow::init has been called,
// Set up the animation with the letters for the
// current word

    if(pzl != NULL)
    {
```

continues

Listing 7.7. continued

```
// Construct a SpriteAnimation with background for the puzzle
        anim = new SpriteAnimation(hdc, pf->ltr_wmax(),
                                    pf->ltr_hmax(),"ltrbg.bmp");
        if(anim == NULL) return;
        if(PuzzleFrame::pzlpcs == NULL) return;

        short i, x = toolwidth, y = lystart;
        for(i = 0; i < pzl->numchars; i++)
        {
            lfname[0] = pzl->word[i];
            PuzzleFrame::pzlpcs[i].ltr_sprite = new
                                    Sprite(hdc, lfname, NULL);
            PuzzleFrame::pzlpcs[i].ltr_sprite->newpos(x, y);
            PuzzleFrame::pzlpcs[i].lx = x;
            PuzzleFrame::pzlpcs[i].ly = y;

// Add sprite to animation
            anim->add(PuzzleFrame::pzlpcs[i].ltr_sprite);
            x += lbmpwidth;
        }
    }
// Add the clock...
    clock[0] = new Sprite(hdc, "clock0.bmp", NULL, 10000);
    clock[1] = new Sprite(hdc, "clock1.bmp", NULL, 10000);

    clock[0]->newpos(pf->ltr_wmax() - bmpheight - 4, 0);
    clock[1]->newpos(pf->ltr_wmax() - bmpheight - 4, 0);
    curclock = 0;
    clock[1]->inactive();

    anim->add(clock[0]);
    anim->add(clock[1]);

// Add the time display
    time = new Sprite(hdc, "time.bmp", NULL, 20000);
    time ->newpos(pf->ltr_wmax() - bmpheight - 4, 0);
    if(time ->width() < 40) time->width(40);
    if(time ->height() < 16) time->height(16);
    DRAWPROC proc = (DRAWPROC) MakeProcInstance(
                                    (FARPROC) disp_time,
                    GetApplication()->hInstance);
    time->drawproc(proc, NULL);
    time->active();
    time->update();

    anim->add(time);
```

SPUZZLE—A Spelling Puzzle

```
// Add the sprites to display tick count...
    char fname[8];
    short i;
    for(i = 0; i < 10; i++)
    {
        sprintf(fname, "%d.bmp", i);
        tickpos0[i] = new Sprite(hdc, fname, NULL, 10000);
        tickpos1[i] = new Sprite(hdc, fname, NULL, 10000);
        tickpos0[i]->newpos(pf->ltr_wmax() - bmpheight - 24, 0);
        tickpos1[i]->newpos(pf->ltr_wmax() - bmpheight - 42, 0);
        tickpos0[i]->inactive();
        tickpos1[i]->inactive();
        anim->add(tickpos0[i]);
        anim->add(tickpos1[i]);
    }

    tickpos0[9]->active();
    tickpos1[9]->active();

// Add a label sprite to the left of the tick display...
    ticklabel = new Sprite(hdc, "ticklbl.bmp", NULL, 10000);
    ticklabel->newpos(pf->ltr_wmax() - bmpheight - 83, 0);
    anim->add(ticklabel);

// Add the "score display sprite"
    score = new Sprite(hdc, "score.bmp", NULL, 10000);
    score->newpos(pf->ltr_wmax() - bmpheight - 83, 17);
    if(score->width() < 80) score->width(80);
    if(score->height() < 16) score->height(16);
    dt.text = msg;
    dt.numchars = strlen(msg);
    proc = (DRAWPROC) MakeProcInstance(
                                    (FARPROC) disp_score,
                    GetApplication()->hInstance);
    score->drawproc(proc, &dt);
    score->active();
    score->update();

    anim->add(score);

// Remember to release the DC
    ReleaseDC(HWindow, hdc);

// Reset cursor to arrow
    SetCursor(LoadCursor(NULL, IDC_ARROW));
    ReleaseCapture();
}
```

continues

Listing 7.7. continued

```
//--------------------------------------------------------
void _FAR PASCAL _export disp_time(HDC hdc, short x, short y,
                                   LPVOID)
{
    SetBkMode(hdc, TRANSPARENT);
    SetTextColor(hdc, RGB(255, 255, 255));

    time_t bintime;
    time(&bintime);
    TextOut(hdc, x, y, ctime(&bintime)+11, 8);
}
//--------------------------------------------------------
void _FAR PASCAL _export disp_score(HDC hdc, short x, short y,
                                    LPVOID data)
{
    TEXT_DATA *td = (TEXT_DATA*)data;
    SetBkMode(hdc, TRANSPARENT);

    SetTextColor(hdc, RGB(0, 0, 0));
    TextOut(hdc, x, y, td->text, td->numchars);
}
//--------------------------------------------------------
// LetterWindow:: s e t _ s c o r e
// Set the score being displayed

void LetterWindow::set_score(short s)
{
    dt.numchars = sprintf(msg, "Score: %d", s);
    score->needs_update();
}
```

ToolWindow Class

The `ToolWindow` class represents the tall and narrow window to the left of the `PuzzleWindow`. This window displays a number of bitmap buttons that the player can press to initiate actions such as start a new puzzle, turn the sound off or on, and exit the game.

Listing 7.8 shows the declaration of the `ToolWindow` class together with a supporting class, `ToolIcon`, that represents a small bitmap image. Each button in the `ToolWindow` display is a `ToolIcon`. Unlike the other child windows, I did

SPUZZLE—A Spelling Puzzle

not use a `SpriteAnimation` to manage the display in the `ToolWindow` class because `ToolWindow`'s contents did not have to animated—they were a static display of images.

Listing 7.8. `toolwin.h`—Declaration of the `ToolWindow` class.

```
//---------------------------------------------------------------
// File: toolwin.h
//
// Declares the ToolWindow class that represents the window
// where a number of buttons for the SPUZZLE game is shown.
//---------------------------------------------------------------
#if !defined(__TOOLWIN_H)
#define __TOOLWIN_H

#include <owl.h>

#define GO_ICON         1
#define QUIT_ICON       2
#define SOUND_ON_ICON   3
#define SOUND_OFF_ICON  4
#define NEXT_PZL_ICON   5

class PuzzleFrame;

struct ToolIcon
{
    ToolIcon() : active(0), id(0), img(NULL),
    xoff(0), yoff(0), x(0), y(0), w(0), h(0) {}

    ToolIcon(char *fname, short nid, short xo, short yo,
            unsigned short wdth, unsigned short hght,
            short xw, short yw, short act) : id(nid),
            xoff(xo), yoff(yo), w(wdth), h(hght),
            x(xw), y(yw), active(act)
    {
        img = Sprite::init_image(fname);
    }

    ~ToolIcon()
    {
        if(img != NULL) delete img;
    }

    short           active; // Displayed only if active
    short           id;     // An integer icon ID
```

continues

Listing 7.8. continued

```
    Image           *img;       // The icon's image
    short           xoff,       // Align this point of image
                    yoff;       // with the point (x,y)
    short           x, y;       // Position in the tools window
    unsigned short  w, h;       // Width and height of icon
};

class ToolWindow : public TWindow
{
public:
    ToolWindow(PTWindowsObject parent, PuzzleFrame* pzlf) :
        TWindow(parent, NULL), pf(pzlf),
        icon_current(NULL)
    {
        Attr.Style = WS_CHILD | WS_BORDER | WS_VISIBLE |
                    WS_CLIPSIBLINGS;
    }

    void Paint(HDC hdc, PAINTSTRUCT& ps);
    void WMSize(RTMessage msg) = [WM_FIRST + WM_SIZE];
    void WMLButtonDown(RTMessage msg) = [WM_FIRST + WM_LBUTTONDOWN];

    unsigned short width() { return w;}
    unsigned short height() { return h;}

    void active(short id);
    void inactive(short id);
private:
    unsigned short w, h; // Size of client area
    ToolIcon        *icon_current;
    PuzzleFrame     *pf;

    ToolIcon* icon_at(short x, short y);
    short get_index(short id);
};


#endif
```

Listing 7.9 shows the implementation of the ToolWindow class. Notice that the icons representing the buttons are defined in a static array of ToolIcon objects. Each icon's image comes from a specified file. The position of the image

SPUZZLE—A Spelling Puzzle

Chapter 7

is specified and a flag indicates whether to display the icon. You can have several icons at a location and turn them on and off to show different buttons. This is how I implemented the sound on-off button.

When the player presses the left mouse button down with the mouse cursor inside a button, a specified action has to take place. I implemented this feature by defining the WMLbuttonDown function to handle the WM_LBUTTONDOWN message that Windows sends when the player presses the left mouse button. The WMLButtonDown function calls another member function, icon_at, to determine if the mouse cursor is on an active icon at the time of the button down event. If icon_at returns a valid icon identifier, WMLButtonDown uses a switch statement to initiate the action corresponding to the icon. You can see the details of these actions in the WMLButtonDown function in Listing 7.9.

Listing 7.9. toolwin.cpp— Implementation of the ToolWindow class.

```
//--------------------------------------------------------------
// File: toolwin.cpp
//
// Implementation of the ToolWindow class.
//--------------------------------------------------------------
#include "pzlframe.h"
#include "sounds.h"

#define XSTART 8
#define YSTART 8
#define YSPACE 4
#define ON     1
#define OFF    0

static ToolIcon icons[] =
{
    ToolIcon("go.bmp", GO_ICON, 0, 0, 32, 32,
                            XSTART, YSTART, ON),
    ToolIcon("sndon.bmp", SOUND_ON_ICON, 0, 0, 32, 32,
                         XSTART, YSTART+YSPACE+32, OFF),
    ToolIcon("sndoff.bmp", SOUND_OFF_ICON, 0, 0, 32, 32,
                         XSTART, YSTART+YSPACE+32, ON),
    ToolIcon("nxtpzl.bmp", NEXT_PZL_ICON, 0, 0, 32, 32,
                         XSTART, YSTART+2*(YSPACE+32), ON),
```

continues

Listing 7.9. continued

```
    ToolIcon("quit.bmp", QUIT_ICON, 0, 0, 32, 32,
                 XSTART, YSTART+5*(YSPACE+32), ON)
};

static short numicons = sizeof(icons) / sizeof(icons[0]);

static short firsttime = 1;
//-----------------------------------------------------------
//  ToolWindow:: P a i n t
//  Draw everything in the window

void ToolWindow::Paint(HDC hdc, PAINTSTRUCT&)
{
// Draw all active tool icons
    if(icons != NULL)
    {
        short i;
        for(i = 0; i < numicons; i++)
        {
            if(icons[i].active && icons[i].img != NULL)
                icons[i].img->show(hdc, icons[i].xoff,
                    icons[i].yoff, icons[i].x, icons[i].y,
                    icons[i].w, icons[i].h, SRCCOPY);
        }
    }
}
//-----------------------------------------------------------
//  ToolWindow:: W M S i z e
//  Save the location and size of the window

void ToolWindow::WMSize(RTMessage)
{
    RECT r;
    GetClientRect(HWindow, &r);
    w = r.left - r.right + 1;
    h = r.bottom - r.top + 1;
}
//-----------------------------------------------------------
//  ToolWindow:: W M L B u t t o n D o w n
//  Handle mouse button press

void ToolWindow::WMLButtonDown(RTMessage msg)
{
    short x = msg.LP.Lo;
    short y = msg.LP.Hi;
    icon_current = icon_at(x, y);
```

SPUZZLE—A Spelling Puzzle

Chapter 7

```
        if(icon_current != NULL)
        {
            switch(icon_current->id)
            {
                case GO_ICON:
                    pf->puzzle_window()->shuffle();
                    PuzzleFrame::start_curpzl = 1;
                    PuzzleFrame::ticks_curpzl = 99;
                    break;

                case SOUND_ON_ICON:
                    PuzzleFrame::sound_on = 1;
                    inactive(SOUND_ON_ICON);
                    active(SOUND_OFF_ICON);
                    break;

                case SOUND_OFF_ICON:
                    PuzzleFrame::sound_on = 0;
                    inactive(SOUND_OFF_ICON);
                    active(SOUND_ON_ICON);
                    break;

                case NEXT_PZL_ICON:
                    PuzzleFrame::cur_puzzle = pf->next_puzzle();
                    PuzzleFrame::done_curpzl = 0;
                    PuzzleFrame::start_curpzl = 0;
                    if(PuzzleFrame::cur_puzzle != NULL &&
                       pf->puzzle_window() != NULL)
                            pf->puzzle_window()->init();
                    if(PuzzleFrame::cur_puzzle != NULL &&
                       pf->letter_window() != NULL)
                            pf->letter_window()->init();
                    break;

                case QUIT_ICON:
// Play the closing music...
                    PuzzleFrame::playmusic(
                        PuzzleFrame::closing_music, TRUE);
                    pf->hi_scores("HISCORE.SPZ");
                    PostQuitMessage(0);
                    break;
            }
        }
}
//-----------------------------------------------------------
// ToolWindow:: i c o n _ a t
// Return pointer to ToolIcon (if any) at a specified location
```

continues

Listing 7.9. continued

```
ToolIcon* ToolWindow::icon_at(short x, short y)
{
    short i;
    ToolIcon *rti = NULL;

    if(icons == NULL) return rti;

    for(i = 0; i < numicons; i++)
    {
        if(!icons[i].active) continue;
        if(icons[i].img == NULL) continue;

        if(x < icons[i].x) continue;
        if(y < icons[i].y) continue;

        if(x > (icons[i].x + icons[i].w - 1)) continue;
        if(y > (icons[i].y + icons[i].h - 1)) continue;

        rti = &icons[i];
        break;
    }
    return rti;
}
//----------------------------------------------------------
// ToolWindow:: g e t _ i n d e x
// Return the index of an icon in the icons array

short ToolWindow::get_index(short id)
{
    short i;
    for(i = 0; i < numicons; i++)
        if(icons[i].id == id) return i;

    return -1;
}
//----------------------------------------------------------
// ToolWindow:: a c t i v e
// Make icon active

void ToolWindow::active(short id)
{
    short i;
    if((i = get_index(id)) >= 0)
        if(!icons[i].active)
        {
```

SPUZZLE—A Spelling Puzzle

```
            icons[i].active = 1;
            InvalidateRect(HWindow, NULL, FALSE);
        }
}
//---------------------------------------------------------------
// ToolWindow:: i n a c t i v e
// Make icon inactive

void ToolWindow::inactive(short id)
{
    short i;
    if((i = get_index(id)) >= 0)
        if(icons[i].active)
        {
            icons[i].active = 0;
            InvalidateRect(HWindow, NULL, FALSE);
        }
}
```

StatusWindow Class

I use the StatusWindow class to liven up SPUZZLE by displaying a grassy scene with a worm, a butterfly, and some bugs crawling across the screen. Listing 7.10 shows the header file statwin.h that declares the StatusWindow class. A SpriteAnimation object manages the animation of the insects over the background scene.

Listing 7.10. statwin.h— Declaration of the StatusWindow class.

```
//---------------------------------------------------------------
// File: statwin.h
//
// Declares the StatusWindow class that represents the window
// where the progress of the SPUZZLE game is shown.
//---------------------------------------------------------------
#if !defined(__STATWIN_H)
#define __STATWIN_H

#include <owl.h>
#include "spranim.h"
```

continues

Listing 7.10. continued

```
class PuzzleFrame;

class StatusWindow : public TWindow
{
public:
    StatusWindow(PTWindowsObject parent, PuzzleFrame *pzlf) :
        TWindow(parent, NULL), pf(pzlf), anim(NULL), s(NULL),
        w(1), h(1), top(0), left(0)
    {
        Attr.Style = WS_CHILD | WS_BORDER | WS_VISIBLE |
                     WS_CLIPSIBLINGS;
    }
    ~StatusWindow();

    void init();
    void update();
    void move_sprites();

    void Paint(HDC hdc, PAINTSTRUCT& ps);
    void WMSize(RTMessage msg) = [WM_FIRST + WM_SIZE];

    unsigned short width() { return w;}
    unsigned short height() { return h;}
    void width(unsigned short _w) { w = _w;}
    void height(unsigned short _h) { h = _h;}

    void set_text(LPSTR t, short n);

private:
    PuzzleFrame    *pf;
    unsigned short w, h;  // Size of client area

// SpriteAnimation to display status information...
    SpriteAnimation *anim;
    Sprite          **s;
    short           top, left;
};

#endif
```

The implementation of the `StatusWindow` class is somewhat similar to that of the `AnimationWindow` class in Chapter 5 (see Listing 7.11). As in `AnimationWindow`, the sprites are defined by a static array of `SpriteInfo` structures named `sprite_data`. Most of the work in `StatusWindow` takes place in the `init`, `update`, and `move_sprites`

SPUZZLE—A Spelling Puzzle

Chapter 7

functions. The `init` function creates the `SpriteAnimation` object, creates a `Sprite` object for each entry in `sprite_data`, and adds each `Sprite` to the `SpriteAnimation`. The `update` function, invoked from `PuzzleFrame`, moves the sprites by calling `move_sprites`, and updates the animation by calling the `animate` function of the `SpriteAnimation` class (Chapter 5).

Listing 7.11. `statwin.cpp`—
Implementation of the `StatusWindow` class.

```cpp
//-------------------------------------------------------------
// File: statwin.cpp
//
// Implementation of the StatusWindow class.
//-------------------------------------------------------------
#include "pzlframe.h"

struct SpriteInfo
{
    SpriteInfo(char* imgfname, char* mskfname,
            short xp, short yp, short xv, short yv,
            short prio, short ia) :
            imagefilename(imgfname), maskfilename(mskfname),
            xpos(xp), ypos(yp), xvel(xv), yvel(yv),
            priority(prio), isactive(ia) {}

    char*   imagefilename;
    char*   maskfilename;
    short   xpos, ypos;     // Initial x-y position
    short   xvel, yvel;     // Initial x- and y-velocity
    short   priority;
    short   isactive;
};
// Declare an array of sprites to be loaded from image files
static SpriteInfo sprite_data[] =
{
    SpriteInfo("worm0.bmp",  "worm0m.bmp", 300,  0, -1, 0,  1, 1),
    SpriteInfo("worm1.bmp",  "worm1m.bmp", 300,  0, -1, 0,  1, 0),
    SpriteInfo("bfly.bmp",   "bflym.bmp",  640, -4, -3, 0,  1, 1),
    SpriteInfo("ant.bmp",    "antm.bmp",   200, 20, -2, 0,  1, 1),
    SpriteInfo("bug.bmp",    "bugm.bmp",   400, 24, -1, 0,  1, 1),
    SpriteInfo(NULL, NULL, 200, 0, -1, 0, 99, 1)
};

// Total number of sprites
static int numsprites = sizeof(sprite_data) /
                        sizeof(sprite_data[0]);
```

continues

Listing 7.11. continued

```
void _FAR PASCAL _export draw_text(HDC hdc, short x, short y,
                                   LPVOID data);

struct TEXT_DATA
{
    LPSTR   text;
    size_t  numchars;
};

static TEXT_DATA dt;
static LPSTR msg = "Click on GO to start puzzle";

const short tpsec = 1000 / DISP_MILLISECONDS;
const short htpsec = tpsec / 5;
static short tcount = 0;
static short curworm = 0;

//----------------------------------------------------------------
//  StatusWindow:: ~ S t a t u s W i n d o w
//  Destructor for the StatusWindow class

StatusWindow::~StatusWindow()
{
    if(anim != NULL) delete anim;
    if(s != NULL) delete s;
}
//----------------------------------------------------------------
//  StatusWindow:: P a i n t
//  Draw everything in the window

void StatusWindow::Paint(HDC hdc, PAINTSTRUCT&)
{
    if(anim != NULL)
    {
        anim->set_refresh(TRUE);
        anim->animate(hdc, top, left);
    }
}
//----------------------------------------------------------------
//  StatusWindow:: u p d a t e
//  Animate the sprites in the puzzle window

void StatusWindow::update()
{
    if(anim != NULL)
    {
```

SPUZZLE—A Spelling Puzzle

Chapter 7

```
            if(tcount++ > htpsec)
            {
                tcount = 0;
// Turn off the other worm sprite...
                curworm = 1 - curworm;
                sprite_data[curworm].isactive = 0;
            }

            move_sprites();

            HDC hdc = GetDC(HWindow);
            anim->animate(hdc, top, left);
            ReleaseDC(HWindow, hdc);
    }
}
//----------------------------------------------------------------
// StatusWindow:: W M S i z e
// Save the location and size of the window

void StatusWindow::WMSize(RTMessage)
{
    RECT r;
    GetClientRect(HWindow, &r);
    w = r.left - r.right + 1;
    h = r.bottom - r.top + 1;
}
//----------------------------------------------------------------
// StatusWindow:: i n i t
// Initialize sprites etc. used in the StatusWindow

void StatusWindow::init()
{
// If a SpriteAnimation exists, delete it...
    if(anim != NULL) delete anim;
    if(s != NULL) delete s;

// Get a DC for this window
    HDC hdc = GetDC(HWindow);

// Construct a SpriteAnimation with background for the puzzle
    anim = new SpriteAnimation(hdc, pf->sts_wmax(),
                               pf->sts_hmax(),
                               "stsbg.bmp");
    if(anim == NULL) return;

// Create the array of sprites
    s = new Sprite*[numsprites];
    int i;
```

continues

Listing 7.11. continued

```
    for(i = 0; i < numsprites; i++)
    {
        s[i] = new Sprite(hdc, sprite_data[i].imagefilename,
                          sprite_data[i].maskfilename);
        s[i]->priority(sprite_data[i].priority);
        s[i]->newpos(sprite_data[i].xpos, sprite_data[i].ypos);
        if(!sprite_data[i].isactive) s[i]->inactive();
// Add sprite to animation
        anim->add(s[i]);
    }

// The last sprite is used to display a text string
// Set up size of sprite based on current font
    TEXTMETRIC tm;
    GetTextMetrics(hdc, &tm);
    short hchar = tm.tmHeight + tm.tmExternalLeading;
    short wchar = tm.tmAveCharWidth;
    s[numsprites-1]->width(30*wchar);
    s[numsprites-1]->height(hchar);
    dt.text = msg;
    dt.numchars = strlen(msg);
    DRAWPROC proc = (DRAWPROC) MakeProcInstance(
                                  (FARPROC) draw_text,
                                  GetApplication()->hInstance);
    s[numsprites-1]->drawproc(proc, &dt);
    s[numsprites-1]->active();
    s[numsprites-1]->update();

// Release the DC
    ReleaseDC(HWindow, hdc);
}
//-------------------------------------------------------------
// StatusWindow:: m o v e _ s p r i t e s
// Move the sprites

void StatusWindow::move_sprites()
{
    int i;
    for(i = 0; i < numsprites; i++)
    {
        sprite_data[i].xpos += sprite_data[i].xvel;

        if(i==2) // Butterfly moves up and down...
            sprite_data[i].ypos = random(10) - 7;

        if(i==3) // ant moves up and down a bit
            sprite_data[i].ypos = 24 - random(4);
```

SPUZZLE—A Spelling Puzzle

```
        if(i==4) // bug moves up and down a bit
            sprite_data[i].ypos = 24 - random(2);

        if(sprite_data[i].xpos <= -40)
            sprite_data[i].xpos = width() + 60;

        s[i]->move(sprite_data[i].xpos - s[i]->xpos(),
                   sprite_data[i].ypos - s[i]->ypos());

        if(i == curworm)
        {
            s[i]->inactive();
            s[i]->update_done();
        }
    }
}
//---------------------------------------------------------------
void _FAR PASCAL _export draw_text(HDC hdc, short x, short y,
                                   LPVOID data)
{
    TEXT_DATA *td = (TEXT_DATA*)data;
    SetBkMode(hdc, TRANSPARENT);

    SetTextColor(hdc, RGB(0, 0, 255));
    TextOut(hdc, x, y, td->text, td->numchars);
}
//---------------------------------------------------------------
// StatusWindow:: s e t _ t e x t
// Set the text to be displayed in the status window

void StatusWindow::set_text(LPSTR t, short n)
{
    dt.text = t;
    dt.numchars = n;
}
```

Data Structures for Puzzle Information

Apart from the main window and the child windows that manage the user interface of SPUZZLE, there are some supporting data structures used to represent the puzzles. Listing 7.12 shows the header file pzlinfo.h that implements the structures PuzzleInfo, PuzzlePick, and PuzzlePiece that are used to store information about the puzzles.

Listing 7.12. `pzlinfo.h`—Definition of data structure for storing information about the puzzles.

```
//----------------------------------------------------------------
// File: pzlinfo.h
//
// Defines the structures to hold information about each puzzle.
//----------------------------------------------------------------
#if !defined(__PZLINFO_H)
#define __PZLINFO_H

class Sprite;

struct PuzzleInfo
{
    PuzzleInfo() : word(NULL), numchars(0), imgfname(NULL) {}

    ~PuzzleInfo()
    {
     if(word != NULL) delete word;
     if(imgfname != NULL) delete imgfname;
    }
    char*   word;       // Word to spell
    short   numchars;   // Number of characters in word
    char*   imgfname;   // Name of image file
};

struct PuzzlePick
{
    PuzzlePick() : index(0), done(0) {}
    PuzzlePick(short i, short d) : index(i), done(d) {}

    short   index; // Index of selected puzzle
    short   done;  // Nonzero when puzzle is finished

};

struct PuzzlePiece
{
    Sprite *sprite; // Sprite denoting this piece
    short  x, y;    // Location of piece in finished puzzle
    short  c;       // Character associated with piece
    Sprite *ltr_sprite; // Sprite showing the letter
    short  lx, ly;  // Location of letter sprite
};


#endif
```

SPUZZLE—A Spelling Puzzle

High Scores Dialog Box

SPUZZLE maintains a list of the players with the top 30 scores. I added this feature because many arcade games have it and it illustrates the steps should you need this for your own games.

The idea of the high scores dialog is to display the top scores in a list and provide two text input fields: one for the player's name and the other for a quotation. Once the player fills in these input fields and presses the OK button, the name and the quote are entered into a file that stores the highest scores.

Listing 7.13 shows the file `hscdial.h` that declares the class `HiscoreDialog` used to display the dialog box. `HiscoreDialog` is derived from the OWL class `TDialog`. It maintains an array of high scores using the `SortedArray` container from Borland's container class library. Each entry in the `SortedArray` is a `HiScore` structure, also declared in Listing 7.13.

The layout of `HiscoreDialog` is defined in the resource file `SPUZZLE.RES`, which is in the companion disk. The `hi_scores` function of the `PuzzleFrame` class creates and uses the `HiscoreDialog`.

Listing 7.13. `hscdial.h`— Declaration of classes for the high scores dialog.

```
//---------------------------------------------------------------
// File: hscdial.h
// Declaration of the HiscoreDialog class. The primary reason
// for this dialog class is to initialize the dialog properly.
//---------------------------------------------------------------
#if !defined __HSCDIAL_H
#define __HSCDIAL_H

#include <owl.h>
#include <sortarry.h>   // For the SortedArray class
#include <sortable.h>   // So that we can sort the HiScore entries

struct HiScore : public Sortable
{
    HiScore() : score(0), name(NULL), quote(NULL) {}

    ~HiScore()
    {
```

continues

Listing 7.13. continued

```
        if(name != NULL) delete name;
        if(quote != NULL) delete quote;
    }

// The next four functions are required because Sprite is
// derived from the Sortable class.

    classType isA() const { return HiScoreClass;}

    char _FAR *nameOf() const { return "HiScore";}

    hashValueType hashValue() const { return 0;}

    void printOn(ostream _FAR& os) const
    {
        os << name << endl;
        os << score << endl;
        os << quote << endl;
    }

// The following function is needed to sort the HiScores
// according to the score.
    int isLessThan(const Object _FAR& ob) const
    { return score > ((HiScore&)ob).score;}

    int isEqual(const Object _FAR& ob) const
    { return score == ((HiScore&)ob).score;}

    Long    score;
    char    *name;
    char    *quote;
    enum { HiScoreClass = __firstUserClass + 2};
};

class HiscoreDialog : public TDialog
{
public:
    HiscoreDialog(PTWindowsObject parent, LPSTR name,
                  SortedArray* hi, short n) :
                  TDialog(parent, name), numentries(n),
                  hiscores(hi) {}

    void WMInitDialog(RTMessage msg) = [WM_FIRST + WM_INITDIALOG];

// The following function takes care of some details when
// the "OK" button is pressed
```

Chapter 7

SPUZZLE—A Spelling Puzzle

```
    virtual void Ok(RTMessage msg) = [ID_FIRST + IDOK];

    HiScore* hi_score() { return hi;}
private:
    SortedArray *hiscores;
    short       numentries;
    HiScore     *hi;
};

#endif
```

Listing 7.14 shows the implementation of the two most important functions of the `HiscoreDialog` class: `WMInitDialog` and `Ok`. Windows calls the `WMInitDialog` function when the `HiscoreDialog` is initialized.

`WMInitDialog` adds the name, score, and quotation of the 30 players with the highest scores into the list box that is a part of the dialog. Windows calls the `Ok` function when the player presses the OK button in the dialog box. The `Ok` function extracts the inputs provided by the player and stores them in a new `HiScore` object. The `hi_scores` function in `PuzzleFrame` takes care of creating and destroying the `HiScore` entries stored in the `SortedArray` named `hiscores`.

Listing 7.14. `hscdial.cpp`—
Implementation of classes for the high scores dialog.

```
//-------------------------------------------------------------
// File: hscdial.cpp
// Member functions of the HiscoreDialog class.
//-------------------------------------------------------------
#include "spzlres.h"
#include "hscdial.h"
//-------------------------------------------------------------
// HiscoreDialog::  W M I n i t D i a l o g
// Initialize the list box in the dialog...

void HiscoreDialog::WMInitDialog(RTMessage)
{
// Add the scores to the list box
    short i;
    char item[80];
    numentries = hiscores->getItemsInContainer();
```

continues

269

Listing 7.14. continued

```
    if(numentries > 30) numentries = 30;
    for(i = 0; i < numentries; i++)
    {
        HiScore& hi = (HiScore&)(*hiscores)[i];
        wsprintf(item, "%s\t%ld\t%s",
                 hi.name, hi.score, hi.quote);
        SendDlgItemMsg(ID_LISTBOX, LB_INSERTSTRING, i,
                            (LPARAM)((LPSTR)item));
    }
// Limit the name edit box to 20 characters max
    SendDlgItemMsg(ID_NAME, EM_LIMITTEXT, 20, 0);

// and the "quote" edit control to 40 chars max
    SendDlgItemMsg(ID_QUOTE, EM_LIMITTEXT, 40, 0);

}
//----------------------------------------------------------------
// HiscoreDialog:: O k
// Called when OK button is pressed

void HiscoreDialog::Ok(RTMessage)
{
// Extract the name and the quote from the edit controls
    short nch = SendDlgItemMsg(ID_NAME, EM_LINELENGTH, 0, 0);

    hi = new HiScore;

    hi->name = new char[nch + 2];
    SendDlgItemMsg(ID_NAME, WM_GETTEXT, nch+1,
                        (LPARAM)((LPSTR)hi->name));
    hi->name[nch+1] = '\0';

    nch = SendDlgItemMsg(ID_QUOTE, EM_LINELENGTH, 0, 0);
    hi->quote = new char[nch + 2];
    SendDlgItemMsg(ID_QUOTE, WM_GETTEXT, nch+1,
                        (LPARAM)((LPSTR)hi->quote));
    hi->quote[nch+1] = '\0';

// Now exit the dialog...
    CloseWindow(IDOK);
}
```

SPUZZLE—A Spelling Puzzle

Resources for SPUZZLE

I prepared the resource file for SPUZZLE, SPUZZLE.RES, with Borland's Resource Workshop application. SPUZZLE.RES is in the companion disk and contains the bitmaps, dialog boxes, and menus used in SPUZZLE. To learn more about the resources, open SPUZZLE.RES from Borland's Resource Workshop.

Some of the resources, such as menu items and strings, have identifiers associated with them. These help you determine which string to load and which menu item is selected, for instance. The header file spzlres.h, shown in Listing 7.15, defines symbolic constants for these resource identifiers.

Listing 7.15. spzlres.h—Resource identifiers for SPUZZLE.

```
//-----------------------------------------------------------
// File: spzlres.h
// Resource identifiers for the SPUZZLE game.
//-----------------------------------------------------------
#if !defined(__SPZLRES_H)
#define __SPZLRES_H

#include <owlrc.h>   // For definitions of OWL IDs

#define IDM_HELP      200
#define IDM_ABOUT     201
#define ID_LISTBOX    101
#define ID_NAME       102
#define ID_QUOTE      103

// String IDs
#define IDS_PRESSGO         1
#define IDS_KEEPGOING       2
#define IDS_UCANDOIT        3
#define IDS_WOW             4
#define IDS_GOODJOB         5
#define IDS_TIMESUP         6
#define IDS_PRESSNEXT       7

#endif
```

Help File

You may have noticed that you can get help in SPUZZLE by pressing the F1 function key or by selecting Index from the Help menu. Adding the help facility is easy, provided you have a help file ready. As you can see from the `Help` function shown in the file `pzlframe.h` (Listing 7.2), once you have the help file, `SPZLHLP.HLP`, you can activate it from the handler for the help menu item as follows:

`WinHelp(HWindow, "SPZLHLP.HLP", HELP_INDEX, 0);`

Preparing the help file involves the following steps:

1. Using a word processor capable of producing a *Rich Text Format (RTF)* output, prepare a file with the help information. I used Microsoft Word for Windows to prepare the help file, which I saved as the RTF file: `SPZLHLP.RTF`. Footnotes and hidden text are used to tie keywords and topics to specific sections of the RTF file. You can find detailed information on preparing the help file in the Help Compiler's documentation in the *Tools and Utilities Guide* that accompanies Borland C++.

2. The RTF file has to be compiled by the Help Compiler (HC) before it can be used by the `WinHelp` function. Essentially, you have to prepare a Help Project File that you provide as input to HC. SPUZZLE's help project file, `spzlhlp.hpj`, shown in Listing 7.16. To create the file `SPZLHLP.HLP`, you have to invoke HC with the following command:

   `HC spzlhlp.hpj`

Listing 7.16. `spzlhlp.hpj`—Project file for the Help Compiler.

```
[OPTIONS]
TITLE=SPUZZLE Help
COMPRESS=true
WARNING=1

[FILES]
spzlhlp.rtf
```

SPUZZLE—A Spelling Puzzle

Other Files

There are a host of other files that SPUZZLE needs. Most are images used for the puzzles, for which I used scanned images. SPUZZLE also needs a small bitmap image of each letter of the alphabet and the digits from 0 through 9. I prepared these images in Borland's Resource Workshop and saved them as .BMP files.

The musical notes come from the files with the .SPM extension. The file format is explained in Chapter 6. I prepared these music files using a text editor.

You can find all these files in this book's companion disk. Because of limited disk space, there may be very few puzzles on the disk. You should add more puzzles to SPUZZLE by editing the SPUZZLE.CFG file as explained in earlier sections of this chapter. If you have access to a scanner, you can scan in the images for the puzzles; otherwise, simply draw simple images using PC PaintBrush.

Summary

This chapter uses the image animation and sound generation techniques presented in the previous chapters and blends everything into an educational game called SPUZZLE, which stands for Spelling Puzzle. The game teaches young children spelling through a jigsaw puzzle. After installing the game from the companion disk and trying it out, you can read this chapter to see how SPUZZLE is implemented. Study Chapters 4, 5, and 6 before going through this chapter because SPUZZLE uses many of the C++ classes that appear in them.

Chapter 8

3-D Graphics

So far you have seen techniques of image animation and how to use them in games designed to run under Windows. Now it is time to turn to 3-D graphics, the staple of many action games. This chapter develops a few C++ classes to represent 3-D shapes and uses the classes in the BLOCKADE game in Chapter 9. Although computer graphics can generate realistic renditions of a scene using ray tracing techniques, this chapter's focus is only on displaying reasonably complex shapes that are defined by three- or four-sided polygons. A brief description of 3-D coordinate transformations and vector operations is provided, followed by the C++ classes that represent 3-D shapes. For more detailed information on 3-D graphics and, in particular, 3-D geometry, consult the books listed at the end of this chapter.

Modeling 3-D Objects

To describe 3-D objects you need a 3-D coordinate system. A good way to describe a 3-D coordinate system is to start with a 2-D one. You are probably familiar with the *2-D Cartesian coordinate system*. If you think of this page as a plane, you define the 2-D coordinate system by first selecting a point as the origin. Following the normal convention, pick the lower left corner of the page as the origin. Then think of the bottom edge of the page as the x-axis and the left edge as the y-axis. Note that the two coordinate axes are perpendicular to each other. Once you have defined the origin and the axes, you can specify the location of any point on the page by specifying its *coordinates*—the distances along the x- and y-axes. As you can see from Figure 8.1, the x-coordinate is the distance of the point along the x-axis and the y-coordinate is the distance along the y-axis. The position of a point on the plane is generally expressed as: (x,y) where x and y are the x- and y-coordinates.

3-D Cartesian Coordinates

The commonly used 3-D Cartesian coordinate system is an extension of the 2-D Cartesian coordinate system with the addition of a third axis—the z-axis—oriented perpendicular to the plane containing the x- and y-axes. If you think of the x- and y- axes with the positive x-axis extending to the right of the page and the positive y-axis extending upward, the positive z-axis could either point

3-D Graphics

into the page or extend out of the page. I use the *right-handed* convention that requires the positive z-axis to point out of the page (see Figure 8.2). The right-handed coordinate system is the standard mathematical convention for expressing and manipulating 3-D coordinates in graphics and engineering disciplines, which is why I use it in this book. Note that it does not matter which coordinate convention you use as long as you are consistent and you know the implications of your choice.

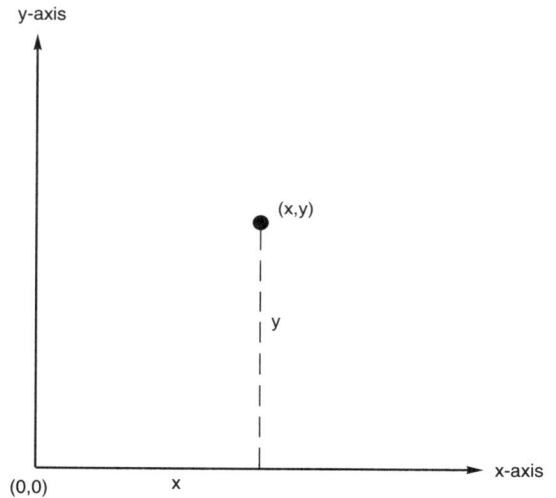

Figure 8.1. *2-D Cartesian coordinate system.*

Boundary Representation of 3-D Objects

One way to model 3-D objects is to specify the surfaces that constitute the boundaries of the object. Although most realistic objects are bounded by curved surfaces, it is possible to use simple polygons to approximate the boundary of any object. In this chapter I represent an object's boundary by a collection of polygons. Of course many simple objects, such as cubes, are naturally bounded by planes, but even objects with curved surfaces, such as a cylinder or a sphere, can be adequately modeled by a large number of planar surfaces. In any case, my focus is not on realistic object models but on models that are simple enough to use in a game. Polygon-bounded objects are used extensively in many computer games such as flight simulators that use 3-D animation. When appropriately shaded, polygons provide adequate realism and yet they are computationally efficient to manipulate.

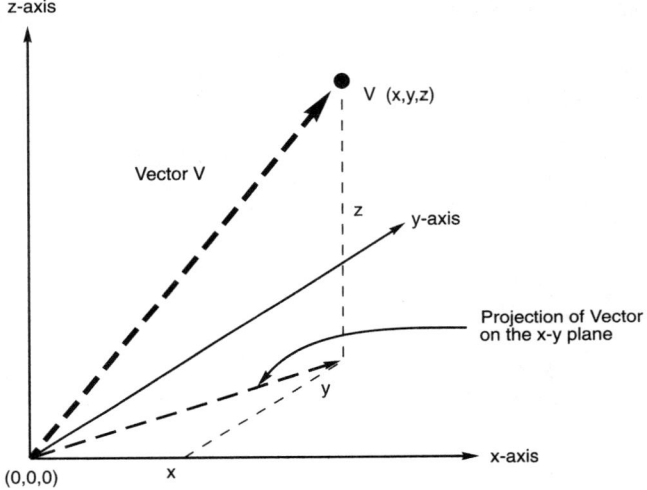

Figure 8.2. *Right-handed 3-D Cartesian coordinate system.*

Constructing Objects with Polygons

A polygon is defined by its corners—the vertices. Each vertex is a 3-D point. Like its 2-D counterpart, a 3-D point is expressed in terms of its x-, y-, and z-coordinates, commonly written as (x,y,z). To define an object with polygons, you have to start with a 3-D coordinate system for the object. Figure 8.3 shows how you might define a unit cube—a cube with sides of length "one."

When constructing a complicated 3-D scene, you might want to place several copies of the same object at different locations in the scene. You might also want to scale and rotate the objects. To do this, you need 3-D coordinate transformations. You have to first define a coordinate system for the scene. Then

Chapter 8

3-D Graphics

you have to scale, rotate, and translate the individual objects so that they are positioned the way you want them. For instance, Figure 8.4 shows a 3-D scene consisting of a plane with two cubes on it—each scaled, rotated, and positioned in a different way.

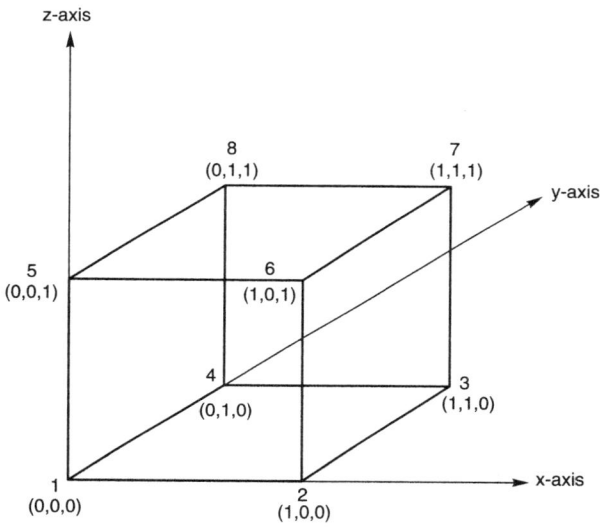

List of Vertices		**List of Polygons**	
Vertex No.	Coordinates	Polygon No.	Vertices
1	(0,0,0)	1	(1,2,3,4)
2	(1,0,0)	2	(5,6,7,8)
3	(1,1,0)	3	(1,5,8,4)
4	(0,1,0)	4	(2,3,7,6)
5	(0,0,1)	5	(1,2,6,5)
6	(1,0,1)	6	(4,3,7,8)
7	(1,1,1)		
8	(0,1,1)		

Figure 8.3. *Vertices and polygons of a unit cube.*

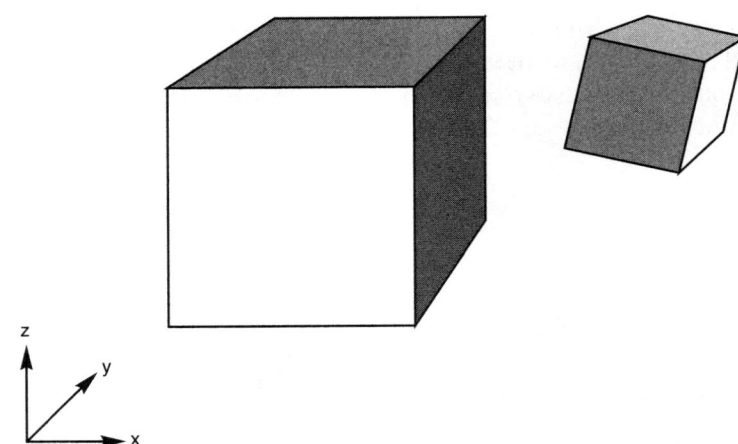

Figure 8.4. *A 3-D scene built with transformed 3-D objects.*

3-D Coordinate Transformations

Scaling, rotating, or translating a polygon-bound 3-D object involves transforming the coordinates of the vertices. Each of the operations is a type of 3-D coordinate transformation. A concise mathematical notation for expressing coordinate transformation is the matrix-vector multiplication. The 3-D point is represented by a three-dimensional column vector, which is simply the x-, y-, and z-coordinates arranged in a column. A matrix is a two-dimensional array of values with a specified number of elements in each row and column. There are specific algebraic rules for multiplying one matrix with another or a matrix with a vector. For example, here is how you would multiply a 3-D vector v by a 3x3 matrix T:

```
       t11  t12  t13                  v1
T  =   t21  t22  t23        v  =      v2
       t31  t32  t33                  v3


           t11 v1 + t12 v2 + t13 v3
T v  =     t21 v1 + t22 v2 + t23 v3
           t31 v1 + t32 v2 + t33 v3
```

3-D Graphics

As you can see, the product of a 3x3 matrix and a 3-D vector is another 3-D vector. You can express any coordinate transformation of a 3-D point in terms of a 3x3 matrix. Then the transformation can be applied by multiplying the vector with the transformation matrix. The following sections describe the three types of coordinate transformations: scaling, translation, and rotation.

Scaling

Scaling the coordinates of a point involves multiplying each coordinate by a constant factor. For instance, if you multiply each coordinate of the unit cube by two, the cube becomes twice as large as its previous size. You can also scale the x-, y-, and z-coordinates unequally to get other effects. If you want to scale the x-, y-, and z-coordinate of a 3-D point by the factors s1, s2, and s3, respectively, the following 3x3 transformation matrix represents the scaling:

```
      s1  0   0
T  =  0   s2  0
      0   0   s3
```

You can easily verify that multiplying a vector by this matrix scales the coordinates in the desired manner. Note that although the scaling is shown in terms of a transformation matrix, you do not have to go through the matrix-vector multiplication in your programs. All you have to do is multiply each coordinate by the appropriate factor.

Translation

Translation refers to moving an object to a new point while keeping its orientation the same. To translate a 3-D point, you simply have to add appropriate offsets to the x-, y-, and z-coordinates to take into account the effect of the movement. Thus, translation is basically an addition of two vectors. You can express translation as a matrix multiplication, but you need another mathematical crutch—the *homogeneous coordinate*. You have to augment each 3-D coordinate with an additional coordinate with a value of 1 like this:

```
      v1
v  =  v2
      v3
      1
```

281

This is known as a point in a homogeneous coordinate system. With this definition, you can achieve a translation by multiplying this vector by a 4x4 transformation matrix whose last column represents the amount of translation:

$$T = \begin{matrix} 1 & 0 & 0 & d1 \\ 0 & 1 & 0 & d2 \\ 0 & 0 & 1 & d3 \\ 0 & 0 & 0 & 1 \end{matrix}$$

If you multiply the four-dimensional vector v by this matrix, you get this result:

$$v = \begin{matrix} v1 + d1 \\ v2 + d2 \\ v3 + d3 \\ 1 \end{matrix}$$

which represents a translation.

In fact, by using this artifact of homogeneous coordinates, you can express all transformations as a series of matrix multiplications. In the rest of the discussion, I revert back to 3x3 transformation matrices.

Rotation

Rotation is the most complicated of the coordinate transformations and the most important because rotation is what gives us the three-dimensional feeling of being able to see behind an object by rotating it. The simplest way to specify rotation is to express it as a sequence of rotations about the x-, y-, and z-axes. Here are the transformation matrices Θ, Φ, and Ψ denoting rotation about the x-, y-, and z-axes of a right-handed coordinate system:

$$\Theta = \begin{matrix} 1 & 0 & 0 \\ 0 & \cos È & -\sin È \\ 0 & \sin È & \cos È \end{matrix} \quad \Phi = \begin{matrix} \cos ø & 0 & \sin ø \\ 0 & 1 & 0 \\ -\sin ø & 0 & \cos ø \end{matrix} \quad \Psi = \begin{matrix} \cos Á & -\sin Á & 0 \\ \sin Á & \cos Á & 0 \\ 0 & 0 & 1 \end{matrix}$$

Here, È, ø, and Á are the angles of rotation about the x-, y-, and z-axis, respectively. Given these transformation matrices, if you rotate the vector v first about the x-axis, then about the y-axis, and finally about the z-axis, the transformed vector is

$$\Psi \cdot \Phi \cdot \Theta \cdot v$$

3-D Graphics

You can multiply Ψ, Φ, and Θ to define a composite transformation matrix R(È,ø,Á) that performs all the rotations:

```
             cosÁcosø    -sinÁcosÈ+cosÁsinøsinÈ    sinÁsinÈ+cosÁsinøcosÈ
R(È,ø,Á)=    sinÁcosø     cosÁcosÈ+sinÁsinøsinÈ   -cosÁsinÈ+sinÁsinøcosÈ
              -sinø            cosøsinÈ                  cosøcosÈ
```

There is only one note of caution in all this. Remember that matrix multiplication is not commutative—that means if A and B are two matrices, the product AB is not the same as BA. Thus, if you apply the rotations about the coordinate axes in a different order, the result is different.

A Few More Vector Operations

In addition to the coordinate transformations, you have to use a few other vector operations when displaying 3-D graphics. So far I have been depicting a 3-D vector as a point in space, but if you draw a line between the origin of the coordinate system and the point, you see that the vector has a magnitude and an orientation (see Figure 8.5). You can compute the magnitude of a vector v as follows:

```
    v1
v = v2                 ||v|| = sqrt(v1*v1 + v2*v2 + v3*v3)
    v3
```

where `sqrt()` denotes the square root.

To *normalize* a vector, you divide each coordinate of the vector by the magnitude.

The *dot product* of two vectors, a.b, yields a single number given by the following expression:

```
    a1       b1
a = a2   b = b2   Dot product: a.b = (a1*b1 + a2*b2 + a3*b3)
    a3       b3
```

The dot product of two normalized vectors is equal to the cosine of the angle between the two vectors.

Another important vector operation is the *cross product* of two vectors, which is a third vector that is perpendicular to the plane containing the other two vectors. The expression for the cross product of a and b, a_b is given by the following:

283

$$a = \begin{matrix} ax \\ ay \\ az \end{matrix} \quad b = \begin{matrix} bx \\ by \\ bz \end{matrix} \quad a \_ b = \begin{matrix} (ay\ bz\ -\ az\ by) \\ (az\ bx\ -\ ax\ bz) \\ (ax\ by\ -\ ay\ bx) \end{matrix}$$

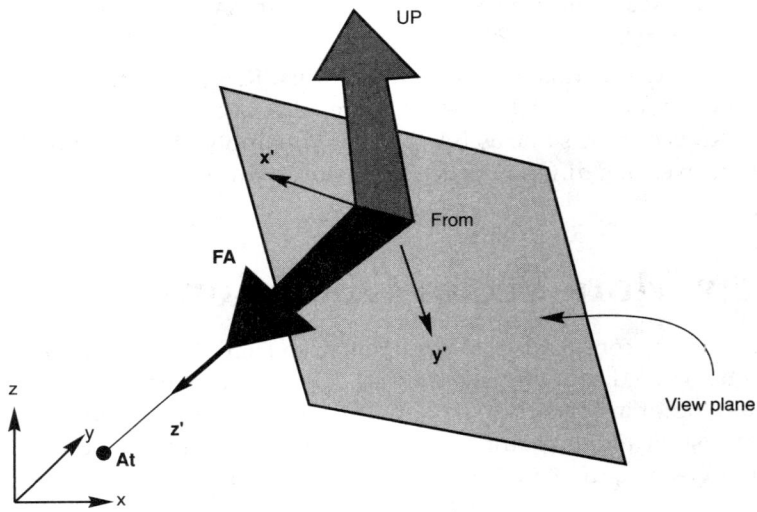

Figure 8.5. *Specifying the view coordinate system.*

If you know the orientation of two axes of a 3-D Cartesian coordinate system, the third axis can be found by taking the cross product of the first two axes. You see this property used when transforming a 3-D scene to the coordinate frame of the viewer.

Viewing a 3-D Scene

So far I have described how you can scale, translate, and rotate objects and place them in a 3-D scene. Now we turn to generating a 2-D representation of a 3-D scene when viewed from a specific point. It is as if you are holding a camera, pointing it toward the scene, and taking a picture. The question is how will the picture look? To find the answer, you have to transform the entire scene into the coordinate frame of the camera and project the 3-D points onto a plane.

3-D Graphics

Transforming to View Coordinates

Using the camera analogy, you can specify the view coordinate frame in terms of two points and a vector. As shown in Figure 8.5, the two important points are

- The point where the camera is located (the *from point*)
- The point in the scene at which the camera looks (the *at point*)

The location of the camera is the origin of the camera's coordinate system. It is customary to define the z-axis of the camera's coordinate system to be the line joining the origin and the point at which the camera is looking. A third parameter, the *up vector*, completely specifies the orientation of the camera's coordinate frame.

We want the z-axis of the view coordinate system to coincide with the line joining the from point to the at point—let us call the normalized version of this vector FA. The plane normal to this axis is the x-y plane of the view coordinate system. The unit vector along the x-axis of the view coordinate system is given by the cross product FA×UP where UP is the normalized up vector. Finally, the unit vector along the z-axis is UP×(FA×UP). As explained in Section 5.7 of the graphics textbook by Foley, van Dam, and others (1990), the transformation matrix to convert the points in a scene to the view coordinate system is given by

```
R = [ FA×UP    UP×(FA×UP)    UP ]
```

where each entry is a column vector, resulting in a 3x3 matrix R. For a given viewing direction, you can transform the points in a 3-D scene by multiplying each point (a 3-D vector) by the transformation matrix R.

Perspective Projection

Once all points in the 3-D scene are transformed into the view coordinate system, you can generate the 2-D representation of the scene by a *projection*, which transforms 3-D coordinates into 2-D. The simplest projection is to drop the z-coordinates after the transformation. Remember that the z-axis of the view coordinate system is along the viewing direction. Thus, dropping the z-coordinates gives you what is known as an *orthographic projection*.

285

Unfortunately, orthographic projections do not provide a sense of depth. Our visual system shows us what is known as a perspective projection of the 3-D world around us. A good example of perspective projection is the view of a straight stretch of railroad tracks. Even though the railroad tracks are parallel lines, they seem to meet at a distance.

For a point (x,y,z) in the view coordinate system, the projected point is:

```
x' = x.d/(d+z)
y' = y.d/(d+z)
```

where d is the distance from the viewing point to the origin of the scene.

C++ Classes for 3-D Modeling

When developing a set of classes for 3-D modeling, I wanted to define a `Scene3D` class that contained one or more 3-D shapes with each shape represented by a `Shape3D` class. Each `Shape3D` consists of a number of planar facets, each modeled by a `Facet3D` class. Each `Facet3D`, in turn, is represented by an ordered list of vertices. A `Vector3D` class is used to encapsulate a vertex. Each `Shape3D` maintains its own array of vertices and a `Facet3D` object refers to its vertices by the index of each vertex in the array. Keeping all vertices of a shape in a single array makes it easier to apply the view transform to the vertices.

Defining the Primitive 3-D Classes

Listing 8.1 shows the file `shape3d.h` that declares the classes `Vector3D`, `Facet3D`, and `Shape3D`. These classes are the primitive building blocks of any 3-D scene represented by a `Scene3D` object.

A `Vector3D` is defined by three coordinates. I used a `typedef` to define the type `Coord`. For now `Coord` is the same as `float`, but this allows us to switch over to some other computationally efficient representation for the coordinates. I wanted to leave open the possibility of using fixed-point arithmetic in the future.

3-D Graphics

The Facet3D has up to four vertices. Instead of storing the Vector3D objects that represent the vertices, Facet3D stores the index of the vertices from the array of Vector3D maintained by the Shape3D class. This scheme allows us to store the vertices without any possibility of duplicating them in the Facet3D objects (because adjacent facets share vertices).

The Shape3D class uses the array named vertices to store Vector3D objects and the array named facets for Facet3D objects. An additional array of Vector3D objects, xfrmv, is used to store coordinates of the vertices after transforming them to the view coordinate system.

The Shape3D class stores the Vector3D and Facet3D objects in container classes of type Array from the Borland Class Library. Additionally, the Scene3D class uses an Array to store the Shape3D objects in a scene. To allow this, all three classes, Vector3D, Facet3D, and Shape3D are derived from the Object class. As a consequence of this, each of these classes requires a handful of extra member functions, such as isA, nameOf, hashValue, and printOn.

Listing 8.1. shape3d.h— Declaration of classes for 3-D primitives.

```
//---------------------------------------------------------------
// File: shape3d.h
// Declares a 3D shape consisting of polygonal facets.
//---------------------------------------------------------------
#if !defined(__SHAPE3D_H)
#define __SHAPE3D_H

#include <windows.h>
#include <fstream.h>
#include <array.h>
#include <math.h>

const unsigned short SHAPE_ACTIVE    = 1;
const unsigned short SHAPE_UPDATE    = 2;
const unsigned short SHAPE_SCALE     = 4;
const unsigned short SHAPE_XLATE     = 8;
const unsigned short SHAPE_ROTATE    = 16;

// Later on we'll replace these with sine and cosine tables
#define TabSin(x)   sin(x)
#define TabCos(x)   cos(x)
```

continues

Listing 8.1. continued

```cpp
#define ToCoord(s)      atoi(s)
#define ModCoord(x,y)   fmod(x,y)

typedef float Coord;
#define abs_coord(x) fabs(x)
const Coord err = 0.001;

class Scene3D;

class Vector3D : public Object
{
friend Scene3D;
friend Shape3D;
friend View3DWindow;
friend void _FAR PASCAL _export draw_shape(HDC hdc,
                      short x, short y,LPVOID data);
public:
    Vector3D() : x(0), y(0), z(0) {}
    Vector3D(Coord a, Coord b, Coord c) :
            x(a), y(b), z(c) {}
    Vector3D(const Vector3D& v) : x(v.x), y(v.y), z(v.z) {}


// The following functions are required because Vector3D is
// derived from Object (which we did to use Borland's
// container class library)
    classType isA() const { return Vector3DClass;}

    char* nameOf() const { return "Vector3DClass";}

    hashValueType hashValue() const
    { return (hashValueType)z;}

    int isEqual(const Object _FAR& ob) const;
    void printOn(ostream& os) const
    {
        os << x << " " << y << " " << z << endl;
    }

// Some operations on Vector3D objects
    Vector3D& operator=(const Vector3D& v)
    {
        if(this != &v)
        {
            x = v.x;
            y = v.y;
```

3-D Graphics

```cpp
            z = v.z;
        }
        return *this;
    }
    Coord abs() { return sqrt(x*x + y*y + z*z);}

    void scale(const Coord s)
    {
        if(abs_coord(s) > 0.0001)
        {
            x /= s;
            y /= s;
            z /= s;
        }
    }

    void diff(const Vector3D& v)
    {
        x -= v.x;
        y -= v.y;
        z -= v.z;
    }
    void normalize()
    {
        Coord s = abs();
        scale(s);
    }
    void cross(const Vector3D& v)
    {
        Coord x1 = y*v.z - v.y*z;
        Coord y1 = z*v.x - v.z*x;
        Coord z1 = x*v.y - v.x*y;
        x = x1;
        y = y1;
        z = z1;
    }
private:
    Coord x, y, z;  // 3D coordinates of the vector

    enum { Vector3DClass = __firstUserClass + 10};
};

// A facet consists of 3 or 4 indices into an array
// of 3D vectors
class Facet3D : public Object
{
friend Scene3D;
friend Shape3D;
```

continues

Listing 8.1. continued

```cpp
    friend void _FAR PASCAL _export draw_shape(HDC hdc,
                        short x, short y, LPVOID data);
public:
    Facet3D() : red(0), green(0), blue(0), flags(0), zavg(0)
    {
        vertex[0] = -1;
        vertex[1] = -1;
        vertex[2] = -1;
        vertex[3] = -1;
    }

// The following are required of every class derived from
// Object (which we must do if we want to use the Borland
// container classes).
    classType isA() const { return Facet3DClass;}
    char* nameOf() const { return "Facet3DClass";}
    hashValueType hashValue() const
    {
        return (hashValueType)(vertex[0] + vertex[1]+
                        vertex[2] + vertex[3]);
    }

    int isEqual(const Object _FAR& ob) const;

    void printOn(ostream& os) const
    {
        os << vertex[0] << " " << vertex[1] << " "
           << vertex[2] << " " << vertex[3] << endl;
        os << red << " " << green << " " << blue  << endl;
    }

    void rgb(unsigned char r, unsigned char g, unsigned char b)
    {
        red   = r;
        green = g;
        blue  = b;
    }
private:
    short           vertex[4];
    Coord           zavg;
    unsigned char   red;
    unsigned char   green;
    unsigned char   blue;
    unsigned char   flags; // For future use

    enum { Facet3DClass = __firstUserClass + 11};
```

3-D Graphics

```cpp
};

// A shape is a collection of facets

class Shape3D : public Object
{
public:
friend Shape3D;
friend Scene3D;
friend void _FAR PASCAL _export draw_shape(HDC hdc,
                        short x, short y, LPVOID data);
    Shape3D();

    ~Shape3D();

    classType isA() const { return Shape3DClass;}

    char* nameOf() const { return "Shape3DClass";}

    hashValueType hashValue() const {return 0;}

    int isEqual(const Object _FAR& ob) const { return 0;}

    void printOn(ostream& os) const
    {
        os << numvertices << endl;
        os << vertices;
        os << numfacets << endl;
        os << facets;
    }
// Functions to manipulate the status of a shape
    unsigned short needs_update()
    { return status & SHAPE_UPDATE;}
    unsigned short is_active()
    { return status & SHAPE_ACTIVE;}
    unsigned short is_scaled()
    { return status & SHAPE_SCALE;}
    unsigned short is_translated()
    { return status & SHAPE_XLATE;}
    unsigned short is_rotated()
    { return status & SHAPE_ROTATE;}

    void active() { status |= SHAPE_ACTIVE | SHAPE_UPDATE;}
    void update() { status |= SHAPE_UPDATE;}
    void mark_scaled()
```

continues

Listing 8.1. continued

```
{ status |= SHAPE_SCALE | SHAPE_UPDATE;}
    void mark_xlated()
    { status |= SHAPE_XLATE | SHAPE_UPDATE;}
    void mark_rotated()
    { status |= SHAPE_ROTATE | SHAPE_UPDATE;}

    void update_done(){ status &= ~SHAPE_UPDATE;}
    void scale_done(){ status &= ~SHAPE_SCALE;}
    void translation_done(){ status &= ~SHAPE_XLATE;}
    void rotation_done(){ status &= ~SHAPE_ROTATE;}
    void inactive() { status &= ~SHAPE_ACTIVE;}

// Read a shape from a file
    read(const char* filename);

// Save a shape in a file
    write(const char* filename);

// Functions to translate and rotate the shapes in the scene.
// These functions simply accumulate in a transformation
// matrix-the actual transformation occurs when you
// call the "do_transform" function

    void scale(Coord sx, Coord sy, Coord sz);
    void translate(Coord tx, Coord ty, Coord tz);
    void rotate(Coord rx, Coord ry, Coord rz);
    void do_transform();
    void find_extents();
    void sort_facets();

    Coord min_xpos() { return xmin;}
    Coord max_xpos() { return xmax;}
    Coord min_ypos() { return ymin;}
    Coord max_ypos() { return ymax;}
    Coord min_zpos() { return zmin;}
    Coord max_zpos() { return zmax;}

private:
    Array       *vertices;  // Vertices in scene coordinates
    Array       *xfrmv;     // Temporary storage used after
                            // transforming the vertices to
                            // the viewer's coordinate frame

    Array       *facets;    // Array of facets

    short       numfacets;
    short       numvertices;
```

3-D Graphics

```
    Coord         xmin, xmax;
    Coord         ymin, ymax;
    Coord         zmin, zmax;

    Coord         xlat[3];        // Translation vector
    Coord         sc[3];          // Scale factors
    Coord         rot3x3[3][3];   // 3x3 rotation matrix
    unsigned short status;

    enum { Shape3DClass = __firstUserClass + 12};
};

#endif
```

Implementing *Shape3D*

Listing 8.2 shows the file `shape3d.cpp` that implements the classes `Vector3D`, `Facet3D`, and `Shape3D`. `Shape3D`'s member functions `scale`, `translate`, and `rotate` transform a shape with respect to the 3-D scene's coordinate frame. These functions do not actually apply the transformation; they simply accumulate the specified transformations in a matrix. Then, a call to the `do_transform` function is necessary to apply the coordinate transformations.

The `find_extents` function finds the lower and upper limits of the `Shape3D`'s coordinates along the x-, y-, and z-axes. The `sort_facets` function sorts the facets in terms of increasing z-coordinates. This function is called before drawing the facets to ensure that facets nearer to the viewing point hide the ones that are further away. The `read` function is meant for loading a 3-D scene from a file.

Listing 8.2. `shape3d.cpp`—
Implementation of the classes representing 3-D primitives.

```
//-------------------------------------------------------------
// File: shape3d.cpp
// Implementation of the 3D shape classes.
//-------------------------------------------------------------
#include <string.h>
#include <stdlib.h>
#include "shape3d.h"
```

continues

Listing 8.2. continued

```cpp
//---------------------------------------------------------
// Vector3D:: i s E q u a l
// Equality test for 3D vectors

Vector3D::isEqual(const Object _FAR& ob) const
{
    Vector3D v = (Vector3D&)ob;
    if(abs_coord(v.x - x) > err) return 0;
    if(abs_coord(v.y - y) > err) return 0;
    if(abs_coord(v.z - z) > err) return 0;
    return 1;
}
//---------------------------------------------------------
// Facet3D:: i s E q u a l
// Equality test for 3D facets--I consider them equal if all
// vertex indices are equal.

Facet3D::isEqual(const Object _FAR& ob) const
{
    Facet3D f = (Facet3D&)ob;
    return ((f.vertex[0] == vertex[0]) &&
            (f.vertex[1] == vertex[1]) &&
            (f.vertex[2] == vertex[2]) &&
            (f.vertex[3] == vertex[3]));
}
//---------------------------------------------------------
// Shape3D:: S h a p e 3 D
// Default constructor for the Shape3D class

Shape3D::Shape3D() : facets(NULL), vertices(NULL), xfrmv(NULL),
        numvertices(0), numfacets(0)
{
// Initialize the translation, rotation, and scaling transforms
    sc[0] = sc[1] = sc[2] = 1;
    xlat[0] = xlat[1] = xlat[2] = 0;
    short i, j;
    for(i = 0; i < 3; i++)
        for(j = 0; j < 3; j++)
        {
            if(i == j) rot3x3[i][j] = 1;
            else rot3x3[i][j] = 0;
        }
}
//---------------------------------------------------------
// Shape3D:: ~ S h a p e 3 D
// Destructor for the Shape3D class
```

Chapter 8

3-D Graphics

```
Shape3D::~Shape3D()
{
    if(vertices != NULL) delete vertices;
    if(xfrmv != NULL) delete xfrmv;
    if(facets != NULL) delete facets;
}
//-------------------------------------------------------------
// Shape3D:: s c a l e
// Store the scale factor for use during "do_transform"

void Shape3D::scale(Coord sx, Coord sy, Coord sz)
{
    sc[0] *= sx;
    sc[1] *= sy;
    sc[2] *= sz;
// Mark shape for update
    mark_scaled();
}
//-------------------------------------------------------------
// Shape3D:: t r a n s l a t e
// Store the translations for use during "do_transform"

void Shape3D::translate(Coord tx, Coord ty, Coord tz)
{
    xlat[0] += tx;
    xlat[1] += ty;
    xlat[2] += tz;
// Mark shape as "translated"
    mark_xlated();
}
//-------------------------------------------------------------
// Shape3D:: r o t a t e
// Update the rotational transformation matrix for later use

void Shape3D::rotate(Coord rx, Coord ry, Coord rz)
{
    Coord cosx = TabCos(rx);
    Coord sinx = TabSin(rx);
    Coord cosy = TabCos(ry);
    Coord siny = TabSin(ry);
    Coord cosz = TabCos(rz);
    Coord sinz = TabSin(rz);
    Coord coszcosy = cosz*cosy;
    Coord sinzcosy = sinz*cosy;
    Coord coszsiny = cosz*siny;
    Coord sinzsiny = sinz*siny;

    rot3x3[0][0] = coszcosy;
```

continues

Listing 8.2. continued

```
    rot3x3[0][1] = sinx*coszsiny - sinzcosy;
    rot3x3[0][2] = sinz*sinx + cosx*coszsiny;
    rot3x3[1][0] = sinzsiny;
    rot3x3[1][1] = coszcosy + sinx*sinzsiny;
    rot3x3[1][2] = cosx*sinzsiny - sinx*cosz;
    rot3x3[2][0] = -siny;
    rot3x3[2][1] = sinx*cosy;
    rot3x3[2][2] = cosx*cosy;

// Mark shape as "rotated"
    mark_rotated();
}
//-------------------------------------------------------------
// Shape3D:: r e a d
// Read a shape from a file

int Shape3D::read(const char* filename)
{
    ifstream ifs(filename, ios::in);
    if(!ifs) return 0;

    char line[80];
// Read and ignore the first line of comment
    ifs.getline(line, sizeof(line));

// Next comes the number of vertices
    ifs.getline(line, sizeof(line));
    numvertices = atoi(line);
    vertices = new Array(numvertices, 0, 8);
    if(vertices == NULL) return 0;
    xfrmv = new Array(numvertices, 0, 8);
    if(xfrmv == NULL)
    {
        delete vertices;
        return 0;
    }

// Read the vertices
    short i;
    char *token;
    for(i = 0; i < numvertices; i++)
    {
        ifs.getline(line, sizeof(line));
        if(!ifs)
        {
            numvertices = i;
```

3-D Graphics

Chapter 8

```cpp
            return 0;
        }
        Vector3D* v = new Vector3D;
// Parse the line...first token
        token = strtok(line, " ");
        v->x = ToCoord(token);

// Second token
        token = strtok(NULL, " ");
        v->y = ToCoord(token);

// Third token
        token = strtok(NULL, " ");
        v->z = ToCoord(token);
// Now insert the vector into the "vertices" array
        vertices->addAt(*v, i);
// Make a copy for the "xfrmv" array
        Vector3D* xv = new Vector3D(*v);
        xfrmv->addAt(*xv, i);
    }

// Now read the facets

    ifs.getline(line, sizeof(line));
    numfacets = atoi(line);
    facets = new Array(numfacets, 0, 8);
    if(facets == NULL) return 0;

    for(i = 0; i < numfacets; i++)
    {
                if(ifs.eof())
        {
            numvertices = i;
            return 0;
        }
        ifs.getline(line, sizeof(line));
        Facet3D* f = new Facet3D;

// Parse the line...first token
        token = strtok(line, " ");
        f->vertex[0] = atoi(token);
// Second token
        token = strtok(NULL, " ");
        f->vertex[1] = atoi(token);
// Third token
        token = strtok(NULL, " ");
        f->vertex[2] = atoi(token);
// Fourth token
```

continues

Listing 8.2. continued

```
            token = strtok(NULL, " ");
            if(token != NULL) f->vertex[3] = atoi(token);

// Colors of the facet follow on the next line
            ifs.getline(line, sizeof(line));

// Parse the line...first token
            token = strtok(line, " ");
            f->red = atoi(token);
// Second token
            token = strtok(NULL, " ");
            f->green = atoi(token);
// Third token
            token = strtok(NULL, " ");
            f->blue = atoi(token);

// Now insert the vector in the array
            facets->addAt(*f, i);
        }

        return 1;
}
//--------------------------------------------------------------
// Shape3D:: w r i t e
// Save a shape in a file

int Shape3D::write(const char* filename)
{
// To be done later...
        return 1;
}
//--------------------------------------------------------------
// Shape3D:: d o _ t r a n s f o r m
// Apply any pending transform

void Shape3D::do_transform()
{
    short i, j;
    short nv = vertices->getItemsInContainer();
    if(nv <= 0) return;

// Scale, rotate, and translate shape.
    if(is_scaled())
    {
        if(is_rotated())
        {
```

3-D Graphics

```
// Accumulate scaling into rotation
            for(i = 0; i < 3; i++)
            {
                for(j = 0; j < 3; j++)
                    rot3x3[i][j] *= sc[i];
            }
        }
        else
        {
// Scale all vertices in this shape
            for(i = 0; i < nv; i++)
            {
                Vector3D& v = (Vector3D&)(*vertices)[i];
                v.x *= sc[0];
                v.y *= sc[1];
                v.z *= sc[2];
            }
        }
        sc[0] = sc[1] = sc[2] = 1;
        scale_done();
    }

// Now do the rotation
    if(is_rotated())
    {
        for(i = 0; i < nv; i++)
        {
            Vector3D& v = (Vector3D&)(*vertices)[i];
            Coord x, y, z;
            x = rot3x3[0][0]*v.x + rot3x3[0][1]*v.y +
                rot3x3[0][2]*v.z;
            y = rot3x3[1][0]*v.x + rot3x3[1][1]*v.y +
                rot3x3[1][2]*v.z;
            z = rot3x3[2][0]*v.x + rot3x3[2][1]*v.y +
                rot3x3[2][2]*v.z;
            v.x = x;
            v.y = y;
            v.z = z;
        }
        for(i = 0; i < 3; i++)
            for(j = 0; j < 3; j++)
            {
                if(i == j) rot3x3[i][j] = 1;
                else rot3x3[i][j] = 0;
            }
        rotation_done();
    }
```

continues

Listing 8.2. continued

```
// Finally, the translation
    if(is_translated())
    {
        for(i = 0; i < nv; i++)
        {
          Vector3D& v = (Vector3D&)(*vertices)[i];
            v.x += xlat[0];
            v.y += xlat[1];
            v.z += xlat[2];
        }
        xlat[0] = xlat[1] = xlat[2] = 0;
        translation_done();
    }

}
//-------------------------------------------------------------
// Shape3D::  f i n d _ e x t e n t s
// Find the minimum and maximum x-y-z coordinates of all facets
// in the viewer's coordinate frame.

void Shape3D::find_extents()
{
    short i, j, vindex;
    xmin = ymin = zmin = -32000;
    xmax = ymax = zmax = 32000;

    for(i = 0; i < numfacets; i++)
    {
        Facet3D& f = (Facet3D&)(*facets)[i];
        for(j = 0; j < 4; j++)
        {
            vindex = f.vertex[j];
            if(vindex < 0) break;
            Vector3D& v = (Vector3D&)(*xfrmv)[vindex];
            if(xmin > v.x) xmin = v.x;
            if(xmax < v.x) xmax = v.x;
            if(ymin > v.x) ymin = v.y;
            if(ymax < v.x) ymax = v.y;
            if(zmin > v.x) zmin = v.z;
            if(zmax < v.x) zmax = v.z;
            f.zavg += v.z;
        }
        f.zavg /= (Coord)j;
    }
}
//-------------------------------------------------------------
```

```
// Shape3D::sort_facets
// Sort the facets in order of descending min-z coord of facets

void Shape3D::sort_facets()
{
// Use a simple bubble sort
    short nf = facets->getItemsInContainer();

    short i, j;
    for(i = 0; i < nf; i++)
    {
        for(j = 0; j < nf-1; j++)
        {
            Facet3D& fj = (Facet3D&)(*facets)[j];
            Facet3D& fjp1 = (Facet3D&)(*facets)[j+1];
            if(fj.zavg < fjp1.zavg)
            {
                facets->detach(fj);
                facets->detach(fjp1);
                facets->addAt(fjp1, j);
                facets->addAt(fj, j+1);
            }
        }
    }
}
```

Defining the 3-D Scene

The 3-D scene is modeled by the Scene3D class. Listing 8.3 shows the file scene3d.h that declares the Scene3D class. The most important component of the Scene3D is the array of 3-D shapes represented by Shape3D objects.

Scene3D also includes a large number of variables for specifying the viewing parameters. Here is a partial list of Scene3D's member variables:

- ■ Array *shape_array; is the array of Shape3D objects.
- ■ Shape3D **shapes; contains the same shapes as shape_array.
- ■ short numshapes; is the number of shapes in the scene.
- ■ unsigned short wview; is the width of the viewing window in pixels (used to ensure that the 3-D view is centered in the window).

- unsigned short hview; is the height of the viewing window in pixels (used to ensure that the 3-D view is centered in the window).
- unsigned short wview_2, hview_2; is half the width and height that are precomputed to avoid unnecessary computations during display.
- Coord view_angle; is an angle in degrees (used to magnify or reduce the perspective view and in the view_transform function).
- Vector3D from; specifies the location of the viewer.
- Vector3D at; specifies the point at which the viewer is looking.
- Vector3D up; specifies the orientation of the view coordinate system (see description earlier in this chapter).
- Coord max_view_angle, min_view_angle; specify the ranges within which the view_angle must lie.
- Coord max_zoom_range, min_zoom_range; specify the maximum and minimum distances of the viewing point from the origin of the scene.

Listing 8.3. scene3d.h—Declaration of the Scene3D class.

```
//----------------------------------------------------------------
// File: scene3d.h
// Declarations for the Scene3D class that represents a 3D
// scenario containing Shape3D objects.
//----------------------------------------------------------------
#if !defined(__SCENE3D_H)
#define __SCENE3D_H

#include <windows.h>

#include "shape3d.h"

#define DEG_TO_RAD 0.0174532

class View3DWindow;

class Scene3D
{
public:
friend View3DWindow;
    Scene3D() : numshapes(0), shape_array(NULL), shapes(NULL),
                wview(640), hview(480), d(0) {}
```

3-D Graphics

```
    Scene3D(unsigned short w, unsigned short h,
            const char* filename) : wview(w),
            hview(h), numshapes(0), shape_array(NULL),
            shapes(NULL), d(0)
    {
        read(filename);
        wview_2 = wview/2;
        hview_2 = hview/2;
    }

    ~Scene3D();

    int read(const char* filename);

    void view_transform();

    void zoomin(short step);
    void zoomout(short step);
    void movein(short step);
    void moveout(short step);
    void calc_from()
    {
// Compute x, y, z coords of "from" point
        Coord elrad = el * DEG_TO_RAD;
        Coord azrad = az * DEG_TO_RAD;
        Coord rcosthta = range * TabCos(elrad);
        from.x = rcosthta * TabCos(azrad);
        from.y = rcosthta * TabSin(azrad);
        from.z = range * TabSin(elrad);
    }
    void azimuth(Coord _az)
    {
        az = _az;
        if(az < min_az) az = min_az;
        if(az > max_az) az = max_az;
        calc_from();
    }
    Coord azimuth() { return az;}
    void az_step(Coord daz)
    {
        az += daz;
        az = ModCoord(az, 360);
        if(az < min_az) az = min_az;
        if(az > max_az) az = max_az;
        calc_from();
    }

    void elevation(Coord _el)
```

continues

Listing 8.3. continued

```
    {
        el = _el;
        if(el < min_el) el = min_el;
        if(el > max_el) el = max_el;
        calc_from();
    }
    Coord elevation() { return el;}
    void el_step(Coord del)
    {
        el += del;
        el = ModCoord(el, 360);
        if(el < min_el) el = min_el;
        if(el > max_el) el = max_el;
        calc_from();
    }

private:
    Array           *shape_array; // array of Shape3D objects
    Shape3D         **shapes;
    short           numshapes;
    unsigned short wview;    // Dimensions of view plane
    unsigned short hview;
    unsigned short wview_2, hview_2;
    Coord           view_angle;
    Vector3D        from;
    Vector3D        at;
    Vector3D        up;

    Vector3D        v1, v2, v3;
    Coord           xoffset, yoffset, zoffset;
    Coord           d;
    Coord           fov;
    Coord           max_view_angle;
    Coord           min_view_angle;
    Coord           max_zoom_range;
    Coord           min_zoom_range;
    Coord           min_az, max_az;
    Coord           min_el, max_el;
    Coord           range, az, el;
};

#endif
```

Listing 8.4 shows the file scene3d.cpp that implements the Scene3D class. The two most important member functions of Scene3D are: read and view_transform.

3-D Graphics

Like the Shape3D class, Scene3D provides the read function for loading a scene from a file.

The view_transform function computes the coordinates of all vertices in the view coordinate system. If you look at the code in Listing 8.4, you see that view_transform loops over all the Shape3D objects in the scene and for each Shape3D, transforms the coordinates in the vertices array. The transformed coordinates are stored in the xfrmv array in each Shape3D object. Thus, all that a 3-D viewing program has to do is call view_transform for a given set of viewing parameters and then draw the facets using the coordinates in the xfrmv array of each Shape3D object in the 3-D scene.

Listing 8.4. scene3d.cpp—
Implementation of the Scene3D class.

```
//---------------------------------------------------------------
// File: scene3d.cpp
// Implementation of the Scene3D class.
//---------------------------------------------------------------
#include <string.h>
#include <stdlib.h>
#include "scene3d.h"
//---------------------------------------------------------------
// Scene3D::  ~ S c e n e 3 D
// Destructor for a Scene3D object

Scene3D::~Scene3D()
{
    if(shape_array != NULL) delete shape_array;
    if(shapes != NULL) delete shapes;
}
//---------------------------------------------------------------
// Scene3D::  r e a d
// Read a 3D scene from a file.

int Scene3D::read(const char* filename)
{
    if(filename == NULL) return 0;

    if(shape_array != NULL) delete shape_array;
    if(shapes != NULL) delete shapes;
    shape_array = NULL;
    shapes = NULL;
```

continues

Listing 8.4. continued

```cpp
// Open file for input
    ifstream ifs(filename, ios::in);
    if(!ifs) return 0;

// Read the scene
    char line[80];
    char *token;

// Read the first line--a comment
    ifs.getline(line, sizeof(line));

// View angle
    ifs.getline(line, sizeof(line));
    token = strtok(line, " ");
    min_view_angle = ToCoord(token);
    token = strtok(NULL, " ");
    max_view_angle = ToCoord(token);
// Set initial view angle to midpoint between max and min
    view_angle = (max_view_angle + min_view_angle) / 2;
    Coord vua_rad = view_angle * DEG_TO_RAD / 2;
    Coord sv = TabSin(vua_rad);
    if(abs_coord(sv) < 0.000001) sv = 0.000001;
    fov = TabCos(vua_rad) / sv;

// Min/Max ranges of "from" point
    ifs.getline(line, sizeof(line));

    token = strtok(line, " ");
    min_zoom_range = ToCoord(token);
    token = strtok(NULL, " ");
    max_zoom_range = ToCoord(token);

// Min/max azimuth
    ifs.getline(line, sizeof(line));
    token = strtok(line, " ");
    min_az = ToCoord(token);
    token = strtok(NULL, " ");
    max_az = ToCoord(token);

// Min/max elevation
    ifs.getline(line, sizeof(line));
    token = strtok(line, " ");
    min_el = ToCoord(token);
    token = strtok(NULL, " ");
    max_el = ToCoord(token);
```

3-D Graphics

```
// The "From" vector
    ifs.getline(line, sizeof(line));

// Parse the line...first token
    token = strtok(line, " ");
    range = ToCoord(token);
// Second token
    token = strtok(NULL, " ");
    az = ToCoord(token);
// Third token
    token = strtok(NULL, " ");
    el = ToCoord(token);
    calc_from();

// The "At" vector
    ifs.getline(line, sizeof(line));

// Parse the line...first token
    token = strtok(line, " ");
    at.x = ToCoord(token);
// Second token
    token = strtok(NULL, " ");
    at.y = ToCoord(token);
// Third token
    token = strtok(NULL, " ");
    at.z = ToCoord(token);

// The "Up" vector
    ifs.getline(line, sizeof(line));

// Parse the line...first token
    token = strtok(line, " ");
    up.x = ToCoord(token);
// Second token
    token = strtok(NULL, " ");
    up.y = ToCoord(token);
// Third token
    token = strtok(NULL, " ");
    up.z = ToCoord(token);

// Number of shapes
    ifs.getline(line, sizeof(line));
    numshapes = atoi(line);

// Allocate arrays
    shape_array = new Array(numshapes, 0, 8);
    shapes = new Shape3D*[numshapes];
```

continues

Listing 8.4. continued

```
    Coord x, y, z;
// Read the shapes from individual files...
    short i;
    for(i = 0; i < numshapes; i++)
    {
        if(ifs.eof())
        {
            numshapes = i;
            return 0;
        }
// First the file from which to read the shape's data
        ifs.getline(line, sizeof(line));
        shapes[i] = new Shape3D;

        if(!shapes[i]->read(line))
        {
            numshapes = i;
            return 0;
        }
        while(strnicmp(line, "END", 3) != 0)
        {
            ifs.getline(line, sizeof(line));
            if(ifs.eof())
            {
                numshapes = i;
                return 0;
            }
            token = strtok(line, " ");

            if(strnicmp(token, "SCALE", 5) == 0)
            {
                token = strtok(NULL, " ");
                x = ToCoord(token);
                token = strtok(NULL, " ");
                y = ToCoord(token);
                token = strtok(NULL, " ");
                z = ToCoord(token);
                shapes[i]->scale(x, y, z);
            }
            if(strnicmp(token, "ROTATE", 6) == 0)
            {
                token = strtok(NULL, " ");
                x = ToCoord(token);
                token = strtok(NULL, " ");
                y = ToCoord(token);
```

3-D Graphics

```
                    token = strtok(NULL, " ");
                    z = ToCoord(token);
                    shapes[i]->rotate(x, y, z);
                }
                if(strnicmp(token, "TRANSLATE", 9) == 0)
                {
                    token = strtok(NULL, " ");
                    x = ToCoord(token);
                    token = strtok(NULL, " ");
                    y = ToCoord(token);
                    token = strtok(NULL, " ");
                    z = ToCoord(token);
                    shapes[i]->translate(x, y, z);
                }
                if(strnicmp(token, "TRANSFORM", 9) == 0)
                {
                    shapes[i]->do_transform();
                }
            }
// Add this shape to the array of shapes
                shape_array->addAt(*(shapes[i]), i);
        }
        return 1;
}
//--------------------------------------------------------------
// Scene3D:: z o o m o u t
// Reduce the image by changing field of view

void Scene3D::zoomout(short step)
{
    Coord dv = (max_view_angle - min_view_angle) / (Coord)step;
    view_angle += dv;
    if(view_angle > max_view_angle)
            view_angle = max_view_angle;
    Coord vua_rad = view_angle * DEG_TO_RAD / 2;
    Coord sv = TabSin(vua_rad);
    if(abs_coord(sv) < 0.000001) sv = 0.000001;
    fov = TabCos(vua_rad) / sv;
}
//--------------------------------------------------------------
// Scene3D:: z o o m i n
// Enlarge the image by changing field of view

void Scene3D::zoomin(short step)
{
    Coord dv = (max_view_angle - min_view_angle) / (Coord)step;
    view_angle -= dv;
    if(view_angle < min_view_angle)
            view_angle = min_view_angle;
```

continues

Listing 8.4. continued

```
    Coord vua_rad = view_angle * DEG_TO_RAD / 2;
    Coord sv = TabSin(vua_rad);
    if(abs_coord(sv) < 0.000001) sv = 0.000001;
    fov = TabCos(vua_rad) / sv;
}
//-------------------------------------------------------------
// Scene3D:: m o v e i n
// Bring the "from" point closer

void Scene3D::movein(short step)
{
    Coord dR = (max_zoom_range - min_zoom_range) / (Coord)step;
    range -= dR;
    if(range < min_zoom_range) range = min_zoom_range;
    calc_from();
}
//-------------------------------------------------------------
// Scene3D:: m o v e o u t
// Move the "from" point farther away

void Scene3D::moveout(short step)
{
    Coord dR = (max_zoom_range - min_zoom_range) / (Coord)step;
    range += dR;
    if(range > max_zoom_range) range = max_zoom_range;
    calc_from();
}
//-------------------------------------------------------------
// Scene3D:: v i e w _ t r a n s f o r m
// Apply the viewing transform (convert all coordinates
// to the view coordinate frame).

void Scene3D::view_transform()
{
    d = range;

    Vector3D from2at = at;
    from2at.diff(from);
    v3 = from2at;
    v3.normalize();

    v1 = from2at;
    v1.cross(up);
    v1.normalize();
```

3-D Graphics

```
    v2 = v1;
    v2.cross(v3);
    v2.normalize();

    xoffset = from.x * v1.x + from.y * v1.y + from.z * v1.z;
    yoffset = from.x * v2.x + from.y * v2.y + from.z * v2.z;
    zoffset = from.x * v3.x + from.y * v3.y + from.z * v3.z;
// Apply the transform to all vertices in all shapes
    short i, j;
    Array *va, *xva;
    Coord fp;
    for(i = 0; i < numshapes; i++)
    {
        va = shapes[i]->vertices;
        xva = shapes[i]->xfrmv;
// Loop over all the vertices in this shape
        for(j = 0; j < shapes[i]->numvertices; j++)
        {
            Vector3D& v = (Vector3D&)(*va)[j];
            Vector3D& xv = (Vector3D&)(*xva)[j];
            xv.z = v.x*v3.x + v.y*v3.y + v.z*v3.z - zoffset;

            fp = fov * d/(d+xv.z);

            xv.x = fp*(v.x*v1.x + v.y*v1.y + v.z*v1.z - xoffset)
                    + wview_2;
            xv.y = hview_2 -
                    fp*(v.x*v2.x + v.y*v2.y + v.z*v2.z - yoffset);
        }
// Sort the facets and find bounding box of the transformed shape
        shapes[i]->find_extents();
    }
}
```

Loading a 3-D Scene from a File

The Shape3D class provides a read function to initialize a Shape3D object from a file. The Scene3D class also provides a read function. To initialize a 3-D scene, you have to use the Scene3D constructor that takes a file name as argument. The constructor calls Scene3D::read to load the 3-D scene from a file.

I use a simple text file format to specify the 3-D scene. One reason for picking this format is that I can create the file with any text editor.

In my scheme, the 3-D scene is specified by two types of files. First a 3-D scene definition file describes the shapes to be placed in the scene. Each shape is defined in its own shape definition file.

As an example, consider the problem of creating a scene with two cubes of different size and orientation. Listing 8.5 shows the file CUBE.SHP that defines the cube shape. This is the file that Shape3D::read interprets to initialize the cube shape.

Listing 8.5. CUBE.SHP—Definition of a cube.

```
This is a 50x50 cube (Naba 2/6/93).
8               Number of vertices
0 0 0           Coordinates of vertex 1
50 0 0          Coordinates of vertex 2
50 50 0         and so on...
0 50 0
0 0 50
50 0 50
50 50 50
0 50 50
6               Number of facets
0 1 2 3         A facet specified by a list of vertices
255 0 0         Color of the facet (R G B)
4 5 6 7
255 255 0
0 4 7 3
0 255 0
1 2 6 5
0 0 255
0 1 5 4
255 255 255
3 2 6 7
0 0 0
```

Now look at the scene description file, SAMPLE.S3D (Listing 8.6), that creates two copies of the cube defined in the file CUBE.SHP (Listing 8.5).

3-D Graphics

Listing 8.6. SAMPLE.S3D—A sample 3-D scene definition file.

```
A sample 3D scene file with two cubes.   (Naba, 2/6/93)
5 120           Ranges of angle that specifies the field of view
150 300         Min and Max ranges of "from" point
0 360           Min and Max azimuth angle
0 50            Min and Max elevation angle
200 270 30      View from this point (Range, azimuth, elevation)
0 0 0           Look at this point
0 0 1           Direction of the Up vector
2               Number of shapes in the scene
cube.shp        ---- A shape ----
scale 2 2 2     Transformations for the shape
translate -150 -150 0
transform       Perform the actual transformations
end             Indicates end of transformations for shape
cube.shp        ---- The next shape ----
translate 100 -20 0
rotate 0 0 45
transform
end
```

The Scene3D::read function reads and interprets files like the one shown in Listing 8.6. Notice that each occurrence of a shape includes the name of a shape definition file (in this case, cube.shp). Scene3D::read calls Shape3D::read to load the shape's definition from the shape file. After a shape is loaded, you can transform it with the statements translate, rotate, and scale. Note that you have to specify the keyword transform to actually apply the transformation. An end keyword marks the end of the specification of each shape in the scene.

Figure 8.6 shows a view of the 3-D scene defined by the files shown in Listings 8.5 and 8.6. This view was generated by a simple viewer application that is similar to what the View3DWindow class does in Chapter 9.

Viewing a 3-D Scene

Once the 3-D shape classes are defined, viewing the 3-D scene is straightforward. The first step is to transform all the vertices in the scene into the view coordinate system. Next, the facets in each shape are sorted in descending order of the average z-coordinate. Then the facets for each shape are drawn using the Windows API function `Polygon`. The facets are drawn in the far-to-near order starting with the ones that are furthest from the viewing point. Although I am not showing any code to display 3-D scenes in this chapter, you can see an example of displaying a 3-D scene in Listing 9.9 in the next chapter.

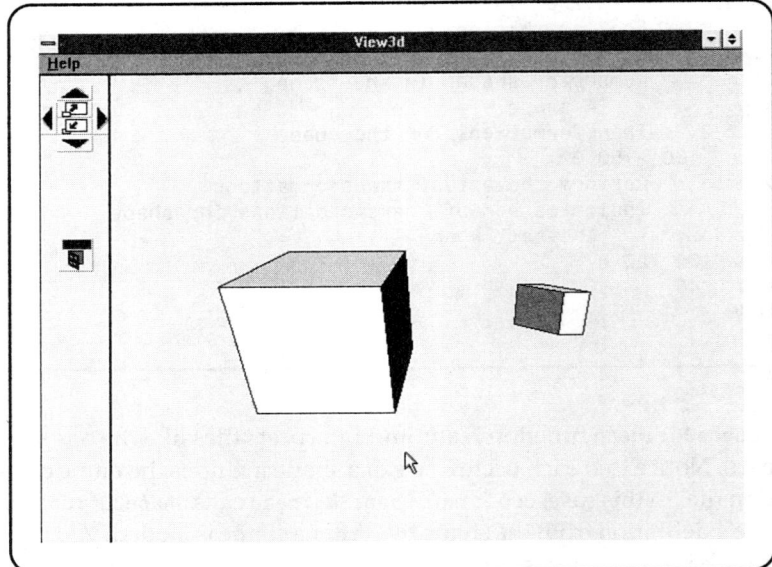

Figure 8.6. *A view of a 3-D scene with two cubes.*

Summary

Many computer games use 3-D representations of objects bound by polygons because polygons are easy to manipulate and display. A polygon is represented by three or more vertices. One way to construct a 3-D scene is to define 3-D shapes with polygons and use 3-D coordinate transformations to place the shapes in the scene. To view the scene from a specified point, all the vertices in the 3-D scene are transformed into the view coordinate system. Then the

3-D Graphics

transformed 3-D points are projected onto a plane normal to the viewing direction. A simple way to hide any hidden surfaces is to draw the polygons starting with the ones furthest from the viewing point to the nearest. Given the direction of a light source, and the reflection coefficient of the surface, the polygons can be shaded to create a reasonably realistic rendition of the 3-D scene.

Further Reading

If you are interested in 3-D graphics, you want a copy of the book by Foley, van Dam, Feiner, and Hughes. This classic textbook covers all aspects of 3-D graphics, including 3-D coordinate transformations and shading models.

If you want ready-to-use code, there are several books that provide code listings of 3-D graphics algorithms. Both Angell and Tsoubelis and Watkins and Sharp include code for generating ray-traced images of 3-D scenes. Both books also show how to display the resulting images on VGA displays.

Loren Heiny also covers 3-D graphics and provides source code for displaying output under Windows.

> Angell, Ian O., and Dimitrios Tsoubelis. *Advanced Graphics on VGA and XGA Cards Using Borland C++*. New York: Wiley, 1992.

> Foley, James D., Andries van Dam, Steven K. Feiner, and John F. Hughes. *Computer Graphics Principles and Practice, Second Edition*. Reading, MA: Addison-Wesley Publishing, 1990.

> Heiny, Loren. *Windows Graphics Programming with Borland C++*. New York: Wiley, 1992.

> Watkins, Christopher D., and Larry Sharp. *Programming in 3 Dimensions*. San Mateo, CA: M&T Books, 1992.

Chapter 9

BLOCKADE— A Game of Modern Naval Simulation

The SPUZZLE game in Chapter 7 illustrates the use of image animation techniques in computer games designed for Windows. Chapter 8 introduces 3-D graphics and shows how to display 3-D shapes defined by polygons. This chapter combines the graphics techniques of previous chapters with simulation techniques to develop a game of modern naval simulation called BLOCKADE—and includes the source code that implements it.

Before you plunge into the description of BLOCKADE, please note that the sheer size of the game made it difficult for me to locate all the bugs and fix them. You are essentially a beta tester for this game. Of course, the difference from other beta products is that you get access to all the source code of the game. That lets you fix bugs on your own and enhance the game any way you want. You also get to see how I implemented some of the features of BLOCKADE.

Playing BLOCKADE

The source code for the BLOCKADE game and an executable version of the game appears on this book's companion disk. The code on the disk is organized by chapter, so the BLOCKADE game appears in the directory named CH09. You should install the code from the disk, run Windows, and start BLOCKADE to get a feel for the game. BLOCKADE has online help, which you can access from the Help menu or by pressing the F1 key.

Overview of BLOCKADE

In BLOCKADE, you command a modern fighting ship assigned to emergency duty enforcing a naval blockade in a troubled part of the world. Other than maintaining some semblance of reality, BLOCKADE does not attempt to simulate real navy ships or tactics. The focus is more on arcade game-style action that pits your ship against enemy patrol boats and aircraft as the enemy tries to protect its cargo ship.

The scenario is as follows: A freighter carrying some valuable cargo is making its way along the coast toward the port. You are instructed to proceed to the general area of the freighter's last reported position and stop it from

Chapter 9

BLOCKADE—A Game of Modern Naval Simulation

reaching port—using force, if necessary. You have to rely on your ship's radar and electronic listening devices to locate the freighter. You win the game if you destroy the freighter before it has a chance to reach the port. While you navigate your ship toward the estimated position of the freighter, enemy patrol boats and attack aircraft try to ambush your ship. As you attempt to locate and stop the freighter from reaching port, you have to pinpoint any approaching enemy ships and aircraft. This is where the game is somewhat similar to the arcade-style "shoot everything in sight" games. You have to use the ship's weapons to destroy the enemy as and where you can. BLOCKADE is programmed to automatically use your ship's guns and missile defense systems should your ship detect any incoming missiles.

At this point I should explain how the BLOCKADE game evolved. Originally I had planned a 3-D simulation of naval combat much like a flight simulator, but as I completed a reasonable simulation of the ships, I realized that it is difficult to convey a feeling of fast action because of the relatively slow speeds at which ships move (when compared with the speed of aircraft, for instance). Also, once I added the map and polar views, the game grew to such a large size (in terms of lines of code) that I could provide only a simple 3-D viewing window. Thus the 3-D aspects of the game are not as well developed as I had originally intended. Even so, BLOCKADE is fairly enjoyable. You play the game from the two other views—the map window and the polar window. The map window shows you the geographic location of your ship and all other ships and aircraft that your ship can detect through its radars. The polar window shows the detected ships and aircraft with respect to your ship's heading. When playing the game, you set course from the map window and shoot at enemy ships from the polar window.

Starting BLOCKADE

When you first run BLOCKADE, you see a screen similar to the one in Figure 9.1. Like many other computer games, the opening screen shows a picture that illustrates the theme of the game. As the opening logo is displayed, BLOCKADE loads bitmaps, creates the windows, and sets up the display. The opening logo goes away after a few seconds or when you click on it.

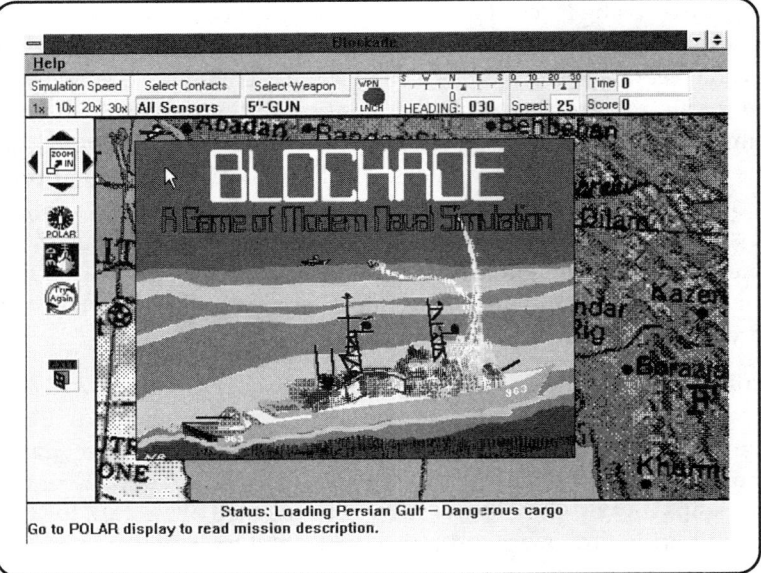

Figure 9.1. *Opening screen in BLOCKADE.*

Terminology of BLOCKADE

Like any game or software product, there are some terms that have special meaning in BLOCKADE. The *scenario* is at the heart of BLOCKADE. A scenario consists of a map and several *platforms*. Platforms refer to ships, aircraft, and any other moving objects, including ammunition rounds and missiles. A platform has *sensors* and weapons. The sensors refer to radar and other electronic listening devices that modern ships and aircraft use to monitor the world around them. The weapons on a ship or aircraft are missiles and various types of guns. The term *engage* is often used to refer to the act of using a weapon against a target.

A scenario may include several *missions*. A mission places the platforms at various locations on the map and specifies how the platforms move about. At start-up, BLOCKADE reads a configuration file named BLOCKADE.CFG and loads one of the scenarios specified in that file. Then, BLOCKADE picks a mission from the scenario file. It is the mission file that indicates which platforms are

BLOCKADE—A Game of Modern Naval Simulation

part of the scenario. BLOCKADE initializes the platforms, sensors, and weapons by reading the database files PLATFORM.DAT, SENSOR.DAT, and WEAPON.DAT respectively. These are text files with information on a variety of platforms, sensors, and weapons.

Components of the BLOCKADE Screen

Once the opening logo is gone, you see a screen like the one in Figure 9.2. The layout is as follows:

- At the top of the screen are a number of controls for adjusting the simulation speed, setting the ship's heading and speed, selecting the weapon and the sensor, and launching the weapon. A counter shows the current simulation time and the current score.

- Status messages are displayed in the window at the bottom of the screen. Note that the initial display prompts you to go to the polar window to read a description of the current mission.

- The scenario is displayed in a large window occupying most of the screen. At the beginning, this window shows a map view of the scenario with icons representing your ship and all other platforms visible from your ship using the currently selected sensor. Other possible views of the scenario include a polar view and a 3-D view.

- The window along the left edge of the screen has the controls associated with the current view, which is initially the map view. The controls include arrows for scrolling, buttons for zooming into a view, and buttons to change the current view.

Views in BLOCKADE

Figure 9.2 shows the map view in BLOCKADE. In this view you see the platforms displayed on a map. Your ship appears as an icon, and all other ships and aircraft that are detected by your ship's sensors are displayed on the map. The map view is useful for setting your ship's heading because you have the map as a reference to guide you. To set the heading, use the mouse to grab and drag the heading indicator in the heading display area in the top window of BLOCKADE. You can set the speed in the same way you set the heading.

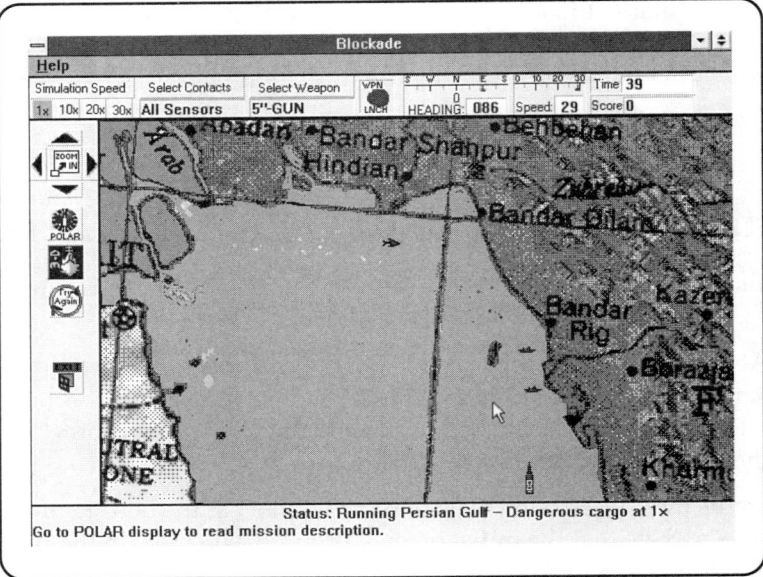

Figure 9.2. *Map view in BLOCKADE.*

3-D View

Figure 9.3 shows a 3-D view of the ship. The 3-D view does not have all the details of the ship and it does not show shading. You do not need further discussion of the 3-D view because all interactions for playing the game occur in the map window or the polar window.

Polar View

The polar view is where you play most of the game. As Figure 9.4 shows, the polar view displays everything with respect to your ship, which is located at the center of a circle. Your ship always points straight up, which is bearing zero degrees. *Bearing* indicates the direction in which the ship is moving. Zero degrees is the bearing convention used by ships and it increases in the clockwise direction. The tick marks along the edge of the circle help you determine the bearing of other platforms with respect to your ship.

Chapter 9

BLOCKADE—A Game of Modern Naval Simulation

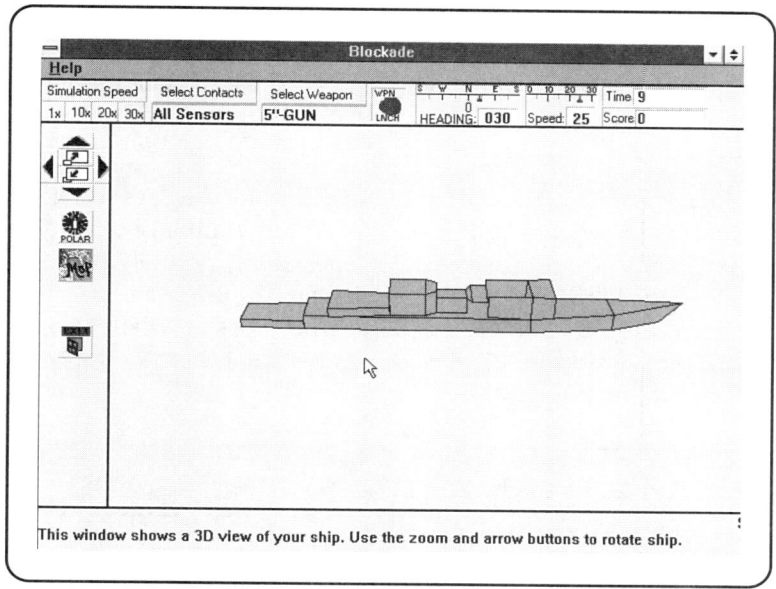

Figure 9.3. *3-D view in BLOCKADE.*

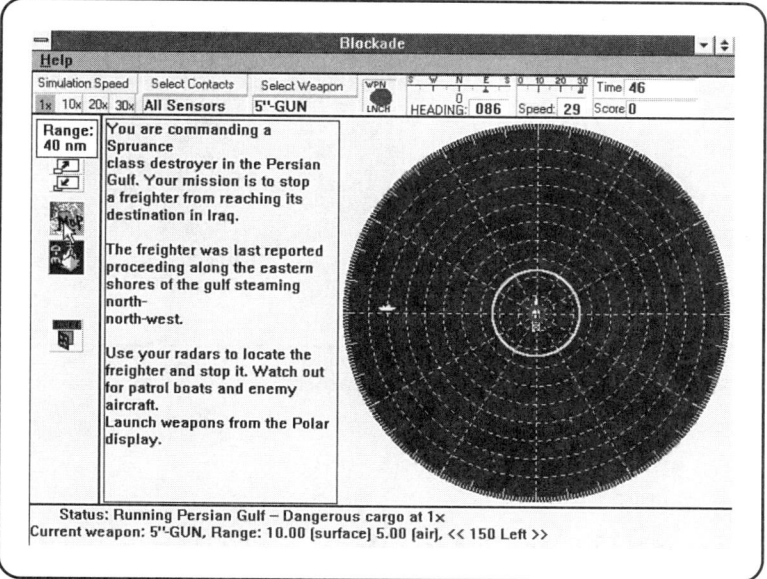

Figure 9.4. *Polar view in BLOCKADE.*

In the polar view, the radial direction represents range from your ship. The entire polar plot is divided into ten circular rings. The range at the outermost edge of the circle is shown in the window at the left edge of the screen. You can zoom in or zoom out by clicking on the buttons that appear beneath the range display.

A window immediately to the left of the polar plot displays some pertinent information. As shown in Figure 9.4, this window initially displays a brief description of the current mission. If you click at any point in the polar view, the window to the left of the polar view displays the range and bearing of this platform from your ship. If there is a platform at the point where you click, the name of that platform is also displayed. Figure 9.5 shows an example of selecting a platform in the polar view.

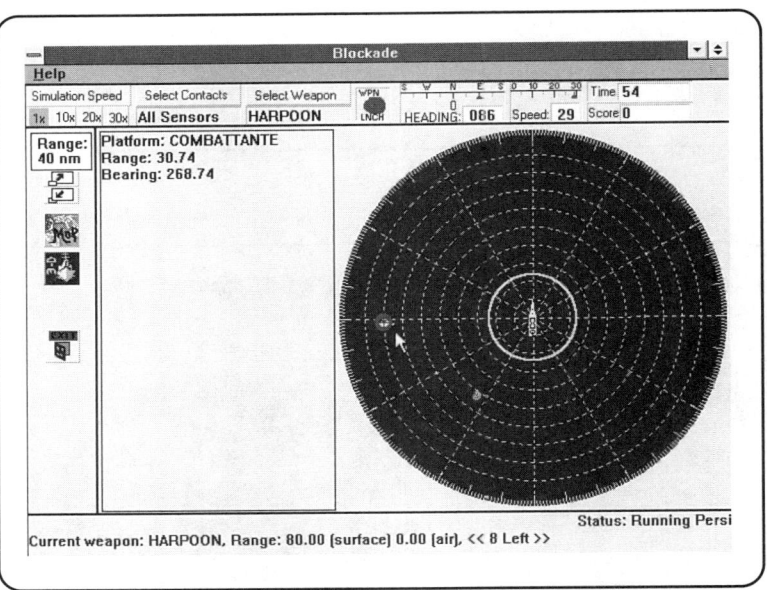

Figure 9.5. *Selecting a platform in the polar view.*

Controlling Simulation Speed

The simulation speed control is at the upper left corner of the main window. There are four buttons labeled 1x, 10x, 20x, and 30x. When 1x is selected, each

BLOCKADE—A Game of Modern Naval Simulation

second of elapsed time is roughly equal to a second of simulation time. On the other hand, selecting 30x causes the simulation to run 30 times faster than real time. Because ships move slowly, you might want to run the simulation at 30x to make everything happen faster.

Launching Weapons

The polar view is where you can select a platform as a target and launch a weapon against it. Of course, the polar view shows only those platforms that are detected by your sensors. To select a weapon, click on the Select Weapon button. The display underneath cycles through all the weapons on your ship. Once you select a target and a weapon, you can initiate the weapon launch by clicking on the button labeled WPN LNCH that appears next to the current weapon display. If the weapon is available, it is used against the selected target.

The availability of a weapon depends on several factors. The target must be within the range of the weapon and the target's bearing must be within the sectors where the weapon can be engaged. Yellow arcs, drawn around your ship, indicate the valid sectors. Additionally, there is a limit on the number of targets that a weapon can engage simultaneously.

There is one condition under which your ship's weapons automatically engage a target. If your ship detects a missile (not one launched by your ship), all available weapon systems engage the missile. This is because missiles move fast and there is very little time for the player to designate a missile as a target and shoot it down.

Designing BLOCKADE

If I decompose the application using the model-view-controller model, you can see that there are two categories of design elements in BLOCKADE:

- Classes to model the scenario
- Classes to view the scenario

325

I need the first set of classes for the simulation of ships, aircraft, and missiles that are at the heart of the BLOCKADE game. The second set of classes are derived from Borland's OWL classes, and these are basically windows where specific views of the scenario are presented. As much as possible, I tried to keep the simulation models separate from the views of the scenario.

Simulating the Scenario

C++ is ideal for simulating the scenario because each physical entity can be represented by a C++ class. In this case, I started with a `Platform` class that represents anything that moves in the scenario. Initially I thought of deriving other platform classes (such as Ship or Aircraft) from `Platform`, but soon I realized that all platforms can be modeled adequately by a generic platform with a large number of parameters.

A `Platform` has arrays of sensors and weapons. Like `Platform`, an all-purpose `Sensor` class models all sensors while a `Weapon` class models the weapons. One peculiarity of a `Weapon` is that when the weapon is engaged, it creates a `Platform` corresponding to the gun round or the missile fired by the weapon.

A `Scenario` class models the battle scenario and has an array of `Platform` objects.

Viewing the Scenario

All in all there are nine different window classes offering a variety of views in BLOCKADE. At any time, there are four different windows visible within BLOCKADE's main window. Some of the windows share the same area of the display screen, so only the topmost window is visible. Here are the nine window classes:

- ■ `BlockadeFrame` is the main window that encloses all other windows.
- ■ `StatusWindow` appears at the bottom part of the main window and it displays status messages.
- ■ `InfoWindow` is the window at the top—it displays a number of controls for changing the ship's speed and course and launching weapons.

BLOCKADE—A Game of Modern Naval Simulation

- `MapWindow`, `PolarWindow`, and `View3DWindow` share the large display area in the right middle part of the main window. Each of these window classes offers a specific view of the scenario.

- `MapToolWindow`, `PolarToolWindow`, and `View3DToolWindow` share the space to the left of the `MapWindow`, `PolarWindow`, and `View3DWindow`, respectively. Each tool window has a number of bitmaps representing tools useful with the corresponding view window. Thus, `MapToolWindow` goes with `MapWindow`, `PolarToolWindow` with `PolarWindow`, and `View3DToolWindow` with `View3DWindow`.

Because the three view windows `MapWindow`, `PolarWindow`, and `View3DWindow` are for similar purposes, they are all derived from a common base class named `DisplayWindow`. Similarly, `MapToolWindow`, `PolarToolWindow`, and `View3DToolWindow` are all derived from the `ToolWindow` class.

Game Definition Files

A series of files control the scenario that is simulated in BLOCKADE. The file `BLOCKADE.CFG` is the configuration file that contains a list of file names defining the scenarios that are available in BLOCKADE.

Each scenario file includes a list of platforms in the scenario and another set of file names—mission files that define specific missions within a scenario. It's the mission file that actually specifies the positions of the platforms.

When initializing a platform, the platform's data comes from a text file named `PLATFORM.DAT`, which stores information on each platform by name. Similarly, the file `SENSOR.DAT` is a text database of sensors and `WEAPON.DAT` holds information on weapons.

Implementing BLOCKADE

Given the list of classes listed in the previous sections, implementing BLOCKADE is a matter of defining and implementing the classes. Nevertheless, the sheer magnitude of the details nearly swamped me. I am convinced that I was able to do so much only because I used object-oriented techniques and the Borland C++ Windows-hosted development environment. First of all, I could use the image animation classes from the previous chapters without any change. The modular decomposition of the application into a number of C++ classes allowed me to write and test the application incrementally—a few classes at a time.

Following the strategy I used when implementing SPUZZLE (see Chapter 7), I started by building a framework for BLOCKADE. My first goal was to get the display up and running. This required definition of the application class `BlockadeApp` and the window classes `StatusWindow`, `InfoWindow`, `MapWindow`, `PolarWindow`, `View3DWindow`, `MapToolWindow`, `PolarToolWindow`, and `View3DToolWindow`. I could leave many of these classes as bare shells and still have an operational framework. Once the framework was available, I added the details in each of the windows. Only after the displays were fairly stable, did I start work on the `Scenario`, `Platform`, `Sensor`, and `Weapon` classes that make up the naval simulation at the heart of BLOCKADE.

In the following sections I present the classes that make up BLOCKADE. Because of the level of detail and the number of views that BLOCKADE offers, the source files are rather lengthy. Each class is described briefly, pointing out the important member functions and variables of each. You have to browse through the source code for specific details.

Taking Stock of the Source Files

A list of all the source files gives you a feel for the size of the source code necessary to implement a game like BLOCKADE. Table 9.1 shows most of the header files that BLOCKADE needs. The table also identifies the listing where the header file appears. This table shows only 15 header files that appear in the CH09 directory on the companion disk. Note that BLOCKADE also needs many header files from the previous chapters.

Table 9.1. Partial list of header files used by BLOCKADE.

Name	Description
BFRAME.H	Defines the `BlockadeFrame` class, which represents the main window of BLOCKADE (Listing 9.2)
BLKDRES.H	Defines the resource identifiers for the BLOCKADE application (Listing 9.29)

Chapter 9

BLOCKADE—A Game of Modern Naval Simulation

Name	Description
DISPWIN.H	Defines the view window classes: `DisplayWindow`, `MapWindow`, `PolarWindow`, and `View3DWindow` (Listing 9.5)
INFOWIN.H	Defines the `InfoWindow` class, the window that appears along the top edge of the screen (Listing 9.15)
LOGOWIN.H	Defines the `LogoWindow` class that represents the window where the opening logo is displayed (Listing 9.4) (see Figure 9.1)
PLATFORM.H	Defines the `Platform` class (Listing 9.23)
SCENARIO.H	Defines the `Scenario` class (a `Scenario` contains several `Platforms`, and the `Scenario` class includes a large number of static variables that store BLOCKADE's global information) (Listing 9.19)
SCENE3D.H	Defines the Scene3D class representing a 3-D scene (Listing 8.3)
SCNINFO.H	Defines a number of structures (`ScenarioInfo` and `MissionInfo`) that store information about the current simulation (Listing 9.20)
SENSOR.H	Defines the `Sensor` class (radars and electronic listening devices are typical sensors) (Listing 9.25)
SHAPE3D.H	Defines 3-D shape classes, Vector3D, Facet3D, and Shape3D (Listing 8.1)
SIMDEFS.H	Defines many macros, `typedefs`, and the `Sector` class (Listing 9.21)
STATWIN.H	Defines the `StatusWindow` class that represents the window at the bottom edge of BLOCKADE's screen (Listing 9.17)
TOOLWIN.H	Defines the classes representing the windows that appear to the left of the view windows: `ToolWindow`, `MapToolWindow`, `PolarToolWindow`, and `View3DToolWindow` (Listing 9.10)
WEAPON.H	Defines the `Weapon` class (platforms have weapons) (Listing 9.27)

Table 9.2 shows the 18 major source files of BLOCKADE. Each entry briefly describes what the source file contains and also indicates the listing where you can find the source code. In addition to these 18 source files, BLOCKADE also uses the source code for image display and animation from previous chapters. Note that the source files shown in Table 9.2 appear in the CH09 directory on the companion disk.

Table 9.2. Partial list of source files for BLOCKADE.

Name	Description
BFRAME.CPP	Implements the BlockadeFrame class (Listing 9.3)
BLOCKADE.CPP	Defines the BlockadeApp class and the WinMain function (Listing 9.1)
DISPWIN.CPP	Implements the view window classes: DisplayWindow, MapWindow, PolarWindow, and View3DWindow (Listing 9.6)
INFOWIN.CPP	Implements the InfoWindow class (Listing 9.16)
MAPTOOL.CPP	Implements the MapToolWindow class that provides the tools to manipulate the map window (Listing 9.12)
MAPWIN.CPP	Implements the MapWindow class that provides the map view in BLOCKADE (Listing 9.7)
PLATFORM.CPP	Implements the Platform class (Listing 9.24)
PLRTOOL.CPP	Implements the PolarToolWindow class that provides the tools to interact with the polar view in BLOCKADE (Listing 9.13)
POLARWIN.CPP	Implements the PolarWindow class that displays the polar view in BLOCKADE (Listing 9.8)
SCENARIO.CPP	Implements the Scenario class (Listing 9.22)
SCENE3D.CPP	Implements the Scene3D class, which represents a 3-D scene (Listing 8.4)
SENSOR.CPP	Implements the Sensor class (Listing 9.26)
SHAPE3D.CPP	Implements the classes (Vector3D, Facet3D, Shape3D) needed for modeling 3-D shapes (Listing 8.2)

Chapter 9

BLOCKADE—A Game of Modern Naval Simulation

Name	Description
STATWIN.CPP	Implements the `StatusWindow` class that displays status messages in a window along the bottom edge of the screen (Listing 9.18)
TOOLWIN.CPP	Implements the `ToolWindow` class, which is the base class of `MapToolWindow`, `PolarToolWindow`, and `View3DToolWindow` classes (Listing 9.11)
VU3DTOOL.CPP	Implements the `View3DToolWindow` class that provides the tools to manipulate the 3-D view displayed in `View3DWindow` (Listing 9.14)
VU3DWIN.CPP	Implements the `View3DWindow` class that shows a 3-D view of the scene (Listing 9.9)
WEAPON.CPP	Implements the `Weapon` class (Listing 9.28)

The *Application* Class

BLOCKADE's main application class, `BlockadeApp`, is based on the `TApplication` class from Borland's OWL classes. Listing 9.1 shows the file `blockade.cpp` that defines the `BlockadeApp` class and includes the `WinMain` function necessary for any OWL-based application. The `WinMain` function creates an instance of `BlockadeApp` and calls the `Run` member function to begin processing events. BLOCKADE's main window is displayed when the `Run` calls the `InitMainWindow` function. `InitMainWindow` creates an instance of `BlockadeFrame` and this, in turn, creates and displays all the child windows in BLOCKADE. `InitMainWindow` also creates the logo window that displays the picture shown in Figure 9.1.

**Listing 9.1. blockade.cpp—
The main function of the BLOCKADE application.**

```
//-----------------------------------------------------------
//  File:    blockade.cpp
//
//  An educational game that teaches spelling through puzzles.
//
```

continues

Listing 9.1. continued

```
//---------------------------------------------------------------
#include "bframe.h"

LogoWindow *logo;
//---------------------------------------------------------------
class BlockadeApp: public TApplication
{
public:
// Constructor that simply calls the base class constructor

    BlockadeApp(LPSTR name, HINSTANCE instance,
        HINSTANCE prev_instance, LPSTR  cmdline, int show) :

        TApplication(name, instance, prev_instance,
                    cmdline, show) {}

// Define function to initialize application's main window
    void InitMainWindow();

// Define function to initialize an instance of this application
    void InitInstance();
};
//---------------------------------------------------------------
// V i e w 3 d A p p : : I n i t M a i n W i n d o w

void BlockadeApp::InitMainWindow()
{
    MainWindow = new BlockadeFrame(NULL, "Blockade", "MainMenu");
    logo = new LogoWindow(NULL, (BlockadeFrame*)MainWindow);
    MakeWindow(logo);
}
//---------------------------------------------------------------
// V i e w 3 d A p p : : I n i t I n s t a n c e

void BlockadeApp::InitInstance()
{
   TApplication::InitInstance();
   HAccTable = LoadAccelerators(hInstance, "MainAccelTable");
}
//---------------------------------------------------------------
// W i n M a i n
//
// Create an instance of the application and "run" it.

int PASCAL WinMain(HINSTANCE instance, HINSTANCE prev_instance,
                LPSTR cmdline, int show)
```

BLOCKADE—A Game of Modern Naval Simulation

```
{
    BlockadeApp Blockade("Blockade", instance,
                    prev_instance, cmdline, show);

    Blockade.nCmdShow = SW_SHOWMAXIMIZED;
    Blockade.Run();

    return Blockade.Status;
}
```

BlockadeFrame Class

The `BlockadeFrame` class is responsible for creating and initializing the child windows that constitute the user interface of the BLOCKADE game. As you can see from the header file bframe.h (Listing 9.2), the `BlockadeFrame` class stores pointers to all its child windows so that it can access and manipulate them. In addition to the child windows, `BlockadeFrame` also contains a pointer to a `Scenario` object that represents the scenario being simulated in BLOCKADE.

Listing 9.2. `bframe.h`—Declaration of the `BlockadeFrame` class.

```
//---------------------------------------------------------------
// File: bframe.h
// Declaration of the BlockadeFrame class, which represents
// the main window of the BLOCKADE game.
//---------------------------------------------------------------
#if !defined(__BFRAME_H)
#define __BFRAME_H

#include <owl.h>
#include "logowin.h"
#include "dispwin.h"
#include "statwin.h"
#include "toolwin.h"
#include "infowin.h"
#include "blkdres.h"

#include "scenario.h"
#include "scninfo.h"
#include "simdefs.h"
```

continues

Listing 9.2. continued

```cpp
const short bmpheight = 40;
const short toolwidth = 64;

#define DISPLAY_TIMER    1

class BlockadeFrame : public TWindow
{
public:
    BlockadeFrame(PTWindowsObject parent, LPSTR title,
                  LPSTR menu): TWindow(parent, title),
                  view3d(NULL), polar(NULL),
                  map(NULL), info(NULL), scene(NULL),
                  status(NULL), polar_tools(NULL),
                  map_tools(NULL), vu3d_tools(NULL),
                  close_logo(-100), logo_displayed(0),
                  numscenarios(0), scenario_data(NULL),
                  nummissions(0), mission_data(NULL),
                  current_scenario(NULL), current_mission(NULL),
                  num_scndone(0), num_msndone(0)
    {
        AssignMenu(menu);
    }

    ~BlockadeFrame();

    Scenario* scenario() { return scene;}
    int load_scenarios(const char *filename);
    int load_missions(const char *filename);
    int pick_scenario();
    int pick_mission();
    void new_scenario();
    ScenarioInfo* scenario_info() { return current_scenario;}
    MissionInfo* mission_info() { return current_mission;}

    void GetWindowClass(WNDCLASS _FAR &wc);
    void WMCreate(RTMessage msg) = [WM_FIRST + WM_CREATE];
    void WMSize(RTMessage msg) = [WM_FIRST + WM_SIZE];
    void WMTimer(RTMessage msg) = [WM_FIRST + WM_TIMER];
    void About(RTMessage msg) = [CM_FIRST + IDM_ABOUT];
    void Help(RTMessage msg) = [CM_FIRST + IDM_HELP]
    {
        WinHelp(HWindow, "BLKDHLP.HLP", HELP_INDEX, 0);
    }

    View3DWindow* view3d_window() { return view3d;}
    MapWindow* map_window() { return map;}
    PolarWindow* polar_window() { return polar;}
```

BLOCKADE—A Game of Modern Naval Simulation

Chapter 9

```
InfoWindow* info_window() { return info;}
StatusWindow* status_window() { return status;}
View3DToolWindow* view3d_tool_window() { return vu3d_tools;}
MapToolWindow* map_tool_window() { return map_tools;}
PolarToolWindow* polar_tool_window() { return polar_tools;}

short view3d_window_visible() { return view3d_visible;}
short map_window_visible() { return map_visible;}
short polar_window_visible() { return polar_visible;}

short max_width() { return wmax;}
short max_height() { return hmax;}
short vu3_wmax() { return wvu3;}
short vu3_hmax() { return hvu3;}
short info_wmax() { return winfo;}
short info_hmax() { return hinfo;}
short sts_wmax() { return wsts;}
short sts_hmax() { return hsts;}

void hide_view3d()
{
    view3d_visible = FALSE;
    ShowWindow(view3d->HWindow, SW_HIDE);
    ShowWindow(vu3d_tools->HWindow, SW_HIDE);
}
void hide_polar()
{
    polar_visible = FALSE;
    ShowWindow(polar->HWindow, SW_HIDE);
    ShowWindow(polar_tools->HWindow, SW_HIDE);
}
void hide_map()
{
    map_visible = FALSE;
    ShowWindow(map->HWindow, SW_HIDE);
    ShowWindow(map_tools->HWindow, SW_HIDE);
}
void show_view3d()
{
    view3d_visible = TRUE;
    ShowWindow(view3d->HWindow, SW_SHOW);
    ShowWindow(vu3d_tools->HWindow, SW_SHOW);
    InvalidateRect(view3d->HWindow, NULL, FALSE);
    InvalidateRect(vu3d_tools->HWindow, NULL, FALSE);
}
void show_polar()
{
```

continues

Listing 9.2. continued

```
        polar_visible = TRUE;
        ShowWindow(polar->HWindow, SW_SHOW);
        ShowWindow(polar_tools->HWindow, SW_SHOW);
        InvalidateRect(polar->HWindow, NULL, FALSE);
        InvalidateRect(polar_tools->HWindow, NULL, FALSE);
    }
    void show_map()
    {
        map_visible = TRUE;
        ShowWindow(map->HWindow, SW_SHOW);
        ShowWindow(map_tools->HWindow, SW_SHOW);
        InvalidateRect(map->HWindow, NULL, FALSE);
        InvalidateRect(map_tools->HWindow, NULL, FALSE);
    }

    void logo_done() { close_logo = -1;}
    void logo_on()   { logo_displayed = TRUE;}
    short hi_scores(const char *filename);

private:
    Scenario           *scene; // The scenario being simulated
    View3DWindow       *view3d;
    MapWindow          *map;
    PolarWindow        *polar;
    InfoWindow         *info;
    StatusWindow       *status;
    PolarToolWindow    *polar_tools;
    View3DToolWindow   *vu3d_tools;
    MapToolWindow      *map_tools;
    unsigned short     wmax, hmax;    // BlockadeFrame's dimensions
    unsigned short     wvu3, hvu3;    // View3DWindow's dimensions
    unsigned short     winfo, hinfo;  // InfoWindow's dimensions
    unsigned short     wsts, hsts;    // StatusWindow's dimensions
    short              timer_id;

    short              view3d_visible;
    short              polar_visible;
    short              map_visible;
    short              close_logo;
    short              logo_displayed;

    short              numscenarios;
    short              nummissions;
    short              num_scndone;
    short              num_msndone;
```

BLOCKADE—A Game of Modern Naval Simulation

```
    ScenarioInfo      *scenario_data;
    ScenarioInfo      *current_scenario;
    MissionInfo       *mission_data;
    MissionInfo       *current_mission;
};

#endif
```

Creating and Initializing the Child Windows

Listing 9.3 shows the file bframe.cpp, which implements the member functions of the BlockadeFrame class. One of the first tasks of the BlockadeFrame class is to create the child windows and position them properly. The child windows are created in the WMCreate member function (see Listing 9.3), which handles the WM_CREATE message that Windows sends when creating the BlockadeFrame window.

The sizes and positions of the child windows depend on the size of the BlockadeFrame window. This size is not known when the window is created, but Windows sends a WM_SIZE message when the BlockadeFrame window is moved or resized. The WMSize function handles the WM_SIZE function. Thus, a good way to handle the resizing and positioning of the child windows is during the first call to the WMSize function. The positions and sizes of the child windows depend on the initial size of the BlockadeFrame window.

Note that in blockade.cpp (Listing 9.1), the BLOCKADE application is started with the nCmdShow parameter set to SW_SHOWMAXIMIZED, which means BLOCKADE's main window, BlockadeFrame, uses the entire display screen.

Loading Scenarios and Missions

BlockadeFrame's WMCreate function calls the load_scenarios function to open the file BLOCKADE.CFG and initialize an array of ScenarioInfo structures (scenario_data) with information on all available scenarios. Next the pick_scenario function selects one of the scenarios and stores a pointer to the selected scenario in the current_scenario variable.

Once a scenario is picked, a call to the `load_missions` function loads information on all available missions into the `mission_data` array. Finally, another function, `pick_mission`, is called to select one of the missions for the current game.

Note that the `ScenarioInfo` and `MissionInfo` structures are declared in the header file `scninfo.h`, shown in Listing 9.20.

The actual initialization of the scenario is done by calling the `new_scenario` function from the `WMTimer` function. A flag, `init_done`, is used to ensure that the scenario is initialized only once.

Updating the Child Windows

All the child windows in BLOCKADE are updated using the image animation techniques illustrated in Chapter 5. I set up a timer and call the update function of each child window in the `WMTimer` function (Listing 9.3) of the `BlockadeFrame` class.

Displaying the High Scores Dialog

The `hi_scores` function of the `BlockadeFrame` class displays the high scores dialog box using the same technique as the one in the SPUZZLE game (see Chapter 7). As you can see from Listing 9.3, the `hi_scores` function gets the top 30 scores from a file and displays them in a list box inside the high scores dialog, which is an instance of the `HiscoreDialog` class (described in Chapter 7). The `hi_scores` function is called from each of the `ToolWindow` classes when the player clicks on the EXIT button.

**Listing 9.3. bframe.cpp—
Implementation of the `BlockadeFrame` class.**

```
//------------------------------------------------------------
// File: bframe.cpp
//
// Implementation of the BlockadeFrame class--the main window of
// the BLOCKADE game.
//------------------------------------------------------------
```

Chapter 9

BLOCKADE—A Game of Modern Naval Simulation

```cpp
#include <string.h>
#include <fstream.h>
#include <strng.h>
#include "bframe.h"
#include "hscdial.h"

static short first_time = TRUE;
static short init_done = FALSE;
extern LogoWindow *logo;
static char *whitespace = " \t";
//---------------------------------------------------------------
// B l o c k a d e F r a m e : : W M C r e a t e
// Initializes the main window of the BLOCKADE game.

void BlockadeFrame:: WMCreate(RTMessage)
{
// Initialize random number generator with a random seed
    randomize();

// Read in scenario definitions from the BLOCKADE.CFG file
    load_scenarios("BLOCKADE.CFG");
    pick_scenario();
    load_missions(current_scenario->defnfile);
    pick_mission();

// Create the child windows
    view3d = new View3DWindow(this, this);
    GetApplication()->MakeWindow(view3d);

    polar = new PolarWindow(this, this);
    GetApplication()->MakeWindow(polar);

    map = new MapWindow(this, this);
    GetApplication()->MakeWindow(map);

    info = new InfoWindow(this, this);
    GetApplication()->MakeWindow(info);

    status = new StatusWindow(this, this);
    GetApplication()->MakeWindow(status);

    vu3d_tools = new View3DToolWindow(this, this);
    GetApplication()->MakeWindow(vu3d_tools);

    polar_tools = new PolarToolWindow(this, this);
    GetApplication()->MakeWindow(polar_tools);
```

continues

Listing 9.3. continued

```
    map_tools = new MapToolWindow(this, this);
    GetApplication()->MakeWindow(map_tools);
}
//---------------------------------------------------------------
// BlockadeFrame:: ~ B l o c k a d e F r a m e
// Destructor for a BlockadeFrame

BlockadeFrame::~BlockadeFrame()
{
// Kill the timer
    if(timer_id) KillTimer(HWindow, timer_id);

// Delete the child windows
    if(view3d != NULL) delete view3d;
    if(polar != NULL) delete polar;
    if(map != NULL) delete map;
    if(map_tools != NULL) delete map_tools;
    if(polar_tools != NULL) delete polar_tools;
    if(vu3d_tools != NULL) delete vu3d_tools;
    if(info != NULL) delete info;
    if(status != NULL) delete status;

// Delete scenario and mission info structures
    if(scenario_data != NULL) delete scenario_data;
    if(mission_data != NULL) delete mission_data;

// Delete the scenario used in the simulation
    if(scene != NULL) delete scene;
}
//---------------------------------------------------------------
//  BlockadeFrame:: G e t W i n d o w C l a s s
//  Set up icon for the Application

void BlockadeFrame::GetWindowClass(WNDCLASS _FAR &wc)
{
// First call the GetWindowClass function of the base class
    TWindow::GetWindowClass(wc);

// Set up icon for this application
    wc.hIcon = LoadIcon(wc.hInstance, "BLOCKADE_ICON");
}
//---------------------------------------------------------------
//  BlockadeFrame:: A b o u t
//  Display the "About..." box
```

BLOCKADE—A Game of Modern Naval Simulation

Chapter 9

```cpp
void BlockadeFrame::About(RTMessage)
{
    TDialog *p_about = new TDialog(this, "ABOUTBLOCKADE");
    PTApplication app = GetApplication();
    app->ExecDialog(p_about);
}
//----------------------------------------------------------------
// BlockadeFrame:: W M S i z e
// Resize/Reposition all child windows when frame changes size

void BlockadeFrame::WMSize(RTMessage)
{
    if(IsIconic(HWindow)) return;

// Get the size of this window
    RECT r;
    GetClientRect(HWindow, &r);

    unsigned short w = r.right - r.left + 1;
    unsigned short h = r.bottom - r.top + 1;

// Resize and reposition child windows
// The info window is across the top
    if(info != NULL)
    {
        MoveWindow(info->HWindow, 0, 0, w, bmpheight, TRUE);
        info->width(w);
        info->height(bmpheight);
    }

// The status window is at the bottom
    if(status != NULL)
    {
        MoveWindow(status->HWindow, 0, h - bmpheight, w,
                   bmpheight, TRUE);
        status->width(w);
        status->height(bmpheight);
    }

// All the tools windows are on the left
    short htool = h - 2*bmpheight;
    if(vu3d_tools != NULL)
    {
        MoveWindow(vu3d_tools->HWindow, 0, bmpheight, toolwidth,
                   htool, TRUE);
    }
    if(polar_tools != NULL)
    {
```

continues

Listing 9.3. continued

```
            MoveWindow(polar_tools->HWindow, 0, bmpheight, toolwidth,
                    htool, TRUE);
    }
    if(map_tools != NULL)
    {
        MoveWindow(map_tools->HWindow, 0, bmpheight, toolwidth,
                    htool, TRUE);
        if(map_window()->image_ready())
            map_tools->set_scroll_buttons();
    }

// view3d, polar, and map windows share the large area in the
// middle to the right of the tools area
    if(view3d != NULL)
    {
        MoveWindow(view3d->HWindow, toolwidth, bmpheight,
                    w - toolwidth, htool, TRUE);
        view3d->width(w-toolwidth);
        view3d->height(htool);
    }
    if(polar != NULL)
    {
        MoveWindow(polar->HWindow, toolwidth, bmpheight,
                    w - toolwidth, htool, TRUE);
        polar->width(w-toolwidth);
        polar->height(htool);
    }
    if(map != NULL)
    {
        MoveWindow(map->HWindow, toolwidth, bmpheight,
                    w - toolwidth, htool, TRUE);
        map->width(w-toolwidth);
        map->height(htool);
    }

    if(first_time)
    {
        first_time = 0;
// Save the maximum dimensions of some windows...
        wmax = w;
        hmax = h;
        wvu3 = w-toolwidth;
        hvu3 = htool;
        winfo = w;
```

BLOCKADE—A Game of Modern Naval Simulation

```
            hinfo = bmpheight;
            wsts = w;
            hsts = bmpheight;

            hide_view3d();
            hide_polar();
            hide_map();

// Set up a timer to update the display and manage the game
            timer_id = SetTimer(HWindow, DISPLAY_TIMER,
                    DISP_MILLISECONDS, NULL);
            if(!timer_id)
                MessageBox(HWindow, "Failed to start Timer!",
                            "View3D: BlockadeFrame",
                            MB_ICONEXCLAMATION | MB_OK);
    }
}
//-------------------------------------------------------------
// BlockadeFrame:: W M T i m e r
// Handle WM_TIMER events

void BlockadeFrame::WMTimer(RTMessage msg)
{
    switch(msg.WParam)
    {
        case DISPLAY_TIMER:
            if(logo_displayed && !init_done)
            {
                new_scenario();
                init_done = TRUE;
            }

// Call the update function of the child windows...
            if(close_logo < 0)
            {
// Make sure the logo window is on the top
                BringWindowToTop(logo->HWindow);
                close_logo++;
                if(close_logo >= 0)
                {
                    delete logo;
                    Scenario::status = RUNNING;
                }
            }

// Update the scenario
            if(scene != NULL) scene->update();
```

continues

Listing 9.3. continued

```
// If Scenario::refresh is set, ensure a refresh
        if(Scenario::refresh)
        {
            polar->refresh_anim();
            map->refresh_anim();
            Scenario::refresh = 0;
        }

// Then update the visible display
        if(view3d != NULL && view3d_visible)
                                             view3d->update();
        if(polar != NULL && polar_visible) polar->update();
        if(map != NULL && map_visible) map->update();
        if(info != NULL) info->update();
        if(status != NULL) status->update();
        break;

    default:
        break;
    }
}
//------------------------------------------------------------
// LogoWindow:: W M L B u t t o n D o w n
// Handle button click in the "logo" window

void LogoWindow::WMLButtonDown(RTMessage)
{
    blockade_frame->logo_done();
    Scenario::status = RUNNING;
}
//------------------------------------------------------------
// LogoWindow:: W M C r e a t e
// Resize and position the logo window in the middle of the
// main window.

void LogoWindow::WMCreate(RTMessage)
{
    SetWindowPos(HWindow, HWND_TOPMOST,
                 100, 100, width(), height(), SWP_DRAWFRAME);
}
//------------------------------------------------------------
// LogoWindow:: P a i n t
// Draw the logo
```

BLOCKADE—A Game of Modern Naval Simulation

Chapter 9

```cpp
void LogoWindow::Paint(HDC hdc, PAINTSTRUCT&)
{
    if(img != NULL)img->show(hdc);
    blockade_frame->logo_on();
}
//-------------------------------------------------------------
// BlockadeFrame :: l o a d _ s c e n a r i o s
// Initialize an array of ScenarioInfo by reading from a file

int BlockadeFrame::load_scenarios(const char* filename)
{
// Open file for reading
    ifstream ifs(filename, ios::in);
    if(!ifs)
    {
// Error reading file. Return 0.
        return 0;
    }

// Read and interpret the contents of the file
    char line[81];

// First line should have the string BLOCKADE.CFG
    ifs.getline(line, sizeof(line));
    strupr(line);
    if(strnicmp(line, "BLOCKADE.CFG",
        strlen("BLOCKADE.CFG")) != 0) return 0;

// Second line has a version number--just in case the
// contents have to change in the future
    ifs.getline(line, sizeof(line));
    short version = atoi(line);
    if(version != 1) return 0;

// Third line has the number of scenarios in this file.
    ifs.getline(line, sizeof(line));
    numscenarios = atoi(line);

// Allocate an array of ScenarioInfo structures
    ScenarioInfo *new_scenarios = new ScenarioInfo[numscenarios];
    if(new_scenarios == NULL) return 0;

// At this point we have an array of ScenarioInfo structures
// allocated. If there is an existing ScenarioInfo array,
// delete it before loading new values
    if(scenario_data != NULL) delete scenario_data;
    scenario_data = new_scenarios;
```

continues

Listing 9.3. continued

```
// Load all the scenario info...
    short i, len;
    char *token;
    for(i = 0; i < numscenarios; i++)
    {
// Ignore first line (it's used as a separator)
        ifs.getline(line, sizeof(line));
// Scenario's name
        ifs.getline(line, sizeof(line));
        len = strlen(line);
        scenario_data[i].name = new char[len+1];
        strcpy(scenario_data[i].name, line);

// Name of scenario definition file
        ifs.getline(line, sizeof(line));
        token = strtok(line, whitespace);
        len = strlen(token);
        scenario_data[i].defnfile = new char[len+1];
        strcpy(scenario_data[i].defnfile, token);

// Name of the map's image file
        ifs.getline(line, sizeof(line));
        token = strtok(line, whitespace);
        len = strlen(token);
        scenario_data[i].mapfile = new char[len+1];
        strcpy(scenario_data[i].mapfile, token);

// Name of zoomed-in version of the map
        ifs.getline(line, sizeof(line));
        token = strtok(line, whitespace);
        len = strlen(token);
        scenario_data[i].zmapfile = new char[len+1];
        strcpy(scenario_data[i].zmapfile, token);

// Map zoom factor
        ifs.getline(line, sizeof(line));
        token = strtok(line, whitespace);
        scenario_data[i].mapzoom = atoi(token);

// Pixels per degree of latitude and longitude
        ifs.getline(line, sizeof(line));
        token = strtok(line, whitespace);
        scenario_data[i].pixperlat = atof(token);
        token = strtok(NULL, whitespace);
        scenario_data[i].pixperlng = atof(token);
```

BLOCKADE—A Game of Modern Naval Simulation

```
// Latitude and longitude of upper left corner of map
        ifs.getline(line, sizeof(line));
        token = strtok(line, whitespace);
        scenario_data[i].orglat = atof(token);
        token = strtok(NULL, whitespace);
        scenario_data[i].orglng = atof(token);

        scenario_data[i].done = FALSE;
    }
    return 1;
}
//-----------------------------------------------------------------
// BlockadeFrame : : l o a d _ m i s s i o n s
// Read the missions for the current scenario

int BlockadeFrame::load_missions(const char* filename)
{
    if(current_scenario == NULL) return 0;

// Open file for reading
    ifstream ifs(filename, ios::in);
    if(!ifs)
    {
// Error reading file. Return 0.
        return 0;
    }

// Read and interpret the contents of the file
    char line[81];

// First line should have the string BLOCKADE.BSN
    ifs.getline(line, sizeof(line));
    strupr(line);
    if(strnicmp(line, "BLOCKADE.BSN",
            strlen("BLOCKADE.BSN")) != 0) return 0;

// Second line has a version number--just in case the
// contents have to change in the future
    ifs.getline(line, sizeof(line));
    short version = atoi(line);
    if(version != 1) return 0;

// Read the basic time period for updating platform positions
// Save it in the static variable: "Scenario::BASIC_PERIOD"
    char *token;
    ifs.getline(line, sizeof(line));
    token = strtok(line, whitespace);
```

continues

Listing 9.3. continued

```
    Scenario::BASIC_PERIOD = atof(token);
    if(Scenario::BASIC_PERIOD < 0.0001)
        Scenario::BASIC_PERIOD = 0.0001;

// Read in a list of rectangles that define the valid regions
// where a ship can go. This is used to ensure that ships
// stay in the water.
    ifs.getline(line, sizeof(line));
    current_scenario->nrects = atoi(line);
    RECT *r = new RECT[current_scenario->nrects];
    if(r == NULL) return 0;
    if(current_scenario->valuesea != NULL)
        delete current_scenario->valuesea;
    current_scenario->valuesea = r;

    short i;
    for(i = 0; i < current_scenario->nrects; i++)
    {
        ifs.getline(line, sizeof(line));
        token = strtok(line, whitespace);
        current_scenario->valuesea[i].left = atoi(token);
        token = strtok(NULL, whitespace);
        current_scenario->valuesea[i].top = atoi(token);
        token = strtok(NULL, whitespace);
        current_scenario->valuesea[i].right = atoi(token);
        token = strtok(NULL, whitespace);
        current_scenario->valuesea[i].bottom = atoi(token);
    }

// Next read the number of missions in this file.
    ifs.getline(line, sizeof(line));
    nummissions = atoi(line);

// Allocate an array of MissionInfo structures
    MissionInfo *new_missions = new MissionInfo[nummissions];
    if(new_missions == NULL) return 0;

// If there is an existing MissionInfo array,
// delete it before loading new values
    if(mission_data != NULL) delete mission_data;
    mission_data = new_missions;

// Load all the mission info...
    short len;
    for(i = 0; i < nummissions ; i++)
    {
```

BLOCKADE—A Game of Modern Naval Simulation

```
        ifs.getline(line, sizeof(line));
        len = strlen(line);
        mission_data[i].name = new char[len+1];
        strcpy(mission_data[i].name, line);

// Name of 3D scene file
        ifs.getline(line, sizeof(line));
        token = strtok(line, whitespace);
        len = strlen(token);
        mission_data[i].s3dfile = new char[len+1];
        strcpy(mission_data[i].s3dfile, token);

// Name of image file for 3D display
        ifs.getline(line, sizeof(line));
        token = strtok(line, whitespace);
        len = strlen(token);
        mission_data[i].bg3dfile = new char[len+1];
        strcpy(mission_data[i].bg3dfile, token);

// Name of mission definition file
        ifs.getline(line, sizeof(line));
        token = strtok(line, whitespace);
        len = strlen(token);
        mission_data[i].defnfile = new char[len+1];
        strcpy(mission_data[i].defnfile, token);

        mission_data[i].done = FALSE;
    }
    return 1;
}
//-------------------------------------------------------------
// BlockadeFrame:: p i c k _ s c e n a r i o
// Pick a scenario to be played

int BlockadeFrame::pick_scenario()
{
    if(num_scndone == numscenarios) return FALSE;
    short index;
    while(1)
    {
        index = random(numscenarios);
        if(!scenario_data[index].done) break;
    }
    current_scenario = &scenario_data[index];
    return TRUE;
}
```

continues

Listing 9.3. continued

```
//---------------------------------------------------------------
// BlockadeFrame:: p i c k _ m i s s i o n
// Pick a mission within a scenario

int BlockadeFrame::pick_mission()
{
    if(num_msndone == nummissions) return FALSE;
    short index;
    while(1)
    {
        index = random(nummissions);
        if(!mission_data[index].done) break;
    }
    current_mission = &mission_data[index];
    return TRUE;
}
//---------------------------------------------------------------
// BlockadeFrame:: n e w _ s c e n a r i o
// Load a new scenario

void BlockadeFrame::new_scenario()
{
// Initialize all the child windows
    if(status != NULL)
    {
        status->init();
        status->update();
    }

// Load scenario...
    if(scene != NULL) delete scene;
    scene = new Scenario();
    scene->init(current_scenario, current_mission);

    if(view3d != NULL) view3d->init(
                    current_mission->s3dfile,
                    current_mission->bg3dfile);
    if(polar != NULL) polar->init();
    if(map != NULL) map->init();
    if(info != NULL) info->init();

    if(map_tools != NULL) map_tools->set_scroll_buttons();
    show_map();
}
//---------------------------------------------------------------
// BlockadeFrame:: h i _ s c o r e s
// Display the high scores and enter current score into the
```

BLOCKADE—A Game of Modern Naval Simulation

```
// table (only if the current score is greater than the
// 30 highest scores in the "high score" file).

short BlockadeFrame::hi_scores(const char *filename)
{
// Load the current hi score table from the file
// Open file for reading
    ifstream ifs(filename, ios::in);
    if(!ifs)
    {
// Create a file with a single entry
        ofstream ofs(filename, ios::out);
        if(!ofs) return 1;
        ofs << "BLOCKADE.HISCORES" << endl;
        ofs << 1 << endl;
        ofs << 1 << endl;
        ofs << "Naba Barkakati" << endl;
        ofs << 999999 << endl;
        ofs << "Hope you like BLOCKADE!" << endl;
        ofs.close();
// Reopen it for reading
        ifs.open(filename, ios::in);
        if(!ifs) return 1;
    }

// Read and interpret the contents of the file
    char line[81];

// First line should have the string BLOCKADE.HISCORES
    ifs.getline(line, sizeof(line));
    strupr(line);
    if(strnicmp(line, "BLOCKADE.HISCORES",
        strlen("BLOCKADE.HISCORES")) != 0) return 1;

// Second line has a version number--just in case the
// contents have to change in the future
    ifs.getline(line, sizeof(line));
    short version = atoi(line);
    if(version != 1) return 1;

// Third line has the number of entries in the file
    ifs.getline(line, sizeof(line));
    short numentries = atoi(line);

// Read all the entries into a SortedArray
    SortedArray* hiscores = new SortedArray(32, 0, 8);
    if(hiscores == NULL) return 1;
    short i;
```

continues

351

Listing 9.3. continued

```
    for(i = 0; i < numentries; i++)
    {
        HiScore *s = new HiScore;
        if(s == NULL)
        {
            delete hiscores;
            return 1;
        }
        if(ifs.eof())
        {
            numentries = i;
        }
        ifs.getline(line, sizeof(line));
        s->name = new char[strlen(line) +1];
        strcpy(s->name, line);

        ifs.getline(line, sizeof(line));
        s->score = atol(line);

        ifs.getline(line, sizeof(line));
        s->quote = new char[strlen(line) +1];
        strcpy(s->quote, line);
// Add the score to the array
        hiscores->add(*s);
    }

// Check if current score is greater than the top 30 scores
    short lastindex = 29;
    if(lastindex > numentries) lastindex = numentries - 1;
    HiScore& last_hi = (HiScore&)(*hiscores)[lastindex];
    if(((lastindex == numentries - 1) && (Scenario::score > 0)) ||
       (Scenario::score > last_hi.score))
    {
// Display the dialog box HISCORES
        HiscoreDialog *p_hiscores = new HiscoreDialog(this,
                        "HISCORES", hiscores, lastindex+1);
        PTApplication app = GetApplication();
        short r = app->ExecDialog(p_hiscores);

        if(r == IDOK)
        {
            HiScore *s = p_hiscores->hi_score();
            s->score = Scenario::score;
// Add this score to the hiscores array
            hiscores->add(*s);
```

BLOCKADE—A Game of Modern Naval Simulation

Chapter 9

```
// Now save the top 30 scores back in the file
            ifs.close();
// Open file for reading
            ofstream ofs(filename, ios::out);
            if(!ofs)
            {
// Error opening file. Return.
                delete hiscores;
                return 1;
            }
            ofs << "BLOCKADE.HISCORES" << endl;
            ofs << 1 << endl;
            short n = hiscores->getItemsInContainer();
            if(n > 30) n = 30;
            ofs << n << endl;
            for(i = 0; i < n; i++)
            {
                HiScore& hi = (HiScore&)(*hiscores)[i];
                ofs << hi;
            }
// Delete the SortedArray hiscores
            delete hiscores;
            return 1;
        }
        if(r == IDCANCEL)
        {
            if(hiscores != NULL) delete hiscores;
            return 0;
        }
    }
    return 1;
}
```

LogoWindow Class

The LogoWindow class is derived from the OWL class TWindow. I create an instance of the LogoWindow class in the InitMainWindow function (see Listing 9.1) to display the opening logo in BLOCKADE. Listing 9.4 shows how the LogoWindow class is declared. The member functions of the LogoWindow class are defined in bframe.cpp (Listing 9.3) together with those of the BlockadeFrame class.

Listing 9.4. `logowin.h`—Declaration of the `LogoWindow` class.

```cpp
//----------------------------------------------------------------
// File: logowin.h
//
// Declares the window where the opening logo of the BLOCKADE
// game is displayed.
//----------------------------------------------------------------
#if !defined(__LOGOWIN_H)
#define __LOGOWIN_H

#include <owl.h>
#include "sprite.h"

class BlockadeFrame;

class LogoWindow : public TWindow
{
public:
    LogoWindow(PTWindowsObject parent, BlockadeFrame* bf) :
        TWindow(parent, NULL), blockade_frame(bf)
    {
        Attr.Style = WS_POPUP | WS_BORDER | WS_VISIBLE;
        img = Sprite::init_image("opening.bmp");
    }

    ~LogoWindow()
    {
        if(img != NULL) delete img;
    }

    void Paint(HDC hdc, PAINTSTRUCT&);

    void WMLButtonDown(RTMessage) = [WM_FIRST + WM_LBUTTONDOWN];

    void WMCreate(RTMessage) = [WM_FIRST + WM_CREATE];

    short width() { return img->width();}
    short height() { return img->height();}


private:
    Image         *img;
    BlockadeFrame *blockade_frame;
};

#endif
```

BLOCKADE—A Game of Modern Naval Simulation

DisplayWindow Classes

BLOCKADE's three view windows: `MapWindow`, `PolarWindow`, and `View3DWindow`, are derived from the base class named `DisplayWindow`. The header file `dispwin.h` declares these classes. As you can see from Listing 9.5, the base class `DisplayWindow` is derived from the OWL class `TWindow`.

Each window class has an `init` function to initialize the window and an `update` function to update the contents of the window. The `new_scenario` function in the `BlockadeFrame` class Listing 9.3) calls the `init` function of each of the view windows. `BlockadeFrame`'s `WMTimer` function calls the `update` functions to keep the view windows updated.

Each of the view windows uses an instance of the `SpriteAnimation` class (described in Chapter 5) to display bitmapped images and other drawings. The `MapWindow` class uses two `SpriteAnimation` objects: one to display the map of the region where the scenario takes place and the other to display a zoomed-in version of the map.

Listing 9.5. `dispwin.h`— Declaration of the `DisplayWindow` classes.

```
//-------------------------------------------------------------
// File: dispwin.h
// Declares the window class that displays various views in
// the BLOCKADE game.
//-------------------------------------------------------------
#if !defined(__DISPWIN_H)
#define __DISPWIN_H

#include <owl.h>
#include <bstatic.h>
#include "scene3d.h"
#include "spranim.h"

#define VIEW_WIREFRAME  0
#define VIEW_SOLID      1

class BlockadeFrame;
class Platform;

class DisplayWindow : public TWindow
{
public:
```

continues

355

Listing 9.5. continued

```cpp
        DisplayWindow(PTWindowsObject parent, BlockadeFrame *bf) :
            TWindow(parent, NULL), blockade_frame(bf),
            top(0), left(0), w(1), h(1),
            anim(NULL), s(NULL), spr_current(NULL)
        {
            Attr.Style = WS_CHILD | WS_BORDER | WS_VISIBLE |
                        WS_CLIPSIBLINGS;
        }

        virtual ~DisplayWindow();

        virtual void set_currents();
        virtual void get_currents();
        virtual void update() = 0;

        virtual void refresh_anim()
        {
            if(anim != NULL) anim->set_refresh(TRUE);
        }

        virtual unsigned short width() { return w;}
        virtual unsigned short height() { return h;}
        virtual void width(unsigned short _w) { w = _w;}
        virtual void height(unsigned short _h) { h = _h;}

        virtual void WMSize(RTMessage msg) = [WM_FIRST + WM_SIZE];

protected:
        BlockadeFrame    *blockade_frame;
        short            top, left;
        unsigned short   w, h; // Size of client area
        SpriteAnimation  *anim;
        Sprite           **s;
        Sprite           *spr_current;
        Platform         *cp;
        short            xp, yp;
        float            brg;
        float            rng;
};

class View3DWindow : public DisplayWindow
{
public:
        View3DWindow(PTWindowsObject parent, BlockadeFrame *bf) :
            DisplayWindow(parent, bf), scene(NULL)
        {
```

BLOCKADE—A Game of Modern Naval Simulation

```cpp
        Attr.Style = WS_CHILD | WS_BORDER | WS_VISIBLE |
                    WS_CLIPSIBLINGS;
    }

    ~View3DWindow(){ if(scene != NULL) delete scene;}

    void init(const char* scenefile, char* bgfile);
    void update();

    void Paint(HDC hdc, PAINTSTRUCT&);

    Scene3D* scene3d() { return scene;}
    void adjust_view_angle(Coord a);
    void adjust_at(Coord x, Coord y, Coord z);

    static short view_type;

private:
    Scene3D         *scene;
};

class PolarAnimation;

class PolarWindow : public DisplayWindow
{
public:
    PolarWindow(PTWindowsObject parent, BlockadeFrame *bf) :
        DisplayWindow(parent, bf), panim(NULL),
        infowin(NULL), infotext(NULL), nm_radius(40)
    {
        Attr.Style = WS_CHILD | WS_BORDER | WS_VISIBLE |
                    WS_CLIPCHILDREN | WS_CLIPSIBLINGS;
    }
    ~PolarWindow();

    void init();
    void update();
    void move_sprites();
    Platform* platform_at(short x, short y);

    void refresh_anim();

    void Paint(HDC hdc, PAINTSTRUCT&);
    void WMLButtonDown(RTMessage) = [WM_FIRST + WM_LBUTTONDOWN];

    short range_scale() { return nm_radius;}
    void range_scale(short n)
```

continues

Listing 9.5. continued

```cpp
    {
        if(n > 0 && n != nm_radius)
        {
            nm_radius = n;
        }
    }
    short xcenter() { return xc;}
    short ycenter() { return yc;}

    void disp_mission();

private:
    PolarAnimation *panim;
    TBStatic       *infowin;    // Window to display some info
    short          nm_radius;   // Nautical miles being displayed
    short          pix_radius;  // Radius in pixels
    short          xc, yc;      // Center of circle
    short          wiwin, hiwin;
    short          nciwin;
    char           *infotext;
    Sprite         *wpncover;   // Sprite to show weapon coverage
    Sprite         *marker;
};

class MapWindow : public DisplayWindow
{
public:
    MapWindow(PTWindowsObject parent, BlockadeFrame *bf) :
        DisplayWindow(parent, bf), zoom_anim(NULL), zoomed(0),
        mouse_captured(0)
    {
        Attr.Style = WS_CHILD | WS_BORDER | WS_VISIBLE |
                     WS_CLIPSIBLINGS;
    }
    ~MapWindow()
    {
        if(zoom_anim != NULL) delete zoom_anim;
    }
    void init();
    void update();
    void move_sprites();
    Platform* platform_at(float lat, float lng);
    void mouse_at(short x, short y);

    void refresh_anim()
    {
```

BLOCKADE—A Game of Modern Naval Simulation

Chapter 9

```cpp
        DisplayWindow::refresh_anim();
        if(zoom_anim != NULL) zoom_anim->set_refresh(TRUE);
    }

    void Paint(HDC hdc, PAINTSTRUCT&);
    void WMLButtonDown(RTMessage) = [WM_FIRST + WM_LBUTTONDOWN];
    void WMLButtonUp(RTMessage msg) = [WM_FIRST + WM_LBUTTONUP];
    void WMMouseMove(RTMessage msg) = [WM_FIRST + WM_MOUSEMOVE];

    short image_width() { return anim->bgimage()->width();}
    short image_height() { return anim->bgimage()->height();}
    short image_ready()
    {
        if(anim != NULL) return TRUE;
        else return FALSE;
    }

    void scroll_right();
    void scroll_left();
    void scroll_up();
    void scroll_down();

    void swap_anim()
    {
        if(zoom_anim == NULL) return;
        SpriteAnimation *t = anim;
        anim = zoom_anim;
        zoom_anim = t;
        anim->set_refresh(TRUE);
        zoomed = ~zoomed;
    }
private:
    SpriteAnimation *zoom_anim;
    short           zoomed;
    Sprite          *marker;
    Sprite          *zmarker;

    short           mouse_captured;
    short           xlo, xhi;
    short           ylo, yhi;
    short           xlast;
    short           ylast;
};

#endif
```

Implementation of *DisplayWindow*

Listing 9.6 shows the implementation of the few common functions of the classes that represent the view windows in BLOCKADE.

Listing 9.6. `dispwin.cpp`—
Implementation of the `DisplayWindow` class.

```
//-------------------------------------------------------------
// File: dispwin.cpp
// Implementation of the DisplayWindow class.
//-------------------------------------------------------------
#include <stdlib.h>
#include "bframe.h"

//-------------------------------------------------------------
//    ~ D i s p l a y W i n d o w
//    Destructor for the window.

DisplayWindow::~DisplayWindow()
{
    if(anim != NULL) delete anim;
    if(s != NULL) delete s;
}
//-------------------------------------------------------------
// DisplayWindow:: W M S i z e
// Save the location and size of the window

void DisplayWindow::WMSize(RTMessage)
{
    RECT r;
    GetClientRect(HWindow, &r);
    w = r.left - r.right + 1;
    h = r.bottom - r.top + 1;
}
```

Implementation of *MapWindow*

The `MapWindow` class represents the map view (see Figure 9.2). In this view of the scenario, you see a map of the region where the game's action takes place. On the map you see the icon of your ship as well as icons representing other ships and aircraft that are detected by your ship's sensors.

BLOCKADE—A Game of Modern Naval Simulation

The companion class `MapToolWindow` provides the controls to manipulate the map view. Among the controls in a `MapToolWindow`, there are buttons to zoom in, zoom out, and scroll the map display.

Listing 9.7 shows the member functions of the `MapWindow` class. Here are the highlights of this class:

- The `init` function prepares the items to be displayed in the window. Note that there are two `SpriteAnimation` objects, one for the map and the other for a zoomed version of the map.

- The variable named `anim` always points to the current animation. The member function `swap_anim` (defined inline in `dispwin.h`) swaps the animations when the player clicks on the zoom button in the `MapToolWindow`.

- The member functions `scroll_right`, `scroll_left`, `scroll_up`, and `scroll_down` scroll the map within the window. Scrolling is done by adjusting what I call the bitmap origin—the point on the background bitmap of the animation that gets mapped to the origin of the display window.

- The `MapWindow` class also handles mouse button press and mouse movement events occurring in its window. The member functions `WMLButtonDown`, `WMMouseMove`, and `WMLButtonUp` handle these events. When you press the left mouse button with the mouse pointer on the map, Windows calls `WMLButtonDown`, which gets the coordinates of the mouse and calls the `mouse_at` function to display a marker at that point and a status message. Mouse movements and button up events are handled in a similar manner.

- The function `platform_at` is called by `mouse_at` to determine the platform, if any, at a specified location of the map.

Listing 9.7. `mapwin.cpp`—
Implementation of the `MapWindow` class.

```
//------------------------------------------------------------
// File: mapwin.cpp
// Implementation of the MapWindow class.
//------------------------------------------------------------
#include <stdlib.h>
#include "bframe.h"
#include <stdio.h>
```

continues

Listing 9.7. continued

```
#define SCROLL_BY 3

static char none[] = "--- NONE ---";
//----------------------------------------------------------------
//  MapWindow:: P a i n t
//  Draw everything in the window

void MapWindow::Paint(HDC hdc, PAINTSTRUCT&)
{
    if(anim != NULL)
    {
        move_sprites();
        anim->set_refresh(TRUE);
        anim->animate(hdc, left, top);
    }
}
//----------------------------------------------------------------
//  MapWindow:: u p d a t e
//  Update the view of the scene in the window

void MapWindow::update()
{
    if(anim != NULL)
    {
        move_sprites();
        HDC hdc = GetDC(HWindow);
        anim->animate(hdc, left, top);
        ReleaseDC(HWindow, hdc);
    }
}
//----------------------------------------------------------------
// MapWindow:: i n i t
// Initialize the map.

void MapWindow::init()
{
// Change the cursor to an hourglass
    SetCapture(HWindow);
    SetCursor(LoadCursor(NULL, IDC_WAIT));

// Clean up existing map, if any
    if(anim != NULL) delete anim;
    if(zoom_anim != NULL) delete zoom_anim;
    if(s != NULL) delete s;
```

BLOCKADE—A Game of Modern Naval Simulation

```
// Get a DC for this window
    HDC hdc = GetDC(HWindow);

// Construct a SpriteAnimation with the specified background
// image file
    anim = new SpriteAnimation(hdc, blockade_frame->vu3_wmax(),
                    blockade_frame->vu3_hmax(),
                    blockade_frame->scenario_info()->mapfile);

    if(anim == NULL)
    {
        ReleaseDC(HWindow, hdc);
        SetCursor(LoadCursor(NULL, IDC_ARROW));
        ReleaseCapture();
    }

// Add sprites to the map
    short i, xpos, ypos;
    Sprite *spr;
    ScenarioInfo *si = blockade_frame->scenario_info();
    for(i = 0; i < blockade_frame->scenario()->numplatform(); i++)
    {
        spr = blockade_frame->scenario()->platform(i).
                                                    map_sprite();
        xpos = (-si->orglng + blockade_frame->scenario()->
                    platform(i).longitude()) * si->pixperlng -
                        spr->width() / 2;
        ypos = (si->orglat - blockade_frame->scenario()->
                    platform(i).latitude()) * si->pixperlat -
                        spr->height() / 2;
        spr->newpos(xpos, ypos);
        if(i > 0) spr->inactive();
// Add sprite to animation
        anim->add(spr);
    }
// Add the sprite to be used as a "marker" in the map
    Platform *po = blockade_frame->scenario()->our_ship();
    marker = new Sprite(hdc, "marker.bmp", "markerm.bmp");
    marker->priority(10000);
    marker->id(-1);
    marker->newpos(po->map_sprite()->xpos() -
                    po->map_sprite()->width() / 2,
                    po->map_sprite()->ypos() -
                    po->map_sprite()->height() / 2);
    marker->inactive();
    anim->add(marker);
```

continues

Listing 9.7. continued

```
// Add sprites to the zoomed version of the map
// Create a "zoomed-in" version of the map
    zoom_anim = new SpriteAnimation(hdc,
                    blockade_frame->vu3_wmax(),
                    blockade_frame->vu3_hmax(),
                    blockade_frame->scenario_info()->zmapfile);
    if(zoom_anim != NULL)
    {
        for(i = 0; i < blockade_frame->scenario()->numplatform();
            i++)
        {
            spr = blockade_frame->scenario()->platform(i).
                                                zmap_sprite();
            xpos = (-si->orglng + blockade_frame->scenario()->
                    platform(i).longitude()) * si->pixperlng *
                    si->mapzoom - spr->width() / 2;
            ypos = (si->orglat - blockade_frame->scenario()->
                    platform(i).latitude()) * si->pixperlat *
                    si->mapzoom - spr->height() / 2;
            spr->newpos(xpos, ypos);
            if(i > 0) spr->inactive();
// Add sprite to animation
            zoom_anim->add(spr);
        }
// Add the sprite to be used as a "marker" in the zoomed map
        zmarker = new Sprite(hdc, "marker.bmp", "markerm.bmp");
        zmarker->priority(10000);
        zmarker->id(-1);
        zmarker->newpos(po->zmap_sprite()->xpos() -
                        po->zmap_sprite()->width() / 2,
                        po->zmap_sprite()->ypos() -
                        po->zmap_sprite()->height() / 2);
        zmarker->inactive();
        anim->add(zmarker);
    }

// Remember to release the DC
    ReleaseDC(HWindow, hdc);

// Reset cursor to arrow
    SetCursor(LoadCursor(NULL, IDC_ARROW));
    ReleaseCapture();
}
//------------------------------------------------------------
// MapWindow:: s c r o l l _ r i g h t
```

Chapter 9

BLOCKADE—A Game of Modern Naval Simulation

```cpp
void MapWindow::scroll_right()
{
    if(anim == NULL) return;
    short x = anim->xbmp_origin();
    x += w / SCROLL_BY;
    if((x + w) > anim->bgimage()->width())
        x = anim->bgimage()->width() - w;
    anim->xbmp_origin(x);
    anim->set_refresh(1);
}
//------------------------------------------------------------
// MapWindow:: s c r o l l _ l e f t

void MapWindow::scroll_left()
{
    if(anim == NULL) return;
    short x = anim->xbmp_origin();
    x -= w / SCROLL_BY;
    if(x < 0) x = 0;
    anim->xbmp_origin(x);
    anim->set_refresh(1);
}
//------------------------------------------------------------
// MapWindow:: s c r o l l _ d o w n

void MapWindow::scroll_down()
{
    if(anim == NULL) return;
    short y = anim->ybmp_origin();
    y += h / SCROLL_BY;
    if((y + h) > anim->bgimage()->height())
        y = anim->bgimage()->height() - h;
    anim->ybmp_origin(y);
    anim->set_refresh(1);
}
//------------------------------------------------------------
// MapWindow:: s c r o l l _ u p

void MapWindow::scroll_up()
{
    if(anim == NULL) return;
    short y = anim->ybmp_origin();
    y -= h / SCROLL_BY;
    if(y < 0) y = 0;
    anim->ybmp_origin(y);
    anim->set_refresh(1);
```

continues

Listing 9.7. continued

```
}
//---------------------------------------------------------------
// MapWindow:: m o v e _ s p r i t e s
// Reposition the platforms in the map window

void MapWindow::move_sprites()
{
    ScenarioInfo *si = blockade_frame->scenario_info();
    short i, xpos, ypos;
    Sprite *spr;
    float scale = 1.0;
    if(zoomed) scale = si->mapzoom;
    for(i = 0; i < blockade_frame->scenario()->numplatform(); i++)
    {
        if(blockade_frame->scenario()->platform(i).is_active())
        {
            spr = blockade_frame->scenario()->platform(i).
                        map_sprite();

// Don't update sprite if it's not marked active
            if(!spr->is_active()) continue;

            if(zoomed) spr = blockade_frame->scenario()->
                                platform(i).zmap_sprite();

            xpos = (-si->orglng + blockade_frame->scenario()->
                        platform(i).longitude()) * si->pixperlng *
                        scale - spr->width() / 2;
            ypos = (si->orglat - blockade_frame->scenario()->
                        platform(i).latitude()) * si->pixperlat *
                        scale - spr->height() / 2;
            short xdel = xpos - spr->xpos();
            short ydel = ypos - spr->ypos();
            spr->move(xdel, ydel);
        }
    }
}
//---------------------------------------------------------------
// MapWindow:: W M L B u t t o n D o w n
// Handle button down events in this window

void MapWindow::WMLButtonDown(RTMessage msg)
{
    short x = msg.LP.Lo;
    short y = msg.LP.Hi;
```

Chapter 9

BLOCKADE—A Game of Modern Naval Simulation

```cpp
    mouse_captured = 1;
    SetCapture(HWindow);

    xlast = x;
    ylast = y;
    spr_current = marker;
    if(zoomed) spr_current = zmarker;
    spr_current->active();
    spr_current->update();

    mouse_at(x,y);
}
//---------------------------------------------------------------
// MapWindow:: W M M o u s e M o v e
// Handle mouse movements in this window

void MapWindow::WMMouseMove(RTMessage msg)
{
    if(!mouse_captured) return;

    short x = msg.LP.Lo;
    short y = msg.LP.Hi;
    mouse_at(x,y);
}
//---------------------------------------------------------------
// MapWindow:: W M L B u t t o n U p
// Handle button up event.

void MapWindow::WMLButtonUp(RTMessage msg)
{
    if(!mouse_captured) return;

    short x = msg.LP.Lo;
    short y = msg.LP.Hi;

    mouse_at(x,y);

    spr_current->inactive();
    Scenario::refresh = 1;
    spr_current = NULL;

// Clear the status message
    LPSTR msgtxt = blockade_frame->status_window()->
                                    get_msgbuf(1);
    msgtxt[0] = ' ';
    msgtxt[1] = '\0';
    blockade_frame->status_window()->set_text(msgtxt, 1, 1);
```

continues

Listing 9.7. continued

```cpp
// Release the mouse
    ReleaseCapture();
    mouse_captured = 0;
}
//----------------------------------------------------------------
// MapWindow::  m o u s e _ a t
// Display appropriate information for mouse at (x,y)

void MapWindow::mouse_at(short x, short y)
{
    if(!mouse_captured) return;
    if(spr_current == NULL) return;

    ScenarioInfo *si = blockade_frame->scenario_info();
    Platform *po = blockade_frame->scenario()->our_ship();
    float scale = 1.0;
    if(zoomed) scale = si->mapzoom;

// Convert (x,y) into (lng,lat)
    float lng = (anim->xbmp_origin() + x) / si->pixperlng /
                scale + si->orglng;
    float lat = - (anim->ybmp_origin() + y) / si->pixperlat /
                scale + si->orglat;

// Find range from player's ship and the heading relative to
// north
    float xdist = lng - po->longitude();
    float ydist = lat - po->latitude();
    float rng;
    float brg;
    if(xdist == 0 && ydist == 0)
    {
        rng = 0;
        brg = 0;
    }
    else
    {
        rng = sqrt(xdist*xdist + ydist*ydist) * DEG2NM;
        brg = atan2(xdist, ydist) * RAD_TO_DEG;
    }
    if(brg < 0) brg += 360;

// Next, find the platform at the position of "mouse click"
    cp = platform_at(lat, lng);

// Display information in status window
```

BLOCKADE—A Game of Modern Naval Simulation

Chapter 9

```cpp
    char *nm = none;
    if(cp != NULL) nm = cp->name();

    LPSTR msgtxt = blockade_frame->status_window()->
                                    get_msgbuf(1);
    short len = sprintf(msgtxt,
                    "Platform: %s "
                    "Range: %.2f "
                    "Bearing: %.2f", nm, rng, brg);
    blockade_frame->status_window()->set_text(msgtxt, len, 1);

// Move the marker sprite
    short xdel = anim->xbmp_origin() + x
               - spr_current->xpos()
               - spr_current->width() / 2;
    short ydel = anim->ybmp_origin() + y
               - spr_current->ypos()
               - spr_current->height() / 2;
    spr_current->move(xdel, ydel);
}
//-------------------------------------------------------------
// MapWindow:: p l a t f o r m _ a t
// Find platform at specified position

Platform* MapWindow::platform_at(float lat, float lng)
{
    int i, np = blockade_frame->scenario()->numplatform();
    Platform *rp = NULL;

    for(i = 0; i < np; i++)
    {
        Platform *p = &(blockade_frame->scenario()->
                        platform(i));
        if(!p->is_active()) continue;

        Sprite *spr = p->map_sprite();
        if(zoomed) spr = p->zmap_sprite();
        if(!spr->is_active()) continue;

        if((fabs(lat - p->latitude()) < 0.05) &&
           (fabs(lng - p->longitude()) < 0.05))
        {
            rp = p;
            break;
        }
    }
    return rp;
}
```

Implementation of *PolarWindow*

Listing 9.8 shows the implementation of the `PolarWindow` class that displays a polar view of the scenario (see Figure 9.4). In the polar view, you see circular regions around your ship. The view shows, in polar coordinates, all platforms detected by your ship. The angles in the polar view are with respect to your ship. Thus, no matter what your ship's true heading is, the polar view always shows your ship heading straight up.

The companion class `PolarToolWindow` provides the controls to manipulate the polar view. Among the controls in a `PolarToolWindow`, there are buttons to zoom in and zoom out of the polar display. The zoom feature changes the range scale; the current maximum range is displayed in an area above the zoom buttons. The following are some of the major features of the `PolarWindow` class:

- The `PolarWindow` class uses a special version of `SpriteAnimation`, called `PolarAnimation`. I specialized `SpriteAnimation` (defined in Chapter 5) with a new member function called `draw_polar_bg` that draws the tick marks and circles that I needed for the polar display. This is a good example of a benefit of object-oriented programming—being able to add new functionality to an existing class through inheritance.

- The `init` function prepares the items to be displayed in the window. Note that the sprites for the platforms are created by calling the `make_sprites` function of the current `Scenario`. I store a pointer to `BlockadeFrame` in each view window and access the current scenario through this pointer. For instance, here is how I call the `make_sprites` function of the current `Scenario`:

```
blockade_frame->scenario()->make_sprites(hdc);
```

- The `init` function creates a `TBStatic` window where useful information is displayed during the game.

- The `PolarWindow` class handles mouse button press events occurring in its window. The member function `WMLButtonDown` handles these events. When you press the left mouse button with the mouse pointer on the polar view, Windows calls `WMLButtonDown`, which gets the coordinates of the mouse, converts them to range and bearing, and calls the `platform_at` function to determine the platform, if any, at that location. Then `WMLButtonDown` displays a marker at that point and a message in a `TBStatic` window showing the range and bearing from your ship to the

BLOCKADE—A Game of Modern Naval Simulation

location of the button press and the name of the platform, if any, at that location.

- The `disp_mission` function is called by `init` to display a description of the current mission. This text is loaded by the `Scenario::init` function and kept in the static array `Scenario::mission_description`.

- The `draw_wpncover` function is used as a callback function by a sprite that displays the sectors where the current weapon can be used. The information necessary to draw the sectors comes from the `Weapon` class.

Listing 9.8. polarwin.cpp— Implementation of the PolarWindow class.

```
//--------------------------------------------------------------
// File: polarwin.cpp
// Implementation of the PolarWindow class.
//--------------------------------------------------------------
#include <stdlib.h>
#include "bframe.h"
#include <stdio.h>

#define MAXCONTACTS   64
#define MARGIN        4

#define WPNCOVERSIZE 40

static short firsttime = 1;
static short done_since = 0;

class PolarAnimation : public SpriteAnimation
{
public:
    PolarAnimation(HDC hdc, unsigned short w,
                   unsigned short h,
                   LPSTR filename) :
        SpriteAnimation(hdc, w, h, filename) {}


    PolarAnimation(HDC hdc, unsigned short w,
                   unsigned short h, Image* bg) :
        SpriteAnimation(hdc, w, h, bg) {}

    void draw_polar_bg(short x, short y, short r);
};
```

continues

Listing 9.8. continued

```
void _FAR PASCAL _export draw_wpncover(HDC hdc,short x, short y,
                                       LPVOID data);
static char none[] = "--- None ---";
//----------------------------------------------------------------
// PolarWindow:: ~ P o l a r W i n d o w
// Destructor for a PolarWindow

PolarWindow::~PolarWindow()
{
    if(panim != NULL) delete panim;
    if(infowin != NULL) delete infowin;
    if(infotext != NULL) delete infotext;
}
//----------------------------------------------------------------
// PolarWindow:: r e f r e s h _ a n i m
// Make sure animation is refreshed

void PolarWindow::refresh_anim()
{
    if(panim != NULL)
    {
        panim->set_refresh(TRUE);
    }
}
//----------------------------------------------------------------
//   PolarWindow:: P a i n t
//   Draw everything in the window

void PolarWindow::Paint(HDC hdc, PAINTSTRUCT&)
{
    if(panim != NULL)
    {
        blockade_frame->scenario()->ownship_xfrm();
        move_sprites();
        panim->set_refresh(TRUE);
        panim->animate(hdc, left, top);
    }
}
//----------------------------------------------------------------
//   PolarWindow:: u p d a t e
//   Update the view of the scene in the window

void PolarWindow::update()
{
    if(panim != NULL)
```

BLOCKADE—A Game of Modern Naval Simulation

```
        {
            blockade_frame->scenario()->ownship_xfrm();
            move_sprites();
            HDC hdc = GetDC(HWindow);
            panim->animate(hdc, left, top);
            ReleaseDC(HWindow, hdc);
        }
    }
//--------------------------------------------------------------
// PolarWindow:: i n i t
// Initialize the polar display.

void PolarWindow::init()
{
    get_currents();
// Change the cursor to an hourglass
    SetCapture(HWindow);
    SetCursor(LoadCursor(NULL, IDC_WAIT));

// Clean up existing data, if any
    if(panim != NULL) delete panim;
    if(s != NULL) delete s;
    if(infowin != NULL) delete infowin;
    if(infotext != NULL) delete infotext;

// Get a DC for this window
    HDC hdc = GetDC(HWindow);

// Construct a PolarAnimation with the specified background
// image file
    panim = new PolarAnimation(hdc, blockade_frame->vu3_wmax(),
                               blockade_frame->vu3_hmax(),
                               "polar.bmp");
    if(panim == NULL)
    {
        ReleaseDC(HWindow, hdc);
        SetCursor(LoadCursor(NULL, IDC_ARROW));
        ReleaseCapture();
        return;
    }

// Draw the polar display's background
// I am assuming that the display height is less than the width
    pix_radius = blockade_frame->vu3_hmax() / 2 - MARGIN;
    xc = blockade_frame->vu3_wmax() - pix_radius - MARGIN;
    yc = pix_radius + MARGIN;
    panim->draw_polar_bg(xc, yc, pix_radius);
```

continues

Listing 9.8. continued

```
// Create the window to display info
    wiwin = xc - pix_radius - 2*MARGIN;
    hiwin = blockade_frame->vu3_hmax() - 2*MARGIN;

// Draw a border around info window
    panim->bg_rect(MARGIN-1, MARGIN-1,
                   MARGIN+wiwin+1, MARGIN+hiwin+1);

// Determine how many characters would fit into the
// info window
    TEXTMETRIC tm;
    GetTextMetrics(hdc, &tm);
    short hchar = tm.tmHeight + tm.tmExternalLeading;
    short wchar = tm.tmAveCharWidth;
    nciwin = (wiwin/wchar) * (hiwin/hchar) + 1;
    infotext = new char[nciwin];
    infotext[nciwin-1] = '\0';

    infowin = new TBStatic(this, 1, "Selected Contact",
                           MARGIN, MARGIN, wiwin, hiwin,
                           nciwin);
    GetApplication()->MakeWindow(infowin);
    disp_mission();

// Create a sprite for each platform
    blockade_frame->scenario()->make_sprites(hdc);
    blockade_frame->scenario()->ownship_xfrm();

// Add the sprites to the polar window's animation
    short i, xpos, ypos;
    Sprite *s;
    for(i = 0; i < blockade_frame->scenario()->numplatform(); i++)
    {
        s = blockade_frame->scenario()->platform(i).sprite();
        xpos = xc - s->width() / 2 +
               (long) blockade_frame->scenario()->platform(i).
                   xo() * (long)pix_radius / (long) nm_radius;
        ypos = yc - s->height() / 2 -
               (long) blockade_frame->scenario()->platform(i).
                   yo() * (long)pix_radius / (long) nm_radius;
        s->newpos(xpos, ypos);
        s->priority(1000);
// Hide all but the first sprite
        if(i > 0) s->inactive();
// Add sprite to animation
        panim->add(s);
    }
```

BLOCKADE—A Game of Modern Naval Simulation

```
// Add a sprite to show the coverage sectors of weapons
    wpncover = new Sprite(hdc, NULL, NULL);
    wpncover->priority(500);
    wpncover->width(2*WPNCOVERSIZE);
    wpncover->height(2*WPNCOVERSIZE);
    wpncover->newpos(xc-WPNCOVERSIZE, yc-WPNCOVERSIZE);
    DRAWPROC proc = (DRAWPROC) MakeProcInstance(
                                (FARPROC) draw_wpncover,
                        GetApplication()->hInstance);
    wpncover->drawproc(proc, blockade_frame);
    wpncover->active();
    wpncover->update();
    panim->add(wpncover);

// Add the sprite to be used as a "marker"
    marker = new Sprite(hdc, "marker.bmp", "markerm.bmp");
    marker->priority(10000);
    marker->id(-1);
    marker->newpos(xc-marker->width()/2, yc-marker->height()/2);
    marker->active();
    marker->update();
    panim->add(marker);

// Remember to release the DC
    ReleaseDC(HWindow, hdc);

// Reset cursor to arrow
    SetCursor(LoadCursor(NULL, IDC_ARROW));
    ReleaseCapture();
}
//-------------------------------------------------------------
// PolarWindow:: W M L B u t t o n D o w n
// Handle button down events in the PolarWindow

void PolarWindow::WMLButtonDown(RTMessage msg)
{
    short x = msg.LP.Lo;
    short y = msg.LP.Hi;

// Ignore button presses outside the polar display's bounds
    long xdel = x - xc;
    long ydel = yc - y;
    unsigned long dist = xdel*xdel + ydel*ydel;
    if(dist > pix_radius*pix_radius) return;

// Compute range and bearing to selected point
```

continues

Listing 9.8. continued

```
        rng = sqrt((double)dist) * (double)nm_radius /
                                    (double)pix_radius;
        Scenario::range_current = rng;
        if(xdel == 0 && ydel == 0)
            brg = 0;
        else
            brg = atan2(xdel, ydel) * RAD_TO_DEG;
        if(brg < 0) brg = 360 + brg;
        Scenario::bearing_current = brg;

// Find the platform at the position of "mouse click"
        cp = platform_at(x, y);
        Scenario::current_platform = cp;
        char *nm = none;
        if(Scenario::current_platform != NULL)
        {
            nm = Scenario::current_platform->name();
        }
        infowin->Clear();
        sprintf(infotext, "Platform: %s\n"
                "Range: %.2f\n"
                "Bearing: %.2f\n",
                nm, Scenario::range_current,
                Scenario::bearing_current);
        infowin->SetText(infotext);

// Move the marker sprite
        xdel = x - marker->xpos() - marker->width() / 2;
        ydel = y - marker->ypos() - marker->height() / 2;
        marker->move(xdel, ydel);

        xp = x;
        yp = y;
        Scenario::xpos_current = xp;
        Scenario::ypos_current = yp;
}
//----------------------------------------------------------------
// PolarAnimation::  d r a w _ p o l a r _ b g
// Draw the background of the polar display

void PolarAnimation::draw_polar_bg(short xc, short yc, short r)
{
    HBRUSH hbluebrush = CreateSolidBrush(RGB(0, 0, 255));
    HBRUSH holdbrush = SelectBrush(hdc_bg, hbluebrush);
    HPEN hpen = GetStockPen(WHITE_PEN);
    HPEN hdotpen = CreatePen(PS_DOT, 1, RGB(192, 192, 192));
```

BLOCKADE—A Game of Modern Naval Simulation

```
    HPEN holdpen = SelectPen(hdc_bg, hpen);
    SetBkMode(hdc_bg, TRANSPARENT);
    Ellipse(hdc_bg, xc-r, yc-r, xc+r, yc+r);

// Tick marks around the circle
    short i, x1, y1, x2, y2, ticklen = r/60;
    if(ticklen < 6) ticklen = 6;
    Coord cosi, sini, angrad;

    for(i = 0; i < 360; i++)
    {
        angrad = i * DEG_TO_RAD;
        cosi = TabCos(angrad);
        sini = TabSin(angrad);
        x1 = xc + r * sini;
        y1 = yc - r * cosi;
        MoveTo(hdc_bg, x1, y1);

        x2 = xc + (r - ticklen) * sini;
        y2 = yc - (r - ticklen) * cosi;

        if(i % 10 == 0)
        {
            x2 = xc + (r - 2*ticklen) * sini;
            y2 = yc - (r - 2*ticklen) * cosi;
        }
        LineTo(hdc_bg, x2, y2);
        if(i % 30 == 0)
        {
            x2 = xc;
            y2 = yc;
            HPEN hpen_tmp = SelectPen(hdc_bg, hdotpen);
            MoveTo(hdc_bg, x1, y1);
            LineTo(hdc_bg, x2, y2);
            SelectPen(hdc_bg, hpen_tmp);
        }
    }
// Draw range rings...
    short step = r / 10, r1 = 0;
    SelectBrush(hdc_bg, GetStockBrush(NULL_BRUSH));
    SelectPen(hdc_bg, hdotpen);
    for(i = 0; i < 9; i++)
    {
        r1 += step;
        Arc(hdc_bg, xc-r1, yc-r1, xc+r1, yc+r1,
            xc-r1, yc-r1, xc-r1, yc-r1);
    }
```

continues

Listing 9.8. continued

```
// Reset the pen and the brush
    SelectPen(hdc_bg, holdpen);
    SelectBrush(hdc_bg, holdbrush);
    DeletePen(hdotpen);
    DeleteBrush(hbluebrush);
}
//----------------------------------------------------------------
// PolarWindow:: m o v e _ s p r i t e s
// Reposition the platforms in the polar window

void PolarWindow::move_sprites()
{
    short i, xpos, ypos;
    Sprite *s;
    float scale = (float)pix_radius / (float)nm_radius;

// Position all the sprites for the active platforms
    for(i = 0; i < blockade_frame->scenario()->numplatform(); i++)
    {
        if(blockade_frame->scenario()->platform(i).is_active())
        {
            s = blockade_frame->scenario()->platform(i).sprite();

// Don't update sprite if it's not marked active
            if(!s->is_active()) continue;

            xpos = xc - s->width() / 2 +
                   (float) blockade_frame->scenario()->platform(i).
                   xo() * scale;
            ypos = yc - s->height() / 2 -
                   (float)blockade_frame->scenario()->platform(i).
                   yo() * scale;
            short xdel = xpos - s->xpos();
            short ydel = ypos - s->ypos();
            s->move(xdel, ydel);
        }
    }
}
//----------------------------------------------------------------
// d r a w _ w p n c o v e r
// Draw the sectors where the current weapon is effective

void _FAR PASCAL _export draw_wpncover(HDC hdc, short x, short y,
                                       LPVOID p)
{
    BlockadeFrame *bf = (BlockadeFrame*)p;
    Platform *os = bf->scenario()->our_ship();
```

BLOCKADE—A Game of Modern Naval Simulation

```
    HPEN hpen_yellow = CreatePen(PS_SOLID, 2, RGB(255,255,0));
    HPEN holdpen = SelectPen(hdc, hpen_yellow);

// Get coordinates of center point of polar display
    short xc = bf->polar_window()->xcenter();
    short yc = bf->polar_window()->ycenter();

// Get current weapon index
    short i = Scenario::weapon_index;

// Display all sectors covered by this weapon
    float a, b;
    short j, x3, y3, x4, y4;
    for(j = 0; j < os->weapon(i).numsector(); j++)
    {
        a = os->weapon(i).sector(j)->angle2;
        b = os->weapon(i).sector(j)->angle1;
        a *= DEG_TO_RAD;
        b *= DEG_TO_RAD;
        x3 = xc + WPNCOVERSIZE*sin(a);
        y3 = yc - WPNCOVERSIZE*cos(a);
        x4 = xc + WPNCOVERSIZE*sin(b);
        y4 = yc - WPNCOVERSIZE*cos(b);
        Arc(hdc, xc-WPNCOVERSIZE, yc-WPNCOVERSIZE,
            xc+WPNCOVERSIZE, yc+WPNCOVERSIZE,
            x3, y3, x4, y4);
//         Pie(hdc, xc-WPNCOVERSIZE, yc-WPNCOVERSIZE,
//             xc+WPNCOVERSIZE, yc+WPNCOVERSIZE,
//             x3, y3, x4, y4);
    }

// Reset brush and pen
    SelectPen(hdc, holdpen);
    DeletePen(hpen_yellow);
}
//-------------------------------------------------------------
// PolarWindow:: p l a t f o r m _ a t
// Find platform at specified position

Platform* PolarWindow::platform_at(short x, short y)
{
    int i, np = blockade_frame->scenario()->numplatform();
    Platform *rp = NULL;

    for(i = 0; i < np; i++)
    {
        Platform *p = &(blockade_frame->scenario()->
                        platform(i));
```

continues

Listing 9.8. continued

```
        if(!p->is_active()) continue;
        Sprite *spr = p->sprite();
        if(!spr->is_active()) continue;

        short xs = spr->xpos();
        short ys = spr->ypos();
        if(x < xs) continue;
        if(y < ys) continue;

        short ws = spr->width();
        short hs = spr->height();
        if(x > (xs + ws - 1)) continue;
        if(y > (ys + hs - 1)) continue;

        rp = p;
        break;
    }
    return rp;
}
//-------------------------------------------------------------
// DisplayWindow:: s e t _ c u r r e n t s
// Copy current location of marker to static variables of the
// Scenario class

void DisplayWindow::set_currents()
{
    Scenario::current_platform = cp;
    Scenario::range_current = rng;
    Scenario::bearing_current = brg;
    Scenario::xpos_current = xp;
    Scenario::ypos_current = yp;
}
//-------------------------------------------------------------
// DisplayWindow:: g e t _ c u r r e n t s
// Copy current location of marker from static variables of the
// Scenario class

void DisplayWindow::get_currents()
{
    cp = Scenario::current_platform;
    rng = Scenario::range_current;
    brg = Scenario::bearing_current;
    xp = Scenario::xpos_current;
    yp = Scenario::ypos_current;
}
//-------------------------------------------------------------
// PolarWindow:: d i s p _ m i s s i o n
// Display the mission description in the info window.
```

BLOCKADE—A Game of Modern Naval Simulation

```
void PolarWindow::disp_mission()
{
    infowin->Clear();
    infowin->SetText(Scenario::mission_description);
}
```

Implementation of *View3DWindow*

The `View3DWindow` class is a 3-D view of your ship (see Figure 9.3). Unfortunately, the 3-D view is not as sophisticated as it could be. For now, you see a polygon-bound ship with no shading. The 3-D scene is defined by the classes `Vector3D`, `Facet3D`, `Shape3D`, and `Scene3D`. These classes are presented in Chapter 8.

A companion class, `View3DToolWindow`, provides the controls to manipulate the 3-D view. Among the controls in a `View3DToolWindow`, there are buttons to zoom in, zoom out, and change the viewpoint.

Listing 9.9 shows the implementation of the `View3DWindow` class. Here are some of its major features:

■ The `init` function initializes the 3-D scene by creating a new `Scene3D` object. Then `init` creates a sprite for each `Shape3D` object in the 3-D scene.

■ The `draw_shape` function is used as a callback function that is called when each of the sprites needs updating. The `draw_shape` function retrieves the transformed coordinates of the vertices of each facet and draws a polygon representing the facet.

Listing 9.9. `vu3dwin.cpp`—Implementation of the `View3DWindow` class.

```
//---------------------------------------------------------------
// File: vu3dwin.cpp
// Implementation of the View3DWindow class.
//---------------------------------------------------------------
#include <stdlib.h>
#include "scene3d.h"
#include "bframe.h"
```

continues

Listing 9.9. continued

```
static short firsttime = 1;
static short done_since = 0;

short View3DWindow::view_type = VIEW_SOLID;

void _FAR PASCAL _export draw_shape(HDC hdc, short x, short y,
                                    LPVOID data);

//----------------------------------------------------------------
// View3DWindow:: P a i n t
// Draw everything in the window

void View3DWindow::Paint(HDC hdc, PAINTSTRUCT&)
{
    if(anim != NULL)
    {
        if(scene != NULL) scene->view_transform();
        anim->set_refresh(TRUE);
        anim->animate(hdc, left, top);
    }
}
//----------------------------------------------------------------
// View3DWindow:: u p d a t e
// Update the view of the scene in the window

void View3DWindow::update()
{
    if(anim != NULL)
    {
        if(scene != NULL) scene->view_transform();
        HDC hdc = GetDC(HWindow);
        anim->animate(hdc, left, top);
        ReleaseDC(HWindow, hdc);
    }
}
//----------------------------------------------------------------
// View3DWindow:: i n i t
// Initialize the scene

void View3DWindow::init(const char* scenefile,
                       char* bgfile)
{
    if(scenefile == NULL) return;

// Change the cursor to an hourglass
    SetCapture(HWindow);
    SetCursor(LoadCursor(NULL, IDC_WAIT));
```

BLOCKADE—A Game of Modern Naval Simulation

```
// Clean up existing puzzle, if any
    if(anim != NULL) delete anim;
    if(scene != NULL) delete scene;
    if(s != NULL) delete s;

// Create and initialize the 3D scene
    scene = new Scene3D(blockade_frame->vu3_wmax(),
                       blockade_frame->vu3_hmax(), scenefile);
    if(scene == NULL) return;
    if(scene->shape_array == NULL) return;

// Get a DC for this window
    HDC hdc = GetDC(HWindow);

// Construct a SpriteAnimation with the specified background
// image file
    anim = new SpriteAnimation(hdc, blockade_frame->vu3_wmax(),
                       blockade_frame->vu3_hmax(), bgfile);
    if(anim == NULL)
    {
        ReleaseDC(HWindow, hdc);
        SetCursor(LoadCursor(NULL, IDC_ARROW));
        ReleaseCapture();
        return;
    }

// Set up a sprite for each shape
    short numshapes = scene->shape_array->getItemsInContainer();

// Create the array of sprites
    s = new Sprite* [numshapes];
    DRAWPROC proc = (DRAWPROC) MakeProcInstance(
                                (FARPROC) draw_shape,
                       GetApplication()->hInstance);
    short i, xpos, ypos, wdth, hght;
    for(i = 0; i < numshapes; i++)
    {
        scene->view_transform();
        xpos = scene->shapes[i]->min_xpos();
        ypos = width() - scene->shapes[i]->min_ypos();
        wdth = scene->shapes[i]->max_xpos() - xpos;
        hght = scene->shapes[i]->max_ypos() - ypos;

        scene->shapes[i]->sort_facets();

        s[i] = new Sprite(hdc, NULL, NULL);
        s[i]->newpos(xpos, ypos);
```

continues

Listing 9.9. continued

```
            s[i]->width(wdth);
            s[i]->height(hght);
            s[i]->drawproc(proc, scene->shapes[i]);
            s[i]->active();
            s[i]->update();
// Add sprite to animation
            anim->add(s[i]);
        }

// Remember to release the DC
    ReleaseDC(HWindow, hdc);

// Reset cursor to arrow
    SetCursor(LoadCursor(NULL, IDC_ARROW));
    ReleaseCapture();
}
//---------------------------------------------------------------
void _FAR PASCAL _export draw_shape(HDC hdc, short x, short y,
                                    LPVOID data)
{
// Sort the facets in each shape

// Find the minimum z coord for each shape

// Sort the shapes in increasing order of transformed z coord

// Draw facets in each shape using the transformed vertices
    short i, j, vindex, red, green, blue;
    Shape3D *s = (Shape3D*)data;
    POINT pt[4];
    for(i = 0; i < s->numfacets; i++)
    {
        short x, y;
        Facet3D& f = (Facet3D&)(*(s->facets))[i];
        red = f.red;
        green = f.green;
        blue = f.blue;
        for(j = 0; j < 4; j++)
        {
            vindex = f.vertex[j];
            if(vindex < 0) break;
            Vector3D& v = (Vector3D&)(*(s->xfrmv))[vindex];
            if(View3DWindow::view_type == VIEW_WIREFRAME)
            {
```

BLOCKADE—A Game of Modern Naval Simulation

```cpp
                if(j == 0)
                {
                    x = v.x;
                    y = v.y;
                    MoveTo(hdc, x, y);
                }
                if(j > 0) LineTo(hdc, (short)v.x, (short)v.y);
            }
            if(View3DWindow::view_type == VIEW_SOLID)
            {
// Prepare a polygon...
                pt[j].x = v.x;
                pt[j].y = v.y;
            }
        }
        if(View3DWindow::view_type == VIEW_WIREFRAME)
                                    LineTo(hdc, x, y);
        if(View3DWindow::view_type == VIEW_SOLID)
        {
            HBRUSH hbr = CreateSolidBrush(
                            RGB(red, green, blue));
            HBRUSH hbr_old = SelectBrush(hdc, hbr);
            Polygon(hdc, pt, j);
            SelectBrush(hdc, hbr_old);
            DeleteBrush(hbr);
        }
    }
}
//------------------------------------------------------------
void View3DWindow::adjust_view_angle(Coord a)
{
    if(scene != NULL) scene->view_angle += a;
    refresh_anim();
}
//------------------------------------------------------------
void View3DWindow::adjust_at(Coord x, Coord y, Coord z)
{
    if(scene != NULL)
    {
        scene->at.x += x;
        scene->at.y += y;
        scene->at.z += z;
    }
    refresh_anim();
}
```

ToolWindow Classes

The `ToolWindow` class hierarchy mirrors the `DisplayWindow` hierarchy. Each of these classes represents the window that appears to the left of the main view window in BLOCKADE. The classes `MapToolWindow`, `PolarToolWindow`, and `View3DToolWindow` provide the tools to manipulate the corresponding view windows `MapWindow`, `PolarWindow`, and `View3DWindow`, respectively.

Listing 9.10 shows the header file `toolwin.h` that declares the classes `MapToolWindow`, `PolarToolWindow`, and `View3DToolWindow`. The `ToolWindow` class is derived from the OWL class `TWindow`. `ToolWindow` manages an array of `ToolIcon` objects that represent the icons appearing in the tool windows. The header file `toolwin.h` also declares the `ToolIcon` structure. As you can see, each `ToolIcon` is represented by a bitmap image.

Listing 9.10. `toolwin.h`— Declaration of the `ToolWindow` classes.

```
//----------------------------------------------------------
// File: toolwin.h
//
// Declares the ToolWindow class that represents the window
// where a number of buttons for the application appears.
//----------------------------------------------------------
#if !defined(__TOOLWIN_H)
#define __TOOLWIN_H

#include <owl.h>

class BlockadeFrame;

struct ToolIcon
{
    ToolIcon() : active(0), id(0), img(NULL),
      xoff(0), yoff(0), x(0), y(0), w(0), h(0) {}

    ToolIcon(char *fname, short nid, short xo, short yo,
             unsigned short wdth, unsigned short hght,
             short xw, short yw, short act) : id(nid),
             xoff(xo), yoff(yo), w(wdth), h(hght),
             x(xw), y(yw), active(act)
    {
        img = Sprite::init_image(fname);
    }
```

BLOCKADE—A Game of Modern Naval Simulation

```cpp
    ~ToolIcon()
    {
        if(img != NULL) delete img;
    }

    short         active; // Displayed only if active
    short         id;     // An integer icon ID
    Image         *img;   // The icon's image
    short         xoff,   // Align this point of image
                  yoff;   // with the point (x,y)
    short         x, y;   // Position in the tools window
    unsigned short w, h;  // Width and height of icon
};

class ToolWindow : public TWindow
{
public:
    ToolWindow(PTWindowsObject parent, BlockadeFrame* bf) :
        TWindow(parent, NULL), blockade_frame(bf),
        icon_current(NULL), icons(NULL), numicons(0)
    {
     Attr.Style = WS_CHILD | WS_BORDER | WS_VISIBLE |
                  WS_CLIPSIBLINGS;
    }

    virtual void Paint(HDC hdc, PAINTSTRUCT&);
    virtual void WMSize(RTMessage msg) = [WM_FIRST + WM_SIZE];

    unsigned short width()  { return w;}
    unsigned short height() { return h;}

    void active(short id);
    void inactive(short id);

protected:
    ToolIcon       *icons;
    unsigned short numicons;
    unsigned short w, h; // Size of client area
    ToolIcon       *icon_current;
    BlockadeFrame  *blockade_frame;

    ToolIcon* icon_at(short x, short y);
    short get_index(short id);
};

class View3DToolWindow : public ToolWindow
{
```

continues

Listing 9.10. continued

```
public:
    View3DToolWindow(PTWindowsObject parent, BlockadeFrame* bf) :
        ToolWindow(parent, bf) {}

    void WMCreate(RTMessage msg) = [WM_FIRST + WM_CREATE];
    void WMLButtonDown(RTMessage msg) = [WM_FIRST +
                                         WM_LBUTTONDOWN];
};

class PolarToolWindow : public ToolWindow
{
public:
    PolarToolWindow(PTWindowsObject parent, BlockadeFrame* bf) :
        ToolWindow(parent, bf) {}
    void Paint(HDC hdc, PAINTSTRUCT&);
    void WMCreate(RTMessage msg) = [WM_FIRST + WM_CREATE];
    void WMLButtonDown(RTMessage msg) = [WM_FIRST +
                                         WM_LBUTTONDOWN];
};

class MapToolWindow : public ToolWindow
{
public:
    MapToolWindow(PTWindowsObject parent, BlockadeFrame* bf) :
        ToolWindow(parent, bf) {}

    void WMCreate(RTMessage msg) = [WM_FIRST + WM_CREATE];
    void WMLButtonDown(RTMessage msg) = [WM_FIRST +
                                         WM_LBUTTONDOWN];

    void set_scroll_buttons();
};
#endif
```

Implementation of *ToolWindow*

Listing 9.11 shows the implementation of the `ToolWindow` class. Here is a summary of the functions in this class:

- The `Paint` function handles drawing the image of each active `ToolIcon` in the window.

Chapter 9

BLOCKADE—A Game of Modern Naval Simulation

- The `icons_at` function returns a pointer to the `ToolIcon` at a specified point. The function returns NULL if there is no icon at the specified point.

- The `active` and `inactive` functions are used to show or hide an icon.

Listing 9.11. `toolwin.cpp`— Implementation of the `ToolWindow` class.

```
//----------------------------------------------------------------
// File: toolwin.cpp
//
// Member functions of the ToolWindow class.
//----------------------------------------------------------------
#include "bframe.h"

//----------------------------------------------------------------
// ToolWindow:: P a i n t
// Draw everything in the window

void ToolWindow::Paint(HDC hdc, PAINTSTRUCT&)
{
// Draw all active tool icons
    if(icons != NULL)
    {
        short i;
        for(i = 0; i < numicons; i++)
        {
            if(icons[i].active && icons[i].img != NULL)
                icons[i].img->show(hdc, icons[i].xoff,
                    icons[i].yoff, icons[i].x, icons[i].y,
                    icons[i].w, icons[i].h, SRCCOPY);
        }
    }
}
//----------------------------------------------------------------
// ToolWindow:: W M S i z e
// Save the location and size of the window

void ToolWindow::WMSize(RTMessage)
{
    RECT r;
    GetClientRect(HWindow, &r);
    w = r.left - r.right + 1;
    h = r.bottom - r.top + 1;
}
```

continues

Listing 9.11. continued

```
//----------------------------------------------------------------
// ToolWindow::  i c o n _ a t
// Return pointer to ToolIcon (if any) at a specified location

ToolIcon* ToolWindow::icon_at(short x, short y)
{
    short i;
    ToolIcon *rti = NULL;

    if(icons == NULL) return rti;

    for(i = 0; i < numicons; i++)
    {
        if(!icons[i].active) continue;
        if(icons[i].img == NULL) continue;

        if(x < icons[i].x) continue;
        if(y < icons[i].y) continue;

        if(x > (icons[i].x + icons[i].w - 1)) continue;
        if(y > (icons[i].y + icons[i].h - 1)) continue;

        rti = &icons[i];
        break;
    }
    return rti;
}
//----------------------------------------------------------------
// ToolWindow::  g e t _ i n d e x
// Return the index of an icon in the icons array

short ToolWindow::get_index(short id)
{
    short i;
    for(i = 0; i < numicons; i++)
        if(icons[i].id == id) return i;

    return -1;
}
//----------------------------------------------------------------
// ToolWindow::  a c t i v e
// Make icon active

void ToolWindow::active(short id)
{
```

BLOCKADE—A Game of Modern Naval Simulation

```
    short i;
    if((i = get_index(id)) >= 0)
        if(!icons[i].active)
        {
            icons[i].active = 1;
            InvalidateRect(HWindow, NULL, FALSE);
        }
}
//-------------------------------------------------------------
// ToolWindow:: i n a c t i v e
// Make icon inactive

void ToolWindow::inactive(short id)
{
    short i;
    if((i = get_index(id)) >= 0)
        if(icons[i].active)
        {
            icons[i].active = 0;
            InvalidateRect(HWindow, NULL, FALSE);
        }
}
```

Implementation of *MapToolWindow*

The `MapToolWindow` class displays the bitmap icons that represent the controls for manipulating the map view shown in a `MapWindow`.

Listing 9.12 shows the implementation of the `MapToolWindow` class. Here are the highlights of this class:

■ The static array of `ToolIcons`, `icon_array`, represents the icons to be displayed in the window. The `WMCreate` function initializes the member variables `icons` and `numicons` with the static array `icon_array` and the static variable `nicons`, respectively.

■ Each icon has an image and an identifying number (ID). When the player presses the left mouse button, Windows calls the `WMLButtonDown` function, which calls `icon_at` to determine the icon, if any, at the location of the button press. If there is a valid icon at the location, the icon's ID determines the action to be performed in response to the button press.

391

Listing 9.12. `maptool.cpp`— Implementation of the `MapToolWindow` class.

```cpp
//----------------------------------------------------------
// File: maptool.cpp
//
// Implementation of the MapToolWindow class.
//----------------------------------------------------------
#include "bframe.h"

#define ZOOMIN          1
#define ZOOMOUT         2
#define UPARROW         3
#define DOWNARROW       4
#define LEFTARROW       5
#define RIGHTARROW      6
#define TOPOLAR         7
#define TO3D            8
#define QUIT_ICON       9
#define AGAIN          10

#define XSTART 16
#define YSTART  8
#define YSPACE  4
#define ON      1
#define OFF     0

static ToolIcon icon_array[] =
{
    ToolIcon("zoomin.bmp", ZOOMIN, 0, 0, 32, 32,
                              XSTART, YSTART+16, ON),
    ToolIcon("zoomout.bmp", ZOOMOUT, 0, 0, 32, 32,
                              XSTART, YSTART+16, OFF),
    ToolIcon("larrow.bmp", LEFTARROW, 0, 0, 16, 32,
                              XSTART-16, YSTART+16, OFF),
    ToolIcon("rarrow.bmp", RIGHTARROW, 0, 0, 16, 32,
                              XSTART+32, YSTART+16, OFF),
    ToolIcon("uarrow.bmp", UPARROW, 0, 0, 32, 16,
                              XSTART, YSTART, OFF),
    ToolIcon("darrow.bmp", DOWNARROW, 0, 0, 32, 16,
                              XSTART, YSTART+48, OFF),

    ToolIcon("topolar.bmp", TOPOLAR, 0, 0, 32, 32,
                              XSTART, YSTART+2*(YSPACE+32), ON),
    ToolIcon("to3d.bmp", TO3D, 0, 0, 32, 32,
                              XSTART, YSTART+3*(YSPACE+32), ON),
    ToolIcon("again.bmp", AGAIN, 0, 0, 32, 32,
                              XSTART, YSTART+4*(YSPACE+32), ON),
```

BLOCKADE—A Game of Modern Naval Simulation

```
    ToolIcon("quit.bmp", QUIT_ICON, 0, 0, 32, 32,
                        XSTART, YSTART+6*(YSPACE+32), ON)
};

static short nicons = sizeof(icon_array) / sizeof(icon_array[0]);

static short firsttime = 1;
//-------------------------------------------------------------
// MapToolWindow:: W M C r e a t e
// Initialize this window

void MapToolWindow::WMCreate(RTMessage)
{
    icons = icon_array;
    numicons = nicons;
}
//-------------------------------------------------------------
// MapToolWindow:: W M L B u t t o n D o w n
// Handle mouse button press

void MapToolWindow::WMLButtonDown(RTMessage msg)
{
    short x = msg.LP.Lo;
    short y = msg.LP.Hi;
    icon_current = icon_at(x, y);
    if(icon_current != NULL)
    {
        switch(icon_current->id)
        {
            case ZOOMIN:
                inactive(ZOOMIN);
                active(ZOOMOUT);
                blockade_frame->map_window()->swap_anim();
                break;

            case ZOOMOUT:
                inactive(ZOOMOUT);
                active(ZOOMIN);
                blockade_frame->map_window()->swap_anim();
                break;

            case LEFTARROW:
                blockade_frame->map_window()->scroll_left();
                break;

            case RIGHTARROW:
                blockade_frame->map_window()->scroll_right();
                break;
```

continues

Listing 9.12. continued

```
            case UPARROW:
                blockade_frame->map_window()->scroll_up();
                break;

            case DOWNARROW:
                blockade_frame->map_window()->scroll_down();
                break;

            case TO3D:
// Make simulation slower before switching to 3D view
                blockade_frame->info_window()->
                                    set_simspeed(1);
                blockade_frame->hide_map();
                blockade_frame->show_view3d();
                break;

            case TOPOLAR:
                blockade_frame->hide_map();
                blockade_frame->show_polar();
                break;

            case AGAIN:
// Restart the game
                blockade_frame->info_window()->
                                    set_simspeed(1);
// Make all platforms go back to initial conditions
                short i;
                for(i = 0; i < blockade_frame->scenario()->
                    numplatform(); i++)
                {
                    blockade_frame->scenario()->platform(i).
                                    goto_stage0();
                }
                Scenario::simulation_running = 1;
                Scenario::status = RUNNING;
                break;

            case QUIT_ICON:
                if(blockade_frame->hi_scores("HISCORE.BLD"))
                            PostQuitMessage(0);
                break;
        }
    }
}
```

Chapter 9

BLOCKADE—A Game of Modern Naval Simulation

```
//---------------------------------------------------------------
// MapToolWindow::   s e t _ s c r o l l _ b u t t o n s
// Turn the scroll arrows on or off

void MapToolWindow::set_scroll_buttons()
{
// Check if map scroll buttons should be visible
    if(blockade_frame->map_window()->image_width() >
       blockade_frame->map_window()->width())
    {
        active(LEFTARROW);
        active(RIGHTARROW);
    }
    else
    {
        inactive(LEFTARROW);
        inactive(RIGHTARROW);
    }
    if(blockade_frame->map_window()->image_height() >
       blockade_frame->map_window()->height())
    {
        active(UPARROW);
        active(DOWNARROW);
    }
    else
    {
        inactive(UPARROW);
        inactive(DOWNARROW);
    }
}
```

Implementation of *PolarToolWindow*

The PolarToolWindow class displays the bitmap icons that represent the controls for manipulating the map view shown in a PolarWindow. Listing 9.13 shows the implementation of the PolarToolWindow class. The PolarToolWindow class is similar to the MapToolWindow class. Here are the major features of the PolarToolWindow class:

- As in MapToolWindow, the static array of ToolIcons, icon_array, represents the icons to be displayed in the window. The WMCreate function initializes the member variables icons and numicons with the static array icon_array and the static variable nicons, respectively.

■ Icons are activated by pressing the left mouse button with the mouse pointer inside the icon. When you press the left mouse button, Windows calls the WMLButtonDown function, which calls icon_at to determine the icon at the location of the button press. If there is a valid icon at that location, the icon's ID is used to determine the action performed in response to the button press.

**Listing 9.13. plrtool.cpp—
Implementation of the PolarToolWindow class.**

```cpp
//-----------------------------------------------------------
// File: plrtool.cpp
//
// Implementation of the PolarToolWindow class.
//-----------------------------------------------------------
#include "bframe.h"

#define ZOOMIN      1
#define ZOOMOUT     2
#define TOMAP       7
#define TO3D        8
#define QUIT_ICON   9

#define XSTART 16
#define YSTART 8
#define YSPACE 4
#define ON     1
#define OFF    0

static ToolIcon icon_array[] =
{
    ToolIcon("hzoomi.bmp", ZOOMIN, 0, 0, 32, 16,
                                 XSTART, YSTART+32, ON),
    ToolIcon("hzoomo.bmp", ZOOMOUT, 0, 0, 32, 16,
                                 XSTART, YSTART+48, ON),

    ToolIcon("tomap.bmp", TOMAP, 0, 0, 32, 32,
                         XSTART, YSTART+2*(YSPACE+32), ON),
    ToolIcon("to3d.bmp", TO3D, 0, 0, 32, 32,
                         XSTART, YSTART+3*(YSPACE+32), ON),


    ToolIcon("quit.bmp", QUIT_ICON, 0, 0, 32, 32,
                         XSTART, YSTART+5*(YSPACE+32), ON)
};
```

Chapter 9

BLOCKADE—A Game of Modern Naval Simulation

```cpp
static short nicons = sizeof(icon_array) / sizeof(icon_array[0]);
//---------------------------------------------------------------
// PolarToolWindow::  W M C r e a t e
// Initialize this window

void PolarToolWindow::WMCreate(RTMessage)
{
    icons = icon_array;
    numicons = nicons;
}
//---------------------------------------------------------------
//  PolarToolWindow::  P a i n t
//  Draw contents of the polar tool window

void PolarToolWindow::Paint(HDC hdc, PAINTSTRUCT& ps)
{
// Call the base class's Paint function
    ToolWindow::Paint(hdc, ps);

    char buf[20];
    Rectangle(hdc, 4, 4, 60, 40);

// Display the current range scale
    wsprintf(buf, "%d nm",
            blockade_frame->polar_window()->range_scale());
    short len = strlen(buf);

    SetBkMode(hdc, TRANSPARENT);
//    SetTextColor(hdc, RGB(0, 0, 255));
    TextOut(hdc, XSTART/2+2, YSTART/2+2, "Range:", 6);
    TextOut(hdc, XSTART/2+2, YSTART/2+16, buf, len);
}
//---------------------------------------------------------------
// PolarToolWindow::  W M L B u t t o n D o w n
// Handle mouse button press

void PolarToolWindow::WMLButtonDown(RTMessage msg)
{
    short x = msg.LP.Lo;
    short y = msg.LP.Hi;
    icon_current = icon_at(x, y);
    if(icon_current != NULL)
    {
        switch(icon_current->id)
        {
            short r;
            case ZOOMIN:
```

continues

Listing 9.13. continued

```
                r = blockade_frame->polar_window()->
                                        range_scale();
                if(r > 10)
                {
                    r /= 2;
                    blockade_frame->polar_window()->
                                        range_scale(r);
                    InvalidateRect(HWindow, NULL, FALSE);
                }
                break;

            case ZOOMOUT:
                r = blockade_frame->polar_window()->
                                        range_scale();
                if(r < 320)
                {
                    r *= 2;
                    blockade_frame->polar_window()->
                                        range_scale(r);
                    InvalidateRect(HWindow, NULL, FALSE);
                }
                break;

            case TO3D:
// Make simulation slower before switching to 3D view
                blockade_frame->info_window()->
                                        set_simspeed(1);
                blockade_frame->hide_polar();
                blockade_frame->show_view3d();
                break;

            case TOMAP:
                blockade_frame->hide_polar();
                blockade_frame->show_map();
                break;

            case QUIT_ICON:
                if(blockade_frame->hi_scores("HISCORE.BLD"))
                            PostQuitMessage(0);
                break;
        }
    }
}
```

BLOCKADE—A Game of Modern Naval Simulation

Implementation of *View3DToolWindow*

The `View3DToolWindow` class displays the bitmap icons that represent the controls for manipulating the map view shown in a `View3DWindow`. Listing 9.14 shows the implementation of the `View3DToolWindow` class, which is very similar to the `PolarToolWindow` class. Here are the major features of the `View3DToolWindow` class:

- As in `PolarToolWindow`, the static array of `ToolIcons`, `icon_array`, represents the icons to be displayed in the window. The `WMCreate` function initializes the member variables `icons` and `numicons` with the static array `icon_array` and the static variable `nicons`, respectively.

- The icons are activated in the same manner as in `PolarToolWindow`.

Listing 9.14. vu3dtool.cpp—
Implementation of the **View3DToolWindow** class.

```
//---------------------------------------------------------------
// File: vu3dtool.cpp
//
// Implementation of the View3DToolWindow class.
//---------------------------------------------------------------
#include "bframe.h"

#define ZOOMIN        1
#define ZOOMOUT       2
#define UPARROW       3
#define DOWNARROW     4
#define LEFTARROW     5
#define RIGHTARROW    6
#define TOPOLAR       7
#define TOMAP         8
#define QUIT_ICON     9

#define XSTART  16
#define YSTART   8
#define YSPACE   4
#define ON       1
#define OFF      0
```

continues

Listing 9.14. continued

```
static ToolIcon icon_array[] =
{
    ToolIcon("hzoomi.bmp", ZOOMIN, 0, 0, 32, 16,
                                    XSTART, YSTART+16, ON),
    ToolIcon("hzoomo.bmp", ZOOMOUT, 0, 0, 32, 16,
                                    XSTART, YSTART+32, ON),
    ToolIcon("larrow.bmp", LEFTARROW, 0, 0, 16, 32,
                                    XSTART-16, YSTART+16, ON),
    ToolIcon("rarrow.bmp", RIGHTARROW, 0, 0, 16, 32,
                                    XSTART+32, YSTART+16, ON),
    ToolIcon("uarrow.bmp", UPARROW, 0, 0, 32, 16,
                                    XSTART, YSTART, ON),
    ToolIcon("darrow.bmp", DOWNARROW, 0, 0, 32, 16,
                                    XSTART, YSTART+48, ON),

    ToolIcon("topolar.bmp", TOPOLAR, 0, 0, 32, 32,
                                XSTART, YSTART+2*(YSPACE+32), ON),
    ToolIcon("tomap.bmp", TOMAP, 0, 0, 32, 32,
                                XSTART, YSTART+3*(YSPACE+32), ON),


    ToolIcon("quit.bmp", QUIT_ICON, 0, 0, 32, 32,
                                XSTART, YSTART+5*(YSPACE+32), ON)
};
static short nicons = sizeof(icon_array) / sizeof(icon_array[0]);
//-------------------------------------------------------------
// View3DToolWindow::  W M C r e a t e
// Initialize this window

void View3DToolWindow::WMCreate(RTMessage)
{
    icons = icon_array;
    numicons = nicons;
}
//-------------------------------------------------------------
// View3DToolWindow::  W M L B u t t o n D o w n
// Handle mouse button press

void View3DToolWindow::WMLButtonDown(RTMessage msg)
{
    short x = msg.LP.Lo;
    short y = msg.LP.Hi;
    icon_current = icon_at(x, y);
    if(icon_current != NULL)
```

BLOCKADE—A Game of Modern Naval Simulation

```
{
    switch(icon_current->id)
    {
        case ZOOMIN:
            blockade_frame->view3d_window()->scene3d()->
                                            zoomin(10);
            blockade_frame->view3d_window()->refresh_anim();
            break;

        case ZOOMOUT:
            blockade_frame->view3d_window()->scene3d()->
                                            zoomout(10);
            blockade_frame->view3d_window()->refresh_anim();
            break;

        case LEFTARROW:
            blockade_frame->view3d_window()->scene3d()->
                                            az_step(-5);
            blockade_frame->view3d_window()->refresh_anim();
            break;

        case RIGHTARROW:
            blockade_frame->view3d_window()->scene3d()->
                                            az_step(5);
            blockade_frame->view3d_window()->refresh_anim();
            break;

        case UPARROW:
            blockade_frame->view3d_window()->scene3d()->
                                            el_step(5);
            blockade_frame->view3d_window()->refresh_anim();
            break;

        case DOWNARROW:
            blockade_frame->view3d_window()->scene3d()->
                                            el_step(-5);
            blockade_frame->view3d_window()->refresh_anim();
            break;

        case TOMAP:
            blockade_frame->hide_view3d();
            blockade_frame->show_map();
            blockade_frame->info_window()->set_simspeed(
                                Scenario::old_simspeed);
            break;

        case TOPOLAR:
            blockade_frame->hide_view3d();
```

continues

Listing 9.14. continued

```
                blockade_frame->show_polar();
                blockade_frame->info_window()->set_simspeed(
                                        Scenario::old_simspeed);
                break;

        case QUIT_ICON:
            if(blockade_frame->hi_scores("HISCORE.BLD"))
                                        PostQuitMessage(0);
            break;
        }
    }
}
```

StatusWindow Class

The StatusWindow class represents the window displaying status messages that appears at the bottom edge of the BLOCKADE's main window. Listing 9.15 shows the file statwin.h that declares the StatusWindow class. StatusWindow uses a SpriteAnimation (see Chapter 5) to display sprites with the status messages.

A SpriteInfo structure, declared in Listing 9.15, is used to store information on the sprites that are displayed in the StatusWindow.

Listing 9.15. statwin.h—
Declaration of the StatusWindow class.

```
//-------------------------------------------------------------
// File: statwin.h
//
// Declares the StatusWindow class that represents the window
// where the progress of the application is shown.
//-------------------------------------------------------------
#if !defined(__STATWIN_H)
#define __STATWIN_H

#include <owl.h>
#include "spranim.h"

#define MSGSIZE 256
```

Chapter 9

BLOCKADE—A Game of Modern Naval Simulation

```cpp
class BlockadeFrame;

// A structure to hold information about sprites used in various
// windows (including the status window)
struct SpriteInfo
{
    SpriteInfo(char* imgfname, char* mskfname,
            short xp, short yp, short xv, short yv,
            short prio, short ia, short _id) :
            imagefilename(imgfname), maskfilename(mskfname),
            xpos(xp), ypos(yp), xvel(xv), yvel(yv),
            priority(prio), isactive(ia), id(_id) {}

    char* imagefilename;
    char* maskfilename;
    short  xpos, ypos;     // Initial x-y position
    short  xvel, yvel;     // Initial x- and y-velocity
    short  priority;
    short  isactive;
    short  id;
};

class StatusWindow : public TWindow
{
public:
    StatusWindow(PTWindowsObject parent, BlockadeFrame *bf) :
        TWindow(parent, NULL), blockade_frame(bf), anim(NULL),
        s(NULL), w(1), h(1), top(0), left(0)
    {
     Attr.Style = WS_CHILD | WS_BORDER | WS_VISIBLE |
                WS_CLIPSIBLINGS;
    }
    ~StatusWindow();

    void init();
    void update();
    void move_sprites();
    void update_msgs();

    void Paint(HDC hdc, PAINTSTRUCT& ps);
    void WMSize(RTMessage msg) = [WM_FIRST + WM_SIZE];

    unsigned short width() { return w;}
    unsigned short height() { return h;}
    void width(unsigned short _w) { w = _w;}
    void height(unsigned short _h) { h = _h;}

    void set_text(LPSTR t, short n, short msgid);
```

continues

Listing 9.15. statwin.h—
Declaration of the `StatusWindow` class.

```
    LPSTR get_msgbuf(short i) { return msgtxt[i];}
    static char msgtxt[2][MSGSIZE];
private:
    BlockadeFrame   *blockade_frame;
    unsigned short w, h; // Size of client area

// SpriteAnimation to display status information.
    SpriteAnimation *anim;
    Sprite          **s;
    short           top, left;
};

#endif
```

Listing 9.16 shows the file `statwin.cpp` that implements the `StatusWindow` class. At the beginning of the file, a `SpriteInfo` array named `sprite_data` is declared. There are only two `SpriteInfo` objects in the array—one for each of the status messages displayed in a `StatusWindow`.

The `init` function, called by `BlockadeFrame`, creates the `SpriteAnimation` object, `anim`, and sets up the sprites to be displayed in the window. The `draw_text` function draws the text that constitutes the message.

`StatusWindow` includes a utility function, `set_text`, to change the text being displayed in the status window.

Listing 9.16. statwin.cpp—
Implementation of the `StatusWindow` class.

```
//-----------------------------------------------------------------
// File: statwin.cpp
//
// Implementation of the StatusWindow class.
//-----------------------------------------------------------------
#include "bframe.h"
#include <stdio.h>

// Declare an array of sprites to be loaded from image files
static SpriteInfo sprite_data[] =
{
// imagefilename, maskfilename, xpos, ypos, xvel, yelv,
```

BLOCKADE—A Game of Modern Naval Simulation

```
// priority, isactive, id
    SpriteInfo(NULL, NULL, 200, 0, -1, 0, 99, 1, 1),
    SpriteInfo(NULL, NULL, 0, 16, 0, 0, 99, 1, 1)
};

// Total number of sprites
static int numsprites = sizeof(sprite_data) /
            sizeof(sprite_data[0]);

void _FAR PASCAL _export draw_text(HDC hdc, short x, short y,
                                    LPVOID data);

struct TEXT_DATA
{
    LPSTR   text;
    size_t  numchars;
};

static TEXT_DATA dt[2];

char StatusWindow::msgtxt[2][MSGSIZE] =
{
    "Status: LOADING...",
    "Go to POLAR display to read mission description."
};

static count = 1;
//-------------------------------------------------------------
// StatusWindow:: ~ S t a t u s W i n d o w
// Destructor for the StatusWindow class

StatusWindow::~StatusWindow()
{
    if(anim != NULL) delete anim;
    if(s != NULL) delete s;
}
//-------------------------------------------------------------
//   StatusWindow:: P a i n t
//   Draw everything in the window

void StatusWindow::Paint(HDC hdc, PAINTSTRUCT&)
{
    if(anim != NULL)
    {
        anim->set_refresh(TRUE);
        anim->animate(hdc, left, top);
    }
}
```

continues

Listing 9.16. continued

```cpp
//--------------------------------------------------------------
//  StatusWindow:: u p d a t e
//  Animate the sprites in the puzzle window

void StatusWindow::update()
{
    if(anim != NULL)
    {
        if(count++ >= MOTION_UPDATE_COUNT)
        {
            count = 1;
            update_msgs();
        }

        move_sprites();
        HDC hdc = GetDC(HWindow);
        anim->animate(hdc, left, top);
        ReleaseDC(HWindow, hdc);
    }
}
//--------------------------------------------------------------
//  StatusWindow:: W M S i z e
//  Save the location and size of the window

void StatusWindow::WMSize(RTMessage)
{
    RECT r;
    GetClientRect(HWindow, &r);
    w = r.left - r.right + 1;
    h = r.bottom - r.top + 1;
}
//--------------------------------------------------------------
//  StatusWindow:: i n i t
//  Initialize sprites etc. used in the StatusWindow

void StatusWindow::init()
{
// If a SpriteAnimation exists, delete it...
    if(anim != NULL) delete anim;
    if(s != NULL) delete s;

// Get a DC for this window
    HDC hdc = GetDC(HWindow);
```

BLOCKADE—A Game of Modern Naval Simulation

```
// Construct a SpriteAnimation with background for the puzzle
    anim = new SpriteAnimation(hdc, blockade_frame->sts_wmax(),
                               blockade_frame->sts_hmax(),
                               "stsbg.bmp");
    if(anim == NULL) return;

// Create the array of sprites
    s = new Sprite*[numsprites];
    int i;
    for(i = 0; i < numsprites; i++)
    {
        s[i] = new Sprite(hdc, sprite_data[i].imagefilename,
                          sprite_data[i].maskfilename);
        s[i]->priority(sprite_data[i].priority);
        s[i]->newpos(sprite_data[i].xpos, sprite_data[i].ypos);
        if(!sprite_data[i].isactive) s[i]->inactive();
// Add sprite to animation
        anim->add(s[i]);
    }

// The first sprite is used to display a text string
// Set up size of sprite based on current font
    TEXTMETRIC tm;
    GetTextMetrics(hdc, &tm);
    short hchar = tm.tmHeight + tm.tmExternalLeading;
    short wchar = tm.tmAveCharWidth;

    s[0]->width(MSGSIZE*wchar);
    s[0]->height(hchar);
    dt[0].text = msgtxt[0];
    dt[0].numchars = strlen(msgtxt[0]);
    DRAWPROC proc = (DRAWPROC) MakeProcInstance(
                                (FARPROC) draw_text,
                    GetApplication()->hInstance);
    s[0]->drawproc(proc, &dt[0]);
    s[0]->active();
    s[0]->update();

// Second sprite displays another status message
    s[1]->width(MSGSIZE*wchar);
    s[1]->height(hchar);
    dt[1].text = msgtxt[1];
    dt[1].numchars = strlen(msgtxt[1]);
    proc = (DRAWPROC) MakeProcInstance(
                            (FARPROC) draw_text,
                    GetApplication()->hInstance);
```

continues

Listing 9.16. continued

```
        s[1]->drawproc(proc, &dt[1]);
        s[1]->active();
        s[1]->update();
// Release the DC
        ReleaseDC(HWindow, hdc);
}
//---------------------------------------------------------------
// StatusWindow:: m o v e _ s p r i t e s
// Move the sprites

void StatusWindow::move_sprites()
{
    int i;
    for(i = 0; i < numsprites; i++)
    {
        sprite_data[i].xpos += sprite_data[i].xvel;

        if(sprite_data[i].xpos <= -40)
            sprite_data[i].xpos = width() + 60;

        s[i]->move(sprite_data[i].xpos - s[i]->xpos(),
                sprite_data[i].ypos - s[i]->ypos());
    }
}
//---------------------------------------------------------------
void _FAR PASCAL _export draw_text(HDC hdc, short x, short y,
                                    LPVOID data)
{
    TEXT_DATA *td = (TEXT_DATA*)data;
    SetBkMode(hdc, TRANSPARENT);

    SetTextColor(hdc, RGB(0, 0, 255));
    TextOut(hdc, x, y, td->text, td->numchars);
}
//---------------------------------------------------------------
// StatusWindow:: s e t _ t e x t
// Set the text to be displayed in the status window

void StatusWindow::set_text(LPSTR t, short n, short msgid)
{
    if(msgid >=0 && msgid < 2)
    {
        dt[msgid].text = t;
        dt[msgid].numchars = n;
    }
```

BLOCKADE—A Game of Modern Naval Simulation

```cpp
}
//--------------------------------------------------------------
// StatusWindow:: u p d a t e _ m s g s
// Update the status messages

void StatusWindow::update_msgs()
{
    short len;
// Set the first status message (depends on Scenario::status)
    switch(Scenario::status)
    {
        case LOADING:
            len =
                sprintf(msgtxt[0], "Status: Loading %s -- %s",
                blockade_frame->scenario_info()->name,
                blockade_frame->mission_info()->name);
            set_text(msgtxt[0], len, 0);
            break;

        case RUNNING:
            len =
                sprintf(msgtxt[0],
                "Status: Running %s -- %s at %dx",
                blockade_frame->scenario_info()->name,
                blockade_frame->mission_info()->name,
                Scenario::simulation_speed);
            set_text(msgtxt[0], len, 0);
            break;

        case YOU_WON:
            len =
                sprintf(msgtxt[0],
                "Status: You did well. "
                "You have stopped the cargo ship from "
                "reaching port");
            set_text(msgtxt[0], len, 0);
            break;

        case YOU_LOST:
            len =
                sprintf(msgtxt[0],
                "Status: You lost. "
                "The cargo ship slipped away.");
            set_text(msgtxt[0], len, 0);
            break;
    }
```

continues

Listing 9.16. continued

```
// Display the second line of status message
    if(!Scenario::simulation_running)
    {
        len = sprintf(msgtxt[1],
            "Go to the MAP view and click on TRY AGAIN "
            " to play again.");
        set_text(msgtxt[1], len, 1);
    }

    if(blockade_frame->polar_window_visible())
    {
        Weapon *w = &(blockade_frame->scenario()->our_ship()->
                    weapon(Scenario::weapon_index));
        len = sprintf(msgtxt[1],
            "Current weapon: %s, Range: %.2f (surface)"
            " %.2f (air), << %d Left >>",
            w->name(), w->range_against_surface(),
            w->range_against_air(), w->ammo_left());

        set_text(msgtxt[1], len, 1);
    }
    if(blockade_frame->view3d_window_visible())
    {
        len = sprintf(msgtxt[1],
            "This window shows a 3D view of your ship. "
            "Use the zoom and arrow buttons to rotate ship.");
        set_text(msgtxt[1], len, 1);
    }

// Check if player's ship is outside the rectangles that define
// the valid region of the sea
    if((blockade_frame->scenario()->ownship_aground() >= 0) &&
       (Scenario::ran_aground >= 0))
    {
        len = sprintf(msgtxt[1],
                    "You avoided running aground!");
        set_text(msgtxt[1], len, 1);
        Scenario::ran_aground = AGROUND_THRESHOLD;
    }
    if(Scenario::ran_aground < 0 &&
       Scenario::ran_aground > AGROUND_THRESHOLD)
    {
```

BLOCKADE—A Game of Modern Naval Simulation

```
// Display status message
        len = sprintf(msgtxt[1],
                    "Change course to avoid running aground!");
        set_text(msgtxt[1], len, 1);
    }
}
```

InfoWindow Class

The `InfoWindow` class represents the window across the top edge of BLOCKADE's main window. This window has a host of controls for controlling the game. As you might infer from Listing 9.17, the controls are implemented using sprites that are managed by a `SpriteAnimation` class. Here are the major controls in `InfoWindow`:

- A set of four buttons to set the simulation speed. The `simspeed` array of sprites denotes these buttons. There are eight sprites because each button uses two sprites—one for the "button active" state and the other for the "button inactive" state.

- A control to select the sensor whose detections are to be shown in the view window. The pointer to this sprite is `selcon`. Another sprite, `condisp`, displays the name of the currently selected sensor.

- A control to select a weapon. The pointer to this sprite is `selwpn`. A second sprite named `wpndisp` displays the name of the currently selected weapon.

- A set of sprites, `hdgdisp` and `hdgpick`, that provides a convenient graphical way to set the ship's heading.

- A set of sprites, `spddisp` and `spdpick`, that provides a way to set the ship's speed.

- A weapon engagement button that the player can press to "shoot" from the currently selected weapon. The pair of sprites, `engbtn` and `engbdn`, implements this button.

- Two more sprites, `timedisp` and `scoredisp`, that display the current timer count and the score.

Listing 9.17. infowin.h—Declaration of the InfoWindow class.

```
//------------------------------------------------------------------
// File: infowin.h
//
// Declares the InfoWindow class that represents the window
// where some pertinent information about the application
// appears.
//------------------------------------------------------------------
#if !defined(__INFOWIN_H)
#define __INFOWIN_H

#include <owl.h>
#include "spranim.h"

const short lbmpwidth = 32;
const short lystart = 4;

class BlockadeFrame;

class InfoWindow: public TWindow
{
public:
    InfoWindow(PTWindowsObject parent, BlockadeFrame* bf);

    ~InfoWindow();

    void update();
    void init();
    void set_score(short s);
    void set_simspeed(short speed);

    void Paint(HDC hdc, PAINTSTRUCT& ps);
    void WMLButtonDown(RTMessage msg) =
                                    [WM_FIRST + WM_LBUTTONDOWN];
    void WMLButtonUp(RTMessage msg) = [WM_FIRST + WM_LBUTTONUP];
    void WMMouseMove(RTMessage msg) = [WM_FIRST + WM_MOUSEMOVE];

    unsigned short width() { return w;}
    unsigned short height() { return h;}
    void width(unsigned short _w) { w = _w;}
    void height(unsigned short _h) { h = _h;}

private:
    BlockadeFrame    *blockade_frame;

    SpriteAnimation  *anim;
    Sprite           *score; // To display the current score
    Sprite           *smslabel;
```

BLOCKADE—A Game of Modern Naval Simulation

```
    Sprite              *simspeed[8];
    Sprite              *selcon;
    Sprite              *condisp;
    Sprite              *selwpn;
    Sprite              *wpndisp;
    Sprite              *hdgdisp;
    Sprite              *hdgpick;
    Sprite              *spddisp;
    Sprite              *spdpick;
    Sprite              *engbtn;
    Sprite              *engbdn;
    Sprite              *timedisp;
    Sprite              *scoredisp;

    short               mouse_captured;
    Sprite              *spr_current;
    short               xlo, xhi;
    short               ylo, yhi;
    short               xlast;
    short               ylast;

    short               top, left;
    unsigned short      w, h;  // Size of client area
};

#endif
```

Listing 9.18 shows the implementation of the InfoWindow class. As in the StatusWindow class (Listing 9.16), a static array of SpriteInfo structures, sprite_data, defines the layout of the sprites in the window. Note that some sprites overlap each other—these sprites are used to change the image in response to an event such as a mouse button press. A flag in the SpriteInfo structure determines whether a sprite is displayed or not.

The init function, called from BlockadeFrame, sets up the SpriteAnimation and the sprites specified in the sprite_data array.

The functions WMLButtonDown, WMMouseMove, and WMLButtonUp handle mouse button press, mouse movement, and button release events, respectively. If the player presses the left mouse button anywhere in the InfoWindow, Windows calls the WMLButtonDown function. The action performed by this function depends on the sprite at the location of the button press. If there is a valid sprite at that location, the ID of the sprite determines how the event is handled. The other functions, WMMouseMove and WMLButtonUp, work similarly.

Listing 9.18. `infowin.cpp`—
Implementation of the `InfoWindow` class.

```cpp
//----------------------------------------------------------------
// File: infowin.cpp
//
// Implementation of the InfoWindow class.
//----------------------------------------------------------------
#include "bframe.h"
#include <time.h>
#include <stdio.h>

#define SIMSPEED    1
#define CONSELECT   2
#define WPNSELECT   3
#define HDGDISP     4
#define HDGPICK     5
#define SPDDISP     6
#define SPDPICK     7
#define ENGAGE      8
#define TIMEDISP    9
#define SCOREDISP   10

#define PIXPERDEG   0.267
#define DEGPERPIX   3.75
#define KTPERPIX    0.5
#define PIXPERKT    2

#define ENGPOS   300
#define HDGPOS   340
#define SPDPOS   440
#define TIMEPOS  510

// Declare an array of sprites to be loaded from image files
static SpriteInfo sprite_data[] =
{
//   image, mask, xpos, ypos, xvel, yvel, priority, isactive, id

    SpriteInfo("1x.bmp",  NULL, 2, 20, 0, 0, 99, 0, 10*SIMSPEED),
    SpriteInfo("1xs.bmp", NULL, 2, 20, 0, 0,99, 1,10*SIMSPEED+1),

    SpriteInfo("10x.bmp", NULL, 26, 20,0, 0, 99, 1,10*SIMSPEED+2),
    SpriteInfo("10xs.bmp",NULL,26, 20,0, 0, 99, 0,10*SIMSPEED+3),

    SpriteInfo("20x.bmp", NULL, 50,20, 0, 0, 99, 1,10*SIMSPEED+4),
    SpriteInfo("20xs.bmp",NULL,50,20, 0, 0, 99, 0,10*SIMSPEED+5),
```

BLOCKADE—A Game of Modern Naval Simulation

```
    SpriteInfo("30x.bmp",NULL, 74,20, 0, 0, 99, 1,10*SIMSPEED+6),
    SpriteInfo("30xs.bmp",NULL,74,20, 0, 0, 99, 0,10*SIMSPEED+7)
};

// Total number of sprites
static int numsprites = sizeof(sprite_data) /
            sizeof(sprite_data[0]);

void _FAR PASCAL _export disp_contact(HDC hdc, short x, short y,
                    LPVOID data);
void _FAR PASCAL _export disp_weapon(HDC hdc, short x, short y,
                    LPVOID data);
void _FAR PASCAL _export disp_heading(HDC hdc, short x, short y,
                    LPVOID data);
void _FAR PASCAL _export disp_speed(HDC hdc, short x, short y,
                    LPVOID data);
void _FAR PASCAL _export disp_time(HDC hdc, short x, short y,
                    LPVOID data);
void _FAR PASCAL _export disp_score(HDC hdc, short x, short y,
                    LPVOID data);
//---------------------------------------------------------------
// InfoWindow:: I n f o W i n d o w

InfoWindow::InfoWindow(PTWindowsObject parent,
        BlockadeFrame *bf) :
        TWindow(parent, NULL), blockade_frame(bf),
        top(0), left(0), w(1), h(1), anim(NULL),
        mouse_captured(0), spr_current(NULL)
{
    Attr.Style = WS_CHILD | WS_BORDER | WS_VISIBLE |
                WS_CLIPSIBLINGS;
}
//---------------------------------------------------------------
// InfoWindow:: ~ I n f o W i n d o w
// Destructor for the InfoWindow class

InfoWindow::~InfoWindow()
{
    if(anim != NULL) delete anim;
}
//---------------------------------------------------------------
// InfoWindow:: P a i n t
// Draw everything in the window

void InfoWindow::Paint(HDC hdc, PAINTSTRUCT&)
{
```

continues

Listing 9.18. continued

```
    if(anim != NULL)
    {
        anim->set_refresh(TRUE);
        anim->animate(hdc, left, top);
    }
}
//----------------------------------------------------------------
// InfoWindow:: u p d a t e
// Animate the sprites in the puzzle window

void InfoWindow::update()
{
    if(anim != NULL)
    {
        timedisp->move(0,0);
        scoredisp->move(0,0);
        HDC hdc = GetDC(HWindow);
        anim->animate(hdc, left, top);
        ReleaseDC(HWindow, hdc);
    }
}
//----------------------------------------------------------------
// InfoWindow:: i n i t
// Initialize the animation for this window

void InfoWindow::init()
{
// Change the cursor to an hourglass
    SetCapture(HWindow);
    SetCursor(LoadCursor(NULL, IDC_WAIT));

// Clean up existing puzzle, if any
    if(anim != NULL) delete anim;

// Get a DC for this window
    HDC hdc = GetDC(HWindow);

// Construct a SpriteAnimation with background for this window
    anim = new SpriteAnimation(hdc, blockade_frame->info_wmax(),
                        blockade_frame->info_hmax(), "infobg.bmp");
    if(anim == NULL) return;

// Add a label sprite for "Simulation Speed"
    smslabel= new Sprite(hdc, "simspeed.bmp", NULL, 10000);
    smslabel->newpos(0, 0);
    anim->add(smslabel);
```

BLOCKADE—A Game of Modern Naval Simulation

```
    short i;
    for(i = 0; i < numsprites; i++)
    {
        simspeed[i] = new Sprite(hdc,
                        sprite_data[i].imagefilename,
                        sprite_data[i].maskfilename);
        simspeed[i]->priority(sprite_data[i].priority);
        simspeed[i]->newpos(sprite_data[i].xpos,
                        sprite_data[i].ypos);
        simspeed[i]->id(sprite_data[i].id);
        if(!sprite_data[i].isactive) simspeed[i]->inactive();
// Add sprite to animation
        anim->add(simspeed[i]);
    }

// Add contact selection sprites
    selcon = new Sprite(hdc, "selcon.bmp", NULL);
    selcon->priority(100);
    selcon->newpos(100, 0);
    selcon->id(10*CONSELECT);
    anim->add(selcon);

    condisp = new Sprite(hdc, "txtdisp.bmp", NULL);
    condisp->priority(100);
    condisp->newpos(100, 20);
    condisp->id(10*CONSELECT+1);
    DRAWPROC proc = (DRAWPROC) MakeProcInstance(
                        (FARPROC) disp_contact,
                    GetApplication()->hInstance);
    condisp->drawproc(proc, blockade_frame);
    condisp->active();
    condisp->update();
    anim->add(condisp);

// Add weapons selection sprites
    selwpn = new Sprite(hdc, "selwpn.bmp", NULL);
    selwpn->priority(100);
    selwpn->newpos(200, 0);
    selwpn->id(10*WPNSELECT);
    anim->add(selwpn);

    wpndisp = new Sprite(hdc, "txtdisp.bmp", NULL);
    wpndisp->priority(100);
    wpndisp->newpos(200, 20);
    wpndisp->id(10*WPNSELECT+1);
    proc = (DRAWPROC) MakeProcInstance(
                        (FARPROC) disp_weapon,
                    GetApplication()->hInstance);
```

continues

Listing 9.18. continued

```
    wpndisp->drawproc(proc, blockade_frame);
    wpndisp->active();
    wpndisp->update();
    anim->add(wpndisp);

// Add a sprite for launching weapon
    engbtn = new Sprite(hdc, "engup.bmp", NULL);
    engbtn->priority(300);
    engbtn->newpos(ENGPOS, 4);
    engbtn->id(10*ENGAGE);
    engbtn->active();
    engbtn->update();
    anim->add(engbtn);
// Pushed version of engage button
    engbdn = new Sprite(hdc, "engdn.bmp", NULL);
    engbdn->priority(300);
    engbdn->newpos(ENGPOS, 4);
    engbdn->id(10*ENGAGE);
    engbdn->inactive();
    anim->add(engbdn);

// Add a sprite for setting the heading...
    hdgdisp = new Sprite(hdc, "heading.bmp", NULL);
    hdgdisp->priority(100);
    hdgdisp->newpos(HDGPOS, 0);
    hdgdisp->id(10*HDGDISP);
    proc = (DRAWPROC) MakeProcInstance(
                            (FARPROC) disp_heading,
                       GetApplication()->hInstance);
    hdgdisp->drawproc(proc, blockade_frame);
    hdgdisp->active();
    hdgdisp->update();
    anim->add(hdgdisp);

// And the marker used to pick new headings...
    hdgpick = new Sprite(hdc, "hdgmrk.bmp", "hdgmrkm.bmp");
    hdgpick->priority(200);
    float hdg = blockade_frame->scenario()->our_ship()->heading();
    short pos;
    if(hdg > 180) pos = HDGPOS + (hdg-180)*PIXPERDEG;
    if(hdg < 180) pos = HDGPOS + hdg*PIXPERDEG + 48;
    hdgpick->newpos(pos, 10);
    hdgpick->id(10*HDGPICK);
    hdgpick->active();
    hdgpick->update();
    anim->add(hdgpick);
```

BLOCKADE—A Game of Modern Naval Simulation

```cpp
// Add sprites for setting the speed...
   spddisp = new Sprite(hdc, "speed.bmp", NULL);
   spddisp->priority(100);
   spddisp->newpos(SPDPOS, 0);
   spddisp->id(10*SPDDISP);
   proc = (DRAWPROC) MakeProcInstance(
                        (FARPROC) disp_speed,
                  GetApplication()->hInstance);
   spddisp->drawproc(proc, blockade_frame);
   spddisp->active();
   spddisp->update();
   anim->add(spddisp);

// And the marker used to pick new speed
   spdpick = new Sprite(hdc, "hdgmrk.bmp", "hdgmrkm.bmp");
   spdpick->priority(200);
   float spd = blockade_frame->scenario()->our_ship()->speed();
   pos = SPDPOS + spd*PIXPERKT - 3;
   spdpick->newpos(pos, 10);
   spdpick->id(10*SPDPICK);
   spdpick->active();
   spdpick->update();
   anim->add(spdpick);

// Add a sprite to display the "simulation time"
   timedisp = new Sprite(hdc, "time.bmp", NULL);
   timedisp->priority(100);
   timedisp->newpos(TIMEPOS, 0);
   timedisp->id(10*TIMEDISP);
   proc = (DRAWPROC) MakeProcInstance(
                        (FARPROC) disp_time,
                  GetApplication()->hInstance);
   timedisp->drawproc(proc, blockade_frame);
   timedisp->active();
   timedisp->update();
   anim->add(timedisp);

// Add a sprite to display the score
   scoredisp = new Sprite(hdc, "score.bmp", NULL);
   scoredisp->priority(100);
   scoredisp->newpos(TIMEPOS, 20);
   scoredisp->id(10*SCOREDISP);
   proc = (DRAWPROC) MakeProcInstance(
                        (FARPROC) disp_score,
                  GetApplication()->hInstance);
   scoredisp->drawproc(proc, blockade_frame);
   scoredisp->active();
   scoredisp->update();
   anim->add(scoredisp);
```

continues

Listing 9.18. continued

```
// Remember to release the DC
    ReleaseDC(HWindow, hdc);

// Reset cursor to arrow
    SetCursor(LoadCursor(NULL, IDC_ARROW));
    ReleaseCapture();
}
//-----------------------------------------------------------------
// InfoWindow:: W M L B u t t o n D o w n
// Handle button down events in the InfoWindow

void InfoWindow::WMLButtonDown(RTMessage msg)
{
    short x = msg.LP.Lo;
    short y = msg.LP.Hi;
    Sprite *s = anim->sprite_at(x, y);

    if(s != NULL)
    {
        short type = s->id() / 10;
        short index = s->id() - 10*type;
        switch(type)
        {
            case SIMSPEED:  // Simulation speed selection
                if(index % 2  == 0)
                {
// Set new simulation speed...
                    short speed = 5*index;
                    if(index == 0) speed = 1;
                    set_simspeed(speed);
                }
                break;

            case CONSELECT: // Select contacts to be displayed
                short maxsensor =
                    blockade_frame->scenario()->our_ship()->
                                                    numsensor();
                if(Scenario::sensor_index < maxsensor)
                                    Scenario::sensor_index++;
                if(Scenario::sensor_index == maxsensor)
                                Scenario::sensor_index = -1;
                Scenario::sensor_changed = 1;
                condisp->move(0,0);
                break;
```

BLOCKADE—A Game of Modern Naval Simulation

```cpp
        case WPNSELECT: // Weapon selection
            short maxweapon =
                blockade_frame->scenario()->our_ship()->
                                            numweapon();
            if(Scenario::weapon_index < maxweapon)
                            Scenario::weapon_index++;
            if(Scenario::weapon_index == maxweapon)
                        Scenario::weapon_index = 0;
            Scenario::weapon_changed = 1;
            wpndisp->move(0,0);
            break;

        case HDGPICK: // Move the marker...
            spr_current = s;
            spr_current->active();
            xlast = x;
            ylast = y;
            xlo = HDGPOS;
            xhi = HDGPOS + 96;
            SetCapture(HWindow);
            mouse_captured = 1;
            break;

        case SPDPICK: // Move the marker...
            spr_current = s;
            spr_current->active();
            xlast = x;
            ylast = y;
            xlo = SPDPOS;
            xhi = blockade_frame->scenario()->our_ship()->
                max_speed() * PIXPERKT + SPDPOS;
            SetCapture(HWindow);
            mouse_captured = 1;
            break;

        case ENGAGE: // Engage weapon (only in polar window)
            if(!blockade_frame->polar_window_visible())
            {
// Clear the status message
                LPSTR msgtxt = blockade_frame->
                        status_window()->get_msgbuf(1);
                short len = sprintf(msgtxt,
                  "Engage weapons from Polar window!");
                blockade_frame->status_window()->
                            set_text(msgtxt, len, 1);
                break;
            }
```

continues

Listing 9.18. continued

```
                spr_current = s;
                xlast = x;
                ylast = y;
                xlo = spr_current->xpos();
                ylo = spr_current->ypos();
                xhi = xlo + spr_current->width();
                yhi = ylo + spr_current->height();
                SetCapture(HWindow);
                mouse_captured = 1;
                engbtn->inactive();
                engbdn->active();
                anim->set_refresh(1);
                break;
            }
        }
}
//----------------------------------------------------------------
// InfoWindow:: W M M o u s e M o v e
// Handle mouse move events

void InfoWindow::WMMouseMove(RTMessage msg)
{
    if(!mouse_captured) return;

    short x = msg.LP.Lo;
    short y = msg.LP.Hi;

    if(spr_current->id() == 10*ENGAGE)
    {
        if(x > xlo && x < xhi && y > ylo && y < yhi)
        {
            engbtn->inactive();
            engbdn->active();
            engbdn->move(0,0);
        }
        else
        {
            engbdn->inactive();
            engbtn->active();
            engbtn->move(0,0);
        }
        return;
    }

    // Don't let the marker move out of the specified xlo/xhi area
    short xs = spr_current->xpos();
    short xdel = x - xlast;
```

Chapter 9

BLOCKADE—A Game of Modern Naval Simulation

```cpp
        if(xs + xdel <= xlo) xdel = 0;
        if(xs + xdel >= xhi) xdel = 0;

// Move sprite
        spr_current->move(xdel, 0);

        xlast = xlast + xdel;

// Update the heading or speed
        if(spr_current->id() == 10*HDGPICK)
        {
            float hdg = (xlast - HDGPOS) * DEGPERPIX;
            if(hdg > 180) hdg -= 180;
            else hdg += 180;
            blockade_frame->scenario()->our_ship()->heading(hdg);
            hdgdisp->move(0,0); // Move forces update
        }
        if(spr_current->id() == 10*SPDPICK)
        {
            float spd = (xlast - SPDPOS) * KTPERPIX;
            blockade_frame->scenario()->our_ship()->speed(spd);
            spddisp->move(0,0); // Move forces update
        }
}
//----------------------------------------------------------------
// InfoWindow:: W M L B u t t o n U p
// Handle button up event

void InfoWindow::WMLButtonUp(RTMessage msg)
{
    if(!mouse_captured) return;

    short x = msg.LP.Lo;
    short y = msg.LP.Hi;

    if(spr_current->id() == 10*ENGAGE)
    {
        if(x > xlo && x < xhi && y > ylo && y < yhi)
        {
// Engage the current weapon of player's ship aganist the
// current target
            blockade_frame->scenario()->engage_ownship_weapon();
        }
        engbdn->inactive();
        engbtn->active();
        engbtn->move(0,0);
        anim->set_refresh(1);
```

continues

Listing 9.18. continued

```
// Deselect the Sprite...and release the mouse
        spr_current = NULL;
        ReleaseCapture();
        mouse_captured = 0;
        return;
    }

// Don't let the marker image move out of the window...
    short xs = spr_current->xpos();
    short ys = spr_current->ypos();

    short xdel = x - xlast;

    if((xs + xdel >= xlo) && (xs + xdel <= xhi))
    {
        spr_current->move(xdel, 0);
        xlast = x;

// Update the heading or speed
        if(spr_current->id() == 10*HDGPICK)
        {
            float hdg = (xlast - HDGPOS) * DEGPERPIX;
            if(hdg > 180) hdg -= 180;
            else hdg += 180;
            blockade_frame->scenario()->our_ship()->heading(hdg);
            hdgdisp->move(0,0); // Move forces update
        }
        if(spr_current->id() == 10*SPDPICK)
        {
            float spd = (xlast - SPDPOS) * KTPERPIX;
            blockade_frame->scenario()->our_ship()->speed(spd);
            spddisp->move(0,0); // Move forces update
        }
    }

// De-select the Sprite...and release the mouse
    spr_current = NULL;
    ReleaseCapture();
    mouse_captured = 0;
}
//--------------------------------------------------------------
void _FAR PASCAL _export disp_contact(HDC hdc, short x, short y,
                                      LPVOID p)
{
    BlockadeFrame *bf = (BlockadeFrame*)p;
    char *nm;
    short len;
```

Chapter 9

BLOCKADE—A Game of Modern Naval Simulation

```
    SetBkMode(hdc, TRANSPARENT);

// Get current sensor index
    if(Scenario::sensor_index == -1)
        TextOut(hdc, x+2, y+2, "All Sensors", 11);
    else
    {
        nm = bf->scenario()->our_ship()->
                    sensor(Scenario::sensor_index).name();
        len = strlen(nm);
        TextOut(hdc, x+2, y+2, nm, len);
    }

}
//------------------------------------------------------------
void _FAR PASCAL _export disp_weapon(HDC hdc, short x, short y,
                                    LPVOID p)
{

    BlockadeFrame *bf = (BlockadeFrame*)p;
    char *nm;
    short len;

    SetBkMode(hdc, TRANSPARENT);

// Get current weapon index
    nm = bf->scenario()->our_ship()->
                weapon(Scenario::weapon_index).name();
    len = strlen(nm);
    TextOut(hdc, x+2, y+2, nm, len);
}
//------------------------------------------------------------
void _FAR PASCAL _export disp_heading(HDC hdc, short x, short y,
                                    LPVOID p)
{
    BlockadeFrame *bf = (BlockadeFrame*)p;
    char buf[8];
    SetBkMode(hdc, TRANSPARENT);

// Get current heading
    float hdg = bf->scenario()->our_ship()->heading();
    wsprintf(buf, "%.3d", (short)hdg);
    TextOut(hdc, x+63, y+23, buf, 3);
}
//------------------------------------------------------------
void _FAR PASCAL _export disp_speed(HDC hdc, short x, short y,
                                    LPVOID p)
```

continues

Listing 9.18. continued

```
{
    BlockadeFrame *bf = (BlockadeFrame*)p;
    char buf[8];
    SetBkMode(hdc, TRANSPARENT);

// Get current speed
    float hdg = bf->scenario()->our_ship()->speed();
    wsprintf(buf, "%.2d", (short)hdg);
    TextOut(hdc, x+43, y+23, buf, 2);
}
//---------------------------------------------------------------
void _FAR PASCAL _export disp_time(HDC hdc, short x, short y,
                                    LPVOID p)
{
    char buf[20];
    SetBkMode(hdc, TRANSPARENT);

// Display the current time in seconds
    short len = sprintf(buf, "%ld", Scenario::simulation_time);
    TextOut(hdc, x+32, y+2, buf, len);
}
//---------------------------------------------------------------
void _FAR PASCAL _export disp_score(HDC hdc, short x, short y,
                                     LPVOID p)
{
    char buf[20];
    SetBkMode(hdc, TRANSPARENT);

// Display the current score
    short len = sprintf(buf, "%ld", Scenario::score);
    TextOut(hdc, x+32, y+2, buf, len);
}
//---------------------------------------------------------------
// InfoWindow:: s e t _ s i m s p e e d
// Sets the simulation speed and adjusts the buttons that
// indicate the simulation speed

void InfoWindow::set_simspeed(short speed)
{
// Reset the sprite corresponding to the current rate of
// simulation
    short index = Scenario::simulation_speed / 5;
    simspeed[index]->active();
    simspeed[index+1]->inactive();
```

BLOCKADE—A Game of Modern Naval Simulation

```
// Save current speed...
    Scenario::old_simspeed = Scenario::simulation_speed;

// Set new simulation speed...
    Scenario::simulation_speed = speed;
    Scenario::update_every = 30 /
                    Scenario::simulation_speed;
    index = speed / 5;
    simspeed[index]->inactive();
    simspeed[index+1]->active();
}
```

Scenario Class

The Scenario class is responsible for creating and initializing the naval simulation that is at the heart of the BLOCKADE game. The most important component of the Scenario class is the array of Platform objects named platforms. These denote the ships and aircraft (and any other moving objects such as missiles and gun ammunition) that populate the scenario.

As you can see from the header file scenario.h (Listing 9.19), the Scenario class has a large set of static variables representing global data for the game. These variables are described later.

Listing 9.19. scenario.h—Declaration of the Scenario class.

```
//-----------------------------------------------------------------
// File: scenario.h
//
// Declaration of the classes that represent the objects in
// the scenario being simulated in BLOCKADE.
//-----------------------------------------------------------------
#if !defined(__SCENARIO_H)
#define __SCENARIO_H

#include <array.h>
#include "platform.h"
#include "scninfo.h"
```

continues

Listing 9.19. continued

```cpp
class Scenario
{
public:
    Scenario() : platforms(NULL), count(0), motion_count(0)
    {}
    ~Scenario();

    void init(ScenarioInfo *current_scenario,
              MissionInfo *current_mission);
    void init_weapons();

    void update();

    short numplatform()
    {
        return platforms->getItemsInContainer();
    }

    Platform& platform(short i)
    { return (Platform&)(*platforms)[i];}

    Platform* our_ship() {return ownship;}

    void make_sprites(HDC hdc);
    void ownship_xfrm();
    void mark_detected_sprites();

    void engage_ownship_weapon();
    void auto_engage_weapon();
    short ownship_aground();

    static float    BASIC_PERIOD;
    static SimTime  simulation_time;
    static SimTime  update_every;
    static short    simulation_running;
    static short    simulation_speed;
    static short    old_simspeed;
    static short    sensor_index;
    static short    weapon_index;
    static short    weapon_changed;
    static short    sensor_changed;
    static short    weapons_engaged;
    static short    status;
    static Platform *current_platform;
    static float    bearing_current;
    static float    range_current;
```

Chapter 9

BLOCKADE—A Game of Modern Naval Simulation

```
    static short    xpos_current;
    static short    ypos_current;
    static short    refresh; // TRUE => animation is redrawn
    static short    ran_aground;
    static long     score;
    static char     mission_description[512];
    static short    random_draw(float prob);
protected:
    Array           *platforms; // Platforms in the scenario
    Platform        *ownship;   // Pointer to player's ship
    ScenarioInfo    *sinfo;
    MissionInfo     *minfo;
    float           future_hdg;
    short           count;
    short           motion_count;
};

#endif
```

Header File: *scninfo.h*

In BLOCKADE, `ScenarioInfo` and `MissionInfo` structures are used to store information on available scenarios as well as information on the missions defined for the current scenario. The header file `scninfo.h`, shown in Listing 9.20, defines these structures.

Listing 9.20. `scninfo.h`— Declaration of some structures used in BLOCKADE.

```
//---------------------------------------------------------------
// File: scninfo.h
//
// Defines the structures to hold information about each
// scenario meant for the BLOCKADE game.
//---------------------------------------------------------------
#if !defined(__SCNINFO_H)
#define __SCNINFO_H

#include <windows.h>
```

continues

Listing 9.20. continued

```cpp
struct ScenarioInfo
{
    ScenarioInfo() : name(NULL), defnfile(NULL),
        mapfile(NULL), zmapfile(NULL), done(0),
        validsea(NULL)
        {}

    ~ScenarioInfo()
    {
     if(name != NULL) delete name;
     if(defnfile != NULL) delete defnfile;
     if(mapfile != NULL) delete mapfile;
     if(zmapfile != NULL) delete zmapfile;
     if(validsea != NULL) delete validsea;
    }
    short done;          // TRUE = scenario played
    char   *name;        // Name of scenario
    char   *defnfile;    // Name of scenario definition file
    char   *mapfile;     // Map image file
    char   *zmapfile;    // Map image--zoomed-in version
    float mapzoom;       // Magnification of zoomed-in map
    float orglat;        // Latitude and longitude of
    float orglng;        // map's upper left corner
    float pixperlat;     // Pixels per degree (latitude)
    float pixperlng;     // Pixels per degree (longitude)
    short nrects;        // Number of rectangles in next array
    RECT  *validsea;     // Places where ships can go
};

struct MissionInfo
{
    MissionInfo() : name(NULL), defnfile(NULL),
        done(0), s3dfile(NULL), bg3dfile(NULL)
        {}

    ~MissionInfo()
    {
     if(name != NULL) delete name;
     if(defnfile != NULL) delete defnfile;
     if(s3dfile != NULL) delete s3dfile;
     if(bg3dfile != NULL) delete bg3dfile;
    }
    short done;          // TRUE = Mission played
    char   *name;        // Name of mission
```

BLOCKADE—A Game of Modern Naval Simulation

```
    char    *defnfile;   // Name of mission definition file
    char    *s3dfile;    // 3D Scenario definition file
    char    *bg3dfile;   // Background image for 3D display
};

#endif
```

Header File: *simdefs.h*

Listing 9.21 shows the header file `simdefs.h` that declares a number of macros and structures used in the simulation of a scenario in BLOCKADE. The macros include conversion factors (`DEG_TO_RAD`, `DEG2NM`) and identifiers for platform types (`SURFACE`, `AIR`), platform sizes (`SMALL`, `MEDIUM`, `LARGE`), and other constants denoting status (`LOADING`, `RUNNING`).

Listing 9.21. `simdefs.h`—
Declaration of macros for BLOCKADE.

```
//-------------------------------------------------------------
// File: simdefs.h
// Definitions for simulation time and events.
//-------------------------------------------------------------
#if !defined(__SIMDEFS_H)
#define __SIMDEFS_H

#include <math.h>

#define AGROUND_THRESHOLD -5

#define LOADING         1
#define RUNNING         2
#define YOU_WON         4
#define YOU_LOST        8

#define WPN_TOLERANCE 1.0
#define MAXHITS 16

#define DEG_TO_RAD 0.0174532
#define RAD_TO_DEG 57.29578

// Timer interval for display updates
#define DISP_MILLISECONDS 60
```

continues

Listing 9.21. continued

```
#define PLATFORM   100
#define SENSOR     200
#define WEAPON     300
#define DETECTION  400

#define INACTIVE 0
#define ACTIVE   1

// Define platform types
#define SURFACE 0
#define AIR     1
#define BOTH    2

// Platform size
#define SMALL  0
#define MEDIUM 1
#define LARGE  2

// Define sensor types
#define RADAR 1
#define ESM   2

// Conversion factors...
#define DEG2NM  60
#define NM2DEG  0.167
#define NM2FT   6076
#define FT2NM   0.00016

typedef unsigned long SimTime;

#define SIMTICK_PER_SEC (1000/DISP_MILLISECONDS)

// Defines an angle sector (clockwise positive, 0 degree along
// ship's axis).
struct Sector
{
    Sector() : angle1(0), angle2(360) {};
    void angles(float a, float b)
    {
        if(a < b)
        {
            angle1 = a;
            angle2 = b;
        }
        else
```

```
        {
            angle1 = b;
            angle2 = a;
        }
    }
    short contains(float a)
    {
        if(a > angle1 && a < angle2)
            return 1;
        else
            return 0;
    }
    float angle1;
    float angle2;
};

struct latlng
{
    latlng() : lat(0), lng(0) {}
    float lat;
    float lng;
};

struct Stage
{
    Stage() : npts(0), pt(NULL) {}
    ~Stage() { if(pt != NULL) delete pt;}
    short  npts;
    latlng *pt;
};

#endif
```

Implementation of *Scenario*

Listing 9.22 shows the file `scenario.cpp`, which implements the member functions and initializes a host of static variables of the Scenario class. The `init` member function initializes the current scenario by reading and interpreting the current mission file. In the process of initializing the scenario, `init` creates and initializes all specified platforms. Each platform, in turn, initializes its sensors and weapons.

The `init_weapons` function does further initializations for each weapon. Specifically, `init_weapons` creates a platform representing the weapon's ammunition (for example, missile or gun projectiles). These platforms (tied to ammunition) are activated when the weapon is used.

Another useful function is `ownship_xfrm`, which computes the coordinates of each platform in terms of the player's ship. These coordinates are used in the `PolarWindow` class to draw the polar display.

Simulating the Scenario

The `update` function of the `Scenario` class ensures that the platforms in the simulation move and interact with each other. If you study the `update` function in Listing 9.22, you see that the function first calls the `update` function of each platform. Then, it loops over the platforms, computes the range between pairs of platforms and calls the detect function of the sensors to determine whether a platform "sees" another. It calls the `mark_detected_sprites` function to ensure that the current view window shows only those platforms that are detected by the current sensor of the player's ship.

Next, update calls `auto_engage_weapon` to let all platforms (other than the player's) shoot at the player's ship. Of course, the platforms can use their weapons only if they are able to detect the player's ship. Finally, update calls the `continue_engagements` function of all the weapons in each platform in the scenario. That function determines if a weapon has hit its target or not.

Drawing a Random Number with Specified Probability

The `Scenario` class includes a static function, `random_draw`, that accepts a probability (between 0 and 1), makes a random draw, and returns TRUE if the draw occurs with the specified level of probability. In BLOCKADE, weapons hit a target with a certain probability. I use the `random_draw` function to determine the success of a weapon. The idea behind `random_draw` is the following: If a uniform random number generator generates numbers between 0 and N-1, each number between 0 and N-1 can occur with probability $1/N$. Then, the probability that a number is less than M, is equal to M/N. For example, if the random number generator generates values between 0 and 999, the probability

BLOCKADE—A Game of Modern Naval Simulation

that a number is less than 800 is $800/1000 = 0.8$. Thus, to check if a random draw with probability 0.8 succeeds, all you have to do is generate a uniform random number between 0 and 999, and return TRUE if the number is less than 800. This is the idea embodied in the `random_draw` function. Note that the function call `random(1000)` returns a uniform random number between 0 and 999.

Static Member Variables in *Scenario*

The `Scenario` class includes the following static member variables that are used as global variables for the BLOCKADE game:

- `static float BASIC_PERIOD;` is the time step in seconds for every 30 ticks of the timer. Because BLOCKADE is set up for a 60-millisecond timer, this should be about 1.8 seconds. This variable is read in from the scenario definition file.

- `static SimTime simulation_time;` is the number of BASIC_PERIOD seconds that has elapsed so far. Remember that when the simulation is running 30 times faster, this is one-thirtieth of the specified number of seconds.

- `static SimTime update_every;` is the number of timer ticks that elapses between each update of the scenario. This variable is set to 30 divided by the `simulation_speed`. Thus, when `simulation_speed` is 1, `update_every` is 30.

- `static short simulation_running;` indicates if simulation is running. It is initially TRUE and becomes FALSE only when the game ends.

- `static short simulation_speed;` is a factor indicating current speed of the simulation. It can be one of 1, 10, 20, or 30. Higher simulation speeds cause the scenario to be updated faster. Initially, `simulation_speed` is set to 1.

- `static short old_simspeed;` is the previous setting of `simulation_speed`.

- `static short sensor_index;` is the currently selected sensor number of the player's ship.

- `static short weapon_index;` is the currently selected weapon number of the player's ship.

- `static short weapons_engaged;` is set to TRUE when any weapon engagement is in progress.
- `static short status;` denotes the status of the simulation.
- `static Platform *current_platform;` is the currently selected platform (the platform in the polar view on which the player has clicked).
- `static float bearing_current;` is the bearing from player's ship to `current_platform`.
- `static float range_current;` is the range from player's ship to `current_platform`.
- `static short xpos_current;` is the x-coordinate of the last button press in the polar window.
- `static short ypos_current;` is the y-coordinate of the last button press in the polar window.
- `static short refresh;` controls if the display is updated. If you set this variable to TRUE, all displays are refreshed.
- `static short ran_aground;` indicates if the player's ship is about to run aground.
- `static long score;` is the current score.
- `static char mission_description[512];` holds a description of the current mission. The description is read from the current mission file in the `init` function.

Listing 9.22. `scenario.cpp`— Implementation of the `Scenario` class.

```
//-------------------------------------------------------------
// File: scenario.cpp
//
// Implementation of the Scenario class.
//-------------------------------------------------------------
#include <stdlib.h>
#include <fstream.h>
#include "scenario.h"
#include <stdio.h>
```

BLOCKADE—A Game of Modern Naval Simulation

```cpp
float Scenario::BASIC_PERIOD = 1.0;
SimTime Scenario::simulation_time = 0L;
short Scenario::simulation_running = 1;
short Scenario::simulation_speed = 1;
short Scenario::old_simspeed = 1;
SimTime Scenario::update_every = 30/Scenario::simulation_speed;
short Scenario::sensor_index = -1;
short Scenario::weapon_index = 0;
short Scenario::sensor_changed = 0;
short Scenario::weapon_changed = 0;
short Scenario::weapons_engaged = 0;
short Scenario::status = LOADING;
Platform *Scenario::current_platform = NULL;
short Scenario::xpos_current = 0;
short Scenario::ypos_current = 0;
float Scenario::bearing_current = 0.0;
float Scenario::range_current = 0.0;
short Scenario::refresh = 0;
short Scenario::ran_aground = AGROUND_THRESHOLD;
long Scenario::score = 0L;
char Scenario::mission_description[512] = " ";

static char *whitespace = " \t";
//----------------------------------------------------------------
// ~ S c e n a r i o

Scenario::~Scenario()
{
    if(platforms != NULL) delete platforms;
}
//----------------------------------------------------------------
// Scenario:: r a n d o m _ d r a w
// Draws a random number and returns 1 if the probability of
// drawing the number is "prob"
short Scenario::random_draw(float prob)
{
    float draw = (float) random(1000);
    if(draw < (float)1000 * prob)
        return 1;
    else
        return 0;
}
//----------------------------------------------------------------
// Scenario:: i n i t
// Initialize a scenario by reading from a file
```

continues

Listing 9.22. continued

```
void Scenario::init(ScenarioInfo *si, MissionInfo *mi)
{
    sinfo = si;
    minfo = mi;
    if(sinfo == NULL || minfo == NULL) return;
// Open the mission file and create the specified scenario
    ifstream ifs(mi->defnfile, ios::in);
    if(!ifs)
    {
// Error reading file.
        return;
    }

// Read and interpret the contents of the file
    char line[81];

// First line should have the string BLOCKADE.MSN
    ifs.getline(line, sizeof(line));
    strupr(line);
    if(strnicmp(line, "BLOCKADE.MSN",
            strlen("BLOCKADE.MSN")) != 0) return;

// Second line has a version number--just in case the
// contents have to change in the future
    ifs.getline(line, sizeof(line));
    short version = atoi(line);
    if(version != 1) return;

// Third line has the number of lines that describe the
// mission.
    ifs.getline(line, sizeof(line));
    short nlines = atoi(line);

// Read the comment lines
    short i, len, count = 0;
    if(nlines > 0)
    {
        for(i = 0; i < nlines; i++)
        {
            ifs.getline(line, sizeof(line));
            len = strlen(line);
            if(count + len < 512)
                count += sprintf(&mission_description[count],
                            "%s\n", line);
```

BLOCKADE—A Game of Modern Naval Simulation

```
            else
                mission_description[count++] = '\n';
        }
    }
// Next line has the number of platforms in this scenario
    ifs.getline(line, sizeof(line));
    short numplat = atoi(line);
    if(numplat == 0) return;

// Allocate an array for the Platforms
    platforms = new Array(numplat, 0, 8);
    if(platforms == NULL) return;

// Set up Platforms
    char *token;
    Platform *p;
    for(i = 0; i < numplat; i++)
    {
// Skip first line
        ifs.getline(line, sizeof(line));

// Next line has name of a platform
        ifs.getline(line, sizeof(line));
        token = strtok(line, whitespace);
        p = new Platform(token);
// Initialize the platform
        p->init();

// Is platform active now?
        ifs.getline(line, sizeof(line));
        token = strtok(line, whitespace);
        if(strnicmp(token, "ACTIVE", 6) == 0)
                                    p->active();
        if(strnicmp(token, "INACTIVE", 8) == 0)
                                    p->inactive();

// Set its position, speed, and bearing
        ifs.getline(line, sizeof(line));
        token = strtok(line, whitespace);
        p->lng = atof(token) /
                sinfo->pixperlng + sinfo->orglng;

        token = strtok(NULL, whitespace);
        p->lat = -atof(token) /
                 sinfo->pixperlat + sinfo->orglat;
        token = strtok(NULL, whitespace);
        p->alt = atof(token);
```

continues

Listing 9.22. continued

```
        ifs.getline(line, sizeof(line));
        token = strtok(line, whitespace);
        p->_speed = atof(token);
        token = strtok(NULL, whitespace);
        p->bearing = atof(token);
        p->bearing_cmd = p->bearing;
        token = strtok(NULL, whitespace);
        p->alt_rate = atof(token);

// Set up the number of stages (these define the motion
// of some platforms), if any.

        ifs.getline(line, sizeof(line));
        token = strtok(line, whitespace);
        p->nstages = atoi(token);
        p->curstage = 0;
        if(p->nstages > 0)
        {
            if(p->stages != NULL) delete p->stages;
            p->stages = new Stage[p->nstages];
            short j;
            for(j = 0; j < p->nstages; j++)
            {
                ifs.getline(line, sizeof(line));
                token = strtok(line, whitespace);
                p->stages[j].npts = atoi(token);
                if(p->stages[j].npts > 0)
                {
                    p->stages[j].pt = new latlng[
                                        p->stages[j].npts];
                    short k;
                    for(k = 0; k < p->stages[j].npts; k++)
                    {
                        ifs.getline(line, sizeof(line));
                        token = strtok(line, whitespace);
                        p->stages[j].pt[k].lng = atof(token) /
                          sinfo->pixperlng + sinfo->orglng;
                        token = strtok(NULL, whitespace);
                        p->stages[j].pt[k].lat = -atof(token) /
                          sinfo->pixperlat + sinfo->orglat;
                    }
                }
            }
        }
```

BLOCKADE—A Game of Modern Naval Simulation

```cpp
// Set platform's heading to a point in the first stage
        if(p->nstages > 0)
        {
            short ip = random(p->stages[0].npts);
            p->lat = p->stages[0].pt[ip].lat;
            p->lng = p->stages[0].pt[ip].lng;
            if(p->nstages > 1)
            {
                ip = random(p->stages[1].npts);
                p->destlat = p->stages[1].pt[ip].lat;
                p->destlng = p->stages[1].pt[ip].lng;
                p->bearing_cmd = atan2(p->destlng-p->lng,
                            p->destlat-p->lat) * RAD_TO_DEG;
                if(p->bearing_cmd < 0)
                        p->bearing_cmd = 360 + p->bearing_cmd;
            }
        }
        if(i == 0) ownship = p;
// Add platform to the array of platforms
        platforms->addAt(*p, i);
    }
// Change ownship image file name...
    if(ownship->imgfile != NULL) delete ownship->imgfile;
    if(ownship->mskfile != NULL) delete ownship->mskfile;
    if(ownship->imgmfile != NULL) delete ownship->imgmfile;
    if(ownship->mskmfile != NULL) delete ownship->mskmfile;
    ownship->imgfile = new char[strlen("OWNSHIP.BMP")+1];
    strcpy(ownship->imgfile, "OWNSHIP.BMP");
    ownship->mskfile = new char[strlen("OWNSHIPM.BMP")+1];
    strcpy(ownship->mskfile, "OWNSHIPM.BMP");
    ownship->imgmfile = new char[strlen("OWNSM.BMP")+1];
    strcpy(ownship->imgmfile, "OWNSM.BMP");
    ownship->mskmfile = new char[strlen("OWNSMM.BMP")+1];
    strcpy(ownship->mskmfile, "OWNSMM.BMP");

// Make sure all platforms from the third one onward keep
// repeating themselves
    for(i = 2; i < numplat; i++)
        platform(i).loop_back = 1;

// Initialize the ammo rounds of the weapons on all platforms
    init_weapons();
}
//--------------------------------------------------------------
// Scenario:: m a k e _ s p r i t e s
// Create a sprite for each platform.
```

continues

Listing 9.22. continued

```
void Scenario::make_sprites(HDC hdc)
{
    short i;
    for( i = 0; i < numplatform(); i++)
    {
        platform(i).make_sprite(hdc);
        platform(i).sprite()->id(i);
        platform(i).map_sprite()->id(i);
        platform(i).zmap_sprite()->id(i);
    }
}
//----------------------------------------------------------------
// Scenario:: o w n s h i p _ x f r m
// Transform all platform's coordinates to the coordinate
// frame of the player's ship (which we call "ownship").

void Scenario::ownship_xfrm()
{
    short i;
    float hdg_rad = ownship->heading() * DEG_TO_RAD;
    float coshdg = cos(hdg_rad);
    float sinhdg = sin(hdg_rad);
    float x, y, xp, yp;

    for( i = 0; i < numplatform(); i++)
    {
        x = DEG2NM * (platform(i).longitude() -
                                ownship->longitude());
        y = DEG2NM * (platform(i).latitude() -
                                ownship->latitude());
        xp = x*coshdg - y*sinhdg;
        yp = x*sinhdg + y*coshdg;
        platform(i).xo(xp);
        platform(i).yo(yp);
        platform(i).zo(platform(i).altitude() -
                        ownship->altitude());
    }
}
//----------------------------------------------------------------
// Scenario:: u p d a t e
// Update the scenario (move platforms, make sensor detections,
// and engage weapons,...)

void Scenario::update()
{
// Do nothing if simulation is not running
    if(!simulation_running) return;
```

Chapter 9

BLOCKADE—A Game of Modern Naval Simulation

```
// Update all platforms
    short i;
    for( i = 0; i < numplatform(); i++)
    {
        platform(i).update();
    }

    if(count++ > Scenario::update_every)
    {
// Reset count
        count = 0;
        Scenario::simulation_time++;
        short updtcount = MOTION_UPDATE_COUNT;
        if(weapons_engaged > 0) updtcount = 0;
        if(motion_count++ > updtcount)
        {
            motion_count = 0;
// Make sensor detections...
            short j;
// Reset all sensor detections
            for(i = 0; i < numplatform() - 1; i++)
            {
                for(j = 0; j < platform(i).numsensor(); j++)
                    platform(i).sensor(j).reset_detections();
            }

            for(i = 0; i < numplatform() - 1; i++)
            {
                for(j = i+1; j < numplatform(); j++)
                {
                    if(!platform(j).is_active()) continue;

// Compute distance between platform i and j in nautical miles
                    float x = platform(i).longitude() -
                              platform(j).longitude();
                    float y = platform(i).latitude() -
                              platform(j).latitude();
// Ignore altitude when computing distance
                    float r;
                    if(x == 0 && y == 0)
                        r = 0;
                    else
                        r = sqrt(x*x+y*y) * DEG2NM;

// Loop over platform i's sensors
                    short k, n = platform(i).numsensor();
                    short detected;
                    if(n > 0)
```

continues

Listing 9.22. continued

```
                        {
                            for(k = 0; k < n; k++)
                            {
                                detected = platform(i).sensor(k).
                                    detect(r,platform(j).type(),
                                            platform(j).size(),
                                            &platform(j));
                                if(i==0)
                                {
                                    if(detected)
                                    {
                                        platform(j).detected();
                                    }
                                    else
                                    {
                                        if(platform(j).is_detected())
                                        {
                                            platform(j).hide_sprite();
                                            refresh = 1;
                                        }
                                        platform(j).not_detected();
                                    }
                                }
                            }
                        }
// Loop over platform j's sensors
                        n = platform(j).numsensor();
                        if(n > 0)
                        {
                            for(k = 0; k < n; k++)
                            {
                                detected = platform(j).sensor(k).
                                            detect(r,
                                                platform(i).type(),
                                                platform(i).size(),
                                                &platform(i));
                            }
                        }
                    }
                }

// Change course/heading of other ships according to some
// logic. Platform(1) -- the cargo carrier tries to hug the
// coastline. Other ships and planes try to stop Platform(0),
// the player's ship. This could be better done with some
// sort of a scripting language or "rules" that define the
```

BLOCKADE—A Game of Modern Naval Simulation

```
// behavior of all computer-controlled platforms. For now, the
// cargo carrier follows a predefined route with some
// randomness.
            if(platform(1).curstage == platform(1).nstages-1)
            {
// Cargo carrier reached detsination. Game's over.
                status = YOU_LOST;
            }
        }
    }
// Make sure only visible platforms are displayed
    mark_detected_sprites();

// Initiate new weapon engagements and continue ongoing
// engagements

    auto_engage_weapon();
    for(i = 0; i < numplatform(); i++)
    {
        short nw = platform(i).numweapon();
        if(nw <= 0) continue;
        short j;
        for(j = 0; j < nw; j++)
        {
            platform(i).weapon(j).continue_engagements();
        }
    }
}
//-------------------------------------------------------------
void Scenario::mark_detected_sprites()
{
// Show the platforms that are visible from the current sensor
// used by the player's ship
    short i;
    for(i = 1; i < numplatform(); i++)
        platform(i).hide_sprite();

    short maxsensor = ownship->numsensor();
    if(maxsensor <= 0) return;

    if(Scenario::sensor_index == -1)
    {
        for(i = 0; i < maxsensor; i++)
        {
            short j;
            for(j = 0; j < ownship->sensor(i).numdetect(); j++)
            {
```

continues

445

Listing 9.22. continued

```
                    (ownship->sensor(i).detections())[j].
                                    platform()->show_sprite();
            }
        }
    }
    else
    {
        i = Scenario::sensor_index;
        short j;
        for(j = 0; j < ownship->sensor(i).numdetect(); j++)
        {
            (ownship->sensor(i).detections())[j].
                                    platform()->show_sprite();
        }
    }
}
//----------------------------------------------------------------
// Scenario:: i n i t _ w e a p o n s
// Initialize the ammo rounds of all weapons on all platforms

void Scenario::init_weapons()
{
    short ip, np = numplatform();
    short pindex = np;
    for(ip = 0; ip < np; ip++)
    {
        Platform *p = &platform(ip);
        if(p->numweapon() <= 0) continue;
        short i;

        for(i = 0; i < p->numweapon(); i++)
        {
            Weapon *w = &(p->weapon(i));

            if(w->engage_count(SURFACE) > 0)
            {
                if(w->ammo[SURFACE] != NULL)
                        delete w->ammo[SURFACE];
                w->ammo[SURFACE] = new Ammunition[w->engage_count
                                                    (SURFACE)];
                short j;
                for(j = 0; j < w->numengage[SURFACE]; j++)
                {
                    Platform *pa = new Platform
                                    (w->platform_name());
```

BLOCKADE—A Game of Modern Naval Simulation

```
                pa->init();
                pa->inactive();
                pa->lng = p->lng;
                pa->lat = p->lat;
                pa->alt = p->alt;
                pa->turnrate = 10;
                pa->_speed = pa->max_speed();
                pa->bearing = p->bearing;
                pa->nstages = 0;
                w->ammunition(SURFACE, j)->platform(pa);
// Add platform to the array of platforms
                platforms->addAt(*pa, pindex++);
            }
        }
        if(w->engage_count(AIR) > 0)
        {
            if(w->ammo[AIR] != NULL)
                    delete w->ammo[AIR];
            w->ammo[AIR] = new Ammunition[w->engage_count
                                                (AIR)];
            short j;
            for(j = 0; j < w->numengage[AIR]; j++)
            {
                Platform *pa = new Platform(
                        w->platform_name());
                pa->init();
                pa->inactive();
                pa->lng = p->lng;
                pa->lat = p->lat;
                pa->alt = p->alt;
                pa->turnrate = 10;
                pa->_speed = pa->max_speed();
                pa->bearing = p->bearing;
                pa->nstages = 0;
                w->ammunition(AIR, j)->platform(pa);
// Add platform to the array of platforms
                platforms->addAt(*pa, pindex++);
            }
        }
    }
}
//---------------------------------------------------------------
// Scenario:: e n g a g e _ o w n s h i p _ w e a p o n
// Use the current weapon against the currently selected target.
```

continues

Listing 9.22. continued

```cpp
void Scenario::engage_ownship_weapon()
{
// Engage weapon selected by player
    short type = SURFACE;
    if(Scenario::current_platform != NULL)
        type = Scenario::current_platform->type();
    ownship->weapon(weapon_index).engage(
                Scenario::current_platform, type,
                Scenario::range_current,
                Scenario::bearing_current);
}
//---------------------------------------------------------------
// Scenario:: a u t o _ e n g a g e _ w e a p o n
// Automatically engage missiles aimed at player's ship

void Scenario::auto_engage_weapon()
{
// If there is an incoming missile, automatically use a
// weapon against the missile.
    short i, j;
    Platform *p;
    for(i = 0; i < ownship->numsensor(); i++)
    {
        if(ownship->sensor(i).numdetect() <= 0) continue;
        for(j = 0; j < ownship->sensor(i).numdetect(); j++)
        {
            p = (ownship->sensor(i).detections())[j].platform();
            float r = (ownship->sensor(i).detections())[j].
                        range();
            if(strncmp(p->name(), "MISSILE", 7) == 0)
            {
// Make sure this missile is not one of those launched by
// the player's ship
                short k;
                if(ownship->numweapon() <= 0) break;
                for(k = 0; k < ownship->numweapon(); k++)
                {
                    short et;
                    for(et = SURFACE; et <= AIR; et++)
                    {
                        short nmax = ownship->weapon(k).
                                        engage_count(et);
                        if(nmax > 0)
                        {
                            short n;
                            for(n = 0; n < nmax; n++)
                            {
```

BLOCKADE—A Game of Modern Naval Simulation

Chapter 9

```
                            Ammunition * am =
                                ownship->weapon(k).
                                    ammunition(et,n);
                            if(am->in_use() &&
                               am->platform() == p)
                            {
                                p = NULL;
                                break;
                            }
                        }
                    }
                }
            }
            if(p != NULL)
            {
                float brg;
                float dlng = p->lng - ownship->lng;
                float dlat = p->lat - ownship->lat;
                if(dlng == 0 && dlat == 0)
                    brg = 0;
                else
                    brg = atan2(dlng, dlat) * RAD_TO_DEG;
                if(brg < 0) brg += 360;
                for(k = 0; k < ownship->numweapon(); k++)
                {
// Engage the first available weapon
                    if(ownship->weapon(k).engage(
                        p, p->type(), r, brg))
                    {
                        break;
                    }
                }
            }
        }
    }
}
//-------------------------------------------------------------
// Scenario:: o w n s h i p _ a g r o u n d
// Checks if player's ship is about to run aground

short Scenario::ownship_aground()
{
// See if player's ship is in one of the "validsea" rectangles.
    short x = (ownship->longitude() - sinfo->orglng) *
                sinfo->pixperlng;
    short y = (-ownship->latitude() + sinfo->orglat) *
                sinfo->pixperlat;
```

continues

Listing 9.22. continued

```
    short i;
    for(i = 0; i < sinfo->nrects; i++)
    {
        if(x-5 > sinfo->validsea[i].left   &&
           x+5 < sinfo->validsea[i].right  &&
           y-5 > sinfo->validsea[i].top &&
           y+5 < sinfo->validsea[i].bottom)
        {
            return i;
        }
    }
    Scenario::ran_aground++;
    return -1;
}
```

Platform Class

The `Platform` class represents ships, aircraft, and anything that moves in the scenario, including missiles and projectiles shot by guns. Listing 9.23 shows the file `platform.h` that declares the `Platform` class.

A `Platform` has a position specified in latitude (degrees), longitude (degrees), and altitude (feet). It has a speed and a bearing. Also, a `Platform` has an array of `Sensor` objects and an array of `Weapon` objects. The `Sensors` are the eyes and ears of the `Platform`. Most modern ships and aircraft use radars and electronic listening devices as sensors. The `Platform` class uses the `Array` container class to store `Sensors` and `Weapons`.

The motion of the player's ship is controlled by the player, but the other platforms are programmed to move along straight line segments. These segments are stored in an array of `Stage` structures (defined in `simdefs.h`, Listing 9.21) named `stages`. If the variable named `loop_back` is `TRUE`, the platform keeps repeating through these stages of motion. As you can see from Listing 9.24, the path taken by a platform is somewhat random because the start and end points of the path are selected at random from a small set of points.

A `Platform` also has several bitmap images associated with it. A pair of image and mask bitmaps defines how the `Platform` appears in the polar view while another pair of bitmaps defines the `Platform`'s appearance in the map view.

Chapter 9

BLOCKADE—A Game of Modern Naval Simulation

The Scenario class stores Platforms in a Borland Class Library's container class (Array). I derived Platform from the Object class because this is a condition that must be met for any object stored in the Array container class.

Listing 9.23. platform.h—Declaration of the Platform class.

```
//---------------------------------------------------------------
// File: platform.h
//
// Declaration of the Platform classes.
//---------------------------------------------------------------
#if !defined(__PLATFORM_H)
#define __PLATFORM_H

#include <strng.h>
#include <array.h>
#include "sprite.h"
#include "sensor.h"
#include "weapon.h"

#define MOTION_UPDATE_COUNT 5

#define IS_ACTIVE     1
#define HAS_MOVED     2
#define IS_DETECTED   4

class Platform : public Object
{
friend Scenario;
public:
    Platform() : sensors(NULL), weapons(NULL), _name(NULL),
        imgfile(NULL), mskfile(NULL), flags(0),
        imgmfile(NULL), mskmfile(NULL), turnrate(2),
        count(0), motion_count(0), stages(NULL),
        nstages(0), curstage(0), _strength(0), _speed(0),
        _full_strength(0), _max_speed(0), loop_back(0)
    {
        motion_update_count(MOTION_UPDATE_COUNT);
    }
    Platform(char *_nm) : sensors(NULL),
        weapons(NULL), imgfile(NULL), mskfile(NULL),
        imgmfile(NULL), mskmfile(NULL), turnrate(2),
        count(0), motion_count(0), stages(NULL),
        nstages(0), curstage(0), _strength(0), _speed(0),
        _full_strength(0), _max_speed(0), loop_back(0)
    {
```

continues

Listing 9.23. continued

```
        if(_nm != NULL)
        {
            _name = new char[strlen(_nm) + 1];
            strcpy(_name, _nm);
        }
        motion_update_count(MOTION_UPDATE_COUNT);
    }

    ~Platform();

    void init();
    void update();
    void hit(short hs);

// The following functions are required because Platform
// is derived from Object (the base class of Borland's
// container class library).

    classType isA() const { return PlatformClass;}

    char* nameOf() const { return "PlatformClass";}

    hashValueType hashValue() const
    { return (hashValueType)(lat+lng+alt);}

    int isEqual(const Object _FAR& ob) const
    { return 0;}

    void printOn(ostream& os) const
    {
        os << lat << " " << lng << " " << alt << endl;
    }

    Sprite* sprite() { return psprite;}
    Sprite* map_sprite() { return pmsprite;}
    Sprite* zmap_sprite() { return pzmsprite;}

    void make_sprite(HDC hdc)
    {
        psprite = new Sprite(hdc, imgfile, mskfile);
        pmsprite = new Sprite(hdc, imgmfile, mskmfile);
        pzmsprite = new Sprite(hdc, imgmfile, mskmfile);
    }
    void show_sprite()
    {
```

BLOCKADE—A Game of Modern Naval Simulation

```
    psprite->active();
    psprite->move(0,0);
    pmsprite->active();
    pmsprite->move(0,0);
    pzmsprite->active();
    pzmsprite->move(0,0);
}
void hide_sprite()
{
    psprite->inactive();
    pmsprite->inactive();
    pzmsprite->inactive();
}

float altitude() { return alt;}
float latitude() { return lat;}
float longitude() { return lng;}
float xo() { return xos;}
float yo() { return yos;}
float zo() { return zos;}
float heading() { return bearing;}
float speed() { return _speed;}
float max_speed() { return _max_speed;}

void altitude(float v) { alt = v;}
void latitude(float v) { lat = v;}
void longitude(float v) { lng = v;}
void xo(float x) { xos = x;}
void yo(float y) { yos = y;}
void zo(float z) { zos = z;}
void heading(float hdg) { bearing_cmd = hdg;}
void speed(float spd) { _speed = spd;}
void max_speed(float spd) { _max_speed = spd;}

short numsensor()
{
    if(sensors != NULL)
        return sensors->getItemsInContainer();
    else
        return 0;
}

short numweapon()
{
    if(weapons != NULL)
        return weapons->getItemsInContainer();
    else
```

continues

Listing 9.23. continued

```cpp
            return 0;
    }

    Sensor& sensor(short i) { return (Sensor&)(*sensors)[i];}
    Weapon& weapon(short i) { return (Weapon&)(*weapons)[i];}


    void moved() { flags |= HAS_MOVED;}
    void move_done() { flags &= ~HAS_MOVED;}
    void active() { flags |= IS_ACTIVE;}
    void inactive() { flags &= ~IS_ACTIVE;}
    void detected() { flags |= IS_DETECTED;}
    void not_detected() { flags &= ~IS_DETECTED;}
    short is_active() { return (flags & IS_ACTIVE);}
    short has_moved() { return (flags & HAS_MOVED);}
    short is_detected() { return (flags & IS_DETECTED);}

    char *name() { return _name;}

    short strength() { return _strength;}
    short full_strength() { return _full_strength;}
    short type() { return _type;}
    short size() { return _size;}

    short motion_update_count() { return mupdt_count;}
    void  motion_update_count(short n);
    float motion_period_hour() { return mperiod_hour;}
    float motion_period_sec() { return mperiod_sec;}
    void goto_stage0();

    void engage_weapons();

protected:
    Sprite *psprite;    // Sprite denoting this platform
    Sprite *pmsprite;   // Sprite for the map window
    Sprite *pzmsprite;  // Sprite for the zoomed map window
    char   *imgfile;
    char   *mskfile;
    char   *imgmfile;
    char   *mskmfile;
    float  lat, lng;    // Latitude and longitude
    float  alt;         // Altitude in feet
    float  _speed;      // Speed in knots
    float  bearing;     // Degrees with respect to north
```

BLOCKADE—A Game of Modern Naval Simulation

```
    float   bearing_cmd;// Commanded bearing
    float   turnrate;   // How fast can the ship turn? (deg/sec)
    float   alt_rate;   // Rate of change of altitude (ft/sec)
    float   xos, yos, zos; // This platform's location
                           // with respect to player's ship
    short   curstage;
    short   nstages;
    Stage   *stages;
    float   destlat, destlng;

    float   _max_speed; // Maximum speed
    float   saved_max_speed;
    short   _strength;
    short   _full_strength;
    short   _type;      // SURFACE or AIR
    short   _size;      // Size of platform as a radar target
                        // can be: SMALL, MEDIUM, or LARGE
    Array   *sensors;
    Array   *weapons;
    char    *_name;     // Name of platform

    short   flags;      // Status flags
    short   loop_back;  // TRUE = platform keeps repeating itself
    short   count;
    short   motion_count;
    short   mupdt_count;
    float   mperiod_hour;
    float   mperiod_sec;

    enum { PlatformClass = __firstUserClass + PLATFORM};
};

#endif
```

Implementation of *Platform*

Listing 9.24 shows the implementation of the Platform class. Two of the important member functions of Platform are init and update. The init function initializes a Platform and update moves a Platform. These are further discussed in the following sections.

455

Initializing a *Platform*

The Scenario::init function initializes a Platform by calling its init function. Before it is called, the name of the Platform must be set. To initialize a Platform, init opens the platform database file, PLATFORM.DAT. This is a text file of specified format that stores information on all available platforms. Once init locates the information on the named platform, it reads and stores the data in appropriate member variables of the Platform. In the course of initializing a Platform, the code in init also calls the init functions of any Sensor and Weapon that the Platform has.

Moving a *Platform*

The update function moves the Platform. As you can see from Listing 9.24, the update function first updates the bearing. Then it updates the position of the Platform, provided enough timer ticks have elapsed since the last update.

If any stages of motion are defined (the stages are defined in the mission definition file) for the Platform, the update function checks if the Platform should go on to the next leg of motion. If the Platform is at the last stage and the loop_back flag is TRUE, the Platform is repositioned at one of the starting points.

Taking a Hit

A Platform object has an associated survival strength. Each Weapon object, on the other hand, has a kill strength. When a Weapon hits a Platform, the Weapon's kill strength is subtracted from the Platform's survival strength. The continue_engagements function of the Weapon class calls the hit function of the Platform to account for the hit. The parameter passed to the hit function is the amount to be subtracted from the Platform's strength. After reducing the Platform's strength, the hit function tries to assess the damage. The speed is degraded for nonfatal hits. If strength falls to an eighth of the full strength, the Platform is considered to be destroyed. If the loop_back flag is TRUE, the platform is revived and placed at the starting position.

BLOCKADE—A Game of Modern Naval Simulation

Listing 9.24. `platform.cpp`— Implementation of the `Platform` class.

```cpp
//----------------------------------------------------------------
// File: platform.cpp
//
// Implementation of the Platform class.
//----------------------------------------------------------------
#include <stdlib.h>
#include <fstream.h>
#include <string.h>
#include "scenario.h"

#define LINES_PER_PLATFORM  8

static char *whitespace = " \t";
//----------------------------------------------------------------
// ~ P l a t f o r m

Platform::~Platform()
{
    if(sensors != NULL) delete sensors;
    if(weapons != NULL) delete weapons;
    if(_name != NULL) delete _name;
    if(imgfile != NULL) delete imgfile;
    if(mskfile != NULL) delete mskfile;
    if(imgmfile != NULL) delete imgmfile;
    if(mskmfile != NULL) delete mskmfile;
}
//----------------------------------------------------------------
// Platform:: i n i t
// Initialize a Platform by reading from the PLATFORM.DAT file

void Platform::init()
{
    if(_name == NULL) return;

// Open the file PLATFORM.DAT and read in platform data.
    ifstream ifs("platform.dat", ios::in);
    if(!ifs)
    {
// Error reading file.
        return;
    }

// Read and interpret the contents of the file
    char line[81];
```

continues

Listing 9.24. continued

```cpp
// First line is a comment; ignore it.
    ifs.getline(line, sizeof(line));

// Second line has the number of platforms in this file
    ifs.getline(line, sizeof(line));
    short numplat = atoi(line);
    if(numplat == 0) return;

// Search for this platform's data
    short i, j, len = strlen(_name);
    char *token;
    for(i = 0; i < numplat; i++)
    {
// Ignore first line of each platform record
        ifs.getline(line, sizeof(line));

// Next line should have platform's name
        ifs.getline(line, sizeof(line));
        if(strnicmp(line, _name, len) != 0)
        {
// Skip the data for this platform
            for(j = 0; j < LINES_PER_PLATFORM; j++)
                ifs.getline(line, sizeof(line));
// Next comes number of sensors
            ifs.getline(line, sizeof(line));
            short n = atoi(line);
            if(n > 0)
                for(j = 0; j < n; j++)
                    ifs.getline(line, sizeof(line));
// Next comes number of weapons
            ifs.getline(line, sizeof(line));
            n = atoi(line);
            short k;
            if(n > 0)
                for(j = 0; j < n; j++)
                {
                    for(k = 0; k < 3; k++)
                        ifs.getline(line, sizeof(line));
                    ifs.getline(line, sizeof(line));
                    short m = atoi(line);
                    for(k = 0; k < m; k++)
                        ifs.getline(line, sizeof(line));
                }
        }
        else
        {
// Yes, the name matches. Read in data.
```

BLOCKADE—A Game of Modern Naval Simulation

```
// Platform type (SURFACE or AIR)
            _type = 0;
            ifs.getline(line, sizeof(line));
            token = strtok(line, whitespace);
            if(strnicmp(token, "SURFACE", 7) == 0) _type = 0;
            if(strnicmp(token, "AIR", 3) == 0) _type = 1;

// Platform size as radar target (SMALL, MEDIUM, or LARGE)
            _size = SMALL;
            ifs.getline(line, sizeof(line));
            token = strtok(line, whitespace);
            if(strnicmp(token, "SMALL", 5) == 0) _size = SMALL;
            if(strnicmp(token, "MEDIUM", 6) == 0) _size = MEDIUM;
            if(strnicmp(token, "LARGE", 5) == 0) _size = LARGE;

// Icon image for the platform (for polar window)
            ifs.getline(line, sizeof(line));
            token = strtok(line, whitespace);
            if(imgfile != NULL) delete imgfile;
            imgfile = new char[strlen(token)+1];
            strcpy(imgfile, token);

            ifs.getline(line, sizeof(line));
            token = strtok(line, whitespace);
            if(mskfile != NULL) delete mskfile;
            mskfile = new char[strlen(token)+1];
            strcpy(mskfile, token);

// Icon image for the platform (for the map window)
            ifs.getline(line, sizeof(line));
            token = strtok(line, whitespace);
            if(imgmfile != NULL) delete imgmfile;
            imgmfile = new char[strlen(token)+1];
            strcpy(imgmfile, token);

            ifs.getline(line, sizeof(line));
            token = strtok(line, whitespace);
            if(mskmfile != NULL) delete mskmfile;
            mskmfile = new char[strlen(token)+1];
            strcpy(mskmfile, token);

// Survival strength
            ifs.getline(line, sizeof(line));
            token = strtok(line, whitespace);
            _full_strength = atoi(token);
            _strength = _full_strength;
```

continues

Listing 9.24. continued

```
// Maximum speed in knots
            ifs.getline(line, sizeof(line));
            token = strtok(line, whitespace);
            _max_speed = atof(token);
            saved_max_speed = _max_speed;
// Set the "motion update count"
            float n = (float)360/(float)_max_speed /
                    (float)Scenario::BASIC_PERIOD;
            motion_update_count((short)n);

// Read sensor list
            ifs.getline(line, sizeof(line));
            token = strtok(line, whitespace);
            short numsensors = atoi(token);
            short j;
            if(numsensors > 0)
            {
// Create an array of sensors
                sensors = new Array(numsensors, 0, 8);
                if(sensors == NULL) return;

                Sensor *s;
                for(j = 0; j < numsensors; j++)
                {
                    ifs.getline(line, sizeof(line));
                    token = strtok(line, whitespace);
                    s = new Sensor(token, this);
                    s->init();
// Add sensor to array of sensors
                    sensors->addAt(*s, j);
                }
            }

// Read weapons list
            ifs.getline(line, sizeof(line));
            token = strtok(line, whitespace);
            short numweapons = atoi(token);
            if(numweapons > 0)
            {
// Create an array of weapons
                weapons = new Array(numweapons, 0, 8);
                if(weapons == NULL) return;

                Weapon *w;
                for(j = 0; j < numweapons; j++)
                {
```

BLOCKADE—A Game of Modern Naval Simulation

Chapter 9

```
                    ifs.getline(line, sizeof(line));
                    token = strtok(line, whitespace);
                    w = new Weapon(token, this);
                    w->init();
// Set number of weapons
                    ifs.getline(line, sizeof(line));
                    token = strtok(line, whitespace);
                    w->count = atoi(token);
// How many weapons can be used simultaneously...
                    ifs.getline(line, sizeof(line));
                    token = strtok(line, whitespace);
                    w->numengage[SURFACE] = atoi(token);
                    token = strtok(NULL, whitespace);
                    w->numengage[AIR] = atoi(token);

// Coverage sectors (because of ship's structure, weapons cannot
// always work all around the ship. A list of sectors keeps track
// of the exact areas where the weapon can work.
                    ifs.getline(line, sizeof(line));
                    token = strtok(line, whitespace);
                    w->nsector = atoi(token);
                    w->sectors = new Sector[w->nsector];
                    short k;
                    float a, b;
                    for(k = 0; k < w->nsector; k++)
                    {
                        ifs.getline(line, sizeof(line));
                        token = strtok(line, whitespace);
                        a = atof(token);
                        token = strtok(NULL, whitespace);
                        b = atof(token);
                        w->sectors[k].angles(a, b);
                    }
// Add sensor to array of sensors
                    weapons->addAt(*w, j);
                }
            }
        }
    }
}
//-------------------------------------------------------------
// Platform:: u p d a t e
// Update1 platform position etc.

void Platform::update()
{
// If platform is not active, do nothing.
    if(!is_active()) return;
```

continues

Listing 9.24. continued

```
        if(count++ > Scenario::update_every)
        {
// Reset count
            count = 0;

// The following code simulates a slow change in ship's heading
            if(fabs(bearing-bearing_cmd) > 0.1)
            {
                if(bearing_cmd > bearing)
                {
                    bearing += turnrate * Scenario::BASIC_PERIOD;
                }
                else
                {
                    bearing -= turnrate * Scenario::BASIC_PERIOD;
                }
                if(bearing > bearing_cmd) bearing = bearing_cmd;
                if(bearing < bearing_cmd) bearing = bearing_cmd;
            }

// If enough time has elapsed, move the platform...
            if(motion_count++ > mupdt_count)
            {
                motion_count = 0;
                float hdg_rad = bearing * DEG_TO_RAD;
                float coshdg = cos(hdg_rad);
                float sinhdg = sin(hdg_rad);
                float dist = speed() * mperiod_hour * NM2DEG;
                lat += dist*coshdg;
                lng += dist*sinhdg;
                alt += alt_rate * mperiod_sec;

// Engage weapons
                engage_weapons();

// Check if it's time to move to next stage
                dist *= 2;
                if(nstages > 0 &&
                    fabs(destlat - lat) <= dist &&
                    fabs(destlng - lng) <= dist)
                {
                    if(curstage == nstages-1 && loop_back)
                        goto_stage0();
                    if(curstage < nstages-1)
                    {
```

BLOCKADE—A Game of Modern Naval Simulation

```
// Set heading to a point in the next stage
                    short ip = random(stages[curstage+1].npts);
                    destlat = stages[curstage+1].
                                              pt[ip].lat;
                    destlng = stages[curstage+1].
                                              pt[ip].lng;
                    float lngdel = destlng - lng;
                    float latdel = destlat - lat;
                    if(latdel == 0 && lngdel == 0)
                        bearing_cmd = 0;
                    else
                        bearing_cmd = atan2(lngdel, latdel) *
                                                  RAD_TO_DEG;
                    if(bearing_cmd < 0)
                            bearing_cmd = 360 + bearing_cmd;
                    curstage++;
                }
            }
        }
    }
}
//--------------------------------------------------------------
// Platform:: h i t
// Take a specified level of hit from a weapon

void Platform::hit(short hs)
{
    _strength -= hs;
    if(_strength <= 0) _strength = 0;

    if(sprite()->id() == 0)
    {
// This is the player's ship. Subtract hit from score.
        if(Scenario::score >= hs)
            Scenario::score -= hs;
    }
    else
    {
// Add hit to score.
        Scenario::score += hs;
    }

// Do some damage assessment
// Reduce platform's maximum speed according to the hit
    _max_speed = saved_max_speed * _strength / _full_strength;
    if(_speed > _max_speed) _speed = _max_speed;
```

continues

Listing 9.24. continued

```cpp
// If strength is an eighth of its full strength, I consider
// the platform to be "dead"
    if(_strength < _full_strength/8)
    {
        if(sprite()->id() > 1)
        {
            Scenario::score += _full_strength - _strength;
            if(loop_back) goto_stage0();
            else
            {
                inactive();
                hide_sprite();
                Scenario::refresh = 1;
            }
        }
// If cargo ship or player's ship is dead, then game is over.
        if(sprite()->id() == 1)
        {
            Scenario::status = YOU_WON;
            Scenario::simulation_running = 0;
        }
        if(sprite()->id() == 0)
        {
            Scenario::status = YOU_LOST;
            Scenario::simulation_running = 0;
        }
    }
}
//----------------------------------------------------------------
// Platform:: g o t o _ s t a g e 0
// Platform returns to a position in stage 0 of its defined
// motion pattern. The Scenario class calls this function to
// reuse platforms.

void Platform::goto_stage0()
{
// Restore the platform's strength and max speed
    _strength = _full_strength;
    _max_speed = saved_max_speed;
    _speed = 9*_max_speed / 10;

// Cannot do anything else if there are no "stages" defined
    if(nstages <= 0) return;

    curstage = 0;
    short ip = random(stages[0].npts);
```

BLOCKADE—A Game of Modern Naval Simulation

```
    lat = stages[0].pt[ip].lat;
    lng = stages[0].pt[ip].lng;
    if(nstages > 1)
    {
        ip = random(stages[1].npts);
        destlat = stages[1].pt[ip].lat;
        destlng = stages[1].pt[ip].lng;
        bearing_cmd = atan2(destlng-lng,
                    destlat-lat) * RAD_TO_DEG;
        if(bearing_cmd < 0)
              bearing_cmd = 360 + bearing_cmd;
    }
}
//-------------------------------------------------------------
void Platform::motion_update_count(short n)
{
    if(n < 0) return;
    mupdt_count = n;
    mperiod_sec = Scenario::BASIC_PERIOD * (mupdt_count+1);
    mperiod_hour = mperiod_sec / 3600;
}
//-------------------------------------------------------------
// Platform:: e n g a g e _ w e a p o n s
// Automatically engage weapons.

void Platform::engage_weapons()
{
    short index = sprite()->id();

    if(index == 0 || index == 1) return;
    if(numsensor() <= 0) return;
    if(numweapon() <= 0) return;

    short i, j, k;
    Platform *p;
    for(i = 0; i < numsensor(); i++)
    {
        if(sensor(i).numdetect() <= 0) continue;
        for(j = 0; j < sensor(i).numdetect(); j++)
        {
            p = (sensor(i).detections())[j].platform();
            index = p->sprite()->id();
            if(index == 0) break;
        }
        if(index == 0) break;
    }
    if(index != 0) return;
```

continues

Listing 9.24. continued

```
// Engage weapon
    float r = (sensor(i).detections())[j].range();
    float brg;
    float dlng = p->lng - lng;
    float dlat = p->lat - lat;
    if(dlng == 0 && dlat == 0)
        brg = 0;
    else
        brg = atan2(dlng, dlat) * RAD_TO_DEG;
    if(brg < 0) brg += 360;

    for(k = 0; k < numweapon(); k++)
    {
// Engage the first available weapon
        if(weapon(k).engage(p, p->type(), r, brg))
        {
            break;
        }
    }
}
```

Sensor Class

Listing 9.25 shows the file sensor.h that declares the Sensor class. A Sensor is characterized by the following important member variables:

- ■ Platform *parent; is the Platform on which the Sensor is located.
- ■ short can_detect[2]; are interpreted as two Boolean variables that respectively determine if the Sensor can detect a SURFACE or an AIR Platform.
- ■ float range[3]; are three ranges (in nautical miles) that respectively specify the ranges at which the Sensor can detect a SMALL, MEDIUM, or LARGE Platform.
- ■ Detection detection[MAXDETECT]; is an array of detections made by the Sensor. The Detection structure is defined in Listing 9.25.
- ■ short ndetect; is the number of detections in the detection array.

BLOCKADE—A Game of Modern Naval Simulation

Chapter 9

The Platform class stores its Sensor objects in an Array, a container class from the Borland Class Library. To facilitate this, I derive the Sensor class from the Object class. A consequence of deriving Sensor from Object is that I had to define a number of additional member functions such as isA, nameOf, hashValue, isEqual, and printOn.

Listing 9.25. sensor.h—Declaration of the Sensor class.

```
//---------------------------------------------------------------
// File: sensor.h
//
// Declarations of the Sensor class.
//---------------------------------------------------------------
#if !defined(__SENSOR_H)
#define __SENSOR_H

#include <object.h>
#include <string.h>
#include "simdefs.h"

#define MAXDETECT    16

class Platform;

class Detection
{
public:
    Detection() : p(NULL), t_detect(0) {}

    Detection(Platform *_p, SimTime t) :
        p(_p), t_detect(t) {}

    void platform(Platform *_p) { p = _p;}
    Platform* platform() { return p;}

    float range() { return r;}
    void range(float _r) { r = _r;}

private:
    Platform    *p;
    float       r;          // Range to this platform
    SimTime     t_detect;   // Tick count at detection

    enum { DetectionClass = __firstUserClass + DETECTION};
};
```

continues

Listing 9.25. continued

```
class Sensor : public Object
{
friend Scenario;
friend Platform;
public:
    Sensor(char *_nm, Platform *p) : parent(p), ndetect(0)
    {
        if(_nm != NULL)
        {
            _name = new char[strlen(_nm) + 1];
            strcpy(_name, _nm);
        }
    }

    ~Sensor();

// The following functions are required because Sensor
// is derived from Object (the base class of Borland's
// container class library).

    classType isA() const { return SensorClass;}
    char* nameOf() const { return "SensorClass";}

    hashValueType hashValue() const
    { return (hashValueType)(1);}

    int isEqual(const Object _FAR& ob) const
    { return 0;}

    void printOn(ostream& os) const
    {
        os << *_name << endl;
    }

    void init();
    char *name() { return _name;}
    void numdetect(short n) { ndetect = n;}
    short numdetect() { return ndetect;}
    void reset_detections() { ndetect = 0;}
    Detection* detections() { return detection;}

    short detect(float r, short type, short size, Platform *p);

protected:
    Platform   *parent;   // Platform where sensor resides
    char       *_name;    // Sensor's name
```

BLOCKADE—A Game of Modern Naval Simulation

```
    short       can_detect[2];
    float       range[3]; // Range at which sensor detects small,
                          // medium and large platforms
    short       type;     // Is this is a radar or ESM sensor?
    Detection   detection[MAXDETECT];
    short       ndetect;

    enum { SensorClass = __firstUserClass + SENSOR};
};

#endif
```

Listing 9.26 shows the file sensor.cpp that implements the member functions of the Sensor class. The init function is responsible for initializing a Sensor. The Platform::init function creates a Sensor with a specific name and then calls its init function. The Sensor::init function opens a database file, SENSOR.DAT, searches for the sensor by name and, if found, initializes the Sensor's member variables.

The detect function is another important member function of Sensor. When the detect function is called with the range to a Platform and the Platform's type and size, the function first checks whether the Sensor can detect that Platform. If the Platform is detectable, the detect function adds that Platform to its detection list.

Listing 9.26. sensor.cpp—Implementation of the Sensor class.

```
//-----------------------------------------------------------
// File: sensor.cpp
//
// Implementation of the sensor class.
//-----------------------------------------------------------
#include <fstream.h>
#include <stdlib.h>
#include <string.h>
#include "platform.h"

#define LINES_PER_SENSOR  3

static char *whitespace = " \t";
//-----------------------------------------------------------
```

continues

Listing 9.26. continued

```
// ~Sensor

Sensor::~Sensor()
{
    if(_name != NULL) delete _name;
}
//------------------------------------------------------------
// Sensor:: init
// Initialize a Sensor by reading from the SENSOR.DAT file

void Sensor::init()
{
    if(_name == NULL) return;

// Open the file SENSOR.DAT and read in Sensor data.
    ifstream ifs("SENSOR.DAT", ios::in);
    if(!ifs)
    {
// Error reading file.
        return;
    }

// Read and interpret the contents of the file
    char line[81];

// First line is a comment; ignore it.
    ifs.getline(line, sizeof(line));

// Second line has the number of Sensors in this file
    ifs.getline(line, sizeof(line));
    short numsensors = atoi(line);
    if(numsensors == 0) return;

// Search for this Sensor's data
    short i, j, len = strlen(_name);
    char *token;
    for(i = 0; i < numsensors; i++)
    {
// Ignore the first line (it's used as a separator)
        ifs.getline(line, sizeof(line));

// Next line should have the sensor's name
        ifs.getline(line, sizeof(line));
        if(strnicmp(line, _name, len) != 0)
        {
// Skip the data for this Sensor
            for(j = 0; j < LINES_PER_SENSOR; j++)
```

BLOCKADE—A Game of Modern Naval Simulation

```cpp
            ifs.getline(line, sizeof(line));
        }
        else
        {
// Yes, the name matches. Read in data.

// Sensor type (RADAR, ESM, or BOTH)
            type = RADAR;
            ifs.getline(line, sizeof(line));
            token = strtok(line, whitespace);
            if(strnicmp(token, "RADAR", 5) == 0) type = RADAR;
            if(strnicmp(token, "ESM", 3) == 0)   type = ESM;
            if(strnicmp(token, "BOTH", 4) == 0)
                                                 type = RADAR+ESM;

// What type of platforms does sensor detect (SURFACE, AIR, or BOTH)
            can_detect[SURFACE] = 0;
            can_detect[AIR] = 0;
            ifs.getline(line, sizeof(line));
            token = strtok(line, whitespace);
            if(strnicmp(token, "SURFACE", 7) == 0)
                                    can_detect[SURFACE] = 1;
            if(strnicmp(token, "AIR", 3) == 0) type = 1;
                                    can_detect[AIR] = 1;
            if(strnicmp(token, "BOTH", 4) == 0)
            {
                can_detect[SURFACE] = 1;
                can_detect[AIR] = 1;
            }

// Next line has detection ranges (for SMALL, MEDIUM, and LARGE
// targets)
            ifs.getline(line, sizeof(line));
            token = strtok(line, whitespace);
            range[SMALL] = atof(token);

            token = strtok(NULL, whitespace);
            range[MEDIUM] = atof(token);

            token = strtok(NULL, whitespace);
            range[LARGE] = atof(token);
        }
    }
}
//---------------------------------------------------------------
// Sensor:: d e t e c t
// See if sensor can detect specified platform
```

continues

Listing 9.26. continued

```
short Sensor::detect(float r, short type, short size,
                     Platform *p)
{
    if(p->is_active() && can_detect[type] && r < range[size])
    {
        if(ndetect < MAXDETECT - 1)
        {
            detection[ndetect].platform(p);
            detection[ndetect].range(r);
            ndetect++;
            return 1;
        }
    }
    else return 0;
}
```

Weapon Class

Listing 9.27 shows the header file weapon.h with declaration of the Weapon class. A Weapon is characterized by the following member variables:

- Platform *parent; is the Platform on which the Weapon is located.
- short strength[2]; are the kill strengths against SURFACE and AIR targets.
- short numengage[2]; are the number of SURFACE and AIR targets that this Weapon can engage simultaneously.
- float range[2]; are the ranges (in nautical miles) at which the Weapon can engage SURFACE and AIR targets.
- float prob_hit[2]; are the probabilities of hitting SURFACE and AIR targets.
- short count; is the number of times the weapon can be engaged.
- short nsector; is the number of sectors where the weapon can engage.
- Sector *sectors; is the array of sectors where the weapon can engage.
- char *pname; is the name of the platform representing ammunition shot by this Weapon. This platform is created and displayed when the Weapon is used.

BLOCKADE—A Game of Modern Naval Simulation

Chapter 9

- `short tracks;` is a flag that indicates if the ammunition shot from the `Weapon` can track a target.
- `Ammunition *ammo[2];` is an array of `Ammunition` structures (defined in Listing 9.27) that denote the ammunition shot by the `Weapon`.

Because the `Platform` class stores `Weapon` objects in an `Array`, a container class from the Borland Class Library, I had to derive the `Weapon` class from the `Object` class. As a consequence of deriving `Weapon` from `Object`, I had to define a number of additional member functions such as `isA`, `nameOf`, `hashValue`, `isEqual`, and `printOn`.

Listing 9.27. `weapon.h`—Declaration of the `Weapon` class.

```cpp
//--------------------------------------------------------------
// File: weapon.h
//
// Declaration of the Weapon classes.
//--------------------------------------------------------------
#if !defined(__WEAPON_H)
#define __WEAPON_H

#include <array.h>
#include "weapon.h"

class Platform;

class Ammunition
{
public:
friend Weapon;
    Ammunition() : p(NULL), t_launch(0), use(0),
        pt(NULL) {}
    ~Ammunition();

    void platform(Platform *_p) { p = _p;}
    Platform* platform() { return p;}
    void target_platform(Platform *_p) { pt = _p;}
    Platform* target_platform() { return pt;}

    float launch_lat() { return latl;}
    float launch_lng() { return lngl;}
    float launch_alt() { return altl;}
```

continues

Listing 9.27. continued

```cpp
        short in_use() { return use;}
        void in_use(short u) { use = u;}

private:
    Platform    *p;     // Platform representing the ammo
    SimTime     t_launch; // Tick count at launch
    short       use;    // TRUE => this ammo is in use
    Platform    *pt;    // Targeted platform (or NULL)
    float       latl;   // Latitude and longitude of the
    float       lngl;   // launch position
    float       altl;   // Launch height (in feet)
                        // = 0 for launches from ships
    float       latt;   // Latitude and longitude of
    float       lngt;   // targeted point
};

class Weapon : public Object
{
friend Scenario;
friend Platform;
public:
    Weapon(char *_nm, Platform *p) :sectors(NULL),
            pname(NULL), parent(p)
    {
        if(_nm != NULL)
        {
            _name = new char[strlen(_nm) + 1];
            strcpy(_name, _nm);
        }
        ammo[SURFACE] = NULL;
        ammo[AIR] = NULL;
    }

    ~Weapon();

// The following functions are required because Weapon
// is derived from Object (the base class of Borland's
// container class library).

    classType isA() const { return WeaponClass;}

    char* nameOf() const { return "WeaponClass";}

    hashValueType hashValue() const
    { return (hashValueType)(1);}

    int isEqual(const Object _FAR& ob) const
    { return 0;}
```

BLOCKADE—A Game of Modern Naval Simulation

Chapter 9

```cpp
    void printOn(ostream& os) const
    {
        os << _name << endl;
    }

    void init();
    short engage(Platform *pt, short type, float r, float b);
    void continue_engagements();

    char *name() { return _name;}
    char *platform_name() { return pname;}
    short numsector() { return nsector;}
    Sector* sector(short i) { return &sectors[i];}
    short engage_count(short type) { return numengage[type];}
    Ammunition *ammunition(short type)
    {
        if(ammo != NULL) return ammo[type];
        else return NULL;
    }
    Ammunition *ammunition(short type, short index)
    {
        if(ammo != NULL) return &(ammo[type][index]);
        else return NULL;
    }
    short can_track() { return tracks;}
    short ammo_left() { return count;}
    float range_against_surface() { return range[SURFACE];}
    float range_against_air() { return range[AIR];}

protected:
    Platform *parent;     // Platform where weapon resides
    char     *_name;      // Weapon's name
    short    strength[2]; // Kill strength against air and surface
    short    numengage[2];// How many targets at a time?
    float    range[2];    // Range at which weapon can engage
    float    prob_hit[2]; // Probability of hitting (air, surface)
    short    count;       // Ammunition count
    short    nsector;     // Sectors where the weapon can
    Sector   *sectors;    // engage targets
    char     *pname;      // Name of platform representing ammo
    short    tracks;      // TRUE = can track target
    Ammunition *ammo[2];

    enum { WeaponClass = __firstUserClass + WEAPON};
};

#endif
```

Listing 9.28 shows the file weapon.cpp with an implementation of the Weapon class. As with the Sensor class, the Platform::init function calls Weapon::init to read the database file WEAPON.DAT and initialize the Weapon.

The engage function takes care of initiating engagements, which is a euphemism that means shooting at a target. The engage function has to be called with a target Platform as well as the target's type (SURFACE or AIR), range, and bearing to the target. If the engage function determines that the Weapon is capable of attacking the target, it activates an Ammunition object, which, in turn, activates a Platform representing the Ammunition.

As the attack continues, the Scenario::update function calls the continue_engagements function to see when to terminate the engagement. As you can see from Listing 9.28, the continue_engagements function applies several tests to determine if an ammunition round has hit its target. When the ammunition hits the target, the target Platform's hit function is called and the ammunition is deactivated.

Listing 9.28. weapon.cpp—Implementation of the Weapon class.

```
//------------------------------------------------------------
// File: weapon.cpp
//
// Implementation of the Weapon class.
//------------------------------------------------------------
#include <stdlib.h>
#include <fstream.h>
#include <string.h>
#include "scenario.h"

#define LINES_PER_WEAPON   4

static char *whitespace = " \t";
//------------------------------------------------------------
// ~ A m m u n i t i o n
Ammunition::~Ammunition()
{
    if(p != NULL) delete p;
}
//------------------------------------------------------------
// ~ W e a p o n

Weapon::~Weapon()
{
```

BLOCKADE—A Game of Modern Naval Simulation

```
        if(sectors != NULL) delete sectors;
        if(_name != NULL) delete _name;
        if(pname != NULL) delete pname;
        if(ammo[SURFACE] != NULL) delete ammo[SURFACE];
        if(ammo[AIR] != NULL) delete ammo[AIR];
}
//-------------------------------------------------------------
// Weapon:: i n i t
// Initialize a weapon by reading from the WEAPON.DAT file

void Weapon::init()
{
    if(_name == NULL) return;

// Open the file weapon.DAT and read in weapon data.
    ifstream ifs("weapon.dat", ios::in);
    if(!ifs)
    {
// Error reading file.
        return;
    }

// Read and interpret the contents of the file
    char line[81];

// First line is a comment; ignore it.
    ifs.getline(line, sizeof(line));

// Second line has the number of weapons in this file
    ifs.getline(line, sizeof(line));
    short numweapons = atoi(line);
    if(numweapons == 0) return;

// Search for this weapon's data
    short i, j, len = strlen(_name);
    char *token;
    for(i = 0; i < numweapons; i++)
    {
// Skip first line of each weapon record
        ifs.getline(line, sizeof(line));

// Next line has weapon's name
        ifs.getline(line, sizeof(line));
        if(strnicmp(line, _name, len) != 0)
        {
// Skip the data for this weapon
            for(j = 0; j < LINES_PER_WEAPON; j++)
```

continues

Listing 9.28. continued

```cpp
            ifs.getline(line, sizeof(line));
        }
        else
        {
// Yes, the name matches. Read in data.

// First the name of platform representing the ammunition
            tracks = 1;
            ifs.getline(line, sizeof(line));
            token = strtok(line, whitespace);
            short len = strlen(token);
            pname = new char[len + 1];
            strcpy(pname, token);

// Range at which weapon can hit SURFACE and AIR targets
            range[SURFACE] = 0;
            range[AIR] = 0;
            ifs.getline(line, sizeof(line));
            token = strtok(line, whitespace);
            range[SURFACE] = atof(token);

            token = strtok(NULL, whitespace);
            range[AIR] = atof(token);

// Probability of hitting SURFACE and AIR targets
            prob_hit[SURFACE] = 0;
            prob_hit[AIR] = 0;
            ifs.getline(line, sizeof(line));
            token = strtok(line, whitespace);
            prob_hit[SURFACE] = atof(token);

            token = strtok(NULL, whitespace);
            prob_hit[AIR] = atof(token);

// Kill strength against SURFACE and AIR targets
            strength[SURFACE] = 0;
            strength[AIR] = 0;
            ifs.getline(line, sizeof(line));
            token = strtok(line, whitespace);
            strength[SURFACE] = atoi(token);

            token = strtok(NULL, whitespace);
            strength[AIR] = atoi(token);
        }
    }
}
```

Chapter 9

BLOCKADE—A Game of Modern Naval Simulation

```cpp
//-------------------------------------------------------------
// Weapon:: e n g a g e
// Start shooting at the designated target

short Weapon::engage(Platform *pt, short type, float r, float b)
{
// If weapon does not have any more ammo, return immediately.
    if(count <= 0) return 0;

// If the weapon can fire in this sector and if there is
// ammunition available, go ahead and release the ammunition
// rounds (these are platforms that fly toward the target)
    short i;
    for(i = 0; i < nsector; i++)
    {
        if(sectors[i].contains(b)) break;
    }
    if(i == nsector) return 0;

// Bearing looks good. Check other conditions.
    if(type != SURFACE && type != AIR) return 0;
    if(numengage[type] <= 0) return 0;
    if(r > range[type]) return 0;

// Use any "engageable" ammo
    for(i = 0; i < numengage[type]; i++)
    {
        if((ammo[type] != NULL) &&
            !ammo[type][i].in_use())
        {
            count--;
            ammo[type][i].in_use(1);
            ammo[type][i].pt = pt;
            Platform *p = ammo[type][i].platform();
            p->latitude(parent->latitude());
            p->longitude(parent->longitude());
            p->altitude(parent->altitude());
            ammo[type][i].latl = p->latitude();
            ammo[type][i].lngl = p->longitude();
            ammo[type][i].altl = p->altitude();
// Compute lat-long of targeted point
            b += parent->heading();
            b = fmod(b, 360);
            float hdgrad = b * DEG_TO_RAD;
            float coshdg = cos(hdgrad);
            float sinhdg = sin(hdgrad);
            ammo[type][i].latt = parent->latitude() +
                                    r*coshdg*NM2DEG;
```

continues

Listing 9.28. continued

```
                ammo[type][i].lngt = parent->longitude() +
                                r*sinhdg*NM2DEG;
                p->heading(b);
// Make sure motion updates occur more often
                p->motion_update_count(0);
// Make the platform (representing the round) active
                p->active();
                p->show_sprite();
                Scenario::weapons_engaged++;
                return 1;
            }
        }
    return 0;
}
//---------------------------------------------------------------
// Weapon:: c o n t i n u e _ e n g a g e m e n t s
// Check any ammo rounds in flight to see if:
//     1. range has exceeded weapon's limits
//     2. ammo hits a platform (determined by a random draw)

void Weapon::continue_engagements()
{
    short i, j;
// Check all ammunitions in flight against any target
    for(i = SURFACE; i <= AIR; i++)
    {
        if(numengage[i] > 0)
        {
            for(j = 0; j < numengage[i]; j++)
            {
                short done = 0;
                if(ammo[i] == NULL) continue;
                if(!ammo[i][j].in_use())continue;
                if(!ammo[i][j].p->is_active())
                {
                    ammo[i][j].in_use(0);
                    Scenario::weapons_engaged--;
                    continue;
                }

// If a platform was targeted, set heading toward the current
// location of that platform
                float destlat = ammo[i][j].latt;
                float destlng = ammo[i][j].lngt;

                if(can_track() && ammo[i][j].pt != NULL)
                {
```

BLOCKADE—A Game of Modern Naval Simulation

```
                destlat = ammo[i][j].pt->latitude();
                destlng = ammo[i][j].pt->longitude();
                float latdel = destlat -
                        ammo[i][j].p->latitude();
                float lngdel = destlng -
                        ammo[i][j].p->longitude();
                float hdg;
                if(lngdel == 0 && latdel == 0)
                    hdg = 0;
                else
                    hdg = atan2(lngdel, latdel) *
                                        RAD_TO_DEG;
                if(hdg < 0) hdg = 360 + hdg;
                ammo[i][j].p->heading(hdg);
            }

// Compute distance between current position of ammo and the
// launch position in nautical miles
                float xdel = ammo[i][j].platform()->longitude() -
                        ammo[i][j].launch_lng();
                float ydel = ammo[i][j].platform()->latitude() -
                        ammo[i][j].launch_lat();
// Note: I am ignoring altitude when computing distance
                float rl = sqrt(xdel*xdel+ydel*ydel) * DEG2NM;

// Find the distance from ammo round to targeted point
                xdel = ammo[i][j].platform()->longitude() -
                        destlng;
                ydel = ammo[i][j].platform()->latitude() -
                        destlat;
// Note: Again, I am ignoring altitude
                float rt = sqrt(xdel*xdel+ydel*ydel) * DEG2NM;

                if(rl > range[i])
                {
// printf("Range %f > %f\n", rl, range[i]);
                    done = 1;
                }
                else
                {
                    if(rt < WPN_TOLERANCE)
                    {
// Draw a random number to determine if the ammo hits the target
                        if(Scenario::random_draw(prob_hit[i]))
                        {
// A successful hit has occurred. Deduct strength from target
// platform. Scenario checks if strength is too low for
// the platform to survive.
```

continues

Listing 9.28. continued

```
                                if(ammo[i][j].pt != NULL)
                                {
                                    ammo[i][j].pt->hit(strength[i]);
                                }
                                done = 1;
// printf("Ammo hit platform %s with prob: %f\n",
// ammo[i][j].pt->name(), prob_hit[i]);
                            }
                            else
                            {
                                done = 1;
// printf("Ammo missed platform %s\n", ammo[i][j].pt->name());
                            }
                        }
                    }
// Reset the variables of this ammo round
                    if(done)
                    {
                        ammo[i][j].pt = NULL;
                        ammo[i][j].p->hide_sprite();
                        ammo[i][j].p->inactive();
                        ammo[i][j].p->goto_stage0();
                        ammo[i][j].in_use(0);
                        Scenario::weapons_engaged--;
                        Scenario::refresh = 1;
// printf("Ammo: %s done\n", ammo[i][j].p->name());
                    }
                }
            }
        }
    }
}
```

Other Files

There are a host of other files needed to build BLOCKADE. You can find all necessary files in the CH09 directory on the companion disk. The last remaining header file, `blkdres.h`, is shown in Listing 9.29. It defines the resource identifiers for the BLOCKADE game.

BLOCKADE—A Game of Modern Naval Simulation

**Listing 9.29. blkdres.h—
Resource identifiers for BLOCKADE.**

```
//-------------------------------------------------------------
// File: blkdres.h
// Resource identifiers for the BLOCKADE game.
//-------------------------------------------------------------
#if !defined(__BLKDRES_H)
#define __BLKDRES_H

#include <owlrc.h>    // For definitions of OWL IDs

#define IDM_HELP    200
#define IDM_ABOUT   201

#endif
```

As I mentioned earlier, BLOCKADE uses a number of text files to set up the scenario that is simulated in the game. Here is a list of the pertinent data files:

- BLOCKADE.CFG is read at the beginning. This file lists all scenarios available for the game. Listing 9.30 shows a sample BLOCKADE.CFG file with a single scenario.

- Scenario files are listed in BLOCKADE.CFG. For instance, in the BLOCKADE.CFG file shown in Listing 9.30, the scenario definition file is PG.BSN. Listing 9.31 shows this scenario file.

- Mission files are listed in the scenario file. For instance, in the scenario file named PG.BSN, shown in Listing 9.31, the mission definition file is CARGO.MSN. Listing 9.32 shows this mission file.

- PLATFORM.DAT is the database file with information on all available platforms. Listing 9.33 shows a typical PLATFORM.DAT file.

- SENSOR.DAT is the database file with information on all available sensors. Listing 9.34 shows a typical SENSOR.DAT file.

- WEAPON.DAT is the database file with information on all available weapons. Listing 9.35 shows a typical WEAPON.DAT file.

- *.BMP files are the bitmap image files.

- *.SHP files are the 3-D shape files (described in Chapter 8).

- *.S3D files are the 3-D scene files (described in Chapter 8).

483

Listing 9.30. `BLOCKADE.CFG`— A typical configuration file for BLOCKADE.

```
BLOCKADE.CFG
1                       The version number
1                       Number of scenarios in file
//////////////////////////////////////////////////////////////
Persian Gulf
pg.bsn                  Scenario definition file
map1c.bmp               Name of normal map image
s_map1c.bmp             Name of "zoomed" map image
2                       Map zoomed in by this factor
165 144                 Pixels per degree of latitude and longitude
30.5 47.1               Lat-Long of left corner of map (in degrees)
//////////////////////////////////////////////////////////////
XXXX                    Next scenario starts here
```

Listing 9.31. `PG.BSN`—A sample scenario file for BLOCKADE.

```
BLOCKADE.BSN
1                       The version number
1.8                     The basic time period for updating positions
10                      Number of rectangles that define the valid sea
85   85  340 221        Pixel coordinates of valid rectangles
175  69  241  84
289  76  335  84
340 117  352 155
340 155  368 205
368 191  395 233
90  221  348 288
347 233  400 288
44  176   84 215
115 290  421 425
1                       Number of missions in file
Dangerous cargo
spruance.s3d            The 3D scene definition file
none                    Background image for 3D display
cargo.msn
```

BLOCKADE—A Game of Modern Naval Simulation

Listing 9.32. `CARGO.MSN`— A sample mission file for BLOCKADE.

```
BLOCKADE.MSN
1                  The version number
16                 Number of lines in mission description
You are commanding a Spruance
class destroyer in the Persian
Gulf. Your mission is to stop
a freighter from reaching its
destination in Iraq.

The freighter was last reported
proceeding along the eastern
shores of the gulf steaming north-
north-west.

Use your radars to locate the
freighter and stop it. Watch out
for patrol boats and enemy aircraft.
Launch weapons from the Polar
display.
4                  Number of platforms
//////////////////////////////////////////////////////////////
SPRUANCE           Ship class (this is player's ship)
ACTIVE
300 340 0          Position (longitude-latitude (in pixels)-altitude)
25 30 0            Speed (knots) and bearing with respect to north
1
10
152 235
170 263
185 282
211 305
238 319
277 334
317 340
357 342
387 339
416 330
//////////////////////////////////////////////////////////////
FREIGHTER          Second ship is the one trying to go through blockade
ACTIVE
395 203 0
20 0 0
4                  Number of stages (of motion)
3                  Point at first stage
```

continues

Listing 9.32. continued

```
389 249
396 203
389 219
3
323 133
332 125
332 114
3
219 113
221 91
221 80
3
90  90
93  83
85  99
//////////////////////////////////////////////////////////////
COMBATTANTE    Third and following platforms are the enemy.
ACTIVE
395 253 0
35 0 0
4              Number of stages (of motion)
4              Point at first stage
397 252
397 242
395 219
391 206
3
282 296
380 312
278 272
3
263 184
292 178
321 172
3
380 187
384 194
388 206
//////////////////////////////////////////////////////////////
MIRAGE
ACTIVE
200 50  2000
1000 180 0
4              Number of stages (of motion)
7              Point at first stage
198 52
```

BLOCKADE—A Game of Modern Naval Simulation

```
237 51
281 53
326 51
366 51
411 50
18  55
5
125 101
99  170
102 236
111 225
114 277
4
216 440
269 440
318 435
365 435
4
413 306
413 273
396 246
391 202
///////////////////////////////////////////////////////////
```

Listing 9.33. PLATFORM.DAT—The platform database file.

```
Platform Data File
6
///////////////////////////////////////////////////////////
SPRUANCE
SURFACE         Type of platform: SURFACE or AIR
LARGE           Platform size as a radar target
ship.bmp        Name of image file
shipm.bmp       Name of image mask
ship2.bmp       Image and mask for
ship2m.bmp      the map window
500             Survival strength
33              Maximum speed in knots
4               Number of sensors
SPS-40
SPS-55
SPQ-9
MK23-TAS
4               Number of weapons
```

continues

Listing 9.33. continued

```
5"-GUN
150             How many times can you use it?
2 2             Simultaneous Surface/Air targets
1               Number of sectors that the weapon covers
0 360           Description of sector
PHALANX
10
1 1
2
0 120
180 360
SEA-SPARROW
8
1 1
1
30 330
HARPOON
8
2 0
1
0 360
/////////////////////////////////////////////////////////
FREIGHTER       A generic cargo carrier
SURFACE
LARGE
ship.bmp        Image and mask for
shipm.bmp       the polar window
ship2.bmp       Image and mask for
ship2m.bmp      the map window
800             Survival strength
22
1               Sensors
NAV-RADAR
0               Weapons
/////////////////////////////////////////////////////////
GUN-ROUND
AIR
SMALL
gunr.bmp        Image and mask for
gunrm.bmp       the polar window
gunr.bmp        Image and mask for
gunrm.bmp       the map window
30              Survival strength
400
0               Sensors
0               Weapons
```

BLOCKADE—A Game of Modern Naval Simulation

```
//////////////////////////////////////////////////////
MISSILE
AIR
SMALL
missile.bmp             Image and mask for
missilem.bmp            the polar window
missile.bmp             Image and mask for
missilem.bmp            the map window
100                     Survival strength
600                     Maximum speed in knots
0                       Sensors
0                       Weapons
//////////////////////////////////////////////////////
COMBATTANTE
SURFACE                 Type of platform: SURFACE or AIR
LARGE                   Platform size as a radar target
ship.bmp                Name of image file
shipm.bmp               Name of image mask
ship2.bmp               Image and mask for
ship2m.bmp              the map window
170                     Survival strength
38                      Maximum speed in knots
1                       Number of sensors
DECCA
3                       Number of weapons
76MM-GUN
120                     How many times can you use it?
1 1                     Simultaneous Surface/Air targets
2                       Number of sectors that the weapon covers
0 150                   Description of sector
210 360
40MM-GUN
120
1 1
1
30 330
HARPOON
2
2 0
2
0 90
270 360
//////////////////////////////////////////////////////
MIRAGE
AIR                     Type of platform: SURFACE or AIR
MEDIUM                  Platform size as a radar target
airp.bmp                Name of image file
airpm.bmp               Name of image mask
```

continues

Listing 9.33. continued

```
airp.bmp      Image and mask for
airpm.bmp     the map window
60            Survival strength
1100          Maximum speed in knots
1             Number of sensors
CYRANO-IV
1             Number of weapons
EXOCET
2             How many times can you use it?
2 0           Simultaneous Surface/Air targets
1             Number of sectors that the weapon covers
0 360         Description of sector
```

Listing 9.34. `SENSOR.DAT`—The sensor database file.

```
Sensor Data File
7             Number of sensors defined in this file
//////////////////////////////////////////////////////////
SPS-40        Name of sensor
RADAR         Type of sensor (RADAR, ESM, or BOTH)
AIR           Detects AIR, SURFACE or BOTH types of platforms
60 120 180    Detection range for SMALL, MEDIUM, and LARGE targets
//////////////////////////////////////////////////////////
SPS-55
RADAR
SURFACE
12 24 36
//////////////////////////////////////////////////////////
SPQ-9
RADAR
SURFACE
6 12 18
//////////////////////////////////////////////////////////
MK23-TAS      A target acquisition system
BOTH          This is a combined radar+ESM system
BOTH          Can detect both surface and air targets
30 60 90
//////////////////////////////////////////////////////////
NAV-RADAR
RADAR
BOTH
10 20 30
```

BLOCKADE—A Game of Modern Naval Simulation

```
//////////////////////////////////////////////////////////
DECCA
RADAR
SURFACE
16 32 48
//////////////////////////////////////////////////////////
CYRANO-IV
RADAR
BOTH
10 20 30
```

Listing 9.35. WEAPON.DAT—The weapon database file.

```
Weapons data file    (Naba, 2/1/93)
7           Number of weapons defined in this file
//////////////////////////////////////////////////////////
5"-gun      Name
GUN-ROUND   Platform representing ammunition
10 5        Range at which it can engage surface and air targets
0.6 0.4     Probablity of hitting surface and air targets
33 9999     Kill strength against surface and air targets
//////////////////////////////////////////////////////////
Phalanx     Anti-air gun
GUN-ROUND
4 4
0.2 0.8
16 9999
//////////////////////////////////////////////////////////
Sea-Sparrow Missile
MISSILE
8 8
0.5 0.6
16 9999
//////////////////////////////////////////////////////////
Harpoon     Missile
MISSILE
80 0
0.8 0
165 0
//////////////////////////////////////////////////////////
Exocet      Missile
MISSILE
35 0
0.7 0
```

continues

Listing 9.35. continued

```
100 0
//////////////////////////////////////////////////////////////
76mm-Gun   Gun
GUN-ROUND
4 3
0.4 0.4
30 9999
//////////////////////////////////////////////////////////////
40mm-Gun   Gun
GUN-ROUND
2 1
0.4 0.1
16 9999
//////////////////////////////////////////////////////////////
```

Building BLOCKADE

You need Borland C++ for Windows to build BLOCKADE. The companion disk has all the files needed to build the executable, BLOCKADE.EXE. In particular, the project file, BLOCKADE.PRJ, lists the source files and library necessary to build the application. There are a few items in the project file that reflect the name of the drive and directory where I installed Borland C++ in my system. Unfortunately, I installed the compiler on a different drive and under a different directory name than the one Borland recommends (C:\BORLANDC). So, all of you who like to go with the defaults, have to make some changes to the project file.

Here are the changes you have to make before using the project file in your system:

1. Run Borland C++ for Windows and open the project file BLOCKADE.PRJ by selecting Open Project... from the Project menu.

2. In the list of items shown in the project window, you will see bwcc.lib listed with a specific drive and directory name. Click on that line and get rid of the line by selecting Delete Item... from the Project Menu.

3. Next select Add Item... from the Project Menu. In the file selection dialog box that appears, go to the directory where you have installed

Chapter 9

BLOCKADE—A Game of Modern Naval Simulation

Borland C++ and select the file `bwcc.lib` (it is in the LIB subdirectory). Click on the Add button to add the library to the project. Click on Done to close the dialog box.

4. Select the Directories item from the Option menu in Borland C++ for Windows. Edit the pathnames to reflect the drive and directory names where you have installed Borland C++.

After making these changes, you should be able to build `BLOCKADE.EXE` by selecting Make from the Compile menu. Once the program is successfully built, you can install its icon under Windows Program Manager by selecting New... from the Program Manager's File menu.

Another file that you need to build a Windows program is a resource file. For the BLOCKADE program, the resource file `BLOCKADE.RES` is included in the companion disk. I prepared the resource file using the Resource Workshop program included with Borland C++.

Summary

This chapter uses much of the classes presented in the previous chapters and adds a framework for a naval scenario to create a modern naval simulation game named BLOCKADE. The theme of the game is that a lone modern combat ship is called upon to enforce a hastily imposed blockade in a troubled region of the world. As a commander of the combat ship, the player has to stop a cargo ship that is trying to break through the blockade. The player relies on the ship's sensors to detect the cargo ship as well as any other enemy ships and aircraft in the region. If any enemy ship or aircraft comes close to the combat ship, the player can use the ship's weapons to attack the enemy. Each enemy ship or aircraft hit by the player earns points that add up to a total score for the game.

The game's source code with all necessary files appears on this book's companion disk.

Index

Symbols

2-D Cartesian coordinate system, 276
2-D graphics, 16-20
3-D Cartesian coordinate system, 276-277
3-D graphics, 16-20
    2-D Cartesian coordinate system, 276
    3-D Cartesian coordinate system, 276-277
    classes, 286-314
        Facet3D, 287-301
        Scene3D, 301-311
        Shape3D, 287-301
        Vector3D, 286-301
    coordinate transformations, 280-282
    defining 3-D scene, 301-311

loading 3-D scene, 311-313
modeling objects, 276-284
objects
    boundary representation, 277-278
    constructing, 278-280
    rotating, 282-283
    scaling, 281
    translating, 281-282
vector operations, 283-284
viewing 3-D scenes, 284-286, 313-314
3-D view (BLOCKADE), 322, 381-385

A

`About` function, 30-32
abstract base classes
    `Image`, 100-101, 105-112
    `Object`, 41
    `TControl`, 52
Abstract Data Type (ADT), 48-49
`AbstractArray` container class, 42
`active` function, 389
adapters, video, 18-19
    colors, displaying, 81
    super VGA, 19
ADT (Abstract Data Type), 48-49
adventure and role playing games, 6-7
aligning text, 33, 78-79
ANIMATE application, 178-187
    animation strategy, 181-185
    `AnimationWindow` class, 178-185
    building, 187
    defining sprites, 181
    initializing animation, 181
    main program, 186-187
    resource identifiers, 180
`animate` function, 165
`animate.cpp` source file, 186-187
`ANIMATE.RES` resource file, 187
`AnimatePalette` GDI function, 84
animation (sprites), 150-151
    ANIMATE application, 178-187
    erase-and-redraw animation, 150-151
    initializing, 158-161
    offscreen bitmap animation, 151
    overlapping, 166-177
    `Sprite` class, 152-161
    `SpriteAnimation` class, 162-177
    SPUZZLE game, 220-231
    updating sprites, 165-166
`AnimationWindow` class, 178-185
`animres.h` header file, 180
`animwin.cpp` source file, 182-185
`animwin.h` header file, 179-180
API functions, *see* GDI functions
application framework, 23
application layer (MVC architecture), 24
applications
    ANIMATE, 178-187
        animation strategy, 181-185
        building, 187
        defining sprites, 181
        initializing animation, 181
        main program, 186-187
        resource identifiers, 180
    ImageView, 136-146
        building, 145-146
        main source file, 137-138
        resource identifiers, 140-141
        starting, 136
    linking files, 35-39

Arc GDI function, 70
arcade games, 6
architecture, MVC (Model-View-Controller), 24-40
Array container class, 42
arrays, 48-49
Association container class, 42
attributes, graphics, 33
    setting up, 63-64
auto_engage_weapon function, 434

B

Bag container class, 42
bags, 48-49
BaseDate simple class, 43
BaseTime simple class, 43
BeginPaint GDI function, 62
bframe.cpp source file, 338-353
bframe.h header file, 333-337
BIDS classes, 40, 46-49
BitBlt GDI function, 89
Bitmap graphics object, 63
BITMAP structure, 92
BITMAPFILEHEADER structure, 113
BITMAPINFOHEADER structure, 101
bitmaps, 17, 58, 86-93
    BITMAP structure, 92
    copying, 89
    DDB (Device Dependent Bitmap) format, 86-92
        converting from DIB format, 106-107
    deleting, 88
    DIB (Device Independent Bitmap) format, 86, 92-93
        converting to DDB format, 106-107
    displaying, 87-88
    drawing on, 89-90
    ROP (raster operation) codes, 90-91
    shrinking, 89
    stretching, 89
blkdres.h header file, 483
BLOCKADE game
    building, 492-493
    child windows
        initializing, 333-353
        sizing, 337
        updating, 338
    classes
        BlockadeApp, 331-333
        BlockadeFrame, 326, 333-353
        InfoWindow, 326, 410-427
        LogoWindow, 353-354
        MapToolWindow, 327, 391-395
        MapWindow, 327, 360-369
        Platform, 450-466
        PolarToolWindow, 327, 370, 395-398
        PolarWindow, 327, 370-381
        Scenario, 427-446
        Sensor, 466-472
        StatusWindow, 326, 402-411
        ToolWindow, 386-402
        View3DToolWindow, 327, 381, 399-402
        View3DWindow, 327, 381-385
        Weapons, 472-482
    controls, 411
        bitmap icons, 391-402
    designing, 325-327
    game definition files, 327
    header files, 328-329
    high scores dialog box, 338-353
    member variables, 435-446

missions, 320
  database file, 485-487
  loading, 337-338
overview, 318-319
platforms, 320, 427-446, 450-466
  database file, 487-490
  hits, 456
  initializing, 456
  moving, 456
  selecting, 324
resource identifiers, 482-483
scenarios, 320
  loading, 337-338
  macros, 431-433
  simulating, 326, 434
  viewing, 326-327
screen components, 321
sensors, 320, 466-472
  database file, 490-491
simulation speed, 324-325
source files, 330-331
starting, 319-320
status messages, 402-411
views, 321-324
  3-D, 381-385
  map, 321-322, 360-369, 391-402
  polar, 370-381
weapons, 472-482
  database file, 491-492
  launching, 325
BLOCKADE.CFG configuration file, 327, 483-484
blockade.cpp source file, 331-333
BlockadeApp class, 331-333
BlockadeFrame class, 326, 333-353
BMP image file format, 99, 113-119
  reading, 114-118
  writing, 118-119

bmphdr member variable, 118
BMPImage class, 113-119
  header file, 113-114
  member functions, 115-118
bmpimage.h header file, 113-114
Borland International Data Structures, *see* BIDS classes
Borland Windows Custom Controls (BWCC), 52
boundaries (3-D graphics), 277-278
Brush graphics object, 63
BTree container class, 42
buffer swapping, 151
building
  ANIMATE application, 187
  BLOCKADE game, 492-493
  ImageView application, 145-146
  puzzles (SPUZZLE), 208
BWCC (Borland Windows Custom Controls), 52

C

CARGO.MSN mission file, 485-487
Carriers at War, 7
cel animation, 150
child windows
  animating (SPUZZLE), 220-231
  initializing
    BLOCKADE game, 333-353
    SUZZLE game, 216-232
  managing, 53
  sizing
    BLOCKADE game, 337
    SPUZZLE game, 219
  SPUZZLE game, 207
  updating (BLOCKADE), 338
Chord GDI function, 71

Index

class libraries, 40-53
  CLASSLIB, 41-46
    container classes, 41-43, 46-49
    iterator classes, 45-46
    simple classes, 43-44
  OWL, 50-53
    control classes, 52-53
    dialog classes, 50-52
    MDI (multiple document interface), 53
    window classes, 50
class templates, 40, 46-49
classes, 23-24
  3-D graphics, 286-314
    `Facet3D`, 287-301
    `Scene3D`, 301-311
    `Shape3D`, 287-301
    `Vector3D`, 286-301
  AnimationWindow, 178-185
  BIDS, 46-49
  BLOCKADE game
    `BlockadeApp`, 331-333
    `BlockadeFrame`, 326, 333-353
    `InfoWindow`, 326, 410-427
    `LogoWindow`, 353-354
    `MapToolWindow`, 327, 391-395
    `MapWindow`, 327, 360-369
    `Platform`, 450-466
    `PolarToolWindow`, 327, 370, 395-398
    `PolarWindow`, 327, 370-381
    `Scenario`, 427-446
    `Sensor`, 466-472
    `StatusWindow`, 326, 402-411
    `ToolWindow`, 386-402
    `View3DToolWindow`, 327, 381, 399-402
    `View3DWindow`, 327, 381-385
    `Weapons`, 472-482

container
  ADT (Abstract Data Type), 48-49
  CLASSLIB class library, 41-43, 46-49
  FDS (Fundamental Data Structure), 47-48
`HelloApp`, 27-29
`HelloModel`, 29-30
`HelloView`, 30-35
image files, 100-135
  `BMPImage`, 113-119
  `Image`, 105-112
  `ImageData`, 101-105
  `PCXImage`, 125-135
  `TGAImage`, 119-124
`ImageViewApp`, 136-138
`ImageViewFrame`, 139-145
`ImageViewWindow`, 139-145
iterator (CLASSLIB class library), 45-46
`Music`, 192-197
MVC (Model-View-Controller) architecture, 24-40
`Note`, 192-197
`Object`, 41
OWL (ObjectWindows Library)
  control, 52-53
  dialog, 50-52
  window, 50
simple (CLASSLIB class library), 43-44
sprite animation
  `Sprite`, 152-161
  `SpriteAnimation`, 162-177
SPUZZLE game
  `HiscoreDialog`, 267-270
  `LetterWindow`, 213, 245-252
  `PuzzleFrame`, 213-232

PuzzlePiece, 214
PuzzleWindow, 213, 232-245
responsibilities, assigning, 213
SpuzzleApp, 214-216
StatusWindow, 213, 259-265
ToolWindow, 213, 252-259
TMDIClient, 53
TMDIFrame, 53
TScroller, 53
TShouldDelete, 42
CLASSLIB class library, 41-46
  container classes, 41-43
    template-based, 46-49
  iterator classes, 45-46
  simple classes, 43-44
CLOSE.SPM file, 210
CloseChildren function, 53
closed figures, drawing, 70-72
Collection container class, 42
color, 18-19, 80-85
  logical palette, 81-85
  pixel, 96-97
  system palette, 81
color palette, 81
CombineRgn GDI function, 75
computer games, *see* games
Computer Gaming World magazine, 20
configuration files
  BLOCKADE.CFG, 327, 483-484
  HELLO.CFG, 35
  SPUZZLE.CFG, 210-211
container classes
  ADT (Abstract Data Type), 48-49
  CLASSLIB class library, 41-43
    template-based, 46-49
  FDS (Fundamental Data Structure), 47-48

Container container class, 42
containers
  accessing contents, 45-46
  ADT (Abstract Data Type), 48-49
continue_engagements function, 434, 476
control classes, 52-53
controls, 52-53
  BLOCKADE game, 411
  BWCC (Borland Windows Custom Controls), 52
coordinate systems
  2-D Cartesian coordinate system, 276
  3-D Cartesian coordinate system, 276-277
  GDI (Graphics Device Interface), 65-68
coordinate transformations, 280-282
copy protection, 17
copying bitmaps, 89
CopyRect GDI function, 73
CreateBrushIndirect GDI function, 72
CreateDIBPatternBrush GDI function, 72
CreateEllipticRgn GDI function, 74
CreateEllipticRgnIndirect GDI function, 74
CreateHatchBrush GDI function, 72
CreatePalette GDI function, 85
CreatePatternBrush GDI function, 72
CreatePolygonRgn GDI function, 74
CreatePolyPolygonRgn GDI function, 74

CreateRectRgn GDI function, 74
CreateRectRgnIndirect GDI function, 74
CreateRoundRectRgn GDI function, 74
CreateSolidBrush GDI function, 72
cross product of two vectors, 283
CUBE.SHP file, 312

D

data structures
   FDS (Fundamental Data Structure), 46-48
   SPUZZLE game, 265-266
Date simple class, 43
DC (device context), 59-65
   contents, 59-61
   device capabilities, 64-65
   for graphics output, 63-64
   getting, 61-62
   graphics objects, 63-64
   persistent, 62-63
   reverting, 63
   storing temporarily, 62
DDB (Device-Dependent Bitmap) format, 86-92
   BITMAP structure, 92
   converting from DIB format, 106-107
   displaying bitmaps, 87-88
   drawing on bitmaps, 89-90
   ROP (raster operation) codes, 90-91
   stretching bitmaps, 89
default values, device context, 59-61
DeleteObject GDI function, 64
deleting
   bitmaps, 88
   graphics objects, 64
Deque container class, 42
deques (double-ended queues), 48-49
detect function, 469
device context, *see* DC
dialog boxes, 50-52
dialog classes, 50-52
DIB (Device-Independent Bitmap) format, 86, 92-93
   converting to DDB format, 106-107
DIBtoDDB function, 105
Dictionary container class, 42
disp_mission function, 371
display adapters, *see* video adapters
displaying
   bitmaps, 87-88
   images, 105
   messages, 30-35
   SPUZZLE puzzle information, 213-214
   text, 77-80
   see also viewing
dispwin.cpp source file, 360
dispwin.h header file, 355-359
dithering, 72
DLLs (dynamic link libraries), MMSYSTEM, 191
dot product of two vectors, 283
DoubleList container class, 42
draw_shape function, 381
draw_wpncover function, 371
drawing
   closed figures, 70-72
   drawing mode, 76-77

ellipses, 71
lines, 69-70
on bitmaps, 89-90
points, 69
polygons, 71
rectangles, 70
regions, 74-75
drawing modes, 76-77
`DrawText` GDI function, 78
drivers, sound, 190-192

E

educational games, 5
    SPUZZLE, *see* SPUZZLE
`Ellipse` GDI function, 71
ellipses, drawing, 71
`EndPaint` GDI function, 62
engage function, 476
`EqualRect` GDI function, 73
`EqualRgn` GDI function, 75
`Error` simple class, 43

F

`Facet3D` class, 287-301
FDS (Fundamental Data Structure), 46-48
figures, closed, drawing, 70-72
files
    `CARGO.MSN`, 485-487
    `CLOSE.SPM`, 210
    configuration
        `BLOCKADE.CFG`, 327, 483-484
        `HELLO.CFG`, 35
        `SPUZZLE.CFG`, 210-211
    `CUBE.SHP`, 312

header
    `animres.h`, 180
    `animwin.h`, 179-180
    `bframe.h`, 333-337
    `blkdres.h`, 483
    BLOCKADE game, 328-329
    `bmpimage.h`, 113-114
    `dispwin.h`, 355-359
    `hellomdl.h`, 29-30
    `hellores.h`, 35, 38
    `hellovw.h`, 31-35
    `hscdial.h`, 267-269
    `image.h`, 102-105
    `imvwres.h`, 141-145
    `imvwwin.h`, 139-140
    `infowin.h`, 412-413
    linking, 35-39
    `logowin.h`, 354
    `ltrwin.h`, 245-246
    `pcximage.h`, 126-127
    `platform.h`, 451-455
    `pzlframe.h`, 216-218
    `pzlinfo.h`, 266
    `pzlwin.h`, 232-233
    `scenario.h`, 427-429
    `scene3d.h`, 302-304
    `scninfo.h`, 429-431
    `sensor.h`, 467-469
    `shape3d.h`, 287-293
    `simdefs.h`, 431-433
    `sounds.h`, 193-194
    `spanim.h`, 162-164
    `sprite.h`, 153-157
    `spzlres.h`, 271
    `statwin.h`, 259-260, 402-404
    `tgaimage.h`, 121
    `toolwin.h`, 253-254, 386-388
    `weapon.h`, 473-475

Index

hello.dlg, 36-39
HELLO.DEF, 35-37
HELLO.EXE, 36-37
HELLO.ICO, 36
image
    C++ classes, 100-135
    characteristics, 97-99
    formats, 96-100
OPEN.SPM, 210
PG.BSN, 484
PLATFORM.DAT, 321, 327, 456, 487-490
PZLDONE.SPM, 209-210
PZLSTRT.SPM, 210
resource
    ANIMATE.RES, 187
    hello.rc, 35-38
    IMAGEVW.RES, 146
SAMPLE.S3D, 313
SENSOR.DAT, 321, 327, 490-491
source
    animate.cpp, 186-187
    animwin.cpp, 182-185
    bframe.cpp, 338-353
    BLOCKADE game, 330-331
    blockade.cpp, 331-333
    dispwin.cpp, 360
    hello.cpp, 27-29
    hellovw.cpp, 32-35
    hscdial.cpp, 269-270
    image.cpp, 107-112
    imagevw.cpp, 137-138
    imvwwin.cpp, 141-145
    ltrwin.cpp, 247-252
    maptool.cpp, 392-395
    mbpimage.cpp, 115-118
    pcximage.cpp, 130-135
    platform.cpp, 457-466
    playsnd.cpp, 198-201
    plrtool.cpp, 396-398
    polarwin.cpp, 371-381
    pzlframe.cpp, 220-231
    pzlwin.cpp, 235-244
    scenario.cpp, 436-446
    scene3d.cpp, 305-311
    sensor.cpp, 469-472
    shape3d.cpp, 293-301
    sounds.cpp, 195-197
    spranim.cpp, 168-177
    sprite.cpp, 158-161
    spuzzle.cpp, 215-216
    statwin.cpp, 261-265, 404-411
    tgaimage.cpp, 122-124
    toolwin.cpp, 255-259, 389-391
    vu3dtool.cpp, 399-402
    vu3dwin.cpp, 381-385
    weapon.cpp, 476-482
spzlhlp.hpj, 272
TICK.SPM, 210
TOCK.SPM, 210
WEAPON.DAT, 321, 327, 491-492
FillRect GDI function, 73
FillRgn GDI function, 75
find_extents function, 293
Font graphics object, 63
fonts, 79-81
formats, image file, 96-100
    BMP, 99, 113-119
    GIF, 100
    PCX, 99, 125-135
    Targa, 99, 119-124
    TIFF, 99
frame animation, 150
FrameRect GDI function, 73
FrameRgn GDI function, 75
friend keyword, 105

functions
  About, 30-32
  active, 389
  animate, 165
  auto_engage_weapon, 434
  BMPImage class, 115-118
  CloseChildren, 53
  continue_engagements, 434, 476
  detect, 469
  DIBtoDDB, 105
  disp_mission, 371
  draw_shape, 381
  draw_wpncover, 371
  engage, 476
  find_extents, 293
  GDI (Graphics Device Interface), 58
    AnimatePalette, 84
    Arc, 70
    BeginPaint, 62
    BitBlt, 89
    Chord, 71
    CombineRgn, 75
    CopyRect, 73
    CreateBrushIndirect, 72
    CreateDIBPatternBrush, 72
    CreateEllipticRgn, 74
    CreateEllipticRgnIndirect, 74
    CreateHatchBrush, 72
    CreatePalette, 85
    CreatePatternBrush, 72
    CreatePolygonRgn, 74
    CreatePolyPolygonRgn, 74
    CreateRectRgn, 74
    CreateRectRgnIndirect, 74
    CreateRoundRectRgn, 74
    CreateSolidBrush, 72
    DC (device context), 59-65
    DeleteObject, 64
    DrawText, 78
    Ellipse, 71
    EndPaint, 62
    EqualRect, 73
    EqualRgn, 75
    FillRect, 73
    FillRgn, 75
    FrameRect, 73
    FrameRgn, 75
    GetDC, 62
    GetDeviceCaps, 64
    GetMapMode, 67
    GetNearestPaletteIndex, 85
    GetPaletteEntries, 85
    GetRgnBox, 75
    GetStockObject, 71
    GetSystemPaletteEntries, 85
    GetSystemPaletteUse, 85
    InflateRect, 73
    InvalidateRgn, 75
    InvertRect, 73
    InvertRgn, 75
    LineTo, 69
    MoveTo, 69
    OffsetRect, 73
    OffsetRgn, 75
    PaintRgn, 75
    Pie, 71
    Polygon, 71, 314
    Polyline, 70
    PtInRect, 73
    RealizePalette, 85
    Rectangle, 70
    ReleaseDC, 62
    ResizePalette, 85
    RoundRect, 70
    SelectClipRgn, 75
    SelectPalette, 85

Index

SetBkMode, 33
SetDIBitsToDevice, 105
SetMapMode, 67
SetPaletteEntries, 85
SetPixel, 69-82
SetRect, 73
SetRectEmpty, 73
SetROP2, 77
SetSysColors, 85
SetSystemPaletteUse, 85
SetTextAlign, 33, 78
StretchBlt, 89
TabbedTextOut, 78-92
TextOut, 33, 78
UnionRect, 73
UpdateColors, 85
UpdateWindow, 62
ValidateRgn, 75
get_string, 29-30
hi_scores, 231, 267, 338-353
icons_at, 389
Image class, 107-112
inactive, 389
init, 234
init_image, 158-161
init_weapons, 434
InitInstance, 27-29
InitMainWindow, 27-29
isA, 153
isLessThan, 153-157
load_missions, 338
load_music, 220
load_puzzles, 219
load_scenarios, 337
make_palette, 105
mark_detected_sprites, 434
mciSendCommand, 191
Music class, 195-197
nameOf, 153
new_scenario, 338
next_puzzle, 219
Ok, 269-270
ownship_xfrm, 434
Paint, 30-35, 61
pick_mission, 338
pick_puzzles, 219
pick_scenario, 337
playmusic, 220
random_draw, 434-435
read, 305-311
redisplay_all, 165
rotate, 293-301
scale, 293-301
show, 105
sort_facets, 293
TileChildren, 53
ToolWindow class, 388-389
translate, 293-301
view_transform, 305-311
WMCreate, 181
WMInitDialog, 269-270
WMLButtonDown, 234-244, 255-259
WMLButtonUp, 234-244
WMMouseMove, 234-244
Fundamental Data Structure (FDS), 46-48

G

games
    adventure and role playing, 6-7
    arcade, 6
    common elements, 15-17
    common themes, 8-14
    copy protection, 17
    educational, 5
    graphics, 16-17
    programming, 18-19

505

real-time action simulation, 6-14
    Gunship 2000, 9-10
    Microsoft Flight Simulator, 8
sound effects, 17
sports, 6
SPUZZLE, *see* SPUZZLE
story line, 15-16
strategic simulation, 7-14
    BLOCKADE, *see* BLOCKADE
    Great Naval Battles, North
        Atlantic 1939-1943, 13-14
    Harpoon, 12-13
    SimCity for Windows, 10-12
traditional, 5-6
GDI (Graphics Device Interface), 22, 58
    coordinate systems, 65-68
    DC (device context), 59-65
        contents, 59-61
        device capabilities, 64-65
        for graphics output, 63-64
        getting, 61-62
        graphics objects, 63-64
        persistent, 62-63
        reverting, 63
        storing temporarily, 62
    drawing functions, 68-80
    drawing modes, 76-77
    mapping mode, 65-68
    ROP (raster operation) codes, 76-77
GDI functions
    `AnimatePalette`, 84
    `Arc`, 70
    `BitBlt`, 89
    `Chord`, 71
    `CombineRgn`, 75
    `CopyRect`, 73
    `CreateBrushIndirect`, 72
    `CreateDIBPatternBrush`, 72
    `CreateEllipticRgn`, 74
    `CreateEllipticRgnIndirect`, 74
    `CreateHatchBrush`, 72
    `CreatePalette`, 85
    `CreatePatternBrush`, 72
    `CreatePolygonRgn`, 74
    `CreatePolyPolygonRgn`, 74
    `CreateRectRgn`, 74
    `CreateRectRgnIndirect`, 74
    `CreateRoundRectRgn`, 74
    `CreateSolidBrush`, 72
    `DrawText`, 78
    `Ellipse`, 71
    `EqualRect`, 73
    `EqualRgn`, 75
    `FillRect`, 73
    `FillRgn`, 75
    `FrameRect`, 73
    `FrameRgn`, 75
    `GetMapMode`, 67
    `GetNearestPaletteIndex`, 85
    `GetPaletteEntries`, 85
    `GetRgnBox`, 75
    `GetStockObject`, 71
    `GetSystemPaletteEntries`, 85
    `GetSystemPaletteUse`, 85
    `InflateRect`, 73
    `InvalidateRgn`, 75
    `InvertRect`, 73
    `InvertRgn`, 75
    `LineTo`, 69
    `MoveTo`, 69
    `OffsetRect`, 73
    `OffsetRgn`, 75
    `PaintRgn`, 75
    `Pie`, 71
    `Polygon`, 71, 314
    `Polyline`, 70

Index

`PtInRect`, 73
`RealizePalette`, 85
`Rectangle`, 70
`ResizePalette`, 85
`RoundRect`, 70
`SelectClipRgn`, 75
`SelectPalette`, 85
`SetBkMode`, 33
`SetDIBitsToDevice`, 105
`SetMapMode`, 67
`SetPaletteEntries`, 85
`SetPixel`, 69-82
`SetRect`, 73
`SetRectEmpty`, 73
`SetROP2`, 77
`SetSysColors`, 85
`SetSystemPaletteUse`, 85
`SetTextAlign`, 33, 78
`StretchBlt`, 89
`TabbedTextOut`, 78-92
`TextOut`, 33, 78
`UnionRect`, 73
`UpdateColors`, 85
`ValidateRgn`, 75
get_string function, 29-30
`GetDC` GDI function, 62
`GetDeviceCaps` GDI function, 64-65
`GetMapMode` GDI function, 67
`GetNearestPaletteIndex` GDI function, 85
`GetPaletteEntries` GDI function, 85
`GetRgnBox` GDI function, 75
`GetStockObject` GDI function, 71
`GetSystemPaletteEntries` GDI function, 85
`GetSystemPaletteUse` GDI function, 85
GIF image file format, 100

graphics, 16-17
  2-D, 16-20
  3-D, 16-20
    2-D Cartesian coordinate system, 276
    3-D Cartesian coordinate system, 276-277
    boundaries, 277-278
    classes, 286-314
    constructing objects, 278-280
    coordinate transformations, 280-282
    defining 3-D scene, 301-311
    loading 3-D scene, 311-313
    rotating objects, 282-283
    scaling objects, 281
    translating objects, 281-282
    vector operations, 283-284
    viewing 3-D scenes, 284-286, 313-314
background mode, 33
color, 18-19
drawing mode, 76-77
GDI functions, 58
  closed figures, drawing, 70-72
  DC (device context), 59-65
  lines, drawing, 69-70
  logical palettes, manipulating, 84-85
  points, drawing, 69
  rectangles, manipulating, 72-73
  regions, 74-75
  system palettes, manipulating, 84-85
  see also GDI functions
images, 16
text alignment, 33

507

graphics attributes, setting up, 63-64
Graphics Device Interface, *see* GDI
Great Naval Battles, North Atlantic 1939-1943, 7, 13-14
Gunship 2000, 7-10

H

Harpoon, 7, 12-13
`HashTable` container class, 42
`hbm_ddb` member variable, 105
`hdr` member variable, 119-121
header files
    `animres.h`, 180
    `animwin.h`, 179-180
    `bframe.h`, 333-337
    `blkdres.h`, 483
    BLOCKADE game, 328-329
    `bmpimage.h`, 113-114
    `dispwin.h`, 355-359
    `hellomdl.h`, 29-30
    `hellores.h`, 35-38
    `hellovw.h`, 31-35
    `hscdial.h`, 267-269
    `image.h`, 102-105
    `imvwres.h`, 141-145
    `imvwwin.h`, 139-140
    `infowin.h`, 412-413
    linking, 35-39
    `logowin.h`, 354
    `ltrwin.h`, 245-246
    `pcximage.h`, 126-127
    `platform.h`, 451-455
    `pzlframe.h`, 216-218
    `pzlinfo.h`, 266
    `pzlwin.h`, 232-233
    `scenario.h`, 427-429
    `scene3d.h`, 302-304
    `scninfo.h`, 429-431
    `sensor.h`, 467-469
    `shape3d.h`, 287-293
    `simdefs.h`, 431-433
    `sounds.h`, 193-194
    `spanim.h`, 162-164
    `sprite.h`, 153-157
    `spzlres.h`, 271
    `statwin.h`, 259-260, 402-404
    `tgaimage.h`, 121
    `toolwin.h`, 253-254, 386-388
    `weapon.h`, 473-475
`HELLO.CFG` configuration file, 35
`hello.cpp` source file, 27-29
`HELLO.DEF` module definition file, 35-37
`hello.dlg` file, 36-39
`HELLO.EXE` file
    dialog definitions, 39
    makefile, 36-37
    module definition file, 37
    resource file, 38
    resource identifiers, 38
    testing, 39-40
`HELLO.ICO` icon file, 36
`hello.rc` resource file, 35-38
`HelloApp` class, 27-29
`hellomdl.h` header file, 29-30
`HelloModel` class, 29-30
`hellores.h` header file, 35-38
`HelloView` class, 30-35
`hellovw.cpp` source file, 32-35
`hellovw.h` header file, 31-35
help (SPUZZLE game), 272
`hi_scores` function, 231, 267, 338-353
high scores dialog box
    SPUZZLE game, 231-232, 267-270
    BLOCKADE game, 338-353

Index

hierarchy
    container classes (CLASSLIB), 41
    `Image` class, 100-101
    OWL classes, 50
    simple classes (CLASSLIB), 44
    SPUZZLE windows, 212
`HiscoreDialog` class (SPUZZLE), 267-270
homogeneous coordinates, 281-282
`hpal` member variable, 105
`hscdial.cpp` source file, 269-270
`hscdial.h` header file, 267-269

I

icon files, `HELLO.ICO`, 36
`icons_at` function, 389
`Image` class, 100-101, 105-112
    header file, 102-105
    member functions, 107-112
image files, 96-100
    BMP format, 99, 113-119
        reading, 114-118
        writing, 118-119
    characteristics, 97-99
    classes, 100-135
        `BMPImage`, 113-119
        `Image`, 105-112
        `ImageData`, 101-105
        `PCXImage`, 125-135
        `TGAImage`, 119-124
    GIF format, 100
    ImageView application, 136-146
    PCX format, 99, 125-135
        reading, 127-135
    Targa format, 99, 119-124
    TIFF format, 99
`image` member variable, 139
`image.cpp` source file, 107-112
`image.h` header file, 102-105
`ImageData` class, 101-105
    header file, 102-105
    member variables, 105
images, 16
    components, 97
    viewing (ImageView), 136-146
    sprites, *see* sprites
ImageView application, 136-146
    building, 145-146
    main source file, 137-138
    resource identifiers, 140-141
    starting, 136
`ImageViewApp` class, 136-138
`ImageViewFrame` class, 139-145
`ImageViewWindow` class, 139-145
`imagevw.cpp` source file, 137-138
`IMAGEVW.RES` resource file, 146
`imvwres.h` header file, 141-145
`imvwwin.cpp` source file, 141-145
`imvwwin.h` header file, 139-140
`inactive` function, 389
`InflateRect` GDI function, 73
`infowin.h` header file, 412-413
`InfoWindow` class, 326, 410-427
`init` function, 234
`init_image` function, 158-161
`init_weapons` function, 434
initializing
    animation (ANIMATE), 181
    child windows (SPUZZLE), 216-232
    instance of application, 27-29
    main application window, 27-29
    platforms (BLOCKADE), 456
    sprites, 158-161
`InitInstance` function, 27-29

509

`InitMainWindow` function, 27-29
interaction layer (MVC architecture), 24
interfaces
    GDI (Graphics Device Interface), *see* GDI
    MDI (multiple document interface), 53
`InvalidateRgn` GDI function, 75
`InvertRect` GDI function, 73
`InvertRgn` GDI function, 75
`isA` function, 153
`isLessThan` function, 153-157
iterator classes (CLASSLIB class library), 45-46

J-K

Jack Nicklaus Signature Edition Golf, 6

keywords, `friend`, 105

L

languages, *see* programming languages
`LetterWindow` class (SPUZZLE), 213, 245-252
libraries, *see* class librairies
lines, drawing, 69-70
`LineTo` GDI function, 69
linking files, 35-39
Links 386 Pro, 6
`List` container class, 43
listings
    2.1 `hello.cpp` source file, 27-29
    2.2 `hellomdl.h` header file, 29-30
    2.3 `hellovw.h` header file, 31-35
    2.4 `hellovw.cpp` source file, 32-35
    2.5 `HELLO.EXE` file, 36-37
    2.6 `HELLO.DEF` module definition file, 37
    2.7 `hellores.h` header file, 38
    2.8 `hello.rc` resource file, 38
    2.9 `hello.dlg` file, 39
    4.1 `image.h` header file, 102-105
    4.2 `image.cpp` source file, 107-112
    4.3 `bmpimage.h` header file, 113-114
    4.4 `mbpimage.cpp` source file, 115-118
    4.5 `tgaimage.h` header file, 121
    4.6 `tgaimage.cpp` source file, 122-124
    4.7 `pcximage.h` header file, 126-127
    4.8 `pcximage.cpp` source file, 130-135
    4.9 `imagevw.cpp` source file, 137-138
    4.10 `imvwwin.h` header file, 139-140
    4.11 `imvwres.h` header file, 140-141
    4.12 `imvwwin.cpp` source file, 141-145
    5.1 `sprite.h` header file, 153-157
    5.2 `sprite.cpp` source file, 158-161
    5.3 `spanim.h` header file, 162-164
    5.4 `spranim.cpp` source file, 168-177
    5.5 `animwin.h` header file, 179-180
    5.6 `animres.h` header file, 180
    5.7 `animwin.cpp` source file, 182-185

Index

5.8 `animate.cpp` source file, 186-187
6.1 `sounds.h` header file, 193-194
6.2 `sounds.cpp` source file, 195-197
6.3 `playsnd.cpp` source file, 198-201
7.1 `spuzzle.cpp` source file, 215-216
7.2 `pzlframe.h` header file, 216-218
7.3 `pzlframe.cpp` source file, 220-231
7.4 `pzlwin.h` header file, 232-233
7.5 `pzlwin.cpp` source file, 235-244
7.6 `ltrwin.h` header file, 245-246
7.7 `ltrwin.cpp` source file, 247-252
7.8 `toolwin.h` header file, 253-254
7.9 `toolwin.cpp` source file, 255-259
7.10 `statwin.h` header file, 259-260
7.11 `statwin.cpp` source file, 261-265
7.12 `pzlinfo.h` header file, 266
7.13 `hscdial.h` header file, 267-269
7.14 `hscdial.cpp` source file, 269-270
7.15 `spzlres.h` header file, 271
7.16 `spzlhlp.hpj` file, 272
8.1 `shape3d.h` header file, 287-293
8.2 `shape3d.cpp` source file, 293-301
8.3 `scene3d.h` header file, 302-304
8.4 `scene3d.cpp` source file, 305-311
8.5 `CUBE.SHP` file, 312
8.6 `SAMPLE.S3D` file, 313
9.1 `blockade.cpp` source file, 331-333
9.2 `bframe.h` header file, 333-337
9.3 `bframe.cpp` source file, 338-353
9.4 `logowin.h` header file, 354
9.5 `dispwin.h` header file, 355-359
9.6 `dispwin.cpp` source file, 360
9.7 `mapwin.cpp` source file, 361-369
9.8 `polarwin.cpp` source file, 371-381
9.9 `vu3dwin.cpp` source file, 381-385
9.10 `toolwin.h` header file, 386-388
9.11 `toolwin.cpp` source file, 389-391
9.12 `maptool.cpp` source file, 392-395
9.13 `plrtool.cpp` source file, 396-398
9.14 `vu3dtool.cpp` source file, 399-402
9.15 `statwin.h` header file, 402-404
9.16 `statwin.cpp` source file, 404-411
9.17 `infowin.h` header file, 412-413
9.18 `infowin.cpp` source file, 414-427

9.19 `scenario.h` header file, 427-429
9.20 `scninfo.h` header file, 429-431
9.21 `simdefs.h` header file, 431-433
9.22 `scenario.cpp` source file, 436-446
9.23 `platform.h` header file, 451-455
9.24 `platform.cpp` source file, 457-466
9.25 `sensor.h` header file, 467-469
9.26 `sensor.cpp` source file, 469-472
9.27 `weapon.h` header file, 473-475
9.28 `weapon.cpp` source file, 476-482
9.29 `blkdres.h` header file, 483
9.30 `BLOCKADE.CFG` configuration file, 483-484
9.31 `PG.BSN` scenario file, 484
9.32 `CARGO.MSN` mission file, 485-487
9.33 `PLATFORM.DAT` file, 487-490
9.34 `SENSOR.DAT` file, 490-491
9.35 `WEAPON.DAT` file, 491-492
`load_missions` function, 338
`load_music` function, 220
`load_puzzles` function, 219
`load_scenarios` function, 337
loading
    3-D scenes, 311-313
    missions (BLOCKADE), 337-338
    scenarios (BLOCKADE), 337-338
logical coordinate system (GDI), 65
logical palette, 81-85

`logowin.h` header file, 354
`LogoWindow` class, 353-354
`LOGPALETTE` structure, 82
`ltrwin.cpp` source file, 247-252
`ltrwin.h` header file, 245-246

M

main application window, initializing, 27-29
MAKE utility, 35-39
`make_palette` function, 105
makefiles, 35-39
map view (BLOCKADE), 321-322, 360-369
    controls, bitmap icons, 391-402
mapping mode (GDI), 65-68
`maptocl.cpp` source file, 392-395
`MapToolWindow` class, 327, 391-395
`MapWindow` class, 327, 360-369
`mark_detected_sprites` function, 434
Math Rabbit, 5
matrix-vector multiplication, 280-282
`mbpimage.cpp` source file, 115-118
MCI (Media Control Interface), 191
`mciSendCommand` function, 191
MDI (multiple document interface), 53
Media Control Interface (MCI), 191
member variables
    `bmphdr`, 118
    `hbm_ddb`, 105
    `hdr`, 119-121
    `hpal`, 105
    `image`, 139
    `Scenario` class, 435-446

`Scene3D` class, 301-302
`Sensor` class, 466
SPUZZLE game, 219
`Weapons` class, 472-473
messages
   displaying, 30-35
   status (BLOCKADE), 402-411
metafiles, 58
Microsoft Flight Simulator, 6-8
Microsoft Windows, *see* Windows
missions (BLOCKADE), 320
   database file, 485-487
   loading, 337-338
`MM_ANISOTROPIC` mapping mode, 65
`MM_HIENGLISH` mapping mode, 66
`MM_HIMETRIC` mapping mode, 66
`MM_ISOTROPIC` mapping mode, 66
`MM_LOENGLISH` mapping mode, 66
`MM_LOMETRIC` mapping mode, 66
`MM_TEXT` mapping mode, 66
`MM_TWIPS` mapping mode, 66
MMSYSTEM Dynamic Link Library, 191
Model-View-Controller (MVC) architecture, 24-40
`MoveTo` GDI function, 69
moving
   platforms (BLOCKADE), 456
   puzzle pieces (SPUZZLE), 234-244
multimedia, 19
multiple document interface (MDI), 53
`Music` class, 192-197
   functions, 195-197
music, *see* sound effects
MVC (Model-View-Controller) architecture, 24-40

N

`nameOf` function, 153
New Math Blaster Plus, 5
`new_scenario` function, 338
`next_puzzle` function, 219
NFL Pro League Football, 6
normalizing vectors, 283
`Note` class, 192-197

O

`Object` class, 41
objects, 3-D
   boundaries, 277-278
   constructing, 278-280
   modeling, 276-284
   rotating, 282-283
   scaling, 281
   translating, 281-282
ObjectWindows Library, *see* OWL
`OffsetRect` GDI function, 73
`OffsetRgn` GDI function, 75
`Ok` function, 269-270
`OPEN.SPM` file, 210
orthographic projections, 285-286
overlapping sprites, 166-177
OWL (ObjectWindows Library)
   classes
      hierarchy, 50
      control, 52-53
      dialog, 50-52
      window, 50
      see also classes
`ownship_xfrm` function, 434

P

`Paint` function, 30-35, 61
`PaintRgn` GDI function, 75
`PAINTSTRUCT` structure, 61
Palette graphics object, 63
`PALETTEENTRY` structure, 82
palettes
    color, 81
    logical, 81-85
    system, 81
PC Games magazine, 20
PCX image file format, 99, 125-135
    reading, 127-135
`PCXHeader` structure, 125
`PCXImage` class, 125-135
    header file, 125-127
`pcximage.cpp` source file, 130-135
`pcximage.h` header file, 126-127
Pen graphics object, 63
`PG.BSN` scenario file, 484
physical coordinate system (GDI), 65
`pick_mission` function, 338
`pick_puzzles` function, 219
`pick_scenario` function, 337
`Pie` GDI function, 71
pixels, 18
    color, 96-97
    drawing, 69-82
`Platform` class, 450-466
`platform.cpp` source file, 457-466
`PLATFORM.DAT` file, 321, 327, 456, 487-490
`platform.h` header file, 451-455
platforms (BLOCKADE), 320, 427-446, 450-466
    database file, 487-490
    hits, 456
    initializing, 456
    moving, 456
    selecting, 324
`playmusic` function, 220
`playsnd.cpp` source file, 198-201
`plrtool.cpp` source file, 396-398
points, drawing, 69
polar view (BLOCKADE), 322-324, 370-381
`PolarToolWindow` class, 327, 370, 395-398
`polarwin.cpp` source file, 371-381
`PolarWindow` class, 327, 370-381
`Polygon` GDI function, 71, 314
polygons, drawing, 71
`Polyline` GDI function, 70
presentation layer (MVC architecture), 24
`PriorityQueue` container class, 43
programming games, 18-19
    color, 18-19
    multimedia, 19
    MVC (Model-View-Controller) architecture, 24-40
programming languages, Smalltalk-80, 24-40
`PtInRect` GDI function, 73
`PuzzleFrame` class (SPUZZLE), 213-232
`PuzzlePiece` class (SPUZZLE), 214
`PuzzleWindow` class (SPUZZLE), 213, 232-245
`PZLDONE.SPM` file, 209-210
`pzlframe.cpp` source file, 220-231
`pzlframe.h` header file, 216-218
`pzlinfo.h` header file, 266
`PZLSTRT.SPM` file, 210
`pzlwin.cpp` source file, 235-244
`pzlwin.h` header file, 232-233

Index

Q-R

Queue container class, 43
queues, 48-49

Railroad Tycoon, 7
random_draw function, 434-435
raster lines, 96
raster operation (ROP), 76-77
read function, 305-311
Reader Rabbit, 5
reading
    BMP image file format, 114-118
    PCX image file format, 127-135
real-time action simulation games, 6-14
    Gunship 2000, 9-10
    Microsoft Flight Simulator, 8
RealizePalette GDI function, 85
RECT structure, 72
Rectangle GDI function, 70
rectangles
    drawing, 70
    manipulating, 72-73
redisplay_all function, 165
reference counting, 101
Region graphics object, 63
regions, 74-75
ReleaseDC GDI function, 62
ResizePalette GDI function, 85
resource files
    ANIMATE.RES, 187
    hello.rc, 35-38
    IMAGEVW.RES, 146
resource identifiers
    ANIMATE application, 180
    BLOCKADE game, 482-483
    HELLO.EXE file, 38
    ImageView application, 140-141
    SPUZZLE game, 271

ROP (raster operation), 76-77
rotate function, 293-301
rotating 3-D objects, 282-283
RoundRect GDI function, 70

S

SAMPLE.S3D file, 313
scale function, 293-301
scaling 3-D objects, 281
scan lines, 96
Scenario class, 427-446
scenario.cpp source file, 436-446
scenario.h header file, 427-429
scenarios (BLOCKADE), 320
    loading, 337-338
    macros, 431-433
    simulating, 326, 434
    viewing, 326-327
Scene3D class, 301-311
scene3d.cpp source file, 305-311
scene3d.h header file, 302-304
scninfo.h header file, 429-431
screens, BLOCKADE game, 321
scrolling windows, 53
SelectClipRgn GDI function, 75
selecting graphics objects, 63-64
SelectPalette GDI function, 85
Sensor class, 466-472
sensor.cpp source file, 469-472
SENSOR.DAT file, 321, 327, 490-491
sensor.h header file, 467-469
sensors (BLOCKADE), 320, 466-472
    database file, 490-491
Set container class, 43
SetBkMode GDI function, 33
SetDIBitsToDevice GDI function, 105
SetMapMode GDI function, 67

`SetPaletteEntries` GDI function, 85
`SetPixel` GDI function, 69-82
`SetRect` GDI function, 73
`SetRectEmpty` GDI function, 73
`SetROP2` GDI function, 77
sets, 48-49
`SetSysColors` GDI function, 85
`SetSystemPaletteUse` GDI function, 85
`SetTextAlign` GDI function, 33, 78
`Shape3D` class, 287-301
`shape3d.cpp` source file, 293-301
`shape3d.h` header file, 287-293
`show` function, 105
shrinking bitmaps, 89
SimAnt, 7
SimCity for Windows, 7, 10-12
`simdefs.h` header file, 431-433
simple classes (CLASSLIB class library), 43-44
sizing child windows
    BLOCKADE game, 337
    SPUZZLE game, 219
Smalltalk-80 programming language, MVC architecture, 24-40
`sort_facets` function, 293
`Sortable` simple class, 44
sorted arrays, 48-49
`SortedArray` container class, 43
sound cards, 190
sound drivers, 190-192
sound effects, 17
    generating, 192
    `Music` class, 192-197
    `Note` class, 192-197
    sample program, 197-201
    sound cards, 190
    sound drivers, 190-192
    SPUZZLE game, 209-210
sound.drv driver, 190
`sounds.cpp` source file, 195-197
`sounds.h` header file, 193-194
source files
    `bframe.cpp`, 338-353
    BLOCKADE game, 330-331
    `blockade.cpp`, 331-333
    `dispwin.cpp`, 360
    linking, 35-39
    `maptool.cpp`, 392-395
    `platform.cpp`, 457-466
    `plrtool.cpp`, 396-398
    `polarwin.cpp`, 371-381
    `scenario.cpp`, 436-446
    `sensor.cpp`, 469-472
    `statwin.cpp`, 404-411
    `toolwin.cpp`, 389-391
    `vu3dtool.cpp`, 399-402
    `vu3dwin.cpp`, 381-385
    `weapon.cpp`, 476-482
`spanim.h` header file, 162-164
Spelling Puzzle, *see* SPUZZLE
sports games, 6
`spranim.cpp` source file, 168-177
`Sprite` class, 152-161
    ANIMATE application, 178-187
    display priority, 152
    header file, 153-157
`sprite.cpp` source file, 158-161
`sprite.h` header file, 153-157
`SpriteAnimation` class, 162-177
    ANIMATE application, 178-187
    data members, 162
    header file, 162-164
    objects, setting up, 164-165
`SpriteInfo` structure, 181

Index

sprites, 6, 150-151
    ANIMATE application, 178-187
    animating, 162-177
    background drawing, 165
    classes
        `Sprite`, 152-161
        `SpriteAnimation`, 162-177
    erase-and-redraw animation, 150-151
    initializing, 158-161
    offscreen bitmap animation, 151
    overlapping, 166-177
    updating animation, 165-166
    see also images
SPUZZLE (Spelling Puzzle) game
    bitmap buttons, 252-259
    child windows, 207
        animating, 220-231
        sizing, 219
    classes
        `HiscoreDialog`, 267-270
        `LetterWindow`, 213, 245-252
        `PuzzleFrame`, 213-232
        `PuzzlePiece`, 214
        `PuzzleWindow`, 213, 232-245
        responsibilities, assigning, 213
        `SpuzzleApp`, 214-216
        `StatusWindow`, 213, 259-265
        `ToolWindow`, 213, 252-259
    designing, 211-214
    help, 206, 272
    high scores dialog box, 231-232, 267-270
    implementing, 214-254
    keeping score, 209
    music, playing, 220
    puzzles
        building, 208
        completion, checking for, 244-245
        data structures, 265-266
        information about, displaying, 213-214
        initializing current, 234
        managing, 219
        moving pieces, 234-244
        resource identifiers, 271
        sound, controlling, 209-210
        starting, 207
        window hierarchy, 212
    words
        adding, 210-211
        displaying letters, 245-252
`SPUZZLE.CFG` configuration file, 210-211
`spuzzle.cpp` source file, 215-216
`SpuzzleApp` class (SPUZZLE), 214-216
`spzlhlp.hpj` file, 272
`spzlres.h` header file, 271
`Stack` container class, 43
stacks, 48-49
starting
    BLOCKADE, 319-320
    ImageView, 136
    SPUZZLE, 207
status messages (BLOCKADE), 402-411
`StatusWindow` class, 326, 402-411
    SPUZZLE game, 213, 259-265
`statwin.cpp` source file, 261-265, 404-411
`statwin.h` header file, 259-260, 402-404

story lines, 15-16
strategic simulation games, 7-14
    Great Naval Battles, North Atlantic 1939-1943, 13-14
    Harpoon, 12-13
    SimCity for Windows, 10-12
StretchBlt GDI function, 89
stretching bitmaps, 89
String simple class, 44
structures
    BITMAP, 92
    BITMAPFILEHEADER, 113
    BITMAPINFOHEADER, 101
    LOGPALETTE, 82
    PAINTSTRUCT, 61
    PALETTEENTRY, 82
    PCXHeader, 125
    RECT, 72
    SpriteInfo, 181
    TARGAHeader, 119-121
super VGA video adapters, 19
system palette, 81

T

TabbedTextOut GDI function, 78-92
Targa image file format, 99, 119-124
TARGAHeader structure, 119-121
TBButton control class, 52
TBCheckBox control class, 52
TBDivider control class, 52
TBGroupBox control class, 52
TBRadioButton control class, 52
TBStatic control class, 52
TBStaticBmp control class, 52
TButton control class, 52
TCheckBox control class, 52
TComboBox control class, 52

TControl abstract base class, 52
TDialog window class, 50
TEdit control class, 53
TEditWindow class, 50
testing HELLO.EXE file, 39-40
text
    alignment, 33, 78-79
    background mode, 79
    font, 79-81
    output functions, 77-80
TextOut GDI function, 33, 78
TFileDialog class, 50
TFileWindow class, 50
TGAImage class, 119-124
    header file, 121
tgaimage.cpp source file, 122-124
tgaimage.h header file, 121
TGroupBox control class, 53
three-dimensional graphics, *see* 3-D graphics
TICK.SPM file, 210
TIFF image file format, 99
TileChildren function, 53
Time simple class, 44
TInput Dialog class, 50
TListBox control class, 53
TMDIClient class, 53
TMDIFrame class, 53
TOCK.SPM file, 210
toolwin.cpp source file, 255-259, 389-391
toolwin.h header file, 253-254, 386-388
ToolWindow class, 386-402
    SPUZZLE game, 213, 252-259
TRadioButton control class, 53
traditional games, 5-6
translate function, 293-301

translating 3-D objects, 281-282
`TScrollBar` control class, 53
`TScroller` class, 53
`TShouldDelete` class, 42
`TStatic` control class, 53
`TWindow` class, 50

U

`UnionRect` GDI function, 73
`UpdateColors` GDI function, 85
`UpdateWindow` GDI function, 62
utilities, MAKE, 35-39

V

`ValidateRgn` GDI function, 75
values, default, device context, 59-61
vector operations (3-D graphics), 283-284
`Vector3D` class, 286-301
vectors, 46-48
VGA video adapters, 18-19
video adapters, 18-19
   colors, displaying, 81
   super VGA, 19
`view_transform` function, 305-311
`View3DToolWindow` class, 327, 381, 399-402
`View3DWindow` class, 327, 381-385
viewing
   3-D scenes, 284-286, 313-314
   images (ImageView application), 136-146
   scenarios (BLOCKADE), 326-327
   see also displaying

views (BLOCKADE), 321-324
   3-D, 381-385
   map, 321-322, 360-369
      controls, bitmap icons, 391-402
   polar, 370-381
voices, 191-192
`vu3dtool.cpp` source file, 399-402
`vu3dwin.cpp` source file, 381-385

W

`weapon.cpp` source file, 476-482
`WEAPON.DAT` file, 321, 327, 491-492
`weapon.h` header file, 473-475
weapons (BLOCKADE), 472-482
   database file, 491-492
   launching, 325
`Weapons` class, 472-482
Where in the U.S.A. is Carmen Sandiego?, 5
Where in the World is Carmen Sandiego?, 5
window classes, 50
Windows
   device independence, 22
   programming games, 18-19
windows, 50
   child
      animating (SPUZZLE), 220-231
      initializing, 216-232, 333-353
      managing, 53
      sizing, 219, 337
      SPUZZLE game, 207
      updating (BLOCKADE), 338
   scrolling, 53
   SPUZZLE, hierarchy, 212

Wing Commander II, 7
`WMCreate` function, 181
`WMInitDialog` function, 269-270
`WMLButtonDown` function, 234-244, 255-259
`WMLButtonUp` function, 234-244
`WMMouseMove` function, 234-244
words (SPUZZLE game)
    adding, 210-211
    displaying letters, 245-252
writing BMP format image files, 118-119

Add to Your Sams Library Today with the Best Books for Programming, Operating Systems, and New Technologies!

The easiest way to order is to pick up the phone and call

1-800-428-5331

between 9:00 a.m. and 5:00 p.m. EST.
For faster service please have your credit card available.

ISBN #	Quantity	Description of Item	Unit Cost	Total Cost
0-672-30168-7		Advanced C (Book/Disk)	$39.95	
0-672-30158-X		Advanced C ++ (Book/Disk)	$39.95	
0-672-30287-X		Tom Swan's Code Secrets (Book/Disk)	$39.95	
0-672-30309-4		Programming Sound for DOS & Windows (Book/Disk)	$39.95	
0-672-30240-3		OS/2 2.1 Unleashed (Book/Disk)	$34.95	
0-672-30288-8		DOS Secrets Unleashed (Book/Disk)	$39.95	
0-672-30299-3		Uncharted Windows Programming (Book/Disk)	$34.95	
0-672-30274-8		Mastering Borland C++ (Book/Disk)	$39.95	
0-672-30226-8		Windows Programmer's Guide to OLE/DDE (Book/Disk)	$34.95	
0-672-30236-5		Windows Programmer's Guide to DLLs & Memory Management (Book/Disk)	$34.95	
0-672-30030-3		Windows Programmer's Guide to Serial Communications (Book/Disk)	$39.95	
0-672-30177-6		Windows Programmer's Guide to Borland C++ Tools (Book/Disk)	$39.95	
0-672-30097-4		Windows Programmer's Guide to Resources (Book/Disk)	$34.95	
0-672-30067-2		Windows Programmer's Guide to MS Foundation Class Library (Book/Disk)	$34.95	
0-672-30106-7		Windows Programmer's Guide to ObjectWindows Library (Book/Disk)	$34.95	
0-672-30137-7		Secrets of the Borland C++ Masters (Book/Disk)	$44.95	
0-672-30190-3		Windows Resource and Memory Management (Book/Disk)	$29.95	
0-672-30249-7		Multimedia Madness! (Book/Disk - CD-ROM)	$44.95	
☐ 3 1/2" Disk ☐ 5 1/4" Disk		Shipping and Handling: See information below.		
		TOTAL		

Shipping and Handling: $4.00 for the first book and $1.75 for each additional book. Floppy disk: add $1.75 for shipping and handling. If you need to have it NOW, we can ship product to you in 24 hours for an additional charge of approximately $18.00, and you will receive your item overnight or in two days. Overseas shipping and handling add $20.00 per book and $8.00 for up to three disks. Prices subject to change. Call for availability and pricing information on latest editions.

11711   N. College Avenue,   Suite 140,   Carmel, Indiana   46032

1-800-428-5331— Orders   1-800-835-3202—FAX   1-800-858-7674 — Customer Service

Book ISBN# 0-672-30292-6

What's on the Disk

The disk contains the complete source code, executable files, and support files for the Windows programs developed in the book. The programs include the following:

- **Spuzzle**—an educational puzzle game
- **Blockade**—a Naval Blockade action game
- **ImageView**—a BMP graphics viewer
- **Animation**—an example of sprite animation
- **PlaySound**—shows how to integrate sound into programs

Installing the Floppy Disk

The software included with this book is stored in a compressed form. You cannot use the software without first installing it to your hard drive. The installation program runs from within Windows.

1. From File Manager or Program Manager, choose **F**ile **R**un from the menu.

2. Type `<drive>INSTALL` and press Enter. `<drive>` is the letter of the drive that contains the installation disk. For example, if the disk is in drive B:, type `B:INSTALL` and press Enter.

Follow the on-screen instructions in the installation program. The files will be installed in the /WINGAMES directory, unless you choose a different directory during installation. When the installation is complete, be sure to read the file README.TXT. This file contains information on the files and programs that were installed.

> To install the files on the disk, you'll need at least 3.8M of free space on your hard drive.